MCSD Visual Basic 6 Desktop

The Cram Sheet

This Cram Sheet contains the distilled, key facts about Visual Basic 6 Desktop. Review this information last thing before you enter the test room, paying special attention to those areas where you feel you need the most review. You can transfer any of these facts from your head onto a blank sheet of paper before beginning the exam.

VARIABLES AND PROCEDURES

1. Know the VB data types and important attributes, especially **Variant**.

2. Know the use of enumerated constants or parameters using **Enum**.

3. Know how to declare object variables. Use **Set** to make assignments. Use **Nothing** to free up assignments.

4. When declaring objects using the **New** keyword, the object is created when first referenced.

5. Using **WithEvents** when declaring an object reference exposes the object's event model.

6. Know that **Erase** initializes fixed-size arrays and reclaims memory from dynamic arrays. **Array (arg1, arg2)** creates arrays of variants.

7. Know how to declare variable and procedure scope and lifetime. Know that **Friend** procedures are in class modules only and are visible to all modules but not to the controlling class.

8. Know about procedure arguments: **ByVal** arguments are passed by value and **ByRef** arguments are passed by address. Use **Any** instead of a specific data type to suppress type checking. Use **ParamArray** as the last argument to a procedure to create an optional array of variants.

9. Know the meaning of: **Null** (value of **Variant** containing no valid data), **Empty** (value of uninitialized **Variant**), and **Nothing** (value of an object variable not referencing an object).

10. Use **IsNull** to test for **Null**. Use **vbNullString** to pass a zero value string to an external module.

CLASSES AND OBJECTS

11. **For Each** iterates through properties of an object and enumerates items in a collection.

12. Early binding resolves objects at compile time; late binding resolves objects at runtime. Vtable and DispID binding are early. Vtable is more efficient and used with type libraries that contain virtual function tables.

13. Define class events with **Event** statements. Use **RaiseEvent** to invoke custom events.

14. Expose class properties via **Property Let**, **Property Get**, and **Property Set**.

15. Container classes obtain all public properties and procedures of child classes via **Implements**.

16. The methods of collections are: **Add**, **Item**, and **Remove**. The property of collections is **Count**.

17. Form's **Initialize** event occurs before the **Load** event. Use **QueryUnload** to intercept an **UnLoad**.

18. When assigning objects to variables, **New** creates a new instance and **Set** assigns object reference.

19. **TypeOf** returns type of object in an **If** statement only.

20. The **Screen** object is the entire Windows desktop. Know the following properties: **ActiveControl**, **ActiveForm**, **Fonts** (array indexed by **FontCont**), **MousePointer**, **MouseIcon**, **Height**, and **Width**.

21. Key **App** object properties include **EXEName**, **HelpFile**, and **hInstance**.

CONTROLS

22. Know the usage of these ActiveX controls:
   - **CommonDialog** Displays various dialogs such as File Save
   - **ImageList** Maintains collection of ListImage objects
   - **ListView** Displays items similar to Windows Explorer
   - **Slider** Sets and displays discrete values
   - **StatusBar** Contains the **Panels** collection and is used to display various pieces of information (date, time, help text, and so on)
   - **TabStrip** Contains multiple **Tab** objects
   - **ToolBar** Contains **Button** objects associated with an application
   - **TreeView** Hierarchical list of **Node** objects
   - **UpDown** Associated with another buddy control to display and set values

23. Be familiar with menus. Key properties include **Checked**, **Enabled**, **Parent**, and **WindowList**.

24. Understand usage of ListBox and ComboBox controls. Key properties include **Columns** (ListBox only), **ItemData**, **List**, **ListIndex**, **ListCount**, **SelCount** (ListBox only), **Selected** (ListBox only), **Sorted**, and **Text**. Key methods include **AddItem** and **Clear**.

EXTERNAL MODULES / WINDOWS API

25. Use **Alias** in a **Declare** statement if the external name is illegal.

26. All objects have a handle returned by the **hWnd** property. Forms have the **hDC** property to return graphical device context. Use **AddressOf** to pass procedure addresses.

27. To access the Registry, use **GetSetting**, **GetAllSettings**, **DeleteSetting**, and **SaveSetting**.

ERROR HANDLING

28. Know the properties of the **Err** object (**Number**, **Description**, **HelpContext**, **HelpContextID**, **LastDLLError,** and **Source**) and the **Err** object's methods (**Clear** and **Raise**).

29. Know how to turn on error handling: **On Error GoTo *linelabel*** or **On Error Resume Next**. To turn off, use **On Error GoTo 0**. Handle errors and then use **Resume**, **Resume Next**, or **Resume *linelabel*.**

DATA HANDLING

30. ADO Connection object contains an **Errors** collection. Transactions are at the Connection level.

31. The **Command** object is used to execute commands. If returning rows, must create Recordset.

32. **Recordset**s can be standalone (can create data without being connected to database). **cmdText** for SQL queries, **cmdTable** for entire tables, **cmdStoreProc** for stored procedure. Contains the **Fields** collection.

33. The **Field** object's default property is **Value**. **UnderlyingValue** is data currently on file. **OriginalValue** is data when originally retrieved.

34. The **Parameters** collection is used to pass parameters to a query or stored procedure.

35. Use **WillConnect** and **WillChangeRecord** to cancel connections and record updates. Use **adStatus = adStatusCancel** to cancel pending action.

36. Know the following about transactions:
   - The **BeginTrans** method of the **Connection** object starts a transaction. Transactions are ended by the **CommitTrans** or **RollbackTrans** methods. Transactions cannot be nested in ADO.
   - Optimistic locking means that rows aren't locked until updated. Pessimistic locking means rows are locked as soon as they are accessed. BatchOptimistic locking sends all updates to the database at one time but requires a client-side cursor.

MCSD
Visual Basic 6
Desktop

Michael MacDonald

MCSD Visual Basic 6 Desktop Exam Cram

Limits Of Liability And Disclaimer Of Warranty

Trademarks

The Coriolis Group, LLC
14455 N. Hayden Road, Suite 220
Scottsdale, Arizona 85260

602/483-0192
FAX 602/483-0193
http://www.coriolis.com

Library of Congress Cataloging-in-Publication Data
MacDonald, Michael (Michael D.)
    MCSD Visual Basic 6 desktop exam cram / by Michael D. MacDonald.
        p.   cm.
    Includes index.
    ISBN 1-57610-376-5
    1. Electronic data processing personnel—Certification.   2. Microsoft software—Examinations—Study guides.   3. Microsoft Visual
Basic.   I. Title.   II. Title: MCSD Visual Basic six desktop exam
cram.   III. Title: Microsoft certified solution developer Visual Basic 6
desktop exam cram.
QA76.3.M322   1999
005.26'8—DC21   98-33444
                                                             CIP

Printed in the United States of America
10 9 8 7 6 5 4 3 2

Publisher
Keith Weiskamp

Acquisitions Editor
Shari Jo Hehr

Marketing Specialist
Cynthia Caldwell

Project Editor
Ann Waggoner Aken

Technical Reviewer
Carl Ganz

**Production
Coordinator**
Meg E. Turecek

Cover Design
Jody Winkler

Layout Design
April Nielsen

14455 North Hayden, Suite 220 • Scottsdale, Arizona 85260

The Smartest Way To Get Certified™

Thank you for purchasing one of our innovative certification study guides, just one of the many members of the Coriolis family of certification products.

Certification Insider Press™ was created in late 1997 by The Coriolis Group to help professionals like you obtain certification and advance your career. Achieving certification involves a major commitment and a great deal of hard work. To help you reach your goals, we've listened to others like you, and we've designed our entire product line around you and the way you like to study, learn, and master challenging subjects. Our approach is *The Smartest Way To Get Certified*.

In less than a year, Coriolis has published over one million copies of our highly popular *Exam Cram*, *Exam Prep*, and *On Site* guides. Our *Exam Cram* books, specifically written to help you pass an exam, are the number one certification self-study guides in the industry. They are the perfect complement to any study plan you have, as well as to the rest of the Certification Insider Press series: *Exam Prep*, comprehensive study guides designed to help you thoroughly learn and master certification topics, and *On Site*, guides that really show you how to apply your skills and knowledge on the job.

Our commitment to you is to ensure that all of the certification study guides we develop help you save time and frustration. Each one provides unique study tips and techniques, memory joggers, custom quizzes, insight about test taking, practical problems to solve, real-world examples, and much more.

We'd like to hear from you. Help us continue to provide the very best certification study materials possible. Write us or email us at **cipq@coriolis.com** and let us know how our books have helped you study, or tell us about new features that you'd like us to add. If you send us a story about how an *Exam Cram*, *Exam Prep*, or *On Site* book has helped you, and we use it in one of our books, we'll send you an official Coriolis shirt for your efforts.

Good luck with your certification exam and your career. Thank you for allowing us to help you achieve your goals.

Keith Weiskamp
Publisher, Certification Insider Press

*As always, to my wife, Patricia, and children, Peter and Amanda.
Also, to some incredible people at Coriolis.*

—*Michael MacDonald*

About The Author

Michael MacDonald of Whitinsville, Massachusetts, is widely published in the area of client/server and general computing, including three books on Visual Basic. With twenty years of professional development experience, Michael has developed large business applications on virtually every platform. His experience with Visual Basic dates to the product's initial release in 1991. Besides his writing, Michael is currently the lead instructor in Client/Server Computing for Worcester Polytechnic Institute, one of the nation's leading technical universities. Michael also keeps busy with an independent consulting practice with private and government clients dealing with client/server, database, and networking/Internet issues. Michael has also developed commercial practice certification exams.

Acknowledgments

Anyone that actually reads the acknowledgments that appear in the front of every book already knows that "books are the product of the efforts of many people" and all that stuff. They are. And I will get to that in a moment.

I feel very fortunate to have been afforded the opportunity to write this book and others before it. My break into writing came some six years ago following what may have been the first "e-zine" on the Internet. You see, I was always a frustrated writer. That short-lived magazine led to an invitation to join the editorial board of a startup magazine and, eventually, to 60+ articles in over a dozen or so magazines. I learned a lot in some of those early efforts. My first book (a Powerbuilder title) was a real wakeup in terms of what it took to pull a book together. I have always been fortunate that many people, too numerous to mention here, took pity on a guy that was trying real hard and taught me both the mechanics of properly organizing thoughts and contents, and also the realities of production schedules, layout, and so on.

Since that time, I have worked with a number of publishers including some of the biggest in the world. I can say with absolute sincerity that my involvement with Coriolis has been consistently pleasurable, professional, and rewarding. The people at Coriolis are 100 percent dedicated to the production of the finest titles possible, and I have personally grown enormously merely by watching them in action.

This book began with Shari Jo Hehr, Acquisitions Editor, who developed *Certification Insider Press* from the ground up to the point where the *Exam Cram* and *Exam Prep* series are market leaders both in terms of technical content and value. More importantly, Shari Jo has empowered people to follow their hearts and consciences to be all they can be (okay—acknowledgments to the U.S. Army for that one) and produce a line of books unrivaled on the shelves of any bookstore.

It was my pleasure to work with Ann Waggoner Aken, Senior Project Editor, on this title. The job of Project Editor is complex, requiring patience, thoroughness, and endless coordination of many parties. Ann does her job with aplomb. Inasmuch as much of this book was written before the VB Desktop certification exam was available, there were many revisions once the exam was available. Chapters were added, pulled, and merged. This was no easy task. Ann somehow pulled it off and for that I am grateful.

Acknowledgments

Every book goes through a variety of edits. Carl Ganz did the technical editing of this one. "Ordinary" technical editors have a difficult task: reading each and every page for technical accuracy, running code samples, eyeballing consistency in naming conventions, and so forth. Carl, though, was much more than a technical editor. He took the exam himself. He offered many insights, suggestions, and more. This book would not be what it is without Carl's gracious sharing of his experience and knowledge (and his corrections of my gaffes).

Then, there is the job of the copyeditor. It is the copyeditor's job to read the text for grammatical accuracy as well as for clarity. On this book, Mary Millhollon did all this and more. Mary works from a "whole-book" approach. Even though she works one chapter at a time, she includes in her job description that not only individual sentences and paragraphs flow well, but that the chapters themselves flow well also. Though it is a natural reaction of an author to want to retain every word he or she wrote, Mary did a great job of gently (or not, as needed) pushing me to a more lucid and readable presentation.

Behind the scenes are many others. Bonnie Trenga proofread the book making incredible pick-ups of small details (such as the transposition of two numbers between the text and a graphic) that a mere human being would have missed. Others for whom acknowledgment is too often overlooked include Meg Turecek, who was the Production Coordinator for the project; Jody Winkler, who designed the cover; April Nielsen, who designed the layout of the book itself; and many others.

Lastly, I must acknowledge the most important contributors of all: you, the reader. I received several hundred emails in reference to the VB5 version of this book. All but two of letters were very positive, and while I certainly appreciate kind words, it was the letters pointing out areas where the book could have (and sometimes should have) been better that were the most helpful. I tried to answer every letter, and criticism and praise alike have been reflected both in the organization of this book as well as in the methodology incorporated for quality control. So, to those of you who took the time to write, this book is as much your effort as it is my own.

Contents At A Glance

Table Of Contents

Introduction

Welcome to the *MCSD Visual Basic 6 Desktop Exam Cram*! This book aims to help you get ready to take—and pass—the Microsoft certification test numbered 70-176, "Designing and Implementing Desktop Applications with Microsoft Visual Basic 6.0." This introduction explains Microsoft's certification programs in general and talks about how the *Exam Cram* series can help you prepare for Microsoft's certification exams.

Exam Cram books help you understand and appreciate the subjects and materials you need to pass Microsoft certification exams. *Exam Cram* books are aimed strictly at test preparation and review. They do not teach you everything you need to know about a topic (such as the ins and outs of database development or all the nitty-gritty details involved in creating remote Automation components). Instead, *Exam Cram* books present and dissect the questions and problems we've found that you're likely to encounter on a test. We've worked from Microsoft's training materials, preparation guides, and tests. Our aim is to bring together as much information as possible about Microsoft certification exams.

Nevertheless, to completely prepare yourself for any Microsoft test, we recommend that you begin your studies with some classroom training, or that you pick up and read one of the many study guides available. We also strongly recommend that you install, configure, and fool around with the software or environment that you'll be tested on, because nothing beats hands-on experience and familiarity when it comes to understanding the questions you're likely to encounter on a certification test. Book learning is essential, but hands-on experience is the best teacher of all.

The Microsoft Certified Professional (MCP) Program

The MCP program currently includes eight tracks, each of which boasts its own special acronym (as a would-be certificant, you need to have a high tolerance for alphabet soup of all kinds):

➤ **MCP (Microsoft Certified Professional)** This is the least prestigious of all the certification tracks from Microsoft. Passing any of the major Microsoft exams (except the Networking Essentials exam) qualifies an individual for MCP credentials. Individuals can demonstrate proficiency with additional Microsoft products by passing additional certification exams.

➤ **MCP+I (Microsoft Certified Professional + Internet)** This midlevel certification is attained by completing three core exams: Windows NT Server 4, TCP/IP, and Internet Information Server (3 or 4).

➤ **MCP+SB (Microsoft Certified Professional + Site Building)** This certification program is designed for individuals who are planning, building, managing, and maintaining Web sites. Individuals with the MCP+SB credential will have demonstrated the ability to develop Web sites that include multimedia and searchable content and Web sites that connect to and communicate with a back-end database. It requires passing two of the following three exams: "Designing and Implementing Commerce Solutions with Microsoft Site Server 3.0, Commerce Edition," "Designing and Implementing Web Sites with Microsoft FrontPage 98," and "Designing and Implementing Web Solutions with Microsoft Visual InterDev 6.0."

➤ **MCSD (Microsoft Certified Solution Developer)** The MCSD credential reflects the skills required to create multi-tier, distributed, and COM-based solutions, in addition to desktop and Internet applications, using new technologies. To obtain an MCSD, an individual must demonstrate the ability to analyze and interpret user requirements; select and integrate products, platforms, tools, and technologies; design and implement code and customize applications; and perform necessary software tests and quality assurance operations.

To become an MCSD, you must pass a total of four exams: three core exams (available Winter and Spring 1999) and one elective exam. The required core exam is "Analyzing Requirements and Defining Solution Architectures." Each candidate must also choose one of two desktop application exams—"Designing and Implementing Desktop Applications with Microsoft Visual C++ 6.0" or "Designing and Implementing Desktop Applications with Visual Basic 6.0"—plus one of two distributed application exams—"Designing and Implementing Distributed Applications with Microsoft Visual C++ 6.0" or "Designing and Implementing Distributed Applications with Microsoft Visual Basic 6.0." This book is devoted to the Visual Basic Desktop exam in this series. Table 1 shows the requirements for the MCSD certification. You are

Table 1   MCSD Requirements*

Core

Choose 1 from the desktop applications development group	
Exam 70-016	Designing and Implementing Desktop Applications with Microsoft Visual C++ 6.0
Exam 70-176	Designing and Implementing Desktop Applications with Microsoft Visual Basic 6.0
Choose 1 from the distributed applications development group	
Exam 70-015	Designing and Implementing Distributed Applications with Microsoft Visual C++ 6.0
Exam 70-175	Designing and Implementing Distributed Applications with Microsoft Visual Basic 6.0
This solution architecture exam is required	
Exam 70-100	Analyzing Requirements and Defining Solution Architectures

Elective

Choose 1 from this group	
Exam 70-015	Designing and Implementing Distributed Applications with Microsoft Visual C++ 6.0
Exam 70-016	Designing and Implementing Desktop Applications with Microsoft Visual C++ 6.0
Exam 70-029	Designing and Implementing Databases with Microsoft SQL Server 7.0
Exam 70-024	Developing Applications with C++ Using the Microsoft Foundation Class Library
Exam 70-025	Implementing OLE in Microsoft Foundation Class Applications
Exam 70-055	Designing and Implementing Web Sites with Microsoft FrontPage 98
Exam 70-057	Designing and Implementing Commerce Solutions with Microsoft Site Server 3.0, Commerce Edition
Exam 70-165	Developing Applications with Microsoft Visual Basic 5.0
	OR
Exam 70-175	Designing and Implementing Distributed Applications with Microsoft Visual Basic 6.0
	OR
Exam 70-176	Designing and Implementing Desktop Applications with Microsoft Visual Basic 6.0
Exam 70-069	Application Development with Microsoft Access for Windows 95 and the Microsoft Access Developer's Toolkit
Exam 70-091	Designing and Implementing Solutions with Microsoft Office 2000 and Microsoft Visual Basic for Applications
Exam 70-152	Designing and Implementing Web Solutions with Microsoft Visual InterDev 6.0

* This is not a complete listing—you can still be tested on some earlier versions of these products. However, we have tried to include the most recent versions so that you may test on these versions and thus be certified longer. We have not included any tests that are scheduled to be retired.

The MCSD program is being expanded to include FoxPro and Visual J++. However, these tests are not yet available and no test numbers have been assigned.

Core exams that can also be used as elective exams can be counted only once toward certification. The same test cannot be used as both a core and elective exam.

required to take and pass three "core" exams—one each from "Desktop Applications Development," "Distributed Applications Development," and "Solution Architecture." You also must take and pass one elective exam listed in the "Elective Exams" section. You cannot use the same exam to satisfy two requirements. For example, if you take and pass "Designing and Implementing Desktop Applications with Microsoft Visual Basic 6.0" to satisfy the core "Desktop Applications Development" requirement, you cannot also use the exam to satisfy your elective requirement.

Elective exams cover specific Microsoft applications and languages, including C++, the Microsoft Foundation Classes, Access, SQL Server, Excel, FrontPage, Visual Basic 6 Desktop (the subject of this book), and more. If you're on your way to becoming an MCSD and have already taken some exams, visit **www.microsoft.com/train_cert** for information about how to proceed with your MCSD certification under this new track.

➤ **MCDBA (Microsoft Certified Database Administrator)** The MCDBA credential reflects the skills required to implement and administer Microsoft SQL Server databases. To obtain an MCDBA, an individual must demonstrate the ability to derive physical database designs, develop logical data models, create physical databases, create data services by using Transact-SQL, manage and maintain databases, configure and manage security, monitor and optimize databases, and install and configure Microsoft SQL Server.

To become an MCDBA, you must pass a total of five exams—four core exams and one elective exam. The required core exams are "Administering Microsoft SQL Server 7.0," "Designing and Implementing Databases with Microsoft SQL Server 7.0," "Implementing and Supporting Microsoft Windows NT Server 4.0," and "Implementing and Supporting Microsoft Windows NT Server 4.0 in the Enterprise."

The elective exams that you can choose from cover specific uses of SQL Server and include "Designing and Implementing Distributed Applications with Visual Basic 6.0," "Designing and Implementing Distributed Applications with Visual C++ 6.0," "Designing and Implementing Data Warehouses with Microsoft SQL Server 7.0 and Microsoft Decision Support Services 1.0," and two exams that relate to NT, "Internetworking with Microsoft TCP/IP on Microsoft Windows NT 4.0" and "Implementing and Supporting Microsoft Internet Information Server 4.0."

➤ **MCSE (Microsoft Certified Systems Engineer)** Anyone who has a current MCSE is warranted to possess a high level of expertise with Windows NT (version 3.51 or 4) and other Microsoft operating systems and products. This credential is designed to prepare individuals to plan, implement, maintain, and support information systems and networks built around Microsoft Windows NT and its BackOffice family of products.

To obtain an MCSE, an individual must pass four core operating system exams plus two elective exams. The operating system exams require individuals to demonstrate competence with desktop and server operating systems and with networking components.

You must pass at least two Windows NT-related exams to obtain an MCSE: "Implementing and Supporting Microsoft Windows NT Server" (version 3.51 or 4) and "Implementing and Supporting Microsoft Windows NT Server in the Enterprise" (version 3.51 or 4). These tests are intended to indicate an individual's knowledge of Windows NT in smaller, simpler networks and in larger, more complex, and heterogeneous networks, respectively.

You must pass two additional tests as well. These tests relate to networking and desktop operating systems. At present, the networking requirement can be satisfied only by passing the Networking Essentials test. The desktop operating system test can be satisfied by passing a Windows 95, Windows NT Workstation (the version must match whichever core NT curriculum you are pursuing), or Windows 98 test.

The two remaining exams are elective exams. An elective exam may fall in any number of subject or product areas, primarily BackOffice components. These include tests on Internet Explorer 4, SQL Server, IIS, SNA Server, Exchange Server, Systems Management Server, and the like. However, it's also possible to test out on electives by taking advanced networking tests, such as "Internetworking with Microsoft TCP/IP on Microsoft Windows NT" (but here again, the version of Windows NT involved must match the version for the core requirements taken).

Whatever mix of tests is completed toward MCSE certification, individuals must pass six tests to meet the MCSE requirements. It's not uncommon for the entire process to take a year or so, and many individuals find that they must take a test more than once to pass. Our primary goal with the *Exam Cram* series is to make it possible, given proper study and preparation, to pass all Microsoft certification tests on the first try.

➤ **MCSE+Internet (Microsoft Certified Systems Engineer + Internet)**
This is a newer Microsoft certification and focuses not just on Microsoft
operating systems, but also on Microsoft's Internet servers and TCP/IP.

To obtain this certification, an individual must pass seven core exams
plus two elective exams. The core exams include not only the server
operating systems (NT Server and Server in the Enterprise) and a
desktop operating system (Windows 95, Windows 98, or Windows NT
Workstation), but also include Networking Essentials, TCP/IP, Internet
Information Server, and the Internet Explorer Administration Kit
(IEAK).

The two remaining exams are electives. These elective exams can be in
any of four product areas: SQL Server, SNA Server, Exchange Server,
and Proxy Server.

➤ **MCT (Microsoft Certified Trainer)** Microsoft Certified Trainers are
individuals deemed able to deliver elements of the official Microsoft
curriculum based on technical knowledge and instructional ability.
Therefore, it's necessary for an individual seeking MCT credentials
(which are granted on a course-by-course basis) to pass the related
certification exam for a course and to take the official Microsoft training
on the subject, as well as to demonstrate an ability to teach.

This latter criterion can be satisfied by proving that one has already
attained training certification from Novell, Banyan, Lotus, the Santa
Cruz Operation, or Cisco, or by taking a Microsoft-sanctioned workshop on instruction. Microsoft makes it clear that MCTs are important
cogs in the Microsoft training channels. Instructors must be MCTs
before Microsoft will allow them to teach in any of its official training
channels, including Microsoft's affiliated Authorized Technical Education Centers (ATECs), Authorized Academic Training Programs
(AATPs), and the Microsoft Online Institute (MOLI).

Certification is an ongoing activity. Once a Microsoft product becomes obsolete,
MCPs typically have 12 to 18 months in which to recertify on current product
versions. (If individuals do not recertify within the specified time period, their
certification becomes invalid.) Because technology keeps changing and new products continually supplant old ones, this should come as no surprise.

The best place to keep tabs on the MCP program and its various certifications
is on the Microsoft Web site. The current root URL for the MCP program is
at **www.microsoft.com/mcp**. However, Microsoft's Web site changes frequently,
so, if this URL doesn't work, try using the search tool on Microsoft's site with
either "MCP" or the quoted phrase "Microsoft Certified Professional program"

as the search string. This will help you find the latest and most accurate information about the company's certification programs.

Taking A Certification Exam

Alas, testing is not free. Each computer-based MCP exam costs $100, and, if you do not pass, you can retest for an additional $100 for each additional try. In the United States and Canada, tests are administered by Sylvan Prometric and Virtual University Enterprises (VUE). Here's how you can contact them:

➤ **Sylvan Prometric** You can sign up for a test through the company's Web site at **www.slspro.com**. You can also register by phone at 800-755-3926 (within the United States or Canada) or at 410-843-8000 (outside the United States and Canada).

➤ **Virtual University Enterprises** You can sign up for a test or get the phone numbers for local testing centers through the Web page at **www.microsoft.com/train_cert/mcp/vue_info.htm**.

To sign up for a test, you must possess a valid credit card or contact either company for mailing instructions to send a check (in the United States). Only when payment is verified, or a check has cleared, can you actually register for a test.

To schedule an exam, call Sylvan or VUE, or sign up online at least one day in advance. To cancel or reschedule an exam, you must call by 7 P.M. (Pacific time) the day before the scheduled test (or you may be charged, even if you don't appear to take the test). When you want to schedule a test, have the following information ready:

➤ Your name, organization, and mailing address.

➤ Your Microsoft test ID. (Inside the United States, this is your Social Security number; citizens of other nations should call ahead to find out what type of identification number is required to register for a test.)

➤ The name and number of the exam you wish to take.

➤ A method of payment. (As mentioned already, a credit card is the most convenient method, but alternate means can be arranged in advance, if necessary.)

After you sign up for a test, you'll be informed as to when and where the test is scheduled. Try to arrive at least 15 minutes early. You must supply two forms of identification to be admitted into the testing room—one of which must be a photo ID.

All exams are completely "closed book." In fact, you will not be permitted to take anything with you into the testing area. However, you will be furnished with a blank sheet of paper and a pen. I suggest that you immediately write down on that sheet of paper all the information you've memorized for the test.

In *Exam Cram* books, this information appears on The Cram Sheet inside the front of each book. You'll have some time to compose yourself, record this information, and even take a sample orientation exam before you must begin the real thing. I suggest you take the orientation test before taking your first exam, but, because they're all more or less identical in layout, behavior, and controls, you probably won't need to do this more than once.

When you complete a Microsoft certification exam, the software will tell you whether you've passed or failed. All tests are scored on a basis of 1,000 points, and results are broken into several topic areas. Even if you fail, I suggest you ask for—and keep—the detailed report that the test administrator should print for you. You can use this report to help you prepare for another go-around, if needed.

If you need to retake an exam, you'll have to call Sylvan Prometric or VUE, schedule a new test date, and pay another $100. (When I sat for the Microsoft Visual Basic 6, the exam center stated that they were now able to schedule retakes on the spot.) Microsoft has the following policy regarding failed tests: The first time you fail a test, you are able to retake the test the next day. However, if you fail a second time, you must wait 14 days before retaking that test. If you fail, I do not recommend taking the exam again the next day unless you just missed a passing grade. To me, a week seems about ideal—it gives you enough time to bone up on those areas in which you had problems while also making sure that the types of questions you encountered are fresh in your mind.

Tracking MCP Status

As soon as you pass any Microsoft exam (other than Networking Essentials), you'll attain Microsoft Certified Professional (MCP) status. Microsoft also generates transcripts that indicate which exams you have passed and your corresponding test scores. You can order a transcript by email at any time by sending an email addressed to mcp@msprograms.com. You can also obtain a copy of your transcript by downloading the latest version of the MCT guide from the Web site and consulting the section titled "Key Contacts" for a list of telephone numbers and related contacts.

After you pass the necessary set of exams (one for MCP, two for MCP+SB, or four for MCSD), you'll be certified. Official certification normally takes anywhere from four to six weeks, so don't expect to get your credentials overnight.

When the package for a qualified certification arrives, it includes a Welcome Kit that contains a number of elements:

➤ An MCP+SB or MCSD certificate, suitable for framing, along with a Professional Program Membership card and lapel pin.

➤ A license to use the MCP logo, thereby allowing you to use the logo in advertisements, promotions, and documents, as well as on letterhead, business cards, and so on. Along with the license comes an MCP logo sheet, which includes camera-ready artwork. (Note that before using any of the artwork, individuals must sign and return a licensing agreement that indicates they'll abide by its terms and conditions.)

➤ A subscription to *Microsoft Certified Professional Magazine*, which provides ongoing data about testing and certification activities, requirements, and changes to the program.

➤ A one-year subscription to the Microsoft Beta Evaluation program. This subscription will get you all beta products from Microsoft for the next year. (This does not include developer products. You must join the MSDN program or become an MCSD to qualify for developer beta products. To join the MSDN program, go to **http://msdn.microsoft.com/developer/join.**)

Many people believe that the benefits of MCP certification go well beyond the perks that Microsoft provides to newly anointed members of this elite group. I'm starting to see more job listings that request or require applicants to have an MCP, MCP+SB, MCSD, and so on, and many individuals who complete the program can qualify for increases in pay and/or responsibility. As an official recognition of hard work and broad knowledge, one of the MCP credentials is a badge of honor in many IT organizations.

How To Prepare For An Exam

Preparing for any Microsoft product-related test (including Visual Basic 6 Desktop) requires that you obtain and study materials designed to provide comprehensive information about the product and its capabilities. Plus, you will need to know any Web site design and maintenance techniques that will appear on the specific exam for which you are preparing. The following list of materials will help you study and prepare:

➤ The Visual Basic 6 product CD-ROM includes comprehensive online documentation and related materials; it should be a primary resource when you are preparing for the test.

➤ The Microsoft TechNet CD-ROM delivers numerous electronic titles on Visual Basic 6. Its offerings include Product Manuals, Product Facts, Technical Notes, Tips and Techniques, Tools and Utilities, and information on how to access the Seminars Online training materials for Visual Basic 6. A subscription to TechNet costs $299 per year but is well worth the price. Visit **www.microsoft.com/technet** and check out the information under the "TechNet Subscription" menu entry for more details. Don't ignore the Microsoft Developer's Network CD-ROM that comes with the Enterprise edition of Visual Basic 6. You can get the latest version online at **www.msdn.microsoft.com**—the materials include technical articles, tips, the Knowledge Base, books, and so on.

➤ Find, download, and use the exam prep materials, practice tests, and self-assessment exams on the Microsoft Training And Certification Download page (**www.microsoft.com/train_cert/download/downld.htm**).

In addition, you'll probably find any or all of the following materials useful in your quest for Visual Basic 6 expertise:

➤ **Study Guides** Several publishers—including Certification Insider Press—offer learning materials necessary to pass the tests. The Certification Insider Press series includes:

> ➤ **The *Exam Cram* series** These books give you information about the material you need to know to pass the tests.

> ➤ **The *Exam Prep* series** These books provide a greater level of detail than the *Exam Cram* books.

> *Note: There currently is no Exam Prep book for Visual Basic 6 Desktop available.*

➤ **Classroom Training** ATECs, AATPs, MOLI, and unlicensed third-party training companies all offer classroom training on Visual Basic 6. These companies aim to help prepare developers to use Visual Basic 6 to pass the Visual Basic 6 Desktop test. Although such training runs upwards of $350 per day in class, most of the individuals lucky enough to partake (including your humble author, who also teaches such courses) find them to be quite worthwhile.

➤ **Other Publications** You'll find direct references to other publications and resources in this text, but there's no shortage of materials available about Visual Basic 6. To help you sift through some of the publications out there, I end each chapter with a "Need To Know More?" section that provides pointers to more complete and exhaustive resources covering the chapter's information. This should give you an idea of where I think you should look for further discussion.

By far, this set of required and recommended materials represents a nonpareil collection of sources and resources for Visual Basic 6 and related topics. I anticipate that you'll find that this book belongs in this company. In the section that follows, I explain how this book works, and I give you some good reasons why this book counts as a member of the required and recommended materials list.

About This Book

Each topical *Exam Cram* chapter follows a regular structure, along with graphical cues about important or useful information. Here's the structure of a typical chapter:

➤ **Opening Hotlists** Each chapter begins with a list of the terms, tools, and techniques that you must learn and understand before you can be fully conversant with that chapter's subject matter. I follow the hotlists with one or two introductory paragraphs to set the stage for the rest of the chapter.

➤ **Topical Coverage** After the opening hotlists, each chapter covers a series of topics related to the chapter's subject title. Throughout this section, I highlight topics or concepts likely to appear on a test using a special Study Alert layout, like this:

 This is what a Study Alert looks like. Normally, a Study Alert stresses concepts, terms, software, or activities that are likely to relate to one or more certification test questions. For that reason, I think any information found offset in Study Alert format is worthy of unusual attentiveness on your part. Indeed, most of the information that appears on The Cram Sheet appears as Study Alerts within the text.

Pay close attention to material flagged as a Study Alert; although all the information in this book pertains to what you need to know to pass the exam, I flag certain items that are really important. You'll find what appears in the meat of each chapter to be worth knowing, too, when preparing for the test. Because this book's material is very condensed, I recommend that you use this book along with other resources to achieve the maximum benefit.

In addition to the Study Alerts, I have provided tips that will help you build a better foundation for Visual Basic 6 knowledge. Although the information may not be on the exam, it's certainly related and will help you become a better test-taker.

This is how tips are formatted. Keep your eyes open for these, and you'll become a Visual Basic 6 guru in no time!

➤ **Practice Questions** Although I talk about test questions and topics throughout each chapter, this section presents a series of mock test questions and explanations of both correct and incorrect answers. I also try to point out especially tricky questions by using a special icon, like this:

Ordinarily, this icon flags the presence of a particularly devious inquiry, if not an outright trick question. Trick questions are calculated to be answered incorrectly if not read more than once—and carefully at that. Although they're not ubiquitous, such questions make regular appearances on the Microsoft exams. That's why I say exam questions are as much about reading comprehension as they are about knowing your material inside out and backwards.

➤ **Details And Resources** Every chapter ends with a section titled "Need To Know More?". These sections provide direct pointers to Microsoft and third-party resources offering more details on the chapter's subject. In addition, these sections try to rank or at least rate the quality and thoroughness of the topic's coverage by each resource. If you find a resource you like in this collection, use it, but don't feel compelled to use all the resources. On the other hand, I recommend only resources I use on a regular basis, so none of the recommendations will be a waste of your time or money (but purchasing them all at once probably represents an expense that many network administrators and would-be MCSDs might find hard to justify).

The bulk of the book follows this chapter structure slavishly, but there are a few other elements I'd like to point out. Chapter 15 is a sample test that provides a good review of the material presented throughout the book to ensure you're ready for the exam. Chapter 16 is an answer key to the sample test that appears in

Chapter 15. Additionally, you'll find a glossary that explains terms and an index that you can use to track down terms as they appear in the text. I think you will find that making sure you understand all of the terms in the glossary is a good step toward successfully passing the exam.

Finally, the tear-out Cram Sheet attached next to the inside front cover of this *Exam Cram* book represents a condensed and compiled collection of facts, fig- ures, and tips that I think you should memorize before taking the test. Because you can dump this information out of your head onto a piece of paper before taking the exam, you can master this information by brute force—you need to remember it only long enough to write it down when you walk into the test room. You might even want to look at it in the car or in the lobby of the testing center just before you walk in to take the test.

How To Use This Book

If you're prepping for a first-time test, I've structured the topics in this book to build on one another. Therefore, some topics in later chapters make more sense after you've read earlier chapters. That's why I suggest you read this book from front to back for your initial test preparation. If you need to brush up on a topic or you have to bone up for a second try, use the index or table of contents to go straight to the topics and questions that you need to study. Beyond helping you prepare for the tests, I think you'll find this book useful as a tightly focused reference to some of the most important aspects of Visual Basic 6.

Given all the book's elements and its specialized focus, I've tried to create a tool that will help you prepare for—and pass—Microsoft Exam 70-176, "De- signing and Implementing Desktop Applications with Microsoft Visual Basic 6.0." Although this exam covers desktop aspects of VB6, you may encounter distributed questions on the exam. If this is a concern to you, you may want to prepare for both exams before you take either.

Please share your feedback on the book, especially if you have ideas about how I can improve it for future test-takers. I'll consider everything you say carefully, and I'll respond to all suggestions.

Please send your questions or comments to me at **mike@mmacdonald.com**, or the publisher at **cipq@coriolis.com**. Please remember to include the title of the book in your message; otherwise, we'll be forced to guess which book you're writing about.

As of this writing, I personally received over 800 emails about the Visual Basic 5 version of this book. I attempted to answer each one (though volume caused me to get backed up several times!). While Certification Insider Press and I strive to make each book perfect, we do discover ambiguities and even mistakes. I am grateful and indebted to the many readers of *Visual Basic 5 Exam Cram* who took the time not just to tell me how they made out on the exam, but also to offer constructive criticism. Those comments are incorporated by myself and the publisher in two ways—the first is in refinements to the approach I took to this book. The second is in errata pages that are created for each book in the Exam Cram series. You can find this at **www.examcram.com/errata/default.cfm**. Please be sure to visit it.

Thanks, and enjoy the book!

Self-Assessment

Based on recent statistics from Microsoft, as many as 250,000 individuals are at some stage of the certification process but haven't yet received an MCP or other Microsoft certification. We also know that three or four times that number may be considering whether or not to obtain a Microsoft certification of some kind. That's a huge audience!

The reason we included a self-assessment in this *Exam Cram* book is to help you evaluate your readiness to tackle MCSD certification. It should also help you understand what you need to master the topic of this book—namely, Exam 70-176, "Designing and Implementing Desktop Applications with Microsoft Visual Basic 6.0." But before you tackle this self-assessment, let's talk about concerns you may face when pursuing an MCSD, and what an ideal MCSD candidate might look like.

MCSDs In The Real World

In the next section, we describe an ideal MCSD candidate, knowing full well that only a few real candidates will meet this ideal. In fact, our description of that ideal candidate might seem downright scary. But take heart: Although the requirements to obtain an MCSD may seem pretty formidable, they are by no means impossible to meet. However, you should be keenly aware that it does take time, requires some expense, and consumes substantial effort to get through the process.

You can get all the real-world motivation you need from knowing that many others have gone before, so you will be able to follow in their footsteps. If you're willing to tackle the process seriously and do what it takes to obtain the necessary experience and knowledge, you can take—and pass—all the certification tests involved in obtaining an MCSD. In fact, we've designed these *Exam Crams*, and the companion *Exam Preps*, to make it as easy on you as possible to prepare for these exams. But prepare you must!

 There is currently no *Exam Prep* available for the Visual Basic Desktop exam.

The same, of course, is true for other Microsoft certifications, including:

➤ MCSE, which is aimed at network engineers and requires four core exams and two electives for a total of six exams.

➤ MCSE+I, which is like the MCSE certification but requires seven core exams and two electives drawn from a specific pool of Internet-related topics, for a total of nine exams.

➤ Other Microsoft certifications, whose requirements range from one test (MCP or MCT) to many tests (MCP+I, MCP+SB, MCDBA).

The Ideal MCSD Candidate

Just to give you some idea of what an ideal MCSD candidate is like, here are some relevant statistics about the background and experience such an individual might have. Don't worry if you don't meet these qualifications, or don't come that close—this is a far from ideal world, and where you fall short is simply where you'll have more work to do.

➤ Academic or professional training in application design and development as well as relevant database design and usage.

➤ Typically, six years of professional development experience (33% of MCSDs have less than four years of experience, 20% have five to eight years of experience, and 48% have eight plus years of experience). This experience will include development tools such as Visual Basic, Visual C++, and so on. This must include application design, requirements analysis, debugging, distribution, and an understanding of the Microsoft Services Model.

➤ Three-plus years in a relational database environment designing and using database tools such as SQL Server and Access. The ideal MCSD will have performed both logical and physical database designs from entity modeling through normalization and database schema creation.

➤ A thorough understanding of issues involved in the creation and deployment of distributed applications to include knowledge of COM and DCOM, issues involved in the usage of in-process and out-of process components, and the logical and physical design of those components.

➤ An understanding of both operating system architectures (Windows 9x, NT) as they relate application as well as network issues to include Internet architectures. (You will not, of course, be expected to demonstrate the level of knowledge that a network engineer needs to have. Instead, you want to be familiar with the issues that networks—particularly the Internet—raise in client/server applications.)

Fundamentally, this boils down to a bachelor's degree in computer science, plus at least three to four years of development experience in a networked environment, involving relational database design and usage, and application architecture design, development, and deployment. Given the relative newness of the technologies involved, there are probably few certification candidates that meet these requirements. Particularly in the area of multi-tiered applications, most meet less than half of these requirements—at least, when they begin the certification process. But because those who have already achieved their MCSD certification have survived this ordeal, you can survive it too—especially if you heed what our self-assessment can tell you about what you already know and what you need to learn.

Put Yourself To The Test

The following series of questions and observations is designed to help you figure out how much work you must do to pursue Microsoft certification and what kinds of resources you may consult on your quest. Be absolutely honest in your answers, or you'll end up wasting money on exams you're not yet ready to take. There are no right or wrong answers, only steps along the path to certification. Only you can decide where you really belong in the broad spectrum of aspiring candidates.

Two things should be clear from the outset, however:

➤ Even a modest background in applications development will be helpful.

➤ Hands-on experience with Microsoft development products and technologies is an essential ingredient to certification success.

Educational Background

1. Have you ever taken any computer-programming classes? [Yes or No]

    If Yes, proceed to Question 2; if No, proceed to Question 5.

2. Have you taken any classes on applications design? [Yes or No]

    If Yes, you will probably be able to handle Microsoft's architecture and system component discussions. You will be expected, in most of the exams, to demonstrate core COM concepts. This will include an understanding of the implications of in-process and out-of process components, cross-process procedure calls, and so forth.

    If No, consider some basic reading in this area. The "Component Tools Guide" in the Visual Basic documentation is actually quite good and covers the core concepts. Third party COM books can also be helpful.

3. Have you taken any classes oriented specifically toward Visual Basic or C++? [Yes or No]

   If Yes, you will probably be able to handle the programming related concepts and terms in the "Desktop Applications" and "Distributed Applications" portions of the MCSD track. Each section allows you to choose between a Visual Basic or a Visual C++ exam. If you feel rusty, brush up on your VB or VC++ terminology by going through the Glossary in this book and the product documentation.

   If No, and if you don't have a good deal of on-the-job experience, you might want to read one or two books in this topic area. *Visual Basic 6 Black Book*, by Steven Holzner, (The Coriolis Group, 1998, ISBN 1-57610-283-1) is really quite good and is at an appropriate level.

4. Have you taken any database design classes? [Yes or No]

   If Yes, you will probably be able to handle questions related to general data access techniques. If you do not have experience specific to Microsoft Access or Microsoft SQL Server, you will want to touch up on concepts specific to either of those two products.

   If No, you will want to look over the exams that you can take from the "Elective Exams" portion of the MCSD. They include such topics as SQL Server and FrontPage. You may have expertise in one of these areas and should, therefore, aim to take one of those exams. All in all, whether you take the SQL Server (or Access) exam, you should consider reading a book or two on the subject. I like *Microsoft SQL Server 6.5 Unleashed*, by David Solomon, Ray Rankins, et al., (Sams Publishing, ISBN 0-672-39856-4), though some of the book covers concepts more appropriate to a DBA.

5. Have you done any reading on application design and development? [Yes or No]

   If Yes, go on to the next section "Hands On Experience."

   If No, be particularly alert to the questions asked in the next section, "Hands On Experience." Frequently, a little experience goes a long way. For any areas where you may be weak, consider doing extra reading as outlined in questions 2, 3, and 4 above. Carefully review the Glossary in this book and take unfamiliar terms as cues to areas you need to brush up on. Look at the "Terms you'll need to know" and "Techniques you'll need to master" lists at the front of each chapter. Again, for any terms or techniques that are unfamiliar, consider boning up on those areas.

Hands-On Experience

The most important key to success on all of the Microsoft tests is hands-on experience, especially with the core tool on which you are testing (Visual Basic or Visual C++), as well as an understanding of COM and ADO. If we leave you with only one realization after taking this self-assessment, it should be that there's no substitute for time spent developing real-world applications. The development experience should range from both logical and physical design to the creation of remote COM services and database programming. The recurring theme through nearly all of the tests will be COM and database techniques.

6. Have you created COM components?

    If Yes, you will probably be prepared for Exam 70-100, " Analyzing Requirements and Defining Solution Architectures." This satisfies the "Solutions Architecture" section of the MCSD requirements. Go to Question 7.

    If No, you need to study COM concepts as outlined in Question 2 earlier.

7. Have you done database programming?

    If Yes, go to Question 8.

    If No, you will be in a weak position on all of the tests. You need to consult a book such as the one recommended in Question 3 above.

8. Have you done ADO development?

    If Yes, go to Question 9.

    If No, you need to consult an ADO reference. Use the MSDN library on your product's (Visual Basic, Visual C++, or Visual Studio) CD-ROM and review the ADO articles. Additionally, check out a book such as the one recommended in Question 4.

9. Have you developed with Visual Basic?

    If Yes, you should be prepared to take Exam 70-176, "Designing and Implementing Desktop Applications with Microsoft Visual Basic 6.0." This will satisfy the Desktop Applications Development requirement. Go to Question 10.

    If No, go to Question 10.

10. Have you developed with Visual C++?

If Yes, you should be prepared to take Exam 70-016, "Designing and Implementing Desktop Applications with Microsoft Visual C++ 6.0". If you also answered yes to Question 9, you can use Exam 70-016 as your Elective requirement (see Question 12). Go to Question 11.

If No and if you also answered No to Question 9, then you probably should consider getting some real-world experience with either Visual Basic or Visual C++. (If you answered Yes to Question 9 and No to this question, you will want to take Exam 70-176.)

11. Have you developed Distributed applications with either Visual Basic or Visual C++?

If Yes, you should be prepared to take either Exam 70-175, "Designing and Implementing Distributed Applications with Microsoft Visual Basic 6.0" or Exam 70-015, "Designing and Implementing Distributed Applications with Microsoft Visual C++ 6.0". Either exam will satisfy the Distributed Applications requirement of MCSD certification. Go to Question 12.

If No, consult the book recommended in Question 3.

12. Have you used one of the products listed in the "Elective Exams" section of the MCSD requirements?

If Yes, go ahead and take the related exam after consulting the Microsoft Web site for a list of the MCSD requirements (see Chapter 1).

If No, consider boning up on Microsoft Access or Microsoft SQL Server, as outlined in Question 4 above, and taking one of those exams. If you are qualified in both Visual Basic and Visual C++, consider taking Exam 70-016 (Visual C++ Desktop) for the Desktop Applications Development section and Exam 70-176 (Visual Basic Desktop) for the Elective.

Testing Your Exam-Readiness

Whether you attend a formal class on a specific topic to get ready for an exam or use written materials to study on your own, some preparation for the Microsoft certification exams is essential. At $100 a try, pass or fail, you want to do everything you can to pass on your first try. That's where studying comes in.

We have included practice questions at the end of each chapter. If you do well on these, take the practice exam in Chapter 15.

For any given subject, consider taking a class if you've tackled self-study materials, taken the test, and failed anyway. The opportunity to interact with an instructor and fellow students can make all the difference in the world, if you can afford that privilege. For information about Microsoft classes, visit the Training and Certification page at **www.microsoft.com/train_cert/** (use the "Find a Course" link).

If you can't afford to take a class, visit the Training and Certification page anyway, because it also includes pointers to free practice exams. And even if you can't afford to spend much at all, you should still invest in some low-cost practice exams from commercial vendors, because they can help you assess your readiness to pass a test better than any other tool. The following links may be of interest to you in locating practice exams:

➤ **SelfTest Software (www.stsware.com)** At the time of this writing, the cost for the first test ordered was $79. The Visual Basic 6 exam was not yet ready. The VB5 exam included 390 questions.

➤ **MeasureUp (www.measureup.com)** At the time of this writing, tests cost $99. The Visual Basic 6 exam was not yet ready. The Visual Basic 5 test included 180 practice questions.

13. Have you taken a practice exam on your chosen test subject? [Yes or No]

If Yes and you scored 70 percent or better, you're probably ready to tackle the real thing. If your score isn't above that crucial threshold, keep at it until you break that barrier. (If you scored above 80, you should feel pretty confident.)

If No, obtain all the free and low-budget practice tests you can find (see the list above) and get to work. Keep at it until you can break the passing threshold comfortably.

When it comes to assessing your test readiness, there is no better way than to take a good-quality practice exam and pass with a score of 70 percent or better. If you pass an exam at 80 percent or better, you're probably in great shape.

Assessing Readiness For Exam 70-176

In addition to the general exam-readiness information in the previous section, there are several things you can do to prepare for the Visual Basic 6 Desktop exam. As you're getting ready for Exam 70-176, you should cruise the Web looking for "braindumps" (recollections of test topics and experiences recorded by others) to help you anticipate topics you're likely to encounter on the test. A good place to start is Durham Software's Web site (**www.durhamsoftware.com/cert**).

 When using any braindump, it's okay to pay attention to information about questions. But you can't always be sure that a braindump's author will also be able to provide correct answers. Thus, use the questions to guide your studies, but don't rely on the answers in a braindump to lead you to the truth. Double-check everything you find in any braindump.

Microsoft exam mavens also recommend checking the Microsoft Knowledge Base (available on its own CD as part of the TechNet collection, or on the Microsoft Web site at **http://support.microsoft.com/support/**) for "meaningful technical support issues" that relate to your exam's topics. Although we're not sure exactly what the quoted phrase means, we have also noticed some overlap between technical support questions on particular products and troubleshooting questions on the exams for those products.

One last note: It might seem counterintuitive to talk about hands-on experience in the context of the Visual Basic Desktop exam. But as you review the material for that exam, you'll realize that real-world, Visual Basic development experience will be invaluable. While there will undoubtedly be some "paper MCSDs" emerging from the examination process, the exams are increasingly being designed to pose real-world problems. For these types of questions, book learning simply can't replace having actually "done it."

Onward, Through The Fog!

Once you've assessed your readiness, undertaken the right background studies, obtained the hands-on experience that will help you understand the products and technologies at work, and reviewed the many sources of information to help you prepare for a test, you'll be ready to take a round of practice tests. When your scores come back positive enough to get you through the exam, you're ready to go after the real thing. If you follow our assessment regime, you'll not only know what you need to study, but when you're ready to make a test date at Sylvan or VUE. Good luck!

Microsoft
Certification Exams

Terms you'll need to understand:

✓ Radio button

✓ Checkbox

✓ Exhibit

✓ Multiple-choice question formats

✓ Careful reading

✓ Process of elimination

✓ Adaptive tests

✓ Fixed-length tests

✓ Simulations

Techniques you'll need to master:

✓ Preparing to take a certification exam

✓ Practicing (to make perfect)

✓ Making the best use of the testing software

✓ Budgeting your time

✓ Saving the hardest questions until last

✓ Guessing (as a last resort)

Exam-taking is not something that most people anticipate eagerly, no matter how well prepared they may be. In most cases, familiarity helps offset test anxiety. In plain English, this means you probably won't be as nervous when you take your fourth or fifth Microsoft certification exam as you'll be when you take your first one.

Whether it's your first exam or your tenth, understanding the details of exam taking (how much time to spend on questions, the environment you'll be in, and so on) and the exam software will help you concentrate on the material rather than on the setting. Likewise, mastering a few basic exam-taking skills should help you recognize—and perhaps even outfox—some of the tricks and snares you're bound to find in some of the exam questions.

This chapter, besides explaining the exam environment and software, describes some proven exam-taking strategies that you should be able to use to your advantage.

The Exam Situation

When you arrive at the testing center where you scheduled your exam, you'll need to sign in with an exam coordinator. He or she will ask you to show two forms of identification, one of which must be a photo ID. After you've signed in and your time slot arrives, you'll be asked to deposit any books, bags, or other items you brought with you. Then, you'll be escorted into a closed room. Typically, the room will be furnished with anywhere from one to half a dozen computers, and each workstation will be separated from the others by dividers designed to keep you from seeing what's happening on someone else's computer.

You'll be furnished with a pen or pencil and a blank sheet of paper, or, in some cases, an erasable plastic sheet and an erasable pen. You're allowed to write down anything you want on both sides of this sheet. Before the exam, you should memorize as much of the material that appears on The Cram Sheet (in the front of this book) as you can, so you can write that information on the blank sheet as soon as you are seated in front of the computer. You can refer to your rendition of The Cram Sheet anytime you like during the test, but you'll have to surrender the sheet when you leave the room.

Most test rooms feature a wall with a large picture window. This permits the exam coordinator to monitor the room, to prevent exam-takers from talking to one another, and to observe anything out of the ordinary that might go on. The exam coordinator will have preloaded the appropriate Microsoft certification exam—for this book, that's Exam 70-176—and you'll be permitted to start as soon as you're seated in front of the computer.

All Microsoft certification exams allow a certain maximum amount of time in which to complete your work (this time is indicated on the exam by an on-screen counter/clock, so you can check the time remaining whenever you like). The fixed-length Visual Basic 6 Desktop exam consists of 70 randomly selected questions. You may take up to 90 minutes to complete the exam.

All Microsoft certification exams are computer generated and use a multiple-choice format. Although this may sound quite simple, the questions are constructed not only to check your mastery of basic facts and figures of Visual Basic 6 with an emphasis on desktop development, but they also require you to evaluate one or more sets of circumstances or requirements. Often, you'll be asked to give more than one answer to a question. Likewise, you might be asked to select the best or most effective solution to a problem from a range of choices, all of which technically are correct. Taking an exam is quite an adventure, and it involves real thinking. This book shows you what to expect and how to deal with the potential problems, puzzles, and predicaments.

Some Microsoft exams employ more advanced testing capabilities than might immediately meet the eye. Although the questions that appear are still multiple choice, the logic that drives them is more complex than that of older Microsoft tests, which use a fixed sequence of questions (called a *fixed-length* computerized exam). Other exams employ a sophisticated user interface (which Microsoft calls a *simulation*) to test your knowledge of the software and systems under consideration in a more or less "live" environment that behaves just like the original.

For upcoming exams, Microsoft is turning to a well-known technique, called *adaptive testing*, to establish a test-taker's level of knowledge and product competence. These exams look the same as fixed-length exams, but an adaptive exam discovers the level of difficulty at and below which an individual test-taker can correctly answer questions. Microsoft is in the process of converting all its older fixed-length exams into adaptive exams as well.

Test-takers with differing levels of knowledge or ability therefore see different sets of questions. Individuals with high levels of knowledge or ability are presented with a smaller set of more difficult questions, whereas individuals with lower levels of knowledge are presented with a larger set of easier questions. Both individuals may answer the same percentage of questions correctly, but the test-taker with a higher knowledge or ability level will score higher, because his or her questions are worth more.

Also, the lower-level test-taker will probably answer more questions than his or her more knowledgeable colleague. This explains why adaptive tests use ranges of values to define the number of questions and the amount of time it takes to complete the test.

Adaptive tests work by evaluating the test-taker's most recent answer. A correct answer leads to a more difficult question (and the test software's estimate of the test-taker's knowledge and ability level is raised). An incorrect answer leads to a less difficult question (and the test software's estimate of the test-taker's knowledge and ability level is lowered). This process continues until the test targets the test-taker's true ability level. The exam ends when the test-taker's level of accuracy meets a statistically acceptable value (in other words, when his or her performance demonstrates an acceptable level of knowledge and ability) or when the maximum number of items has been presented (in which case, the test-taker is almost certain to fail).

Microsoft tests come in one form or the other—either they're fixed-length or they're adaptive. Therefore, you must take the test in whichever form it appears—you can't choose one form over another. However, if anything, it pays off even more to prepare thoroughly for an adaptive exam than for a fixed-length one: The penalties for answering incorrectly are built into the test itself on an adaptive exam, whereas the layout remains the same for a fixed-length test, no matter how many questions you answer incorrectly.

 The biggest difference between an adaptive test and a fixed-length test is that, on a fixed-length test, you can revisit questions after you've read them over one or more times. On an adaptive test, you must answer the question when it's presented, and you'll have no opportunities to revisit that question thereafter. As of this writing, the Visual Basic 6 Desktop exam was fixed-length, consisting of 70 questions that I had 90 minutes to complete. Because Microsoft can switch test formats at any time, you must prepare as if it were an adaptive exam to ensure the best possible results.

In the section that follows, you'll learn more about what Microsoft test questions look like and how they must be answered.

Exam Layout And Design

Some exam questions require you to select a single answer, whereas others ask you to select multiple correct answers. The following multiple-choice question requires you to select a single correct answer. Following the question is a brief summary of each potential answer and why it is either right or wrong.

Question 1

> Assume that you want to store a large bitmap in the database.
> Which ADO method will be of interest to you?
>
> ○ a. **AddBlob**
>
> ○ b. **AppendChunk**
>
> ○ c. **LoadPicture**
>
> ○ d. **SavePicture**

The correct answer is b. The **AppendChunk** method is used to store very large character and binary data in a **Field** object. Answer a is incorrect because there is no **AddBlob** method. Answer c is incorrect because **LoadPicture** is a VB function not particularly helpful for this task. Answer d is incorrect because **SavePicture** is a Visual Basic statement that is also not particularly helpful for this task.

This sample question format corresponds closely to the Microsoft certification exam format—the only difference on the exam is that questions are not followed by answer keys. To select an answer, position the cursor over the radio button next to the answer. Then, click the mouse button to select the answer.

Let's examine a question that requires choosing multiple answers. This type of question provides checkboxes rather than radio buttons for marking all appropriate selections.

Question 2

> Under ADO, which of the following are valid collections? [Check all correct answers]
>
> ❑ a. **Connections**
>
> ❑ b. **Fields**
>
> ❑ c. **Parameters**
>
> ❑ d. **Recordsets**

The correct answers are b and c. **Fields** and **Parameters** are valid collections (as are **Errors** and **Properties**). Answers a and d are incorrect because **Connect** and **Recordset** objects are standalone—they are not part of collections (nor is the **Command** object).

For this type of question, more than one answer is required. Some feel, and Microsoft won't comment, that such questions aren't scored unless all the required selections are chosen. In other words, no partial credit is given. Microsoft has stated that for the time being, all quesions are given equal weight. Given that, I believe that Microsoft does give partial credit for multiple answer questions. I base this on five separate sittings for VB exams. In only one instance could I divide my score by 1000 and get a round number of questions.

For Question 2, you have to check the boxes next to items b and c to obtain complete credit for a correct answer. Notice that picking the right answers also means knowing why the other answers are wrong.

Although these two basic types of questions can appear in many forms, they constitute the foundation on which all the Microsoft certification exam questions rest. More complex questions include so-called *exhibits*, which are usually screenshots of various Visual Basic dialogs or screens. On some product exams, you'll be asked to make a selection by clicking on a checkbox or radio button on the screenshot itself. For others, you'll be expected to use the information displayed therein to guide your answer to the question. In my experience with the VB exams, you always use the exhibits to guide your answer to the question (I was never required to interact with the exhibit itself). Familiarity with the underlying tool or utility is your key to choosing the correct answer(s). Be prepared to toggle frequently between the exhibit and the question as you work.

Recognizing Your Test Type: Fixed-Length Or Adaptive

When you begin your exam, the software will tell you the test is adaptive, if in fact the version you're taking is presented as an adaptive test. If your introductory materials fail to mention this, you're probably taking a fixed-length test. However, when you look at your first question, you'll be able to tell for sure. If the first question includes a checkbox that lets you mark the question (for later return and review), you'll know you're taking a fixed-length test, because adaptive test questions can be visited (and answered) only once, and they include no such checkbox.

The Fixed-Length Test-Taking Strategy

A well-known principle when taking fixed-length exams is to first read over the entire exam from start to finish while answering only those questions you feel absolutely sure of. On subsequent passes, you can dive into more complex questions more deeply, knowing how many such questions you have left. On adaptive tests, you get only one shot at the question, which is why preparation is so crucial for such tests.

In contrast, the Microsoft exam software for fixed-length tests makes the multiple-visit approach easy to implement. At the top-left corner of each question is a checkbox that permits you to mark that question for a later visit. (Note that marking questions makes review easier, but you can return to any question if you're willing to click the Forward or Back buttons repeatedly.) As you read each question, if you answer only those you're sure of and mark for review those that you're not sure of, you can keep working through a decreasing list of questions as you answer the trickier ones in order.

There's at least one potential benefit to reading the exam over completely before answering the trickier questions: Sometimes, information supplied in later questions will shed more light on earlier questions. Other times, information you read in later questions might jog your memory about Visual Basic facts or behavior that also will help with earlier questions. Either way, you'll come out ahead if you defer those questions about which you're not absolutely sure.

My own strategy is to at least take a guess at every single question, marking for review those that I am not 100 percent positive of or those that seem to take a long time. When I complete all the questions, I then use the Review feature to look at each question I marked. As noted, very often a later question will have wording that will shed light on an earlier question that you may have guessed at. For example, an early question might offer choices of using the **KeyPress** event or the **PressKey** event (which, of course, doesn't exist). A later question may make reference to the **KeyPress** event in a different context. So, if you are torn between **KeyPress** and **PressKey** on the earlier question, your memory will be jogged by the later question. I have encountered such a scenario on a number of exams that I have sat for.

Here are some question-handling strategies that apply only to fixed-length tests. Use them if you have the chance:

➤ When returning to a question after your initial read-through, read every word again—otherwise, your mind can fall quickly into a rut. Sometimes, revisiting a question after turning your attention elsewhere lets you see something you missed, but the strong tendency is to see what you've seen before. Try to avoid that tendency at all costs.

➤ If you return to a question more than twice, try to articulate to yourself what you don't understand about the question, why the answers don't appear to make sense, or what appears to be missing. If you chew on the subject for awhile, your subconscious might provide the details that are lacking, or you might notice a "trick" that will point to the right answer.

➤ Here's a strategy to use if all else fails. Use the sheet of paper you have been given to write down why all of the answers provided seem wrong. You may find that taking the time to articulate your thought process gives you insights into what the question is really asking. I mention this because I objected to a question on the VB6 beta exam. (After completing a beta exam, you are afforded an opportunity to write comments about the questions.) As I was complaining about how none of the answers made sense, I walked through my reasoning process and then I realized why one of the answers did make sense after all. (For what it is worth, I believe that the "guess" I had made was wrong. Oh, well.)

One of the things that has always bothered me about certification exams—Microsoft or not—is that you do not find out which questions you got wrong. No one (that I know of, at least) scores 100 percent. On my most recent sitting for the Visual Basic 6 Desktop exam, there was one question that drove me absolutely nuts. I knew in my heart that I was supposed to select a certain object, but the way the question was worded, I felt that another choice was correct. I marked the question, came back to it, and changed my answer several times. I still do not know if I chose the correct response. Based on the feedback that I received for the VB5 version of this book (as well as in working on other certification exams), I know that developing questions is difficult. My advice is to go with your gut and stick with your first answer.

As you work your way through the exam, another counter that Microsoft thankfully provides will come in handy—the number of questions completed and questions outstanding. For fixed-length tests, it's wise to budget your time by making sure that you've completed one-quarter of the questions one-quarter of the way through the exam period (or the first 17 or 18 questions in the first 22 minutes or so) and three-quarters of the questions three-quarters of the way through (or 52 or 53 questions in the first 67 minutes or so).

If you're not finished when 85 minutes have elapsed, use the last 5 minutes to guess your way through the remaining questions. Remember, guessing is potentially more valuable than not answering because blank answers are always wrong, but a guess may turn out to be right. If you don't have a clue about any of the remaining questions, pick answers at random, or choose all a's, b's, and so on. The goal is to submit an exam for scoring that has an answer for every question.

At the very end of your exam period, you're better off guessing than leaving questions unanswered.

The Adaptive Test-Taking Strategy

If there's one principle that applies to taking an adaptive test, it could be summed up as "Get it right the first time." You cannot elect to skip a question and move on to the next one when taking an adaptive test, because the testing software uses your answer to the current question to select whatever question it plans to present to you next. Also, you cannot return to a question once you've moved on, because the software gives you only one chance to answer the question.

When you answer a question correctly, you are presented with a more difficult question next to help the software gauge your level of skill and ability. When you answer a question incorrectly, you are presented with a less difficult question, and the software lowers its current estimate of your skill and ability. This continues until the program settles into a reasonably accurate estimate of what you know and can do, and it takes you through somewhere between 25 and 35 questions, on average, as you complete the test.

The good news is that if you know your stuff, you'll probably finish most adaptive tests in 30 minutes or so. The bad news is that you must really, really know your stuff to do your best on an adaptive test. That's because some questions are so convoluted, complex, or hard to follow that you're bound to miss one or two, at a minimum, even if you know your stuff. Therefore, the more you know, the better you'll do on an adaptive test, even accounting for the occasionally weird or unfathomable question that appears on these exams.

As of this writing, Microsoft has not advertised which tests are strictly adaptive. You'll be best served by preparing for the exam as if it were adaptive. That way, you should be prepared to pass no matter what kind of test you take. If you end up taking a fixed-length test, remember the tips from the preceding section. They should help you improve on what you could do on an adaptive test.

If you encounter a question on an adaptive test that you can't answer, you must guess an answer. Because of the way the software works, you may have to suffer for your guess on the next question if you guess right because you'll get a more difficult question next.

Exam-Taking Basics

The most important advice about taking any exam is this: Read each question carefully. Some questions are deliberately ambiguous, some use double negatives, and others use terminology in incredibly precise ways. I have taken numerous exams—both practice and live—and, in nearly every one, I have missed at least one question because I didn't read it closely or carefully enough.

Here are some suggestions on how to deal with the tendency to jump to an answer too quickly:

➤ Make sure you read every word in the question. If you find yourself jumping ahead impatiently, go back and start over.

➤ As you read, try to restate the question in your own terms. If you can do this, you should be able to pick the correct answer(s) much more easily.

Above all, try to deal with each question by thinking through what you know about Visual Basic 6 as well as application design, testing, and deployment—the characteristics, behaviors, and facts involved. By reviewing what you know (and what you've written down on your information sheet), you'll often recall or understand concepts sufficiently to determine the answer to the question.

Question-Handling Strategies

Based on exams I have taken, some interesting trends have become apparent. For those questions that take only a single answer, usually two or three of the answers will be obviously incorrect, and two of the answers will be plausible—of course, only one can be correct. In my experience, a large portion of the questions offer four choices where two are related to each other and the other two are related to each other. For example, you might be asked an ADO-related question and two of the answers may mention the **Workspace** object and two may mention the **Connection** object. This is helpful in narrowing down the potential correct answer. Because ADO does not have a **Workspace** object (which is a DAO object), you need only consider the two answers related to the **Connection** object.

Unless the answer leaps out at you (if it does, reread the question to look for a trick; sometimes those are the ones you're most likely to get wrong), begin the process of answering by eliminating those answers that are most obviously wrong, as in the preceding example with the **Workspace** and **Connection** objects.

Other items to look for in obviously wrong answers include spurious menu choices or utility names, nonexistent software options, and terminology you've never seen. If you've done your homework for an exam, no valid information should be completely new to you. In that case, unfamiliar or bizarre terminology probably indicates a totally bogus answer.

Numerous questions assume that the default behavior of a particular object or control is in effect. Knowing the defaults and understand what they mean will help you cut through many Gordian knots.

Mastering The Inner Game

In the final analysis, knowledge breeds confidence, and confidence breeds success. If you study the materials in this book carefully and review all the practice questions at the end of each chapter, you should become aware of those areas where additional learning and study are required.

Next, follow up by reading some or all of the materials recommended in the "Need To Know More?" section at the end of each chapter. The idea is to become familiar enough with the concepts and situations you find in the sample questions that you can reason your way through similar situations on a real exam. If you know the material, you have every right to be confident that you can pass the exam.

After you've worked your way through the book, take the practice exam in Chapter 15. This will provide a reality check and help you identify areas to study further. Make sure you follow up and review materials related to questions you miss on the practice exam before scheduling a real exam. Only when you've covered all the ground and feel comfortable with the whole scope of the practice exam should you take a real exam.

 If you take the practice exam and don't score at least 80 percent correct, you'll want to practice further. Though one is not available for Visual Basic 6 yet, Microsoft usually provides free Personal Exam Prep (PEP) exams and the self-assessment exams from the Microsoft Certified Professional Web site's download page (its location appears in the next section). If you're more ambitious or better funded, you might want to purchase a practice exam from a third-party vendor.

Armed with the information in this book and with the determination to augment your knowledge, you should be able to pass the certification exam. However, you need to work at it, or you'll spend the exam fee more than once before you finally pass. If you prepare seriously, you should do well. Good luck!

Additional Resources

A good source of information about Microsoft certification exams comes from Microsoft itself. Because its products and technologies—and the exams that go with them—change frequently, the best place to go for exam-related information is online.

If you haven't already visited the Microsoft Certified Professional site, do so right now. The MCP home page resides at **www.microsoft.com/mcp/** (see Figure 1.1).

> *Note: This page might not be there by the time you read this, or it might have been replaced by something new and different because the Microsoft site changes regularly. Should this happen, please read the sidebar titled "Coping With Change On The Web."*

The menu options in the left column of this site point to the most important sources of information in the MCP pages. Here's what to check out:

➤ **Certifications** Use this menu entry to pick whichever certification program you want to read about.

Figure 1.1 The Microsoft Certified Professional Web site.

➤ **Find Exam** Use this menu entry to pull up a search tool that lets you list all Microsoft exams and locate all exams relevant to any Microsoft certification (MCP, MCP+SB, MCSD, and so on) or those exams that cover a particular product. This tool is quite useful not only to examine the options but also to obtain specific exam-preparation information, because each exam has its own associated preparation guide.

➤ **Downloads** Use this menu entry to find a list of the files and practice exams that Microsoft makes available to the public. These include several items worth downloading, especially the Certification Update, the Personal Exam Prep (PEP) exams, various assessment exams, and a general exam study guide. Try to make time to peruse these materials before taking your first exam.

These are just the high points of what's available in the Microsoft Certified Professional pages. As you browse through them—and we strongly recommend that you do—you'll probably find mentioned other informational tidbits that are every bit as interesting and compelling.

Coping With Change On The Web

Sooner or later, all the information we've shared with you about the Microsoft Certified Professional pages and the other Web-based resources mentioned throughout the rest of this book will go stale or be replaced by newer information. In some cases, the URLs you find here might lead you to their replacements; in other cases, the URLs will go nowhere, leaving you with the dreaded "404 File not found" error message. When that happens, don't give up.

You can always find what you want on the Web if you're willing to invest some time and energy. Most large or complex Web sites—and Microsoft's qualifies on both counts—offer a search engine. On all of Microsoft's Web pages, a Search button appears along the top edge of the page. As long as you can get to Microsoft's site (it should stay at **www.microsoft.com** for a long time), use this tool to help you find what you need.

The more focused you can make a search request, the more likely the results will include information you want. For example, search for the string "training and certification" to produce a lot of data about the subject in general, but if you're looking for a preparation guide for Exam 70-176, "Designing and Implementing Desktop Applications with Microsoft Visual Basic 6.0," you'll be more likely to get there quickly if you use a search string similar to the following:

```
"Exam 70-176" AND "preparation guide"
```

Likewise, if you want to find the Training and Certification downloads, try a search string such as this:

```
"training and certification" AND "download page"
```

Finally, feel free to use general search tools—such as **www.search.com**, **www.altavista.com**, and **www.excite.com**—to look for related information. Although Microsoft offers great information about its certification exams online, there are plenty of third-party sources of information and assistance that need not follow Microsoft's party line. Therefore, if you can't find something where the book says it lives, start looking around. If worse comes to worst, you can email us. We just might have a clue.

Visual Basic Data Types

. . . .

Terms you'll need to understand:

√ Objects

√ Variables

√ Variable scope, precision, and accuracy

√ Order of operations

√ Number types

√ Visual Basic variable defaults

√ Arrays

√ **Variant** arrays

√ Dynamic arrays

√ **Public**, **Private**, **ReDim**, **Dim**, **Static**, and **Friend**

Techniques you'll need to master:

√ Understanding the limitations of the different numeric data types

√ Correctly identifying those data types that slow down an application

√ Converting one data type to another

√ Understanding the difference between explicit and implicit variable declaration

√ Understanding the limitations of **Option Explicit**

√ Declaring variables with different scopes and lifetimes

√ Declaring procedures with different scopes

√ Declaring and manipulating static and dynamic arrays

In this chapter, you begin your trek towards Visual Basic certification with the very basic essentials—the Visual Basic data types. This chapter mainly focuses on the intrinsic data types: **Integer**, **String**, and so on. Although I touch on the **Object** data type in this chapter, it is discussed more extensively in Chapters 3 and 4. The **Variant** data type is a special case and figures prominently in this chapter as well as Chapter 3. Of course, **Variant**s also play a major role in the certification exam.

I also use this chapter to summarize key points in variable handling, declaration, scope, and lifetime.

Data Types Introduced

Visual Basic has many data types from which you can choose for your variables. These can be thought of in terms of *simple*, *complex*, and *object* data types. Simple data types, such as **Integer** and **String**, are those that Visual Basic supplies for you. Complex data types encompass user-defined data types, as well as more advanced implementations, such as arrays. Simple and complex data types are referred to as *intrinsic* data types. Finally, object data types are actual Visual Basic objects, such as forms and command buttons, as well as objects that you create yourself. I introduce each briefly and expand on some as we go through this chapter and the remainder of the book.

Table 2.1 summarizes each of the intrinsic data types.

In the following sections, I will summarize each of the data types available to the Visual Basic developer; then I will present topics that discuss how VB manipulates those data types.

Table 2.1	**Visual Basic intrinsic data types.**				
Type	**Length**	**Min Value**	**Max Value**	**Conversion Function**	**Notes**
Boolean	16 bits	False	True	**CBool**	Used for "truth" statements.
Byte	8 bits	0	255	**CByte**	Is equivalent to C's **char** data type.
Currency	64 bits	-9 trillion	9 trillion	**CCur**	Used for monetary calculations.
Date	64 bits	1 Jan 100	31 Dec 9999	**CDate**	Used for date and time calculations.
Decimal	96 bits	See Note 1	See Note 1	**CDec**	Used for huge real numbers.

(continued)

Type	Length	Min Value	Max Value	Conversion Function	Notes
Table 2.1					
Double	64 bits	See Note 2	See Note 2	**CDbl**	Used for floating-point calculations.
Integer	16 bits	-32,768	32,767	**CInt**	Used for most integer operations.
Long	32 bits	-2.1 billion	2.1 billion	**CLng**	Used for large integer operations.
Single	32 bits	See Note 3	See Note 3	**CSng**	Used for moderate size floating-point operations.
String	Varies	0 chars	231 chars	**CStr**	Can be fixed or variable length.

*Note 1: The **Decimal** data type can hold a number of +/-79,228,162,514,264,337,593,543,950,335 if no decimal positions are used. The number of decimal positions can be from 0 through 28.*

*Note 2: The **Double** data type can hold numbers from -1.79769313486232E308 through -4.94065645841247E-324 for negative values and from 4.94065645841247E-324 through 1.79769313486232E308 for positive values.*

*Note 3: The **Single** data type can hold numbers from -3.402823E38 through -1.401298E-45 for negative values and from 1.401298E-45 through 3.402823E38 for positive values.*

The Variant Data Type

The **Variant** data type is the default data type in Visual Basic—if you create a variable without specifying a type, it becomes a **Variant**. It can store any other type of data, including objects and arrays. When a **Variant** stores string data, its *sub-type* is said to be **String** but its data type is still **Variant**. Likewise, if the variable is storing a date, its sub-type is **Date** but its data type is still **Variant**. **Variants** offer a lot of flexibility in usage but it comes at the expense of being an inefficient data type. You can also occasionally get into trouble with **Variants** when making assignments, such as unexpected values. I show you an example of this later in this chapter in the "Visual Basic Defaults" section. Also, I discuss the **Variant** data type more extensively later in this chapter in the "More About **Variants**" section.

Numeric Data Types

Visual Basic supports two types of numeric variables: whole numbers and floating-point numbers. *Whole numbers* store no decimal or fraction and, as such, are most useful for pointers, handles, counters, and so on. Their advantages are speed of operation and minimal storage requirements. Visual Basic provides two whole number data types: **Integer** and **Long**. The **Integer** is 2 bytes long while the **Long** is 4 bytes long. Both are signed (positive or negative). Visual Basic reserves 1 bit for the *mantissa* (the mantissa is the sign of a number). Thus, an **Integer** has a range from -32,768 through 32,767. The **Long** data type has a range of approximately +/- 2.1 billion.

Additionally, the **Byte** data type can be used for any small (0 through 255) unsigned (positive) value.

Moving a fractional number into an integer (**Integer** or **Long** VB data types) results in unexpected behavior. If the decimal portion is below .5 (for example, 1.49), the number is rounded down. If the decimal portion is above .5 (for example, 3.51), the number is rounded up. But, when the decimal portion is exactly .5, VB rounds even numbers down and odd numbers up. (No kidding!)

You can also observe this behavior with VB6's new **Round** function. **Round (5.5)** returns 6; **Round (6.5)** also returns 6.

Scaled integers are data types that look like real numbers but are actually integers. Visual Basic implements the **Currency** and **Decimal** data types this way: When you set **currAmount = 1.14**, Visual Basic actually stores it as 11400 (the **Currency** data type supports four pseudo-decimal points). The **Decimal** data type works similarly except that Visual Basic scales it by storing a power of 10, which specifies the number of digits to the right of the decimal point. The **Decimal** data type was introduced with Visual Basic 5. With Visual Basic 6, it is still not fully implemented—to use it, you must declare a variable of type **Variant** and then use the **CDec** function when storing a value: **myVar = CDec (101.24)**.

The advantage of scaled integers is that you get the speed of integer operations and avoid the rounding errors inherent in floating-point operations. The disadvantage is that true floating-point operations are not possible.

Real numbers are those that can be represented with a fixed number of decimal places. The numbers 14 and 1½ (1.5) are real numbers, but 1⅓ isn't, because it cannot be represented in a fixed number of decimal places. Visual Basic does not have a real data type per se; it uses *floating-point numbers* instead.

Floating-point numbers approximate non-real numbers (called *irrational* numbers) by storing them in exponential format—often called *scientific format*—where the exponent signifies where the decimal point should be. For instance, 1.14E-7 means the decimal point should be moved 7 positions to the left (0.000000114) whereas 1.14E+7 means the decimal point should be moved 7 places to the right (11400000). This represents a compact way to store very large and very small numbers with a high degree of precision.

Visual Basic has two floating-point data types: **Single** and **Double**. The **Single** data type is 4 bytes long while the **Double** data type is 8 bytes long. The **Double** data type can store much smaller and much larger numbers than can the **Single** data type (see Table 2.1).

Program Accuracy And Numeric Variables

Because Visual Basic can only approximate floating-point numbers, it stands to reason that some calculations can produce errors. There are two types of errors that the developer needs to be concerned with:

➤ **Rounding errors** Occur when Visual Basic (or any programming language) does not have enough digits available to adequately store a very large or very small number.

➤ **Overflows and underflows** Occur when a number is so large or so small that the variable cannot hold them at all.

The String Data Type

The **String** data type is used to store any character data. Most programming languages use what are known as *null-terminated* strings: The end of the string is indicated by a null character. VB strings, though, are not null-terminated. Instead, VB maintains an internal table of the start and end of each string that it is keeping track of. VB supports variable-length strings (which can be of any length from empty to approximately two billion characters) and fixed-length strings. If the data is not long enough to fill the fixed-length string, the remainder is padded with spaces.

Other Intrinsic Data Types

The **Boolean** data type is used for truth tests—it stores either of the values **True** or **False**. Inexplicably, it is 2 bytes long.

The **Date** data type stores date and time data with a range from 1 Jan 100 (AD) through 31 Dec 9999.

The **Object** data type is used to declare a variable that will hold a Visual Basic object. The variable itself is actually a 4-byte pointer to the underlying object. Unlike with Visual Basic's other data types, you need to use the **Set** statement when assigning object variables:

```
Dim myVar As Object
Set myVar = Textbox
```

I discuss the **Object** data type extensively throughout much of this book, because it is an underpinning of Visual Basic's approach to object-oriented development.

The **Byte** data type is suitable for small, unsigned whole numbers. The **Byte** data type is 1 byte long. It is suitable for storing a single character or a whole number from 0 to 255.

Data Type Defaults

All numerical data types default to zero when first declared. **Boolean** defaults to **False**; **Date** defaults to midnight, 30 Dec 1899. A fixed-length **String** defaults to spaces while a variable-length **String** defaults to an empty string. The **Object** data type has an initial value of **Nothing** until assigned and the **Variant** has an initial value of **Empty**.

Don't get confused with ambiguous terminology on the exam. An empty string is not equal to the Visual Basic values **Null**, **Empty**, or **Nothing**. These are special values used with the **Variant** and **Object** data types.

Visual Basic Operators

To manipulate data, Visual Basic uses *operators*, such as the addition operator (+) and the equals operator (=). These operators can be used in assignments or in comparisons and are summarized in Table 2.2. The exam will expect you to understand the basic operators as well as **Mod**. The **Boolean** operators **And**, **Or**, **XOr**, **Not**, **Eqv**, and **Imp** work at the bit level, and you will not be expected to demonstrate a knowledge of these. However, **And**, **Or**, and **Not** are used to join comparisons, and, though they are still working at the bit level, their use is intuitive. You will be expected to follow complex tests such as this:

```
If (a = 1 And B = 2) Or (a = 2 And Not B = 2) Then
```

Or, in particular, is a valuable aid in interpreting bit-mapped values. Assume that you had a Textbox control and you set its **ScrollBars** property to **vbSBBoth** (which has a value of 3). Later, your code needs to find out if the Textbox has a vertical scrollbar. The constant **vbVertical** has a value of 2. The following test will fail because the **ScrollBars** property is *not* equal to 2:

```
If Text1.ScrollBars = vbVertical Then
```

Table 2.2	Visual Basic operators.
Operator	**Use**
-	Indicates a number is negative: **-1** Subtracts one number from another: **a = b - c**
+	Adds two numbers together: **a = b + c** Concatenates two strings but is unreliable because of the potential for mismatch errors: **string3 = string1 + string2**
&	Concatenates two strings: **a = b & c**
*	Multiplies two numbers together: **a = b * c**
/	Divides one number by another: **a = b / c** where **c** is the divisor and **b** is the numerator
\	Divides one number (an integer) by another and truncates the answer: **a = b \ c** (**b** and **c** are rounded down to integers first)
^	Raises a number by the exponent: **a = b^c** where **c** is the exponent
Mod	Divides two numbers and returns the remainder (**15 Mod 2** returns 1): **a = b Mod c**
<	Indicates a less than comparison: **If a < b Then** (for numbers or strings)
>	Indicates a greater than comparison: **If a > b Then** (for numbers or strings)
<=	Indicates a less than or equal to comparison: **If a <= b Then** (for numbers or strings)
>=	Indicates a greater than or equal to comparison: **If a >= b Then** (for numbers or strings)
=	Indicates an equal to comparison: **If a = b Then** (for numbers or strings) Is the assignment operator: **a = b** (for numbers or strings)
<>	Indicates a not equal to comparison: **If a <> b Then** (for numbers or strings)
And	Performs the logical conjunction of two variables: **a = b And c** or **If b And c Then**
Not	Performs logical negation: **a = Not b** or **If Not b**
Or	Performs logical disjunction of two variables: **a = b Or c** or **If a Or b Then**
XOr	Performs exclusive **Or** on two variables (the result has to be numeric): **a = b XOr c** or **If b XOr c Then**
Eqv	Performs logical equivalency on two variables: **a = b Eqv C** or **If b Eqv c**
Imp	Performs logical implication on two variables: **a = b Imp c** or **If b Imp c Then**

You should use the **Or** operator instead to see if the appropriate bits are set:

```
If Text1.ScrollBars Or vbVertical Then
```

You will also need to understand Visual Basic order and precedence of operations. This refers to the order in which operations are performed in complex statements, similar to algebraic order of operations in math. Consider the following statement:

```
x = 5 + 2 * 6 / 3 - 4
```

In this example, x is equal to 5. Operations within parentheses are performed before operations outside of parentheses. Inner (nested) parentheses are evaluated before outer parentheses. Within that constraint, division and multiplication operations are performed before addition and subtraction. Finally, operations are performed from left to right. Since there are no parentheses in the above equation, Visual Basic first multiplies 2 by 6 (12) and divides the result by 3 (4). Next, it adds 5 to the result (9) and subtracts 4 to come up with the end result of 5. The equation above would be better written as:

```
x = (5 + (2 * (6 / 3))) - 4
```

Variable Coercion

When Visual Basic encounters assignments of incompatible data types, it attempts to coerce them into something that is compatible. If it is unsuccessful, a mismatch error is generated. Consider the following example:

```
Dim a As Single
Dim b As String
b = "1.17"
a = b + 1.1
```

The variable **b** is clearly a **String** even though it is storing a number. When Visual Basic sees the assignment of character data to the numeric variable **a**, it attempts to coerce the values into something that will not generate an error. In this case, it attempts to convert the **String** to a **Single**. Because the variable **a** does, in fact, contain a number, VB succeeds, and the variable **a** becomes 2.27 (1.17 + 1.1). The same is true in reverse. If VB encounters the assignment of numeric data to a string, it coerces the numeric data into character data:

```
Dim a As Single
Dim b As String
a = 1.17
b = a
```

The variable **b** is now equal to "**1.17**". Visual Basic will also allow you to coerce numeric data types into strings, such as: **text1.text = 4.2 * 3**.

Data Conversion And Promotion

When Visual Basic makes an assignment involving two or more values, such as multiplying two numbers and adding the result to a third, it might need to perform intermediate calculations or do various type conversions and promotions. For instance, examine the following lines of code:

```
Dim a As Integer, b As Integer
a = 18000
b = (a * 2) - 4000
```

Remember that the maximum size of an integer is 32,767 and operations inside of parentheses are performed first. In this case, there is an intermediate result of 36,000 (18,000 * 2), which will normally cause an overflow. Visual Basic handles this by promoting the temporary result to a **Long**. If, after completing the calculation, the result is still too large to be held in an **Integer**, an overflow error will result.

The following summarizes VB conversion and promotion rules:

➤ **Compare** All numbers are promoted to the more complex data type. Example: If you compare **Single** to **Double**, **Single** is converted to **Double**.

➤ **Variant Compare** If the underlying data types are the same, comparisons work as described in Table 2.2. If one is a number and the other is a string, the number is less than the string. If one **Variant** is **Empty** and the other is a number, compare as though the **Empty Variant = 0**. If one **Variant** is **Empty** and the other is **String**, compare as though the **Empty Variant = Space(0)**.

➤ **Concatenate** If either variable being concatenated is a **Variant**, the result is **Variant**.

➤ **+ and -** If the first **Variant** is numeric, the result is numeric. If the first **Variant** is **String**, the result is concatenated **String**. If either **Variant** is **Empty**, the result is equal to the other variable. If either variable is **Null**, the result is **Null**. **Single** and **Long = Double**. If the result overflows, convert to **Double**.

➤ **+, -, *, or /** VB will attempt to maintain the same underlying data type promoting in the case of an overflow. **Byte** is converted to **Integer**. **Integers** are promoted to **Long**. **Long** and **Single** are promoted to **Double**. If the underlying data type is **Currency**, **Decimal**, or **Double** and an overflow is encountered, an error results.

➤ *** and /** If either variable is **Single** or **Long**, the result is **Double**. If the result is variant **Single, Double,** or **Date**, the result is **Variant Double**.

➤ **/ or MOD** If any variable is **Null**, the result is **Null**. Otherwise, it's the smallest of **Byte, Integer,** or **Long** that will contain the result.

➤ **^** If any variable is **Null**, the result is **Null**. Otherwise, the result is **Double** or **Variant Double**.

Conversion Functions

Visual Basic has a conversion function to map any value to a specific data type. The function for each is listed in Table 2.1 earlier in this chapter. Conversion functions include **CInt** (convert to **Integer**), **CStr** (convert to **String**), and so on. The two most obvious implications of the conversion function are in VB intermediate calculations and in assigning to **Variant**s. For intermediate calculations, you may want to suppress VB's normal promotion and conversion rules as outlined in the prior section. Where **Variant**s are concerned, you may need to suppress the default behavior of type conversions when assigning to **Variant**s. Finally, to access the **Decimal** data type, you must create a variable of type **Variant** and then use the **CDec** function when assigning a number:

```
Dim myVar As Variant
myVar = cDec (10.15)
```

More About Variants

The **Variant** data type is a 16-bit pointer to the underlying data—*it does not actually store the value assigned to it*. However, it *is* a data type unto itself. It is capable of storing any valid Visual Basic data type, including **Object**. Though its underlying data type might be **String** or **Integer**, its own data type remains **Variant**. When declared but not initialized (prior to having data assigned to it), it has a value of **Empty** (*not* **Null**).

When a value is assigned to it, the **Variant** takes its type from the data and will usually use the most compact appropriate data type, promoting as needed. However, if you assign a number with a fractional component, VB uses the **Double** data type for the underlying data type. If you need to alter the underlying data type, you can do so with one of the conversion functions listed earlier in Table 2.1. You can use the **VarType** function to determine the underlying data type:

```
If VarType(myVar) = vbDouble Then
  myVar = CCur(myVar)
End If
```

Table 2.3	Visual Basic constants to determine data type.	
Constant	**Value**	**Meaning**
vbEmpty	0	Empty
vbNull	1	Null
vbInteger	2	Integer
vbLong	3	**Long** integer
vbSingle	4	Single-precision floating-point number
vbDouble	5	Double-precision floating-point number
vbCurrency	6	**Currency** value
vbDate	7	**Date** value
vbString	8	**String**
vbObject	9	**Object**
vbError	10	Error value
vbBoolean	11	**Boolean** value
vbVariant	12	**Variant** (used only with arrays of **Variant**s)
vbDataObject	13	A data access object
vbDecimal	14	**Decimal** value
vbByte	17	**Byte** value
vbArray	8192	**Array**

The valid constants for data types are listed in Table 2.3.

If you assign a value that is inconsistent with the underlying value (such as assigning a **String** to a **Variant** that had been storing an **Integer**), the **Variant**'s underlying data type changes to accommodate the new value. The **Variant** cannot be used for fixed-length **String** data types.

 To force a **Variant** to recognize a date, use the pound sign modifier:

```
vValue = #1-July-1998#
```

The Object Data Type

Object is a Visual Basic data type that stores a 32-bit reference to any Visual Basic object such as a form. When initialized, an **Object** variable has a value of **Nothing**.

You can use one or more variables to refer to a Visual Basic object. Unlike with other Visual Basic data types, you must use the **Set** keyword to make any assignments. To reinitialize the variable, you set it to **Nothing**. Memory is not freed until all variables pointing to an object are reinitialized, even if you think you have destroyed the object. For instance, if you **Load** a form and then reference it with a variable of type **Object**, the memory occupied by the form is not released until you both **Unload** the form *and* reinitialize the variable (**Set myVar = Nothing**). You can see this illustrated in the next example:

```
' Load and display Form1
Form1.Show
' Declare object variable
Dim oNewForm1 As Object
' This creates a pointer to Form1
Set oNewForm1 = Form1
' This sets the caption of form1
oNewForm1.Caption = "Hello World"
' This unloads Form1
Unload Form1
' "Form1" is not visible but it is still
' in memory. Now, free up the memory
Set oNewForm1 = Nothing
```

Early And Late Variable Binding

When you declare explicit data types, the compiler can perform type checking, verify properties, and so on. This is called *early binding*. When you use a data type such as **Object**, VB cannot know how you will use the variable and so is forced to resolve properties (and so on) at runtime. This is called *late binding*. I discuss VB binding behavior at length in Chapter 7.

The Is Functions

Visual Basic has a number of functions that can help to determine the type of a variable. They are most useful in determining the underlying data type of a **Variant**. The **Is** functions are as follows:

➤ **IsNumeric** Returns **True** for all data types except for **String** and **Object**. Note that VB considers **Date**, **Boolean**, and **Byte** to be numeric. VB returns **True** for the **Variant** data type if the underlying data type is any VB numeric data type.

➤ **IsDate** Returns **True** for **Date** and for **Variant** if the underlying data type is **Date**.

➤ **IsEmpty** Returns **True** only for a **Variant** that has not been initialized.

➤ **IsObject** Returns **True** for the **Object** data type and for **Variant** if the underlying data type is **Object.**

➤ **IsNull** Returns **True** if a variable's value is **Null.**

Always use the **IsNull** function to determine whether a **Variant** is **Null.** Because the two expressions **If MyVar = Null** and **If MyVar <> Null** are both **Null** themselves, they always return **False.**

Visual Basic is flexible in allowing the developer to create special data types. In the following sections, I discuss the use of user-defined types, constants, and enumerated data types.

User-Defined Types

The Visual Basic user-defined type (UDT) isn't a data type, per se. It's a mechanism using the **Type...End Type** construct that allows VB developers to create their own data types. It is used to create "collections" of data, similar to what is called a "record" in COBOL and a "structure" in many other languages. The individual members of the **Type** can be of any data type themselves, including arrays. When *instantiated* (created) in a program, the UDT can be declared as an array of the **Type** itself. For instance, if a **Type SignOnRec** were declared (via **Type...End Type**), it might be created in the application as an array **Dim strRecIn (14) As SignOnRec.** You cannot declare a UDT as **Public** in a class module.

The UDT members can be of any data type, including arrays and other UDTs:

```
Type EmpRec
   FName As String
   LName As String
   DOB As Date
   Children () As String
End Type
```

New to Visual Basic 6 is that you can pass a UDT as an argument to a procedure and as a return value from a function.

Constants

Visual Basic constants (called *intrinsic* constants) are very powerful—they can make a program very readable. They usually yield significant performance gains because Visual Basic resolves their values at compilation, instead of at runtime. The trade-off is that once a variable has been designated as a constant, it cannot be changed at runtime (hence the term *constant*).

Visual Basic 5 added many new built-in constants that are enumerated in the Help file (search using the term "constant"). Typical Visual Basic constants are **vbNormal** (indicates a file attribute), **vbSaturday** (indicates a day of the week), and **vbCalGreg** (indicates the Gregorian calendar is being used). Table 2.3 lists some VB constants to denote a data type, including **vbSingle** with a compiler-assigned value of 4. You can, however, define a constant **vbSingle** with a different value (**Const vbSingle = 10189**). This does not generate an error—instead, the value you assign overrides that which Visual Basic normally would have assigned.

You can also create your own constants (called *symbolic* constants) using the following syntax:

```
[Public|Private] Const varname As data type = value
```

Constants default to **Private**. You can specify **Public** or **Private** when constants are defined at the module level but not when they are defined at the procedure level.

Enum

Enum allows you to create enumerated variables, similar to constants. The following code snippet shows an **Enum** being used to declare a month structure and then being used in an array:

```
Enum SalesMonth
  Jan = 1
  Feb = 2
  ' etc.
End Enum

Dim Sales (Jan To Dec) As Currency
Sales (May) = 184622.33
```

Enum structures really have two significant advantages over constants. First, you can declare a variable to be an enumerated data type. In other words, using the **SalesMonth** code snippet above, you can declare a variable to be of type

SalesMonth. Second, the **Enum** structure becomes part of the type library of any ActiveX component that you create and is available to the user of that component.

 If you do not assign a value to the enumerated variable, VB assigns a value beginning with zero.

Visual Basic Defaults

Visual Basic does not require that you declare any variables. Use **Option Explicit** to force VB to require that all variables in the module be explicitly declared. Otherwise, any use of a variable in your program causes an *implicit* declaration and creation of that variable the first time it is used.

 Relying on VB to create the variables for you is called *implicit declaration.* Using **Dim**, **ReDim**, and so on to declare variables is called *explicit declaration.*

If you do not assign a data type when you declare a variable, or if you allow a variable to be declared implicitly, it defaults to type **Variant**.

VB infers the underlying data type from its context, as discussed earlier. In other words, the statement

```
my_variable = "CAT"
```

creates a **Variant** whose underlying data type is **String**.

Letting Visual Basic assign your data type is normally a bad programming practice, because, at best, the **Variant** is inefficient relative to other data types. Worse, this can sometimes result in subtle, hard-to-find errors. Consider this code snippet:

```
Option Explicit
Dim myVariant, myString As String
' assumes there is a control named text1
text1.text = "Hello World"
myString = text1
myVariant = text1
```

There are two gotchas in the preceding code. The first is the declaration of **myVariant**. Because I did not supply a data type, it defaults to **Variant**. *Even though* **Option Explicit** *is set, it enforces explicit declaration of variables only—not their data types!*

The second gotcha is in the last two lines. **myString** has a value of "**Hello World**" because the default property of the text box is **Text**. So, you might assume the same would be true of **myVariant**. No. Instead, Visual Basic assigns to **myVariant** a reference to the control itself. This is normally handy behavior (I discuss references to controls and other objects throughout this book) as long as it is intentional. In this case, you can see where a bug could be easily introduced because of an unintentional creation of a **Variant**.

Allowing Visual Basic to create variables on the fly is an even worse habit. The mistyping of a previously used variable results in very difficult-to-find bugs, which is a notorious weakness in the Visual Basic language. This can be surmounted, however, by the explicit declaration of all variables, which can be done through the **Dim**, **ReDim**, **Static**, **Public**, and **Private** keywords. I explore this in a moment.

Explicit Variable Declaration

There are two schools of thought on where to declare variables (setting aside matters of scope, which is discussed later in this chapter). The first is to declare all variables at the top of the procedure or module. The second is to declare variables right before using them. Visual Basic supports either convention as long as the declaration precedes the variable's first use.

Variable Declaration

The five keywords used to declare a variable are **Dim**, **ReDim**, **Static**, **Public**, and **Private**. The syntax of each is as follows:

➤ **Dim** [**WithEvents**] *varname* [(subscripts)] [**As** [**New**] *vartype*] [, ...]

➤ **ReDim** [**Preserve**] *varname* [(subscripts)] [**As** *vartype*] [, ...]

➤ **Static** *varname* [(subscripts)] [**As** [**New**] *vartype*] [, ...]

➤ **Public** [**WithEvents**] *varname* [(subscripts)] [**As** [**New**] *vartype*] [, ...]

➤ **Private** [**WithEvents**] *varname* [(subscripts)] [**As** [**New**] *vartype*] [, ...]

Dim

Most variables will be declared with the **Dim** keyword. Variables declared with **Dim** at the module level (in the General Declarations section) are *visible* to all procedures within the module, whereas variables declared with **Dim** at the *procedure* level are visible only within that procedure.

 Though **Dim** and **Private** are essentially synonymous when used in the General Declarations section of a module (that is, a form), I recommend using **Private** because it is more explicit about your intentions.

The **WithEvents** clause creates an object that can respond to events generated in an ActiveX control. I illustrate this in Chapters 7 and 9. The *varname* is the name you assign to the variable. Subscripts declare that the variable is an array (see "Visual Basic Arrays" later in this chapter). **New** is used to implicitly create an object the first time the object is referenced (the object will not exist until **New** is first used, whereas omitting it causes the object to be created and storage allocated immediately). Therefore, the variable is not created until it is actually assigned a value. **New** cannot be used with intrinsic data types, nor can it be used in conjunction with the **With Events** clause. *vartype* declares that the variable will be a certain data type.

 A quick look at the **New** keyword is a good opportunity to discuss some of the subtleties that can lead to success or failure on the VB test. As seen above, you can use **New** when declaring a variable. No memory is reserved by the compiler and the performance penalty is minimal. The variable has a value of **Nothing**, which implies that it is an object. When you make an assignment to the variable (such as **Set myVar = form1**), memory is then allocated and the object created. On the surface, it seems equivalent to these lines of code:

```
Dim myVar As Form1
Set myVar = New Form1
myVar.Caption = "Hello World"
```

But it is not the same. Using **New** in the variable declaration is more akin to an implicit test for the value of **Nothing**, as seen below:

```
Dim myVar As Form1
If myVar Is Nothing Then
   Set myVar = New Form1
End If
myVar.Caption = New Form1
```

What are the pros and cons of using **New** on the variable declaration line instead of in the **Set** statement? The main reason against this is that it is a kind of late binding that exacts some performance penalty, though the penalty is trivial. (On the other hand, if you declared the variable to be of type **Object,** to which you later used **Set** to assign the form, the penalty would be much higher.) The main reason to use **New** in the variable declaration is that you manage resources better by not allocating memory until and unless it is needed.

ReDim

ReDim is mostly used to resize arrays previously declared as dynamic (see the section titled "Dynamic Arrays" later in this chapter). The **Preserve** keyword is used only in conjunction with **ReDim**. Otherwise, its syntax is similar to **Dim**'s.

 ReDim can also be used to declare a variable not previously declared, even if you've used **Option Explicit**. This can lead to hard-to-find bugs, so it should not be used.

Static

Static is used to declare a variable at the procedure level. The variable retains its value as long as your program is running. It is otherwise identical to **Dim** except that the **With Events** clause is not supported. **Static** can also be used to declare an entire procedure as being **Static** (for example, **Static Sub mySub**), in which case all variables within the procedure are also automatically **Static**.

 Be careful of the context of the **Static** keyword. A procedure that is declared as **Static [Static Function calcTotal (iX As Integer, iY As Integer)]** causes all locally declared variables within that procedure to be static (to retain their values between executions of the procedure). A variable that is declared **Static** within a non-static procedure (a procedure that has not been declared as **Static**) retains its value between executions, but other locally declared variables do not.

Public

Public variables are declared at the module level. By default, they are then available to *all* modules being executed. If **Option Private Module** has been declared, then the variable is visible only to the current project.

You cannot use **Public** to declare a fixed-length string in a class module.

Private

Private is used to declare variables at the module level. It makes these variables visible to all procedures within that module, but they cannot be seen by procedures outside of that module. Otherwise, it is identical in use to **Public** and **Dim**. Also, see the tip in the "**Dim**" section earlier in this chapter.

Variable Scope And Lifetime

When you refer to a variable scope, you refer to its visibility—that is, who can "see" it and who can change it. When we discuss variables in this context, the same rules apply to object data types and intrinsic data types. This is a confusing topic for many developers. I have attempted to summarize visibility rules as succinctly as possible in the next paragraph.

As noted, a variable declared as **Public** can be "seen" by all modules running on your system. If you have the **Option Private Module** clause in effect, variables are visible only within the current project. Thus, if a variable is declared as **Public**, a standard module can read and change the variables declared in another standard module. If the variable is declared as **Private**, however, it can be accessed only by procedures within the module in which it is declared. When **Dim** is used to declare a variable at the procedure level, the variable is *local* in scope, meaning that it cannot be seen or changed by any other procedure in any module. When the procedure is exited, the variable is destroyed. **Static** can also be used to declare variables at the procedure level (and not at the module level). In this case, it is functionally equivalent to **Dim**, except that the variable is not destroyed and retains its value between calls to the procedure.

The same variable name can be used in multiple locations in the project. VB uses the one most local in scope.

As a final note, Visual Basic once supported the **Global** keyword to declare variables as global in scope. It has been retained for backward compatibility, but it is no longer documented and is reported to cause inconsistent results.

Procedure Scope

Procedures also have scope. When you place a command button on a form and then double-click on it, Visual Basic opens the program editor and creates a procedure **Sub Command1_click** (or a similar name). Because procedures default to global visibility, all modules in all projects can access that procedure. (When you create an event procedure by double-clicking on a control, VB inserts **Private**, which overrides the default behavior.)

Procedure scope can be altered with the **Private**, **Public**, and **Friend** keywords. If the **Option Private** (not to be confused with the **Option Private Module** variable visibility modifier) option is used, **Public** procedures are visible only within the current project. Procedures declared as **Private** are visible only within the module in which they are defined.

The **Friend** keyword (see Figure 2.1) is used to declare procedures but only within class modules. These procedures are visible to all modules within the project but not to a class that instantiated the class with the **Friend** procedure. (If class A instantiates class B, the procedures within class B declared with **Friend** are not available to class A nor do they appear in the type library of class A.) It is a strange implementation. **Friend** is a concept used in other languages, but those languages typically allow you to say whom you will be "friendly" with (in other words, what other classes can access the procedure). Its purpose is to expose a **Private** variable within the class under control of that class. (Essentially, this means that though the variable may be visible outside of the class, only the class itself can change it. This is a process called *encapsulation*, which is defined in Chapter 3.)

Visual Basic Arrays

An array is a collection of *logically related* data. The data elements stored in the array do not need to have any physical relationship with each other—they can be grouped together merely for the convenience of the developer.

 New to Visual Basic 6 is that you can return arrays from functions. For example, if you have an array named **sNames**, you can declare a function such as the following:

```
Private Function SortNames () As String ()
```

Arrays can have any Visual Basic data type, including any Visual Basic object. When you copy an existing control on a form and select Paste, you are implicitly creating an array of that control. Thus, if you have a command button named **cmdProcess** and copy and paste it, you have created an array of type **cmdProcess**.

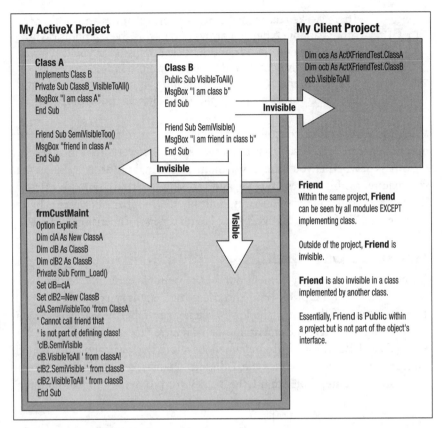

Figure 2.1 An illustration of how Visual Basic implements **Friend** procedures.

 Each element in an array of controls is always the same "type" as the base element and, thus, inherits all of its properties from that base element.

Each item in an array is an *element* and is referenced by its *subscript*, often called its *index*. When you create an array of command buttons, for instance, Visual Basic automatically increments the array's subscript so that each command button can be individually referenced.

To declare an array, simply follow the variable name with the number of elements, enclosed in parentheses:

```
Dim myArray (21) As Integer
```

There is a key difference between control arrays and arrays of other variable types. For arrays of controls, the elements do not need to be numbered contiguously. For instance, you can have an array of five command buttons with the **Index** properties set to 2, 4, 6, 8, and 10. To change the index number of each control, use the control's property page, and alter its **Index** property.

With the exception of control arrays, when you create an array of a certain number of elements, Visual Basic reserves space for every item in that array, regardless of whether you actually use them. Avoid making an array larger than you require, as this wastes memory and can slow your program. To calculate the storage requirements of an array, multiply the number of elements by the variable size. To that, add 20 bytes, plus 4 bytes for each dimension in the array.

Array Subscripts

Arrays always begin with element number zero unless explicitly declared otherwise. You can use **Option Base 1** to cause the default start number to be 1. The beginning of the array (the lowest element number) is referred to as its *lower bound*. The highest element number is referred to as its *upper bound*. The Visual Basic **LBound** and **UBound** functions return the lower and upper bounds of an array, respectively. For example, **LBound (sNames)** returns the lower bound of the array **sNames**. You can use the **To** keyword to modify the numbering:

```
Dim sVar (3 To 8) As String
```

The subscripts can be any valid Visual Basic **Long**, and thus they can be as low as -2,147,483,648 and as high as 2,147,483,647. The subscripts can be numeric *literals* (a literal is any specific value, rather than a value stored in a variable) or any variable previously declared as a constant (**Const**). You cannot use a non-constant variable or any function returning a numeric result to size an array except with the **ReDim** statement (see the section titled "Dynamic Arrays" later in this chapter). If the number is fractional, it is rounded (1.49 becomes 1 and 1.5 becomes 2).

The entire array can be "deleted" (and the memory space reclaimed) with the Erase keyword: **Erase (array)**.

Array Scope

The same rules about visibility with non-subscripted objects also apply to arrays. To make an array visible throughout a project, use the **Public** keyword when declaring the array. To limit its scope to the current module, use the **Private** keyword.

Multidimensional Arrays

By default, arrays have one dimension. The number of dimensions is indicated by the number of subscripts. A three-dimensional array might look like this:

```
Dim iTotals (2 To 4, 1 To 2, -18 To 57)
```

I like to teach students to use enumerated variables (see the "**Enum**" section earlier in this chapter) to declare arrays because doing so makes arrays easier to understand and work with. For instance: **Dim Sales (Alaska To Wyoming, Jan To Dec)**.

Dynamic Arrays

You can dynamically resize an array so that it can grow or shrink as needed. To declare a dynamic array, omit the number of elements in the **Dim** (or **Public**, **Private**, or **Static**) statement:

```
Dim iDynamic ( ) As Integer
```

When you determine the number of elements required, you allocate the storage with the **ReDim** keyword. You can repeatedly use **ReDim** to alter the number of elements in an array, and the subscript can be specified as a literal (as with **Dim**), a variable, or the result of a function returning a numeric result. Re-dimensioning the array destroys all the data contained in the array (effectively reinitializing it) unless you use the **Preserve** keyword. If you increase the number of elements in an array and use **Preserve**, all the data in the array is preserved and the new elements are initialized. If you shrink the size of the array, only the data in the remaining elements is retained.

Technically, you do not need to specify the data type of an array when re-dimensioning the array, because it retains its original data type. However, it is good practice to do so because it serves as one more check so that you do not inadvertently create a new variable by using **ReDim** in its declarative mode. For instance, the last line in the following code was meant to resize **iArray**. However, because of the misspelling, a new array of **Variant**s was created:

```
Dim iArray () As Integer
' Resize
ReDim iArray (0 To 12) As Integer
' Resize again—oops, created new array of Variants!
ReDim iAray (1)
```

When you use the **Preserve** keyword, only the upper bound of the last dimension can be modified. You can, however, change the number of dimensions if you are not using **Preserve**, as seen in the following code:

```
' More on resizing arrays
Dim sArray () As String
' Redimension the array
ReDim sArray (2, 4) As String
' Redimension the last element
ReDim Preserve sArray (2,8) As String
' This causes a runtime error
ReDim Preserve sArray (3, 8) As String
' This also causes a runtime error
ReDim Preserve sArray (4) As String
' Without Preserve, you can change both the
' upper and lower bounds
ReDim sArray (3 To 5, 2 To 10)
```

 Use **Erase** to clear the contents of an array (**Erase myArray**). If the array is fixed, all values are initialized. If the array is dynamic, all memory is reclaimed. To use the array again, you will have to **ReDim** it. Erasing a fixed array does *not* mean you can now **ReDim** it!

New to VB6 is the ability to make assignments directly to a dynamic array. Assume you have two arrays, **myArray1** and **myArray2**; you can assign one to the other as:

```
myArray1=myArray2
```

Variant Arrays

You can never change the data type of an array unless that data type is part of a **Variant** array (and even with an array of **Variant**s, you can change only the underlying data type). However, each element in a **Variant** array can hold a different underlying data type. Further, if a **Variant** is equal to an array, you can change the data type of that array.

You can dynamically create an array of **Variant**s with the **Array** function. Each element can be of any data type. The following code creates a one-dimensional array of three items. The underlying data types are **Integer**, **Date**, and **String**, respectively:

```
Dim vArray As Variant
vArray = Array(3, #1/19/98#, "cat")
```

Arrays Of Arrays

You can create arrays of arrays by employing an array of **Variants**. These can be nested as deeply as you need. Assume, for instance, that you have an array of type **String**:

```
Dim sNames (10) As String
```

Assume also that you have two arrays of **Variant**s:

```
Dim vArray1 (10) As Variant, vArray2 (10) As Variant
```

You can then set any element of the first **Variant** array equal to the entire contents of the **String** array:

```
vArray1 (1) = sNames
```

You can then nest array references by setting an element of the second **Variant** array equal to the first **Variant** array:

```
vArray2 (1) = vArray1
```

To reference an item in the **String** array nested in the second **Variant** array, you append the appropriate subscripts, such as:

```
MsgBox vArray2 (1) (1) (3)
```

In this example, the message box will display the contents of the first element of **vArray2**, which contains **vArray1**. A further reference is made to the first element of **vArray1**, which contains the **String** array **sNames**. Finally, a reference is made to the third element of **sNames**. If **sNames (3)** is equal to "Visual Basic", then that is what will display in the message box.

Practice Questions

Question 1

> What is the data type of "a" below?
>
> ```
> Dim a, b, c As Integer
> ```
>
> ○ a. **Integer**
>
> ○ b. **Variant**
>
> ○ c. User-defined
>
> ○ d. None of the above

The correct answer is b. Each variable needs to be declared explicitly or it defaults to type **Variant**. Only "c" is defined as type **Integer**. Because "a" is not explicitly declared, answers a, c, and d are incorrect. The trick is not to make the (easy-to-do) mistake of looking at the declaration and jumping to the conclusion that all three variables are of type **Integer**.

Question 2

> What is the visibility and lifetime of **lCount** in the following code found inside of a standard module?
>
> ```
> Static Sub Calculate (arg1, arg2)
> Public lCount As Long
> lCount = arg1 + arg2
> End Sub
> ```
>
> ○ a. Global and permanent
>
> ○ b. Global and lifetime of the module only
>
> ○ c. Local and permanent
>
> ○ d. None of the above

Answer d is the correct choice. You cannot have a **Public** statement inside of a sub or function; **Public** statements are only declared at the module level. Answer a would have been correct if the variable had been declared **Public** at the module level. Answer b is a bit ambiguous and should have given a tip-off to the correct answer. Once a standard module is loaded, it does not "go away" until the application is ended, thus making answer b essentially the same as answer a. Answer c would have been correct had the variable been declared as **Static**.

Question 3

> What is the value of **myVar**?
> ```
> Dim myVar As Single
> Dim anotherVar As Single
> anotherVar = 16
> myVar = 4 + anotherVar / 4
> myVar = myVar Mod 4
> ```
> ○ a. 0
> ○ b. 1
> ○ c. 1.25
> ○ d. 2

Answer a is correct. To calculate the answer, you need to be aware of the order of operations (precedence). In the second to last line, the division occurs first even though there are no parentheses. So, 16 divided by 4 equals 4. Then, add 4 to that for an answer of 8. In the last line, the **Mod** operator returns the remainder of a division operation, which, in this case, is 8 divided by 4. There is no remainder, so the answer is 0. You may have guessed answer c if you were not aware that multiplication and division operations occur prior to additions and subtractions. Answers b and d are not reasonable.

Question 4

> What is the value of **myVar**?
> ```
> Dim myVar As Variant
> myVar = ((9 \ 2) \ 9)
> ```
> ○ a. 0
> ○ b. 1
> ○ c. 2
> ○ d. 9

Answer a is correct. The backward slash performs integer division. The parentheses are irrelevant, as is using a **Variant** data type. The inner calculation, 9 \ 2, results in an answer of 4. The other calculation integer divides 4 by 9, which, because it is less than 1, truncates to 0.

Question 5

> What is the data type of the following?
> ```
> Dim vValue
> ```
> ○ a. **Integer**
>
> ○ b. **Variant**
>
> ○ c. **Empty**
>
> ○ d. There is no data type until a value is assigned

Answer b is correct. This question is merely designed to make you doubt what you probably already know: **Variant** is a data type. Answer a is incorrect because no assignment of type **Integer** has been made. Answer c is incorrect because **Empty** is a value and not a data type. Answer d is incorrect because **Variant** is a data type although the underlying data type is not determined until an assignment is made.

Question 6

> You have a class module in which the following is coded:
> ```
> Public Type EmpRec
>   EmpID As String * 5
>   EmpName As String * 30
> End Type
> ```
> You later instantiate **EmpRec** in the following code:
> ```
> Dim strEmpRec As EmpRec
> strEmpRec.EmpID = "123456"
> MsgBox strEmpRec.EmpID
> ```
> What is displayed?
> ○ a. 12345
>
> ○ b. 23456
>
> ○ c. Nothing—the value was too big!
>
> ○ d. None of the above

Answer d is the correct answer because the code will not run. You cannot declare a user-defined data type **Public** in a class module. The trick here is to look at what the answer choices actually mean and to ignore the extraneous detail. Answer d seems to imply that what will be displayed is actually something else. When taking the Microsoft exam, look at the code sample very carefully, with an eye towards whether it will even run at all! Answers a, b, and c are all incorrect for the same reason that answer d is correct. If the user-defined data type had been declared **Private**, then answer a would have been correct. When an assignment of a literal that is too long is made to a fixed-length string, the string is truncated at the right side. Answer b would have been wrong (had the type been declared **Private**) because strings are not left-truncated. Answer c would have been incorrect because Visual Basic truncates when a string that is too long is assigned to a fixed-length string variable.

Need To Know More?

 Aitken, Peter J. *Visual Basic 6 Programming Blue Book*, Coriolis Group Books, Scottsdale, AZ, 1998. ISBN 1-57610-281-5. Peter is an excellent writer and manages to demystify that which Microsoft makes seem mysterious. While *Visual Basic 6 Programming Blue Book* is aimed more at the beginning to intermediate VB developer, this book is a good resource for those migrating from earlier version of Visual Basic (particularly versions 4 and back) as well as those coming from another language. For purposes of exam preparation, Peter hits many of the concepts with which you will want to be familiar. In Chapter 4, Peter covers all of the key aspects of most VB data types building toward Chapter 5 where he expands on the **Variant** data type with some neat examples.

 Craig, John Clark and Jeff Webb. *Microsoft Visual Basic 6.0 Developer's Workshop*, Microsoft Press, Redmond, WA, 1998. ISBN 1-57231-883-X. A good intermediate-level VB6 resource, I found this whole volume interesting and educational. The authors take a "How do I?" approach to explaining various VB techniques. Chapter 3, which covers variables, is a must read for VB developers and is excellent preparation for the materials covered in this chapter.

 Siler, Brian and Jeff Spotts. *Special Edition Using Visual Basic 6*, Que, Indianapolis, IN, 1998. ISBN 0-7897-1542-2. Brian and Jeff's book is a good intermediate-level text. Chapter 8 is devoted to Visual Basic variables, data types, declarations, and so on. Chapter 9 continues with some subjects covered in this chapter such as operator precedence.

 In the online books on the VB CD-ROM, go to Part 1 ("Visual Basic Basics") and browse through the "Variables, Constants, And Data Types" subject.

Application Components

Terms you'll need to understand:

√ Event model

√ Object-oriented development

√ Class and object

√ Instantiation

√ Reuse and delegation

√ Encapsulation

√ Polymorphism

√ **Me**, **ActiveForm**, and **ActiveControl**

√ Form, standard, and class modules

√ Services model

√ COM and DCOM

√ Two-tiered and three-tiered architectures

√ **Function**s

√ **ByVal** and **ByRef**

√ **Sub** procedures

Techniques you'll need to master:

√ Understanding object-oriented concepts in Visual Basic

√ Obtaining references to objects

√ Using the **Forms** and **Controls** collections

√ Using methods and properties of objects with **CallByName**

√ Choosing the proper VB module based on the Microsoft services model

√ Understanding the scope and lifetimes of different modules and objects

√ Understanding the instantiation and life of the **Form** object

√ Mastering VB project startup

√ Declaring subs and functions

√ Using **TypeOf**

This chapter reviews the design of your application from a building-blocks point of view. By building blocks, I mean those modules and components that make up the Visual Basic application. We'll examine the design from the aspect of maintainability and efficiency with an eye towards object-oriented techniques. First, we'll review basic Windows programming principles in the way of background for the application design. Then, we'll review the concept of the Microsoft *services model*. Next, we'll look at the physical components of the application. Finally, we'll review the methodology of designing your application from a physical point of view as opposed to the logic of the business problem being solved.

Visual Basic Development

The following sections guide you through the concepts of *event-driven* and *object-oriented* development. The concepts covered in the next few sections are crucial to the understanding of topics that appear on the exam. Furthermore, an understanding and appreciation of object-oriented concepts can only enhance your skills as a VB developer.

Event-Driven Vs. Object-Oriented

A graphical user interface (GUI) sports an array of controls with which the user interacts. The user dictates program flow rather than the other way around. For instance, the user clicks on a command button, and Windows adds the **Click** event to its *event queue*. Code is written to react to that event, thus the term *event-driven programming*.

Event-driven programming can pose some challenging problems. The developer needs to be especially astute as to what is happening, both in the application itself and in the system as a whole. For instance, consider a situation where you are performing a lengthy operation (perhaps a sort). If you do not change the mouse pointer to an hourglass, the user might think the machine has locked up, and the user might reboot. If you don't put the **DoEvents** function in your sort's loop, the user might not be able to use any other programs (because your program will tie up the CPU). If you don't disable the Sort button (assuming that is how the user invoked the sort routine), the user could inadvertently start a second instance of the sort with undesirable results.

One of the key challenges facing the developer is determining to which events to attach code. Some of the decisions are more art than science—adhering to common user interface (CUI) principles. For example, I generally try to discourage students from attaching code to the **Click** events of the OptionButton control because the purpose of the control is to indicate a choice and not initiate an action. (Obviously, there are exceptions to every rule.) Other decisions are more science than art. As an example, it is common for the developer to need to perform house cleaning when a form is about to close. Your only real opportunity to do so is in the **QueryUnload** event. Here, you can place code to prompt a user to save a file, cancel the closing of the form, and so on.

Another aspect of choosing which event to use is based on knowledge of the event model exposed by various objects. For the ADO **Recordset** object, the developer needs to know that the **FetchComplete** event is triggered after a lengthy asynchronous retrieve of records from the database. Thus, this becomes a likely event in which to attach code that enables edit controls.

Object-oriented development is an entirely different concept than event-driven programming. Object-oriented development seeks to maximize reusability and reliability of previously written code, as you'll see in the next section.

Object-Oriented Development

The benefits of object-oriented development aren't always easy to describe to the uninitiated. In fact, object-oriented development usually requires an up-front cost whose payback might not be realized for months or, sometimes, years. And yet, even the naysayers are employing object-oriented development each time they fire up any modern fourth-generation language (4GL). Each time you draw a command button on a form, you are employing one of the pillars of object-oriented development—*reuse*. The Visual Basic development team at Microsoft has prewritten an object that you can use over and over again, changing only those behaviors (such as caption and event scripts) that need to be customized. In the meantime, you are working with the sure knowledge that the code behind the control has been thoroughly debugged. If designers "rolled their own" command button on every form, productivity would go down just as surely as the number of bugs would soar.

So, let's explore what object-oriented development means. Later, we'll discuss how it is implemented in Visual Basic. In order to understand the concepts of object-oriented development, one must master the terms. You will see these on your Microsoft certification exam.

The term *object-oriented development* is fairly new and is essentially synonymous with the more traditional term *object-oriented programming.* It symbolizes the move away from the term *programming,* which is more indicative of a third-generation language, towards *software engineering* and *application development.* The new terminology better describes the lifecycle of creating an application, from the design of the GUI and the database, to integrating the various components into the finished application.

Objects

An *object* is a "thing" that encompasses both data and behavior. The data is not necessarily records from a database. Data can simply be variables used to calculate screen size or some other custodial function. Behaviors are the object's manifestations—how it appears (if it has a graphical representation at all), and its properties and methods. Every object has three items in common:

➤ **Properties** What is it about the object that defines it? Examples include **Caption, Visible,** and **Sorted.**

➤ **Methods** What can the object do? Methods are services that an object provides. Examples include **Print, Retrieve,** and **Show.**

➤ **Events** What types of things can happen to the object? Examples include **Click, Scroll,** and **Load.**

Collectively, an object's properties, methods, and events make up its *interface.* The interface is the mechanism by which you interact with the object. The interface can be broken into two subcategories:

➤ **Public** Properties, methods, and events exposed for users of the object to use. An example is the **Click** event of a CommandButton control.

➤ **Private** Properties, methods, and events not exposed to users of the object. An example might be a variable declared as **Private** in a class module.

Properties make up the data portion of an object. While we tend to think of properties as public interface items, such as **form1.Visible** and **text1.text,** properties also encompass variables declared within an object. Methods and events make up the behavior of the object.

A *class* is a definition of an object. Take your pet cat (better yet, take mine!). It is an object whose class is cat. Open a dictionary and look up the word "cat" and you will see the definition of what a cat is—it has four legs, it has fur, and it scratches the furniture. But, the dictionary does not contain a living, breathing cat. Instead, it merely presents a definition of what a cat is. The process of modeling real-world objects is called *abstraction.* When you create a class in Visual Basic—such as in a class module—you are creating an abstraction of a real-world object.

The term *instantiate* refers to the process of creating an object from a class. If you design a form named **frmMain** in the development environment, it is a *class* of type **frmMain.** It does not become an object until it is instantiated, which happens when you **Load** it. If you have several copies of **frmMain** in memory, each is called an *instance* of the class **frmMain.**

In the following sections, I detail the handling of objects in Visual Basic.

Manipulating Object Properties

Visual Basic provides a few methods for interacting with the attributes of an object. The brute force method is something like:

```
cmdGo.Caption = "Go!"
cmdGo.Enabled = True
cmdGo.Default = True
cmdGo.Visible = True
```

You can make your code somewhat more readable and efficient using the **With...End With** construct, where the object being operated on is the **With** argument:

```
With cmdGo
   .Caption = "Go!"
   .Enabled = True
   .Default = True
   .Visible = True
End With
```

The object-dot-interface method is called *dot notation*. Using the **With...End With** method, as shown in the previous example, is more efficient because VB only has to resolve the object address once. Consider, as an example, the following statement:

```
text1.text = myObjectA.myObjectB.myObjectC.Value
text2.text = myObjectA.myObjectB.myObjectD.Value
```

This is called a *nested reference.* **myObjectB** is a property of **myObjectA** (similar to how, for instance, the **Fields** collection is a property of the **Recordset** object), and **myObjectC** and **myObjectD** are both properties of **myObjectB**. Resolving nested references is time-consuming for Visual Basic. It is more efficient to create variables to resolve frequently referenced nested object references, like this:

```
Dim vObjC As Variant
Dim vObjD As Variant
Set vObjC = myObjectA.myObjectB.myObjectC
Set vObjD = myObjectA.myObjectB.myObjectD
text1.text = vObjC.Value
text2.text = vObjD.Value
```

Additionally, Visual Basic controls have default attributes. Thus, if you are setting the default property of a control, you don't need to reference it in your assignment. The default property of the TextBox control is **Text**. You can set the control's **Text** property simply by coding:

```
txtResult = "Successful!"
```

If you assign a control to a variable of type **Variant**, the variable can be treated as though it has properties. Assuming you define a **Variant** as type **Object**, you can use the **Set** keyword to make the variable equal to any valid VB control:

```
Set vObject = txtResult
```

Then, you can access the control's **Text** property:

```
vObject.text = "Successful!"
```

However, if instead you code

```
vObject = "Success!"
```

you would not get the expected results (which would be to set the **Text** property). Instead, you would change the underlying data type of **vObject** from **txtResult** to **String** with the assignment. This underscores the concept presented in Chapter 2 that a **Variant** is of data type **Variant**, *not* whatever the underlying variable type is. Therefore, it is not of type **Object**.

 As this example shows all too clearly, you need to pay *very* close attention to variables of type **Variant**, both in your code (where unexpected things can happen) and on your certification exam (where very unpleasant things can happen). Follow the life of a **Variant** line by line and watch out for the ones that change their nature by becoming a new data type.

Examining The Identity Of An Object

Sometimes, you need to know the identity of the object you are dealing with. You do so by examining the **Name** property. Every Visual Basic object has a **Name** property, which is not to be confused with the **Caption** or **Text** properties. If you create a form, its **Name** property might be **frmCustMaint**. Although you can change the **Name** of an object at design time, it is generally read-only at runtime.

The **Me** keyword returns a *reference* to the current object, and the **ActiveControl** keyword returns a reference to whatever object currently has focus. The following code shows the use of both keywords in a trivial application shown in

Figure 3.1 Demonstrating the **Me** keyword and **ActiveControl**
property of the form.

Figure 3.1. In the code, **Me.Name** returns the **Name** property of the form,
whereas **Me.ActiveControl.Name** returns the **Name** property of whatever control currently has focus:

```
Private Sub cmdAsk_Click()
txtMe = Me.Name
txtActControl = Me.ActiveControl.Name
End Sub
```

 In a given module, if you reference a method or property without
an object qualifier, **Me** is assumed. Thus, if you code **Caption =
"Hello World"** in a form, Visual Basic interprets the line of code
as **Me.Caption = "Hello World"**. This is not true of event procedures, however. Visual Basic does not recognize either **Load()** or
Me_Load() as being synonymous with **Form_Load()**.

At design time, you can have only one control for any **Name** property. In other
words, you cannot give two controls the same name. You can, of course, create
a control array with each element differentiated by its **Index** property.

At runtime, you can create new instances of an object, each sharing the same
name, by using the **New** keyword:

```
Dim f As New frmCustMaint
```

This line of code creates a new instance of **frmCustMaint**. Each instance has
the same name. So, how do you differentiate between the two? Put in object-
oriented development terms, how do you obtain a *reference* to the instance that
you want to deal with? The most direct way to reference an instance is to use
Visual Basic's built-in **Forms** collection. **Forms** contains a reference to the
MDIForm (if present), any MDI child forms, and any non-MDI forms. (Similarly, Listing 3.1 illustrates iterating through the **Controls** collection to obtain
a reference to a control.)

Each form object, in turn, has its own **Controls** collection made up of all controls on the form. You can obtain a reference to each form and control in a
project by iterating through these collections using code similar to the following:

```
Dim vForm As Variant
Dim vControl As Variant
For Each vForm In Forms
  Debug.Print vForm.Name; "-"; vForm.Caption
  For Each vControl In vForm.Controls
    Debug.Print vControl.Name
  Next
Next
```

The code iterates through all loaded forms and through all controls on each of those forms that print the name and caption of the form and the name of the controls to the Intermediate window in Visual Basic.

 Many of Visual Basic's built-in collections, such as **Forms** and **Collections**, are zero-based. The **Forms** collection and the **Controls** collection each have one property—**Count**. If you wanted to iterate through the collections using a **For...Next** loop, you would use a syntax something like **For I = 0 to Forms.Count - 1**. Because some collections are zero-based and other collections are one-based, you are better off using the **For Each** loop construct. (**For Each** is more efficient anyway.)

Because multiple objects can have the same **Name** property, it is good practice to use generic calling syntax. For example, examine the following code:

```
Dim f1 As New frmIdentityCrisis
Dim f2 As New frmIdentityCrisis
f1.Show
f2.Show
frmIdentityCrisis.Caption = "Hello World"
```

The two **Dim** statements create new instances of **frmIdentityCrisis**, and the next two lines **Show** the forms. The last line sets the **Caption** property to "Hello World". But, which form is changed—the one referenced by **f1** or **f2**? Alas, neither! The last line of code creates a *third* instance of the form, but it is not seen until you use the **Show** method (it is loaded into memory, however). If you are managing multiple instances of an object, you are better off referencing the object via a variable rather than the object name.

 There are other tricks that developers use to manage multiple instances of an object. For example, assume your application allows multiple customer maintenance screens to be opened. Developers commonly set the **Caption** property to the customer name and/or customer number. Sometimes, developers will use the **Tag** property to manage multiple instances of a form. By setting the

Tag property to a given customer number, it is easy to iterate through the **Forms** collection to find the form that maintains customer 101 or to see if there is already a form opened for maintaining customer 101.

Using *CallByName*

CallByName is a function new to Visual Basic 6. It allows you to call a method or access a property of an object even if you do not know the name of the object at design time (it also allows a user to set properties at runtime). The function's syntax follows:

```
CallByName (Object, Procedure, Calltype,[Arguments()])
```

Object is a valid object reference, such as a control. *Procedure* is the name of the method or property being accessed. *Calltype* is a VB constant of type **vbCallType**. Possible values are **vbGet** (to retrieve a property value), **vbLet** (to assign a non-object value), **vbSet** (to assign an object), or **vbMethod** (to invoke a method). *Arguments* is an optional array of required argument(s) to the property or method being called. For example, if you were setting the **Text** property of a TextBox control, you would pass one string argument.

As a simplistic example, the form shown in Figure 3.2 has the code in Listing 3.1 attached to the **Click** event of **cmdQuery**.

Listing 3.1   Demonstration of CallByName.

```
Private Sub cmdQuery_Click()
Dim sType As String
Dim vControl As Variant
On Error GoTo errorhandler
For Each vControl In Controls
  If vControl.Name = txtObject.Text Then
    Exit For
  End If
Next

If chkProp.Value = vbChecked Then
  If chkLet.Value = vbChecked Then
    CallByName vControl, txtPropMeth.Text, _
      VbLet, txtValue
  Else
    txtValue = CallByName(vControl, txtPropMeth, _
      VbGet)
  End If
```

```
Else
  CallByName vControl, txtPropMeth.Text, _
    VbMethod
End If
Exit Sub
errorhandler:
MsgBox Err.Description
End Sub
```

The code uses the checkboxes to determine if the user desires to access a property (and, if so, whether to assign a value or set the value) or method. The documentation does not show any way of dynamically creating an object reference—using the examples in the Help file, you need to know the object ahead of time. The example allows a user to type in the name of an object and the code searches through the **Controls** collection to obtain a reference to the object. If the user is setting a property, the code sets the specified property to the value in **txtValue**. If the user is retrieving a value (as shown in Figure 3.2), the value is listed in **txtValue**. If the user is invoking a method, the code simply calls the method as shown in the code. For purposes of brevity, the code assumes no arguments are required by the method. A simplistic error handler handles the situation when a user types an invalid control, property, or method name.

Examining The Nature Of An Object

The **TypeOf** keyword helps you to look at an object and evaluate from what class it is derived. When using **TypeOf**, you use the **Is** keyword as a comparison operator instead of the equal sign (=). Any comparison must be done in an **If** statement:

```
If TypeOf myControl Is CommandButton Then ...
```

You cannot assign an object reference to another variable using **TypeOf**.

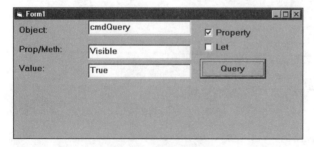

Figure 3.2   Demonstration of the **CallByName** function.

More About Classes

As defined earlier, a class is an abstraction of an object. As an example of a class, examine Visual Basic's **Form** object. It has certain properties, such as **Visible** and **Caption**. When you create a form in the development environment and then customize it (changing the **Caption**, adding controls, and so on), you are doing what is known as *subclassing*—customizing a class definition to create a new class. When your application invokes the form's **Show** method, you are instantiating the class to create an object. If the form's **Name** property is **frmCustMaint**, you are instantiating an object of type **frmCustMaint**.

There are three pillars of object orientation—reuse, encapsulation, and polymorphism—that are discussed briefly in the upcoming sections. The Visual Basic certification exam will not ask questions about the definition of object-oriented development, per se. Instead, the exam will frame questions about Visual Basic with the assumption that you have a general understanding of object-oriented concepts.

Reuse

The holy mantra of object-oriented development is *reuse*. The goal of reuse is obvious—to reduce development time by reusing previously written code. Effective reuse goes beyond merely reusing some aging Accounts Receivable algorithm. You seek to reuse objects and all their associated attributes. Doing so means that you can, for instance, save time or increase productivity by adding a previously written module of Accounts Receivable routines to projects, as needed. You further gain by the knowledge that the routines have been pretested and debugged. Also, you have security knowing that one program will process past-due balances the same as the next. Finally, if there is a need to modify a routine, you have only one place to change it, and then, by recompiling all programs in which that routine appears, the change *propagates* (flows down) through all of those programs that use the reused code.

Object-oriented development purists will tell you that the terms *reuse* and *inheritance* are one and the same. Inheritance may be the best way to *implement* reuse, but the two terms are not the same. Inheritance is simply one method that you can use to accomplish the goal of reuse. (With inheritance, an object is descended from another object. Not only does it assume all of the attributes of the ancestor object, but changes to the ancestor object are propagated to descendents.) Recall that the beginning of this section states that every time you draw a command button on a form, you are implementing reuse. You are doing that without the use of inheritance. Instead, you are instantiating an object of the class (type) command button.

Unfortunately, Visual Basic does not support inheritance. There are other methods to achieve reuse. You can sort of simulate the best of inheritance through the use of containment in a process known as *delegation*. Chapter 5 illustrates the use of delegation.

 If there were a fourth pillar of object-orientation, it would be *multiple inheritance*. Multiple inheritance is the process of inheriting from two or more objects to create a new object comprised of the base objects (it's kind of like inheriting from *tractor* and *trailer* to create a *tractor-trailer* object). It is a confusing concept not implemented in some languages that are otherwise fully object-oriented. Ironically, although Visual Basic does a poor job of simulating inheritance, its process of combining classes and achieving reuse via delegation is actually a pretty good stab at multiple inheritance.

The only true way to reuse code in Visual Basic 6 is by encapsulating the functionality that you need to reuse in a standard module, user class, or other object, and add it to other projects as needed. Visual Basic 6 has improved in the area of encapsulation by leaps and bounds. Consider an application that processes a database. Assume that you need three forms to manipulate customer data. Under prior versions of VB, you had little choice but to embed some or all of the logic in all three forms. If you needed to make a change, you had to make the change to all three forms. In Visual Basic 6, you can use the **DataEnvironment** object or create data-aware classes that can then be reused by as many forms as required. Chapter 10 discusses data-aware objects in more detail. For now, let's take a closer look at encapsulation.

Encapsulation

Encapsulation is another pillar of object-oriented development. Encapsulation refers to the process of hiding attributes from prying eyes. Specifically, encapsulation embeds data and the methods to operate on that data within an object. The object is responsible for manipulating that data. Imagine you have a routine that accepts an encrypted string and decrypts the string to verify whether a password is correct. You don't want the unencrypted data visible to unauthorized use. So, you create an object—perhaps a user class—in which you have a routine with the sole purpose of decrypting a password and comparing it to what is stored in the database. To the extent that you do not make the class's variables public, the object "owns" the data, and the data is "hidden" from others.

When I teach college students or lecture in the corporate environment, I often liken a properly constructed object to a selfish child—it does not allow others to play with its "toys" without first asking permission. An object owns data, and other objects have to go through the first object to access that data.

A great example of encapsulation is the new data-aware class. Let's return to the example of the need for multiple forms to manipulate customer data. Let's say that you create a class that performs all the necessary steps to connect to the database, read records, edit values, and so on. In the class, you implement such business rules as "all customers must be either male or female". If a form needs a customer record, it asks your class for that data. If the form makes a change to the customer's gender, it sends the data to a publicly exposed method or property of the class. The class validates the data and refuses to allow any value other than male or female to be updated to the database. All the code is encapsulated in the object whose job it is to manipulate customer records. That's not the form's job—the form's job is simply to interact with the user. If Congress passes legislation that recognizes other genders, then the code needs to be changed in only one place.

Recall our discussion of visibility or scope in Chapter 2. We discussed *access modifiers*, such as **Public** and **Private**. These allow you to properly protect attributes from unauthorized and (more importantly) unintended use. Recall also that the access modifiers were not restricted to only variables. You could also indicate the scope of subs and functions. If you make a form's procedures visible, another object can invoke those procedures to modify the data while ensuring that the form has complete control over the process.

You really tame the encapsulation tiger when you encapsulate your data, methods, and so on into a class module. Much of Chapter 5 is devoted to this subject.

Polymorphism

The third pillar of object orientation is described by the difficult-to-grasp term *polymorphism*. Polymorphism refers to a process whereby an object invokes a method of another object in a common manner (with the same name), without understanding or caring how it is accomplished. Consider, as an example, VB's **Print** method. When invoked in a form, output is to the form itself. When invoked by the **Debug** object, output is to the Immediate Window. The same command is used to accomplish two different tasks.

You saw polymorphic behavior earlier in this chapter when we iterated through the **Controls** collection to obtain the name of each object. The code did not know which object it was talking to—it merely depended on the polymorphic behavior of those controls to obtain their names.

You may take advantage of polymorphic behavior without even knowing it. Perhaps you have a Data control on a form. In the **Validate** event, you loop through the bound controls looking for any control whose data is invalid and then invoke the **SetFocus** method on it. Your code doesn't specify **text1.SetFocus**. Instead, your code uses the **SetFocus** method not knowing or caring what object it is dealing with.

Armed with a basic knowledge of object-oriented terminology, let's review the components that make up a Visual Basic project. First, we'll review the Microsoft *services model*, then we'll look at the types of modules available to you as a VB developer. Finally, we'll delve into properties, events, and procedures.

Service, Please

The Microsoft services model is not so much a technology as it is a philosophical approach to the technology of client/server development. When you hear the term *services model*, it is the development philosophy that lies at the heart of COM and DCOM. Specifically, a services model refers to the segregating of an application into three distinct sets of services, often called *layers*:

➤ **User Services** Those portions of the application that deal directly with the user—the forms and controls. There is minimal or no business logic encompassed in the user layer.

➤ **Business Services** The logic of the application. Whereas the user layer is concerned with displaying and collecting data, the business layer is concerned with applying business rules in validating and processing that data.

➤ **Data Services** That portion of the client/server application that physically maintains the database. It processes requests from the business layer to retrieve or update data.

That the services model looks like a three-tiered architecture is no coincidence. When you are designing a client/server system, user services are deployed to the client's computer (the desktop), whereas business services are centralized on an application server. Data services, of course, are maintained on the database server.

In the early days of client/server, we had what has become known as *fat clients*, so called because so much of the processing was done at the client level. A good example is the Visual Basic form with a Data control placed on it and all processing occurring within the form. This type of design might be adequate for many applications. But, it is not particularly scalable (*scalable* refers to the ability to "grow" an application to support many users) nor is it easy to maintain. Assume, for example, that you have 1,000 users and that a change needs to be made to how a customer is validated. With the fat-client architecture—called *two-tier*—the change needs to be made on the computers of all 1,000 users.

With the three-tiered architecture, business services are removed from the desktop and relocated to a middle-tier, usually called an *application server*. Assume the same scenario in which a change needs to be made to how a customer is validated. With the three-tiered architecture implemented in the Microsoft services model, the change is made to a business object that runs on the application server. In other words, the change is made on just 1 computer (instead of 1,000).

Figure 3.3 shows the physical structure of the three-tiered architecture that makes up the services model. The logical structure is shown in Table 3.1. In Figure 3.3, we have a number of client computers connected via the network to a server. In turn, the server is connected to the database server. In Table 3.1, the application logic is shown separated into the three components. The user services are strictly concerned with dealing with the user interface, whereas the business services request data from the database, edit the data, and send the data to the database server for updating.

The services model leads to something called the *thin client*, so called because so little processing is done on the client computer. Besides the obvious advantage of maintainability, other advantages are realized at every layer of the model. For instance, because clients have less processing done on them, the need for ever bigger and faster computers is reduced. Because the clients do not interact with the database directly, network traffic can often be reduced. The business layer (the application server) can often manage the multiple connections to the database server more efficiently—sharing multiple connections between clients and thereby reducing the database server's load.

There is no reason why the network shown in Figure 3.3 cannot be the Internet (or an intranet). The Internet is really just another network (albeit with some special considerations for performance reasons). An Internet-based application leads to the logical culmination of the thin client—no application on the client at all. This is accomplished by placing the user interface entirely within a Web browser, such as Internet Explorer. There is also no reason why the application server cannot also be a Web server, such as Microsoft IIS.

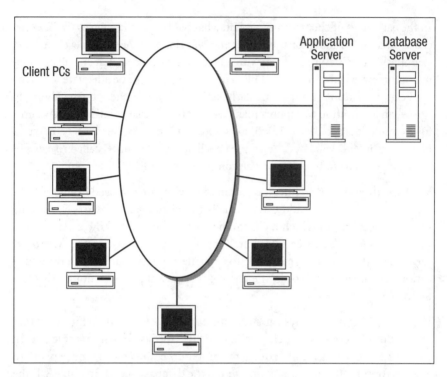

Figure 3.3 The physical structure of a three-tiered client/server architecture.

Table 3.1	The logical structure of an application using the Microsoft services model.	
User Services	**Business Services**	**Data Services**
Multiple document interface		
Form navigation	Get customer information	Select customer
Customer maintenance	Edit customer information	
	Send update request	Update customer
Address maintenance	Get address information	Select address
	Edit address information	
	Send update request	Update address

I was a little surprised to see that the Visual Basic Desktop exam contained questions about three-tiered architectures—I would have expected those types of questions to appear only on the Visual Basic Distributed Applications exam. However, in my test-taking, there were no questions relating to Internet-based applications.

Distributing an application over three layers is overkill for many developers and organizations. Where there are only one, two, or three users, it makes little sense to make the investment in hardware to implement three separate layers. But many of the principles that make up the services model benefit the desktop developer as well. For example, the business layer is usually implemented as an ActiveX server that comprises business objects comprised of class modules. These can be implemented on the desktop as well, yielding productivity and reliability gains.

COM stands for Component Object Model, and *DCOM* stands for Distributed Component Object Model. COM gives ActiveX objects interoperability, whereas DCOM allows those objects to communicate over a network. COM also represents a development philosophy—assembling applications through the use of preassembled objects (components). This concept—the reuse of objects—brings us full circle to our earlier discussion of object-oriented development in Visual Basic. COM, and, more generally, the Microsoft services model fulfills the needs of object-oriented development by providing mechanisms for reuse, encapsulation, and polymorphism.

 The terms *ActiveX* and *COM* are essentially synonymous. In fact, the certification exam does not even refer to ActiveX EXEs or ActiveX DLLs. Instead, they are referred to as COM EXEs and COM DLLs.

The following sections discuss the module and object types available to you as you build Visual Basic applications. We'll take a look at the organization of the application at the project level and then examine each of the components. When designing an application, you will want to keep an eye toward the development of reusable objects and toward the separation of user and business services.

The Visual Basic Project

The basic unit of work in a Visual Basic application is the project. The *project* encompasses all modules, objects, and so on. Analogous to C++ Make files, Visual Basic projects are maintained in the VB project file with an extension of .VBP.

The project file itself contains a list of all modules, ActiveX components, and library references that make up the project as well as project options as specified in the Project Properties dialog box.

You can have multiple projects loaded at once. When you do so, Visual Basic creates a group file with the .VGP extension.

The following sections discuss the different types of modules and files that can appear in a VB project.

Table 3.2 lists the file types that you will run into using Visual Basic. File types ending in *X*, such as FRX, are binary representations of other files. For example, FRX is a binary form file (FRM).

Table 3.2	Visual Basic file types.
Extension	**Description**
.BAS	Basic module
.CLS	Class module
.CTL	User Control
.CTX	User Control binary file
.DCA	Active Designer cache
.DDF	CAB information file
.DEP	Dependency file
.DOB	ActiveX document form file
.DOX	ActiveX document binary form file
.DSR	Active Designer file
.DSX	Active Designer binary file
.DWS	Deployment Wizard script file
.FRM	Form file
.FRX	Binary form file
.LOG	Log file for load errors
.OCA	Control TypeLib cache file
.PAG	Property page file
.PGX	Binary property page file
.RES	Resource file
.TLB	Remote Automation TypeLib file
.VBG	Visual Basic group project file
.VBL	Control licensing file
.VBP	Visual Basic project file
.VBR	Remote Automation registration file
.VBW	Visual Basic project workspace file
.VBZ	Wizard launch file
.VGP	Visual Basic project file
.WCT	WebClass HTML template

Modules And Forms

So, now we get to the nitty-gritty. What is a module anyway? The following sections discuss the various types of Visual Basic code modules and the implications of using each.

 The certification exam will expect you to have mastered the use of the types of code modules and when to use each. It will also expect that you thoroughly understand what happens when a VB application is invoked and begins to run.

 The VB documentation lists the three types of code modules as form, standard, and class. To me, Active Designer files (such as for the **DataEnvironment** object) are clearly modules as well. They have their own format apart from class, form, and standard modules; however, like those three, they include code, references to other objects, and so on. The format is closest to, but not identical to, that of class modules. I think it is safe to say that Active Designer files are a fourth type of code module.

Form Modules

A *form* is a Visual Basic object that is analogous to a window in other programming environments (although note that the operating system considers *all* controls to be windows). The form contains Visual Basic controls, and it exposes various methods, properties, and events.

 A Visual Basic form is an object. This means that a form, as with any other object, can be passed to a sub or function as an argument.

Each form in your project is a module. The form module contains code to react to various events (event procedures) and *general procedures*, which are subs and functions not related to any individual control. In object-oriented development terms, general procedures are methods of the form itself. Forms typically contain form-level declarations of constants, variables (including user-defined types), and objects. Forms can also declare external procedures as well as user-defined events and properties.

The MDIForm

The MDIForm is a special kind of form that contains all other forms whose **MDIChild** property is set to **True**. If you open an MDI child form without first opening the MDIForm, the MDIForm is automatically opened. A project can have only one MDIForm.

The Life And Times Of The Form Object

When *form*.**Show** is issued, Visual Basic does an implicit **Load** first, which creates an instance of the form in memory but *does not display it*. Next, the **Initialize** event of the form is executed, followed by the **Load** event. If there is any code attached to these events, then the code is run prior to the form being displayed. However, you can force the form to display in the **Load** event by using the **Show** method. This might be desirable if you have a lengthy startup script. After the **Load** event, the form is finally made visible (if you have not otherwise forced it to **Show**).

You can load a form (**Load** *formname*) without displaying it. This causes all variables and controls in the form to be initialized. If an attribute of a form is referenced (**form**.*propertyname* = *value*), the form is loaded but not displayed.

When the form is closed (as a result of a user clicking the Close button or an **Unload** statement), the **QueryUnload** event is triggered. In an MDI application where the MDIForm is closed, the MDIForms's **QueryUnload** event is triggered, followed by the **QueryUnload** event of all MDI child forms. You use the **QueryUnload** event to perform any necessary housecleaning, such as verifying that the user has saved all changes to the database.

The **QueryUnload** event is passed two parameters—**cancel** and **unloadmode**. The first, **cancel**, allows you to stop the form (or MDIForm) from unloading by setting the parameter to **True**: **cancel = True**. The **unloadmode** parameter is used to determine why the form (or MDIForm) is closing. Possible reasons include **vbFormControlMenu** (in which case, the user selected the Close button on the control menu), **vbFormCode** (the **Unload** statement was invoked), **vbAppWindows** (Windows is closing), **vbAppTaskManager** (the Windows Task Manager is closing the application), **vbFormMDIForm** (the MDI parent is closing), or **vbFormOwner** (the form's owner is closing).

The **Unload** event is triggered after the **QueryUnload** event. In an MDI application, the MDI child forms' **Unload** events are triggered before the MDIForm itself. The event is passed one parameter—**cancel**—that you can use in the **QueryUnload** event to prevent a form from closing. However, setting **cancel** in the MDIForm does not prevent other forms from closing.

The last event to occur when a form is closing is the **Terminate** event. When this event occurs, it is too late to prevent a form from closing.

 The **QueryUnload** and **Unload** events are not triggered if the **End** statement is encountered. If you need access to those events, use the **Unload** statement to close a form.

Standard Modules

Prior to VB4, *standard modules* were referred to as *code modules*. Because standard modules, form modules, and class modules can also contain code, they are collectively known as code modules. A standard module is a collection of Visual Basic procedures, declarations, and so on. It can have subs and functions, but unlike a form module, data in a standard module defaults to program scope. Further, procedures in a standard module default to **Public** visibility, whereas form-level subs and functions default to **Private** visibility. Of course, use of the **Private** keyword in standard module declarations allows you to make items module level in scope.

If a general procedure is not unique to the form—that is, it could be used elsewhere—it should be put into a standard or class code module.

Except perhaps in your startup module, you should avoid making any references to forms. This allows you to reuse the code in other projects. In modules that need to reference a form (such as the module containing the **Sub Main** procedure), you should not place any other procedures that could be used in other projects.

A key difference between a standard module and a class module is that there can be only one instance of the former and, therefore, only one copy of the module's data. There can be many instances of a class and, therefore, many copies of the class module's data.

Class Modules

Recall the definition of a *class*: an abstraction of an object, including its methods, properties, and attributes. A form is also an object. But there is nothing in the definition of an object that dictates that it has to have a visible component. A *class module* is essentially a user-defined control that does not require a visible component or manifestation. At its simplest, a class module's data consists of the variables declared within the class module, and the class module's methods are the subs and functions declared within it. In that sense, a class module has more in common with a form module than it does with a standard module. Like a form, a class module doesn't expose its data or its methods unless explicitly declared that way.

There can be only one instance of the data encompassed in a standard module, because there can be only one instance of the module itself. However, you can have multiple instances of a form and, thus, multiple instances of the form's data. The same duplication is true of a class.

In Chapter 5, we'll review the construction and instantiation of a class. We'll also discuss how to add properties, events, and methods to a class, as well as how to combine a class with other classes. In addition, we'll discuss some of the specialized classes provided by Visual Basic.

ActiveX Designer Modules

ActiveX designers are add-ins to the Visual Basic IDE that allow you to create specialized objects. For instance, the DataEnvironment Designer allows you to create **DataEnvironment** objects. The designer exposes a class from which you develop the object. As with a class, you can add custom properties, methods, and events although the class contains its own interface as well. The resultant object may have a visible component, but that is not necessary. The ActiveX designer has separate runtime and design-time behaviors. Because the object created by the ActiveX designer typically allows the addition of ActiveX controls, the objects in many ways combine the best of forms and class modules.

To use an ActiveX designer, you need to add it from the Project menu. If you are creating two separate ActiveX designer objects, you need to add two instances of the designer to your project. If the designer is not on the Project menu (Visual Basic automatically places some designers on the menu, depending on the project type), you can add it via the Project|Components menu. The Project menu allows for four designers—if there are more than four, they are listed on the More ActiveX designers submenu.

The Visual Basic Startup Object

One of the project properties is a declaration of the *startup object*—the object that loads when the application starts. Depending on the project type, your choices are generally the different forms and something called **Sub Main**. Chapter 14 discusses the use of the Project Properties dialog box in more detail.

The startup object must be an object that is visible at runtime or must be the **Sub Main** procedure. If it's used, there can be only one **Sub Main** in a project. Most commonly, **Sub Main** is placed in a standard module and used as a means of performing initialization chores and loading the first form.

A typical **Sub Main** procedure looks like the following:

```
' this is in the declarations section
Option Explicit
Public fMainForm As frmMain
```

```
Sub Main()
    Set fMainForm = New frmMain
    fMainForm.Show
End Sub
```

A Visual Basic application does not need to contain a form. The typical "Hello World" program, without a form, would look similar to:

```
Sub Main()
    MsgBox "Hello World!"
End Sub
```

Now that we have examined the module types that make up the Visual Basic project, we can examine the code elements of those modules.

Visual Basic Procedures

In Visual Basic, a *procedure* is a logical component of an application that can be called by name to perform one or more specific operations. For instance, you could write a procedure to compute the total of two numbers. You might give it a name, such as **Add2**.

All procedures can accept arguments (the rules for doing so are discussed in the section titled, "Functions And Sub Procedures," later in this chapter). The procedure uses the arguments in its internal computations. Using the addition example shown earlier, **Add2** would have two arguments. For instance, **Add2 (8, 16)** would mean that the **Add2** procedure is going to sum the numbers 8 and 16.

The key difference between a sub procedure and a function procedure is that a function procedure can return a value, whereas a sub procedure cannot. If **Add2** were defined to return a result, it would be called with syntax similar to:

```
myResult = Add2 (8, 16)
```

There are three types of procedures:

➤ **Event Procedure** A procedure that executes as the result of an event, such as clicking on a command button. The event can be a standard event (supplied by the object or control) or a custom event (added by the developer). (Chapter 5 covers custom events.) The procedure name takes the form **object_procedure**, such as **Command1_Click**.

➤ **Property Procedure** A procedure that executes as the result of a custom property being accessed in code. (See Chapter 5 for more information about custom properties.)

➤ **General Procedure** Any procedure that you write that is not specifically related to a control or object.

 In Windows development, the terminology is sometimes seemingly contradictory. In the Windows API, everything is called a function whether it returns a value or not. If you search through the Help file for the term "method," you will find the following definition: *An invocable function that is defined to be a member of an interface.* This is really a reference to the underlying nature of the object or control because each is derived from the Windows API. VB methods do not truly return values, so they are not functions in the VB sense. For purposes of the certification exam, you should use the definitions that I have just supplied. Throughout this book, I attempt to use the VB terminology and point out where I am departing from that terminology.

Functions And Sub Procedures

Chapter 2 shows you the syntax to declare a **Sub** or **Function** within your VB program, concentrating on the issue of scope. Now, let's examine the syntax of the arguments and the return value:

```
[Private | Public | Friend] [Static] Sub subname [(arglist)]
[Private | Public | Friend] [Static] Function subname [(arglist)]
[As type]
```

In Chapter 2, we discussed the use of the declarative statements **Private, Public, Friend,** and **Static**. A function must return one value whose data type is specified by the **As** clause. Each procedure can take arguments defined with the following syntax:

```
[Optional] [ByVal | ByRef] [ParamArray] varname[( )] _
    [As type] [= defaultvalue]
```

ByVal and **ByRef** are mutually exclusive (**ByRef** is the default). **ByVal** means that you are passing a copy of the variable, and **ByRef** means that you are passing an address to the variable. The implication is that by using **ByRef**, the procedure can alter the value of the variable. **As** defines the data type of the variable being passed.

You can define a default value for the variable being passed as an argument if the **Optional** clause is used. If the variable being passed is any type of object (including a VB control), the only acceptable default value is **Nothing**.

Optional indicates that the following arguments are not required. If you use **Optional** and do not supply a default value, the arguments are assigned as a type **Variant** with the value **Empty**. You can use the **IsMissing** function to test for arguments not provided. **Optional** can appear anywhere in the argument list unless **ParamArray** is used.

ParamArray allows you to define a procedure with a variable number of arguments. You cannot use **ByVal** or **ByRef** with **ParamArray**. The data type is always **Variant** and omits the **As** keyword.

The following code snippet illustrates the use of **ParamArray**:

```
' a function to add some numbers using ParamArray
Function AddEmUp (ParamArray vVars ()) As Integer
   Dim vNumber As Variant
   Dim iRslt As Integer
   For Each vNumber In vVars
      iRslt = iRslt + vNumber
   Next
   AddEmUp = iRslt
End Function
```

You can use *named arguments* when calling procedures. Named arguments are covered in the Chapter 5 discussion of collections.

The other parts that make up your application are ActiveX components, such as ActiveX controls added to the project or ActiveX DLLs and ActiveX EXEs referenced by the application. Chapter 4 covers ActiveX controls, and Chapter 7 covers other ActiveX components.

Practice Questions

Question 1

> What are valid procedure types? [Check all correct answers]
>
> ❑ a. Class
>
> ❑ b. Event
>
> ❑ c. Object
>
> ❑ d. Property

Answers b and d are correct—Visual Basic supports event, property, and general procedures. Event procedures are triggered as the result of a specific event. Property procedures are invoked as the result of a user-defined property being accessed. Answer a is incorrect because, although a class can have procedures (like any other module), there is no such thing as a class procedure. Likewise, answer c is incorrect because there is no such thing as an object procedure.

Question 2

> Which of the following declarations in a standard module is likely to work? [Check all correct answers]
>
> ❑ a. `Private Sub openCustFile (sFile As String)`
>
> ❑ b. `Public Sub openCustFile (sFile As String)`
>
> ❑ c. `Private Sub openCustFile _`
>   `(sFile As String) As Integer`
>
> ❑ d. `Friend Sub openCustFile ()`

Answers a and b are correct. Answer a is a **Private Sub**, which is valid in a standard module. It is passed a single parameter—a string (presumably containing the name of the file to open). Answer b is identical to answer a except that it is defined as **Public**—also valid. Answer c is incorrect because it returns a value (an **Integer**), which is not valid for a **Sub**. Instead, it should have been defined as a **Function**. Answer d is incorrect because the procedure type is **Friend**, which is invalid in a standard module.

Question 3

Which of the following function declarations in a form module is correct?

○ a. `Private Sub openfiles(ParamArray As _`
`String)`

○ b. `Private Sub openfiles(Optional ListCount _`
`As Integer, ParamArray VarList())`

○ c. `Private Sub openfiles(Optional ListCount _`
`As Integer, FileTypes As String)`

○ d. `Friend Sub openfiles(ParamArray _`
`fileList())`

Answer d is correct. Form modules allow you to declare **Friend** procedures (you can declare them in any object module), and the **ParamArray** parameter is defined correctly. The **fileList** variable is, by definition, an array of type **Variant**. Answer a is incorrect because the **As** keyword is used and because it attempts to use the **String** data type—the data type is omitted because only type **Variant** is valid. Answer b is incorrect because you cannot mix **Optional** and **ParamArray** in the same declaration. Also, when **Optional** is used, all following parameters must also be defined as **Optional**. Answer c is incorrect because, although the first parameter is defined as **Optional**, the second parameter isn't. All parameters listed after the first **Optional** parameter must also be defined as **Optional**.

Question 4

> You have an MDIForm named **frmMDI** and another form named **frmChild**, whose **MDIChild** property is set to **True**. You click the Close button on the control menu of **frmMDI**. In what order do the **QueryUnload** and **Unload** of the two forms occur?
>
> ○ a. 1.) frmMDI QueryUnload
>
>   2.) frmMDI Unload
>
>   3.) frmChild QueryUnload
>
>   4.) frmChild Unload
>
> ○ b. 1.) frmChild QueryUnload
>
>   2.) frmChild Unload
>
>   3.) frmMDI QueryUnload
>
>   4.) frmMDI Unload
>
> ○ c. 1.) frmMDI QueryUnload
>
>   2.) frmChild QueryUnload
>
>   3.) frmChild Unload
>
>   4.) frmMDI Unload
>
> ○ d. None of the above

Answer c is correct because the MDIForm's **QueryUnload** event fires first. This is followed by the **QueryUnload** events for all MDI child forms and then the **Unload** event for all the MDI child forms. Finally, the **Unload** event of the MDIForm is triggered. Answer a is incorrect because the MDI child forms close before the MDIForm. Answer b is incorrect because the MDIForm's **QueryUnload** event is fired before the child forms close. Answer d is incorrect because the correct answer is given.

Question 5

A function is: [Check all correct answers]

❏ a. Another type of module

❏ b. A procedure

❏ c. Different from a sub in that it can return a value

❏ d. Different from a sub in that it allows arguments or parameters

The correct answers are b and c. Answer b is correct because both subs and functions are procedures. Answer c is correct because a function procedure can return a value, whereas a sub procedure does not return a value. Answer a is incorrect because a function is not a module. Answer d is incorrect because functions and subs both allow arguments or parameters.

Question 6

Which of the following code snippets are valid? [Check all correct answers]

❏ a.
```
If TypeOf myObject = CommandButton Then
    End If
```

❏ b.
```
If TypeOf (myObject) = CommandButton Then
        myString = "ABC"
    End If
```

❏ c.
```
Select Case TypeOf myObject
        Case = CommandButton
            myString = "ABC"
    End Select
```

❏ d. None of the above

Answer d is the correct answer because none of the choices provided is valid. The correct syntax is **If TypeOf myObject Is CommandButton Then**. Answer a is incorrect because you need to use the keyword **Is** instead of using the equal sign. Answer b is incorrect for the same reason as a, and because you do not enclose the object in parentheses. Answer c is incorrect for the same reason as answer a, and also because you can use **TypeOf** only in an **If...Then...End If** construct.

Need To Know More?

 Craig, John Clark and Jeff Webb. *Microsoft Visual Basic 6.0 Developer's Workshop*, Microsoft Press, Redmond, WA, 1998. ISBN 1-57231-883-X. A good intermediate-level VB6 resource I found this entire volume interesting and educational. The authors take a "How Do I?" approach to explaining various VB techniques. Chapter 4 is devoted entirely to the subject of parameters, whereas Chapter 5 delves into object-oriented techniques.

 Davis, Harold. *Visual Basic 6 Secrets*, IDG Books Worldwide, Foster City, CA, 1998. ISBN 0-7645-3223-5. Harold has done a nice job with this book. Because Harold takes a different organizational approach to his book than I do in this book, the materials from this chapter that you will be interested in are spread throughout *Visual Basic 6 Secrets*. Chapter 3 picks up with events, properties, and procedures. Chapter 4 discusses the **CallByName** function, whereas Chapter 14 covers the meat of the object-oriented approach to applications and objects.

 Siler, Brian and Jeff Spotts. *Special Edition Using Visual Basic 6*, Que, Indianapolis, IN, 1998. ISBN 0-7897-1542-2. Brian and Jeff's book is a good intermediate-level text. Chapters 3, 5, 11, and 17 will be of most interest for topics covered in this chapter.

 Search the online books on the VB CD-ROM for the terms "object", "events", "procedure", and the like. Also, check out the "Programming With Objects" section in the online programmer's guide.

 premium.microsoft.com/msdn/library/ This site contains many good articles on object-oriented development techniques with Visual Basic.

Interacting With The User

Terms you'll need to understand:

- √ Intrinsic control
- √ ActiveX control
- √ **ZOrder**
- √ **TabIndex**
- √ **SetFocus**
- √ **GotFocus** and **LostFocus**
- √ **KeyDown, KeyUp,** and **KeyPress**
- √ **KeyPreview**
- √ Container
- √ Access key

Techniques you'll need to master:

- √ Using the **Global** objects
- √ Using methods, properties, and events of the form and MDIForm objects
- √ Handling keyboard events at the form level
- √ Using the menu control
- √ Using the graphical styles of controls
- √ Performing drag-and-drop operations
- √ Performing OLE drag-and-drop operations
- √ Using the ListBox and ComboBox controls
- √ Adding ActiveX controls to your project
- √ Using the CommonDialog control
- √ Using the ImageList control
- √ Using the TreeView and ListView controls
- √ Creating a toolbar

My original title for this chapter was "Creating The User Interface," and, indeed, that is the central focus of the chapter. However, several topics—such as using the **App** object—seemed best included here as well. Strictly speaking, objects that aren't seen by end users cannot be considered to be part of the user interface. Nevertheless, this chapter covers the elements of interacting with the user, beginning with application-level objects, such as **Global, App,** and **Screen.** From there, we'll discuss forms and menus, and we'll drill down through various intrinsic and ActiveX controls. Please note that the assumption is made that you are essentially familiar with the Visual Basic development platform. This chapter concentrates on drawing out the topics that are likely to appear on the exam.

The Global Object

The **Global** object is an application-level object that is automatically created and referenced whenever a VB project is run. **Global**'s properties include:

➤ App

➤ Clipboard

➤ Forms

➤ Licenses

➤ Printer

➤ Printers

➤ Screen

Global is referenced automatically, so you can use its properties without referencing the **Global** object. **Global** also has these methods:

➤ Load

➤ UnLoad

➤ LoadPicture

➤ SavePicture

➤ LoadResData

➤ LoadResPicture

➤ LoadResString

The last three methods—**LoadResData, LoadResPicture,** and **LoadResString**—are used to load data from a resource file. **Load** and **UnLoad** are used to load and unload objects, such as forms or controls. **LoadPicture** and **SavePicture** are used to load graphics or save graphics. For example, to load a graphic to the PictureBox control, you use the **LoadPicture** method: **Picture1.Picture = LoadPicture ("mypic.bmp")**.

The key properties of the **Global** object are discussed in the following sections.

The App Object

The **App** object is a **Global** object created when the VB application begins execution, and it provides general information about the application. Much of the information is the same as seen in the Project Properties dialog box and in the project file. For example, the **Title** property returns the name of the project as seen in the Windows task listing. You can prevent the application from being listed in the task listing by setting the **TaskVisible** property to **False** (the default is **True**). The **ExeName** property returns the name of the executable file, whereas the **Major, Minor,** and **Revision** properties return version information.

The **LogMode** and **LogPath** properties allow you to perform application logging of any messages. The **LogFile** property indicates the name of the file to which events should be logged. Use the **StartLogging** method to begin logging. Use the **LogEvent** method to log a message to the log file. You must supply a message to be logged and can optionally specify a severity flag using one of the following constants:

➤ **vbLogEventTypeError** Error

➤ **vbLogEventTypeInformation** Informational message, such as:

```
App.LogEvent "Unexpected result encountered!",
vbLogEventTypeInformation
```

➤ **vbLogEventTypeWarning** Warning

The **hInstance** property returns a handle to the instance of the application. The **PrevInstance** property of the **App** object returns **True** if there is another instance of the application already running.

There are a number of **App** properties relating to automation, as well. These control the text that will be displayed if an Automation server is busy but receives keyboard or mouse input (**OLERequestPendingMsgText** and **OLERequestPendingMsgTitle**), the timeout delay before generating an error when attempting to make an automation request (**OLEServerBusyTimeout**), and so on.

The Screen Object

The **Screen** object allows Visual Basic developers to control visible manifestations of the entire Windows environment. Put another way, the **Screen** object is the entire Windows desktop. **Screen** has a number of useful properties:

➤ **ActiveControl** Returns a reference to the control that currently has focus. If you preface the property with a form name (**form1.ActiveControl**), a reference to the control that would have focus if the form were active is returned. This is a convenient way to access a control's properties and methods, because it also represents a reference to the active control.

➤ **ActiveForm** Provides a reference to whichever form is currently active (if the form is an MDIForm, then the active **MDIChild** is returned).

➤ **FontCount** Returns the number of fonts currently available for the display, whereas **Fonts** enumerates them.

➤ **Height** Returns the height of the **Screen** object in units of *twips*. A twip is 1/1440 of an inch or 1/567 of a centimeter.

➤ **MouseIcon** Allows you to load an icon or cursor file and use it as a new cursor, as seen in this example:

```
MouseIcon = LoadPicture ("c:\windows\cursors\mygarish.cur")
```

➤ **MousePointer** Allows you to change the current pointer.

The **ActiveControl**, **ActiveForm**, **MouseIcon**, and **MousePointer** properties also apply to forms.

➤ **TwipsPerPixelX** Combines with the **Width** property to determine the **Screen** object's current resolution height. This is done by performing the following formula:

```
Screen.Width / Screen.TwipsPerPixelX
```

➤ **TwipsPerPixelY** Combines with the **Height** property to determine the resolution height of the **Screen** object. This is accomplished by performing the following formula:

```
Screen.Height / Screen.TwipsPerPixelY
```

➤ **Width** Returns the width of the **Screen** object in units of twips.

The Licenses Collection

The **Licenses** collection contains license keys (**LicenseInfo** objects) of unreferenced controls. For user controls that require a license key, you must add a license key using the collection's **Add** method, like this:

```
Licenses.Add "myproject.mycontrol", "123abc"
```

The Clipboard Object

The **Clipboard** object provides access to the system clipboard. You can place text or binary data (such as graphics) onto the clipboard, copy the data, and so on. The clipboard can contain more than one piece of data at a time if the items are in different formats. For instance, you can store a string and a picture on the clipboard at the same time, but not two pictures. If you put a picture on the clipboard, any picture previously placed there is erased. The **Clipboard** object's methods include:

➤ **Clear** Removes all data from the clipboard.

➤ **GetData** Retrieves binary data from the clipboard.

➤ **GetFormat** Determines the type of data on the clipboard.

➤ **GetText** Retrieves text data from the clipboard.

➤ **SetData** Adds binary data to the clipboard.

➤ **SetText** Adds text data to the clipboard.

Examples of valid clipboard formats include **vbCFBitmap** and **vbCFText**, indicating that the clipboard contains a bitmap or text respectively.

The following code example tests to see if there is text data on the clipboard and moves it to a text box or rich text box. The argument that follows **GetText** is optional:

```
If Clipboard.GetFormat (vbCFText) Then
   Text1.Text = Clipboard.GetText (vbCFText)
ElseIf Clipboard.GetFormat (vbCFRTF) Then
   RichText1.Text = Clipboard.GetText (vbCFRTF)
End if
```

The Printers Collection And Printer Object

The **Printers** collection returns information about all the available printers on the system. It is a zero-based collection of **Printer** objects. If you reference the **Printer** object directly, the system default printer is used. With the **Printer** object, you can set various properties and use various methods. For instance, you can specify the **ColorMode** property to print in color if available (**Printer.ColorMode = vbPRCMColor**) or to print in black and white (**Printer.ColorMode = vbPRCMMonochrome**). You can use the **Copies** properties to set how many copies of a report will be printed. Use the **KillDoc** method to cancel a currently running print job.

Forms And MDIForms

The form object is the window with which you will most often interact with your user. Most developers taking the exam are familiar enough with forms, so I won't belabor the point here except to point out the items I think you might see on the exam.

Form Properties

The **ShowInTaskbar** property is available at design time. Setting **ShowIn-Taskbar** to **False** causes a form not to show on the Windows Taskbar. **True** causes the control to appear on the Taskbar.

The **Appearance** property determines if controls are displayed with a 3D effect. Setting the property to 0 causes controls to be displayed without 3D (flat) as in Internet Explorer. Setting the property to 1 causes the controls to be displayed with 3D. If the form's **BorderStyle** property is set to **vbFixedDouble**, then the caption and border are also painted with 3D effects.

BorderStyle determines the appearance and behavior of the form. Possible values are:

➤ **vbBSNone** No border or control menu, title bar, and so forth.

➤ **vbFixedDouble** Fixed dialog box. Can have a control menu but cannot be minimized or maximized. Not resizable.

➤ **vbFixedSingle** Fixed single. Cannot be resized except to be minimized and maximized.

➤ **vbFixedToolWindow** Fixed tool window. Not resizable, and has a Close button and a title bar with reduced font. Does not appear in the Taskbar.

➤ **vbSizable** The default. Fully resizable.

➤ **vbSizableToolWindow** Same as **vbFixedToolWindow** but resizable.

The **ControlMenu** property sets whether a control menu is on the form. The **ControlMenu** property is valid only for fixed-single, sizable, or fixed-double border styles. If there is a control menu, you can also set **MinButton** and **MaxButton** to **True** or **False** to determine whether the Minimize and Maximize buttons are present.

The **KeyPreview** property is set to **True** to cause the form to receive keystrokes before the controls. For instance, if the focus is on a TextBox control and the form's **KeyPreview** property is set to **False**, then the TextBox receives all keystrokes. Intercepting keystrokes is covered later in this chapter in the section titled, "Form Events."

The **NegotiateMenus** property determines whether the form incorporates the menu of an active object on the form into the form's menu. The form must have a menu, even if it is not visible. If the form's **MDIChild** property is set to **True**, the menu is incorporated into the MDIForm's menu. (You can use the **NegotiatePosition** property of individual menu controls to determine what menus the form displays along with the active object's menus.)

The **ClipControls** property applies to any container, including the Frame and PictureBox controls, and it controls how Windows handles paint operations.

In any container, controls can be broken into two categories: graphical and non-graphical. Graphical controls include the Image, Line, and Shape controls as well as the Label control. Other controls, such as TextBox, are non-graphical. Outlines of non-graphical objects are maintained in memory, and it is usually not necessary to constantly repaint them.

Setting the **ClipControls** property to **False** can often significantly reduce the time it takes to display or redisplay a container object, such as a form. However, if non-graphical controls are placed inside or overlap graphical controls, setting **ClipControls** to **False** can cause the non-graphical controls to be drawn incorrectly. You see this most often when a container that has its **ClipControls** property set to **True** is nested inside another container that has its **ClipControls** property set to **False**. This effect is shown in Figure 4.1.

In Figure 4.1, the form has a **ClipControls** property set to **True**, and the PictureBox and Frame controls each have the property set to **False**. In the figure, the left side shows the form when it is first opened, and the right side shows the form after the form's **Picture** property is refreshed (I simply reloaded the same bitmap). As you can see, Windows first drew the background of the form (the bitmap) and then redrew the containers and the graphical controls. But, the non-graphical controls were not redrawn. Because a clipping region was created around the non-graphical controls, the background shows through.

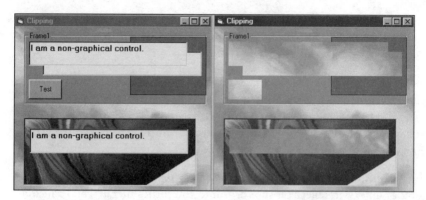

Figure 4.1 Because the embedded containers' **ClipControls** properties have been set to **False**, the form on the right has not been properly repainted.

If the **ClipControls** property is set to **True**, the entire container is repainted each time the form is redrawn on the screen (as the result of being moved, resized, and so forth). As an example, the background is drawn over non-graphical controls and then those are redrawn on top of the background. If **ClipControls** is set to **True**, Windows creates a *clipping region*, which includes all non-graphical controls. The clipping region is repainted with each paint event.

The **AutoRedraw** property can also impact how fast a form redraws. With this property set to **True**, Windows maintains a bitmap of the form (or other container) in memory. If the form has complex graphic methods, Windows repaints the entire form in memory and then copies it to the screen. This can be a lengthy process and can consume a lot of memory. The documentation states that if you use complex graphical methods but do not do so frequently, then setting **AutoRedraw** to **True** is appropriate. However, if the form performs a lot of heavy graphical processing, you are better off setting this property to **False** and performing the graphical methods in the **Paint** event.

My own experience is this: If you set **AutoRedraw** to **False** and use a graphical method, such as **Line**, the form will not be redrawn properly when it receives focus. For example, let's say you use the **Line** method to draw a simple line on a form:

```
Line (0, 0)-(2000, 2000), vbBlue
```

Next, you minimize the form and then restore it. With **AutoRedraw** set to **False**, the line will not be redisplayed. When it's set to **True**, the form will be correctly redrawn, including the line.

Form Events

Chapter 3 reviews key events involved in opening and closing a form. When a form becomes active, the **Activate** event is first triggered followed by the **GotFocus** event. These events occur only if the form is visible. The **Activate** event is triggered only by moving within an application. In other words, the event is not triggered if focus is received as the result of switching from another application. The **Deactivate** event is triggered when the form is no longer active. Like the **Activate** event, **Deactivate** is not triggered as the result of switching to another application. **Deactivate** is not triggered when the form is closed either. The **LostFocus** event occurs when the form is no longer active.

The **Resize** event is triggered whenever the form is resized. This is useful if you want to place code to move or resize controls, ensure that certain controls are visible, and so forth.

When a control has focus and a key is pressed, three events are triggered—**KeyDown**, **KeyUp**, and **KeyPress**. **KeyDown** occurs when the user presses a key but has not yet released it. **KeyUp** occurs when the user releases the key. **KeyPress** occurs after the user has pressed *and* released the key.

You can handle keystrokes (such as the user pressing the F1 key) in the form's **KeyPress** and **KeyDown** events. As noted earlier, for the form to receive keystrokes, there must be no controls on the form, or **KeyPreview** must be set to **False**. If a CommandButton on the form has its **Default** property set to **True**, then the **KeyDown** or **KeyUp** events are not triggered. Likewise, if a CommandButton has its **Cancel** property set to **True**, then the **KeyDown** or **KeyUp** events are not triggered. The Tab key never triggers the **KeyDown** or **KeyUp** events.

The **KeyPress** event is defined as a sub procedure

```
Sub object_KeyPress (keyAscii As Integer)
```

where *keyAscii* is the ASCII value of the key pressed. To determine the character itself, use the syntax **Chr (***keyAscii***)**. **KeyPress** detects all printable characters, the Ctrl key combined with any alphabetic character, and the Enter and Backspace keys (in other words, ANSI characters). You can use the **KeyPress** event to test for characters keyed in and change them (by altering *keyAscii*) before they are echoed to the control.

KeyDown and **KeyUp** are defined as sub procedures:

```
Sub object_KeyPress (keycode As Integer, shift As Integer)
Sub object_KeyUp (keycode As Integer, shift As Integer)
```

Both **KeyDown** and **KeyUp** indicate which key was pressed. **KeyPress** is more flexible for standard ANSI characters. *keycode* is returned as a Visual Basic constant, such as **vbKeyF1** for the F1 key. This means that alphabetic characters are not distinguished as upper- or lowercase. Shift evaluates to **vbShiftMask** if the Shift key was pressed, **vbCtlMask** if the Ctrl key was pressed, and **vbAltMask** if the Alt key was pressed.

Setting **KeyAscii** to 0 in the **KeyPress** event or setting **KeyCode** to 0 in the **KeyDown** event prevents the control from receiving the keystroke. You can change *keyAscii* (for **KeyPress)** and *keycode* (for **KeyDown** and **KeyUp)** to alter the character echoed.

Form Methods

The **PrintForm** method sends a bitmapped image of the form to the printer. The **Refresh** method causes the form to be completely repainted (see also the discussion of **ClipControls** and **AutoRedraw** earlier in this chapter in the "Form Properties" section). The **PopupMenu** method displays a pop-up menu on the form. The menu name supplied might be, for example, **mnuFile**. This would cause the menu and all cascading menus to be displayed. Optional arguments allow you to specify the menu's location, alignment, and which menu item is to be boldfaced. You can also supply the **vbPopupMenuRightButton** argument to cause the menu to react only to the right mouse button (instead of the default left button).

The **Show** method causes the form to be loaded (if not already loaded) and displayed. Chapter 3 discusses the life cycle of a form. Note that referencing a property or method (other than **Show)** of an unloaded form causes that form to be loaded into memory but not displayed. The **Show** method supports two option arguments: **mode** and **owner. mode** refers to whether the form is to be opened *modally*, and **owner** allows you to specify that the current object, denoted with the **Me** keyword, is the owner of the form.

A form opened modally is *application modal*, meaning that no other form in the application can receive keyboard or mouse input. Further, in the object that opens a form modally, no code runs until the modal form has been closed. The following line of code opens a form modally and denotes that the current object is the owner:

```
form1.Show vbModal, Me
```

MDIForm Objects

For the most part, an MDIForm looks and behaves similar to forms, with these exceptions:

➤ There can be only one MDIForm per project. It acts as a container to all forms that have the **MDIChild** property set to **True**. When the MDI-Form is closed, all MDI child forms are also closed.

➤ The MDIForm can act as a container only to forms, the PictureBox control, and any custom controls that have an **Align** property.

➤ An MDIForm cannot be displayed modally.

➤ If the MDI child has a menu, its menu replaces the MDIForm's menus when the MDI child is active.

➤ The MDIForm's **Controls** property is a collection of all controls on the object but does not include child forms.

*Note: The MDIForm is part of the **Forms** collection.*

Menu Control

All forms and MDIForms can have a menu control attached. The **Parent** property returns the parent of the menu (typically the form or MDIForm). The **Visible** property allows you hide or show specific menu items at runtime:

```
' make invisible
mnuDataSort.Visible = False
```

The **Enabled** property allows you to enable and disable menu items at runtime. For instance, you might want to disable the Copy menu if no text is highlighted. Assume you have a menu Edit (**mnuEdit**) with a submenu Copy (**mnuEditCopy**), you might code:

```
Private Sub mnuEdit_Click()
mnuEditCopy.Enabled = Text1.SelLength > 0
End Sub
```

The code is evaluated whenever the Edit menu is clicked. If **Text1.SelLength > 0** evaluates to **True**, then **mnuEditCopy.Enabled** is set to **True** (else it is set to **False**).

The **Checked** property is a **Boolean** that indicates the setting or returns whether the menu item is checked or not. Assume you have a menu named **mnuView-WhiteOnBlue**. The following code would toggle its status and change the background and foreground colors of **Text1** appropriately:

```
Private Sub mnuViewWhiteOnBlue_Click()
mnuViewWhiteOnBlue.Checked = Not mnuViewWhiteOnBlue.Checked
```

```
If mnuViewWhiteOnBlue.Checked Then
  Text1.BackColor = vbBlue
  Text1.ForeColor = vbWhite
Else
  Text1.BackColor = vbWhite
  Text1.ForeColor = vbBlack
End If
End Sub
```

The **WindowList** property can be set to **True** to cause the top-level menu to maintain a list of all open MDI child windows.

You can have separator bars in your menu by using a single dash (-) as the menu **Caption**. Note that the item still needs to have its **Name** property set and that the **Name** property has to be unique. You can have an array of menus, as with any other control, to simplify naming menu items, but the array of menu items must be contiguous.

Methods, Properties, Events, And Controls

The following sections first discuss methods, properties, and events that are common to a number of controls and that you stand a good chance of seeing on the exam. Then, specific controls that are likely to appear on the exam are addressed.

ZOrder Method

The **ZOrder** method places the form, MDIForm, or control in the front or back of the z-order at runtime. The *z-order* refers to how overlapping objects are displayed—which objects are in front of the others. Basically, any control that is visible at runtime has a **ZOrder** method.

To move an object to the back of the z-order, you specify a value of 1. To move an object to the front, you specify a value of 0. If you omit the value, 0 is assumed (the object is moved to the front of the z-order). For example, Figure 4.2 shows two forms opened. In the first, **Command2** is on top of **List1**, which is on top of **Command1**, which, in turn, is on top of **Text1**. In the second form, the following code has been executed:

```
Command1.ZOrder
List1.ZOrder 1
Text1.ZOrder 0
```

Figure 4.2   Demonstration of the **ZOrder** method.

Command1.ZOrder places the **Command1** control as the top-most control. **List1.Zorder 1** puts the list box at the bottom of the z-order. **Text1.Zorder 0** moves the text box to the top of the z-order, and, because it was executed after **Command1.ZOrder**, **Text1** is on top of **Command1**.

GotFocus And LostFocus Events

The **GotFocus** event occurs when a form or control receives the focus. **LostFocus** occurs when the form or control has lost the focus. The MDIForm does not have these events (though it can receive focus). Forms can receive focus only when all controls are invisible or disabled. Only controls that can receive focus generate these events. For instance, the Line, Shape, and Label controls do not have the **GotFocus** and **LostFocus** events. Further, the Menu control does not generate the **GotFocus** and **LostFocus** events.

SetFocus Method

The **SetFocus** method is used to set the focus to a form, MDIForm, or control. The object must be able to receive focus. To set focus to a text box, code this:

```
Text1.SetFocus
```

TabIndex Property

The **TabIndex** property sets or returns the Tab order for most controls on a form. All intrinsic controls have a **TabIndex** property except Menu, Timer, Data, Image, Line, and Shape. Controls that can't receive focus (the Frame and Label controls) as well as controls that are not enabled or that are not visible retain their **TabIndex** properties, but they are skipped when the user tabs through the controls.

The first control in Tab order has a **TabIndex** value of 0. Controls are numbered sequentially from that point. At design time or runtime, you can alter the **TabIndex** property of any control. All controls are resequenced accordingly.

Note that **TabIndex** is unaffected by z-order. You can tab to and interact with a control that is entirely hidden by another control. (In other words, even a control at the bottom of the z-order can receive focus.)

Container Property

When taking the exam, you will be expected to know what a *container* is and what can act as a container. A container is an object that can hold other controls. This includes the form and MDIForm as well as the PictureBox, Frame, SSTab, and UserControl controls.

Controls have a **Container** property that sets or returns the control's container. To change a control's container, use the **Set** statement, like this:

```
Set Text1.Container = Picture1
```

The **Container** property also returns a reference to the object's container:

```
Text1.Text = Text1.Container.Name
```

This code moves the text box to Picture1 and then references the container's container, in this case the form:

```
Set Text1.Container = Picture1
Text1.Text = Text1.Container.Container.Caption
```

The UserControl control has the **ContainedControls** property (listed incorrectly several places in the Help file as **ContainedVBControls**), which is a collection of all controls contained within UserControl.

Enabled, Visible, And Locked Properties

The **Enabled** property sets or returns whether the user can interact with a form, MDIForm, or control. In general, if a control has user-invoked methods or events, then the control has the **Enabled** property. However, the Timer control also has the **Enabled** property. Setting **Enabled** to **False** for the Timer control causes the **Interval** property's countdown to stop.

The **Visible** property controls whether the form, MDIForm, or control is visible. In general, any object that can be seen at runtime has this property. Controls such as Timer or CommonDialog do not have this property.

Locked is a property of the TextBox and ComboBox controls (as well as the Column object). For the TextBox control and **Column** object, setting **Locked** to **True** means the user cannot edit the contents of the control. For the ComboBox control, setting **Locked** to **True** means the user *can't* type into the box but can highlight the data and copy it.

KeyUp, KeyDown, And KeyPress Events

An object that can receive focus generally has the **KeyUp, KeyDown,** and **KeyPress** events. The **KeyUp** and **KeyDown** events are used to handle keyboard states and special keys. For instance, the **KeyPress** event can be used to determine if the user pressed the number 1 on the keyboard, but the **KeyUp** and **KeyDown** events can determine if it was done on the numeric keypad or the regular keypad. The **KeyPress** event intercepts ANSI characters generated from the keyboard (such as typing the *A* character) including Backspace and Enter. The usage of these events is discussed earlier in this chapter in the "Form Events" section.

UseMnemonic And ForwardFocus Properties And Access Keys

For controls that can receive focus, you can place an ampersand (&) in their **Caption** properties to create an access key for that control. For instance, if the **Caption** property of **Command1** is set to **&Close**, then you can use Alt+C as an access key to that control (**Command1**). For most controls, this causes the focus to be shifted to that control. For CommandButton controls, use of the access key at runtime causes the **Click** event procedure to be executed in addition to moving focus to the object.

Not all controls that you want to have an access key to have the **Caption** property (such as the TextBox control). You can use a Label control to supply an access key for a TextBox (or other control). To use a Label control, set the Label control's **UseMnemonic** property to **True**. Then, set the Label control's **TabIndex** property to be one less than the property of the control that you want to supply focus to. For example, assume **Label1.TabIndex** is equal to three and **Text1.TabIndex** is equal to four. Set **Label1.UseMnemonic = True,** and set its **Caption** property to (as an example) **&Name:.** When the user presses Alt+N, focus goes to **Text1** because that is the next control in the Tab order.

ForwardFocus is used for user controls and is set by the control's author. If **ForwardFocus** is set to **True,** then, if an access key for the user control is pressed, the next control in the Tab order receives focus. If **ForwardFocus** is **False** and the **CanGetFocus** property is **True,** then the user control gets the focus.

Index Property

As discussed in Chapter 2, you can create an array of controls that share the same **Name** property. To address a control that is part of an array of controls, use the syntax

```
control (index)
```

where *control* evaluates to the control's **Name** property and *index* is a positive **Integer** (from 0 through 32,767). Specifying an invalid *index* causes a runtime error. Unlike regular arrays, the indexes for arrays of controls do not have to be sequential. Note that every control also has a **Tag** property of type **String** that Visual Basic does not use for any purpose. You can use the **Tag** property to identify a control (or for any other suitable purpose).

 You can use the **Index** property to create a new instance of a control using the **Load** statement. Assuming you have an array of a TextBox control named **txtResult**, you can add a new instance of **txtResult** dynamically using the syntax

```
Load txtResult (newIndex)
```

where *newIndex* is an unused index number.

SelText, SelStart, And SelLength Properties

SelText, **SelStart**, and **SelLength** are properties of the TextBox and ComboBox controls. **SelText** returns the currently highlighted text. You can also assign a string to **SelText**, which causes the currently highlighted text to be replaced by the new string. **SelStart** sets or returns the first position to be highlighted (beginning with zero). **SelLength** sets or returns the number of characters to highlight. If you replace the highlighted text with **SelText**, **SelLength** is set to zero. The following code snippet places focus on **Text1** and highlights (selects) all of the text:

```
With Text1
  ' Move focus to text1
  .SetFocus
  ' Highlight all of the text
  .SelStart = 0
  .SelLength = Len(.Text)
End With
```

The Style Property

The **Style** property controls the appearance and behavior of the CheckBox, CommandButton, and OptionButton controls. (The ComboBox and ListBox controls also have a **Style** property, which is discussed later in this chapter in "The ListBox And ComboBox Controls" section.) The **Style** property defaults to **vbButtonStandard**, meaning that the controls behave like standard CheckBox, CommandButton, and OptionButton controls. If you set **Style** to **vbButtonGraphical**, then the controls behave graphically. For each, the control looks like a button. For the CheckBox and OptionButton controls, the **Caption** property is displayed on the button and there is no box or circle. When the value of the control is **False** (or zero), the control is shown in a raised state. (The CommandButton control has a value of **True** while the **Click** event is running and becomes **False** when the event procedure is complete.) When the value of the control is **True** (or non-zero), the control appears depressed. Figure 4.3 shows the three controls. In the figure, the left-hand versions of the controls are non-graphical, and the right-hand versions are graphical. When **Style** is set to **vbButtonGraphical**, you can set properties such as **Picture** and **BackColor**.

Drag-And-Drop Operations

You can program your application to support drag-and-drop operations. For instance, you can drag the currently selected item in a file list box to a printer icon to initiate the actions necessary to print a document.

Most controls, including the Label and Frame controls (but not Menu, Shape, Line, and Timer), can be the source of a drag operation (in other words, can be dragged). The **DragMode** property is set to **vbManual** or **vbAutomatic**. When a control is set to **vbAutomatic**, clicking the object automatically invokes a drag operation. With **vbManual**, you must use the object's **Drag** method.

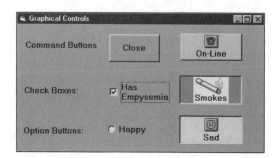

Figure 4.3   The CommandButton, CheckBox, and OptionButton controls shown in their non-graphical and graphical styles.

When a control such as the CommandButton has its **DragMode** property set to **vbAutomatic,** you lose access to the control's **Click** event. This is because the control goes into drag mode before any click or double-click can occur.

You set the control's **DragIcon** property to an icon, another control's **Drag-Icon** property, or the result of the **LoadPicture** function. You can also set **DragIcon** equal to the **Picture** property of a PictureBox control as long as the picture is an icon (ICO) file. To clear the **DragIcon** property, use **LoadPicture** with no argument:

```
text1.DragIcon = LoadPicture ()
```

The **Drag** method initiates a drag operation. Normally, the code is placed inside the **MouseDown** event (though you can place the code anywhere—such as the result of a key press) when **DragMode** has been set to **vbManual**. When invoking the **Drag** method, change the **DragIcon** property, as discussed earlier. You can also change the **MouseIcon** property—it will be used if **DragIcon** has not been set. Supply the **vbCancel** argument to cancel a drag operation, **vbBeginDrag** to start a drag operation, and **vbEndDrag** to end a dragging operation. This code snippet initiates a drag operation from **Text1**:

```
text1.Drag vbBeginDrag
```

Note that although drag operations normally occur in a synchronous manner, using the **Drag** method while **DragMode** is **vbNormal** causes the operation to occur asynchronously.

The **DragOver** event occurs when a drag operation is in process and the mouse pointer enters, leaves, or pauses over a control. The procedure has the following syntax:

```
object_DragOver(Source As Control, X As Single, Y As Single, _
    state As Integer)
```

Source returns a reference to the object being dragged. **X** and **Y** specify the current horizontal and vertical positions of the mouse pointer within the control. **State** returns the reason that the event occurred, such as:

➤ **vbEnter** The mouse pointer entered the control.

➤ **vbLeave** The mouse pointer has left the control.

➤ **vbOver** The mouse pointer is paused over the control.

You normally use the **DragOver** event to change the drag icon to indicate whether the object can be dropped.

The **DragDrop** event of an object is triggered when a dragging operation is in progress and the user drops an object on the control. The syntax of the event is:

```
object_DragDrop(Source As Control, X As Single, _
  Y As Single)
```

Source returns a reference to the object being dragged, whereas **X** and **Y** specify the X and Y coordinates within the object in which the dragged object has been dropped. To determine the source's type, you use the **TypeOf** keyword. To return a reference to the source's object, you use **Source** itself. For example:

```
If TypeOf Source Is FileListBox Then
  sFile = Source.FileName
  ' do something with the file
```

OLE Drag-And-Drop Operations

OLE drag and drop is similar to normal drag and drop, except that instead of dragging an object to invoke some program code, you actually drag *data*. For example, using OLE drag and drop, you can drag the contents of a text box to another control. Because it is an OLE operation, you can drag the contents of the text box to any OLE container, such as Microsoft Word. Likewise, you can drag data from Microsoft Word to a VB control.

To provide automatic drag-and-drop operations for a control within your Visual Basic application, set the **OLEDragMode** and **OLEDropMode** properties of the control to **Automatic**. The ComboBox, DirListBox, FileListBox, Image, PictureBox, ListBox, and TextBox controls support the **OLEDragMode** and **OLEDropMode** properties.

If you set the **OLEDragMode** property to **Manual**, you must use the **OLEDrag** method. This triggers the **OLEStartDrag** event. The **OLEStartDrag** event has the following syntax:

```
object_OLEStartDrag(Data As DataObject, AllowedEffects As Long)
```

Data is a **DataObject** object that contains data formats and/or the actual data from the object. If there isn't any data in the object, it can be obtained using the **DataObject** object's **GetData** method. To clear the data, use the **ClearData** method. The data can be supplied in a variety of formats, which are listed in the Object Browser and the Help file (see "GetData Method" in the Help file).

As an example, the following code gets data from a PictureBox and puts it into a device-independent format. When dropped into another application (or another control), the data will be copied:

```
Private Sub Picture1_OLEStartDrag(Data As DataObject, _
  AllowedEffects As Long)
AllowedEffects = vbDropEffectCopy
Data.SetData Picture1.Picture, vbCFDIB
End Sub
```

The **AllowedEffects** parameter allows you to set effects, such as **vbDropEffect-Copy** or **vbDropEffectMove**. If you use the latter to drag a picture from one PictureBox to another, the image will be moved from the first control to the second. If you do not use **SetData**, most drop targets will request it.

The **OLESetData** event occurs when a drop target requests data. This provides an opportunity to use the **SetData** method and can be advantageous, because moving large amounts of data can be time consuming and resource intensive. Unless the amount of data is small, you may wish to not use the **SetData** method in the **OLEStartDrag** event and wait until the **OLESetData** event instead.

Controls

The following sections review the controls that I believe are most likely to appear on the exam. Note that the previous section discusses many properties, methods, and events common to a number of controls. Because of the nature of this book, certain properties, methods, and events are discussed in other chapters, as well. Because an *Exam Cram* cannot cover every conceivable possibility, this section includes Table 4.1, which lists most key controls along with important attributes.

Visual Basic controls are broken into two categories: *intrinsic controls* and *ActiveX controls*. An intrinsic control is one that is automatically part of any Visual Basic application. It is part of the VB Library (open VB's Object Browser to examine the library in more detail). ActiveX controls are controls added to the toolbox via the Components selection in the Project menu.

The Intrinsic Controls

If you examine the VB library in the Object Browser, it includes the Form and MDIForm classes. Strictly speaking, Visual Basic considers these to be objects and not controls in your application. The Object Browser also lists the Menu

Table 4.1   Visual Basic intrinsic controls.

Control	Purpose	Important Attributes	Type
ADO Data (ADC)	Manipulate database records	**ConnectionString**	Property
		Error	Event
		Recordset	Property
		RecordSource	Property
		WillMove	Event
CheckBox	Set an option	**Caption**	Property
		Style	Property
		Value	Property
ComboBox	Combine a ListBox and a TextBox	See ListBox	
CommandButton	Initiate a process	**Caption**	Property
		Default, Cancel	Property
		Click	Event
DirListBox	Display a hierarchical list of directories	**List, ListCount, ListIndex**	Property
		Path	Property
		Refresh	Method
		Click	Event
DriveListBox	Display a list of disk drives	See DirListBox	
FileListBox	Display a list of files	Same as DirListBox plus	
		Pattern	Property
		PathChange	Event
		PatternChange	Event
Form	Act as the interface for the application	**ActiveControl**	Property
		AutoRedraw	Property
		Caption	Property
		ClipControls	Property
		Controls	Property
		CurrentX, CurrentY	Property
		Height, Width	Property
		hWnd	Property
		MDIChild	Property
		Visible	Property
		PopupMenu	Method
		PrintForm	Method
		Refresh	Method
		Show	Method
		Activate, Deactivate	Event
		Initialize	Event
		Load, UnLoad	Event
		QueryUnload	Event
		ReSize	Event
		Terminate	Event

(continued)

Table 4.1	Visual Basic intrinsic controls *(continued)*.		
Control	**Purpose**	**Important Attributes**	**Type**
Frame	Group related controls, particularly OptionButtons	**Caption**	Property
HScrollBar	Scroll horizontally or represent relative position	**LargeChange**	Property
		SmallChange	Property
		Max, Min	Property
		Change	Event
		Scroll	Event
Image	Display a graphic	**Picture**	Property
		Click, DblClick	Event
Label	Display text	**Alignment**	Property
		Caption	Property
Line	Display a line on the form	**DrawMode**	Property
		X1, Y1, X2, Y2	Property
ListBox	Display data in a scrolling box	**ItemData**	Property
		List, ListCount, ListIndex	Property
		MultiSelect	Property
		NewIndex	Property
		Selected, SelCount	Property
		Sorted	Property
		Text	Property
		AddItem, RemoveItem	Method
		Clear	Method
		Click, DblClick	Event
		ItemCheck	Event
		Scroll	Event
MDIForm	Act as an MDI frame for the application	**ActiveControl**	Property
		ActiveForm	Property
		AutoShowChildren	Property
		Caption	Property
		Controls	Property
		hWnd	Property
		Picture	Property
		Arrange	Method
		PopupMenu	Method
		Show	Method
		Activate, Deactivate	Event
		Initialize	Event
		Load, UnLoad	Event
		QueryUnload	Event
		ReSize	Event
		Terminate	Event

(continued)

Table 4.1	Visual Basic intrinsic controls *(continued)*.		
Control	**Purpose**	**Important Attributes**	**Type**
Menu	Display a custom menu	**Caption**	Property
		Checked	Property
		Enabled	Property
		NegotiatePosition	Property
		Shortcut	Property
		WindowList	Property
		Click	Event
OLE Container	Add insertable objects to forms	**Action**	Property
		ApplsRunning	Property
		AutoActivate	Property
		Class, Container	Property
		MiscFlags	Property
		FileNumber	Property
		SourceDoc, SourceItem	Property
		Close	Method
		Copy	Method
		DoVerb, FetchVerbs	Method
		InsertObj	Method
		SaveToOLE1File	Method
		Click, DblClick	Event
		Updated	Event
OptionButton	Select mutually exclusive options	See CheckBox	
PictureBox	Display graphic; more functional than Image	**CurrentX, CurrentY**	Property
		Image	Property
		Palette	Property
		Circle, CLS, Point, PSet	Method
		PaintPicture	Method
		Click	Event
		Paint	Event
Shape	Place a geometric shape on a form or control	**BackColor, ForeColor**	Property
		DrawMode	Property
		FillColor, FillStyle	Property
		Shape	Property
		Refresh	Method
TextBox	Display or capture data	**DataChanged**	Property
		DataRecord, DataSource	Property
		DataFormat, DataMember	Property
		Enabled, Locked	Property
		Multiline	Property

(continued)

Table 4.1   Visual Basic intrinsic controls *(continued)*.

Control	Purpose	Important Attributes	Type
		PassWordChar	Property
		SelLength, SelStart	Property
		SelText	Property
		Text	Property
		Change	Event
Timer	Execute code at regular intervals	Interval	Property
		Timer	Event

class. VB considers Menu to be a control but it is not part of the toolbox—use the Menu Editor instead. **App** and **Screen** objects are listed as part of the VB Library, and like Form and MDIForm, they are objects—not controls. There is only one occurrence of each in a VB project. (**App** and **Screen** objects are discussed at the beginning of this chapter.)

Image Vs. PictureBox Controls

Visual Basic developers often confuse the Image and PictureBox controls because the controls' functionality overlaps. The Image control is used to display a graphic (such as a bitmap, icon, and so on). It has fewer features than the PictureBox control. However, an Image control uses fewer resources than the PictureBox control and refreshes more rapidly. The Image control can react to **Click, DblClick,** and the usual drag-and-drop events. PictureBox will do all of this and more, including acting as a container for other controls. PictureBox can be used to house graphic methods, such as **Circle, PSet,** and so on, that are used to draw images programmatically. PictureBox can also act as the target for another control's **Print** method. You can place a PictureBox control on an MDIForm to act as a container, and the PictureBox control can be part of a DDE communication. PictureBox has an **AutoSize** property, which, when set to **True,** causes the control to adjust its size to match the graphic's size. On the other hand, the Image control has the **Stretch** property. When **Stretch** is set to **True,** the graphic is resized to fit the control. If **Stretch** is set to **False,** the control is resized to fit the graphic.

The ListBox And ComboBox Controls

Both the ListBox and ComboBox controls display a list of items. A ListBox has a fixed size on the form and scrolls if there are more items in the list than can be displayed at one time. A ComboBox drops down to display the items in the list. A user can select items from each control. The user can type into the ComboBox control but can only select items from the ListBox control.

The following list summarizes the key properties, methods, and events of the ListBox and ComboBox controls:

➤ **Style Property** Indicates how the ListBox or ComboBox control looks and behaves. For the ListBox control, **vbListBoxStandard** means the list box is just a list of items, whereas **vbListBoxCheckbox** means the list box displays items with a checkbox next to them—the user can select multiple items by checking and unchecking the checkboxes. For the ComboBox control, **vbComboDropdownList** causes the control to behave just like a list box except that it collapses after the user has made a selection—the user cannot type into the text box area. **vbComboSimple** is displayed as a drop-down list box with a text box that the user can type into. **vbComboDropDown** expands when the user selects the drop-down arrow, collapses after the user makes a selection, and allows the user to type into the text box area. Figure 4.4 shows the three styles of ComboBox controls.

➤ **List Property** Represents an array of items in the control, where **List (0)** is the first item.

➤ **ListCount Property** Returns the total number of items in the control.

➤ **ListIndex Property** Returns the item number that is currently selected. **ListIndex** returns 0 if the first item is selected, 1 for the second item, and so on. For the ListBox control, if it is equal to -1, there is no item currently selected. For the ComboBox, -1 indicates that the user has entered new text into the text box portion of the control.

➤ **NewIndex Property** Returns the index number of the item most recently added to the list box or combo box.

➤ **TopIndex Property** Returns the item number displayed in the top-most position of the drop-down display area. For example, if a ListBox or ComboBox control has 100 items in it and the user has scrolled so that the eighteenth item is at the top of the display, **TopIndex** returns 17 (it is zero-based). You can also use this property to programmatically scroll the list. Setting **TopIndex** to 20 will cause the ComboBox or ListBox control to scroll so that the twenty-first item is at the top of the control.

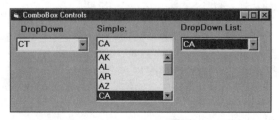

Figure 4.4 ComboBox controls have three presentation styles.

➤ **Text Property** Returns the currently selected item of the ComboBox or ListBox control.

➤ **MultiSelect Property (ListBox Control Only)** Sets or returns the selection mode of the list box. If it's equal to **vbMultiSelectNone**, then only one item can be selected at a time. Selecting an item in the list box deselects any previously selected item. **vbMultiSelectSimple** indicates *simple multiple selection*—the user can select and deselect items by clicking with the mouse or pressing the spacebar. Either action toggles the selected status. **vbMultipleSelectExtended** indicates *extended selection* similar to Windows Explorer. Holding down the Shift key allows contiguous selection, and holding down the Ctrl key allows noncontiguous selection.

➤ **Selected Property (ListBox Control Only)** Represents a zero-based array of type Boolean that indicates whether the item is currently selected. For instance, if **Selected (3)** is **True**, then the fourth item in the list box is selected. The **Selected** property is useful with multiple selections.

➤ **SelCount Property (ListBox Control Only)** Returns the number of items selected in a ListBox control.

➤ **Columns Property (ListBox Control Only)** Sets or returns the number of columns of data to be *displayed* in the ListBox control. Figure 4.5 shows four ListBox controls that display state abbreviations. The bottom two list boxes have their **Columns** properties set to 2 and 3 respectively. The columns are snaked like listings in a telephone directory and the cursor goes down the first column until it reaches the bottom. Then, it goes to the top of the second column.

➤ **Sorted Property** Sets or returns whether the contents of the ListBox or ComboBox control are sorted. The property can be set only at design time. If **Sorted** is set to **True**, then the items in the list box are sorted in alphabetical order. If new items are added, they are inserted into their correct sort order, as well. However, if you insert an item into a specific place in the list (see the **AddItem** method entry later in this list), Visual Basic will not move the item to maintain sort order. In Figure 4.5, the two ListBox controls in the middle of the form have their **Sorted** property set to **True**. Note that using **Sorted** does not preclude duplicate entries (in Figure 4.5, AZ appears in the list twice).

➤ **IntegralHeight** property When set to **True**, causes the ListBox or ComboBox control to resize itself as necessary in order to make sure that no partial rows are displayed. Figure 4.5 shows the effect of this property, where the two right-most list boxes have a font size of 36. The bottom list box displays a partial row.

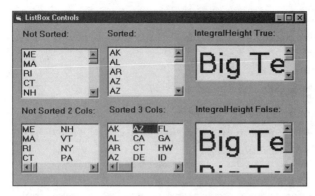

Figure 4.5   Demonstration of the **Sorted, Columns,** and **IntegralHeight** properties of the ListBox control.

➤ **ItemData Property** Is an underused array of type **Long**. For each item in the **List** array, there is a corresponding element in the **ItemData** array. You can, for instance, use this property to store part numbers that correspond to the part descriptions listed in the list box or combo box.

➤ **AddItem Method** Adds an item to the ListBox or ComboBox control. You can optionally specify in what position the item should be inserted. In the following code snippet, the first line adds an item to the ListBox control.

```
List1.AddItem "TX"
List1.AddItem "MN", 0
```

If the ListBox control's **Sorted** property is **False,** the item will be added to the end of the list. If the **Sorted** property is **True,** then the item will be inserted alphabetically. The second line inserts an item at the top of the list. Even if **Sorted** is **True,** the item will not be moved.

➤ **Clear Method** Clears all items from the ComboBox or ListBox control.

➤ **RemoveItem Method** Removes the specified item from the ComboBox or ListBox control. For example, **List1.RemoveItem 8** removes the ninth item in **List1.**

➤ **Change Event** Occurs when the contents of a ListBox or ComboBox control have changed.

➤ **Scroll Event** Occurs when the ComboBox or ListBox controls are scrolled. Note that *scrolling* means that the *display* area has scrolled. For instance, in Figure 4.5, the top-left list box has five items. If you select the top one and press the down arrow four times, the **Scroll** event will not fire because the display has not changed. If you press the down arrow one more time, the contents of the box change, and the **Scroll** event is fired.

ActiveX Controls

You can add ActiveX controls to your project and make them available via the toolbox for use in your development. To do so, click Project|Components, and select the controls that you wish to use.

 The controls that you are likely to run into on the certification exam are referenced where appropriate in the book. For example, the data-aware ActiveX controls (such as DataGrid) are covered in Chapter 10, and the StatusBar control is covered in Chapter 11.

The CommonDialog Control

Visual Basic's CommonDialog control is a Windows dialog customized by the parameters and messages sent to it. Visual Basic shields the developer from most of the complexities involved in setting up the dialog by providing a number of methods to perform the desired service(s), which are discussed in a moment. In general, the dialogs that you present to your users are identical to those presented by other Windows applications, lending your application a professional and common "look and feel."

To add the CommonDialog control to your project, select Project|Components, and then choose Microsoft CommonDialog Control 6.0. The control is then included in the toolbox. To use it, you should place it on the form in which it is going to be used. An icon—not visible at runtime—appears on the form.

The CommonDialog's methods that you invoke dictate the actual dialog that is presented. Table 4.2 summarizes a number of CommonDialog's properties, but CommonDialog has no events associated with it. (Properties related to Help are listed in Chapter 11 in the section titled "Using The CommonDialog To Display Help.") None of the control's methods returns a value. To determine what the user has selected from the dialog presented, the application has to query the control's properties, as outlined in the following sections.

Open, Save, And Save As

Perhaps the most common use of the CommonDialog control is to present an Open File, Save File, or Save File As dialog box. These are invoked by using the **ShowOpen** or **ShowSave** methods of the control, as shown:

```
' Prompt the user to save a file
CommonDialog1.ShowSave
```

Table 4.2   Key CommonDialog properties.

Property	Type	Meaning
CancelError	True or False	Generate or do not generate an error if the user clicks Cancel in a dialog
DefaultExt	String	Default file extension to display
FileName	String	Name of the file(s) that the user selected, delimited by a space
Filter	String	Control what file(s) to be displayed, such as: "Text Files (*.txt)|*.txt"
Flags	Long	Various constants that control the behavior of dialogs
InitDir	String	Specify the initial directory

Alternatively, you can use the control's **Action** property to dictate what dialog will be displayed. The use of **Action** is included for backward compatibility with prior versions of Visual Basic and does not provide all the functionality of CommonDialog's various methods.

To determine the name of the file to open or save, you need to query the **FileName** property of the CommonDialog control. If the user selects or types a valid file name, this property will contain a fully qualified path and file name. It is the application's responsibility to actually open or create the file. If **CancelError** is set to **True**, a runtime error is generated if the user presses Cancel. Handling the runtime error is the only way to determine if the Cancel button was clicked.

Show Fonts

The **ShowFont** method (**CommonDialog1.ShowFont**) displays all the fonts installed on the user's computer or printer. However, you must supply a constant to the **Flags** property of the CommonDialog control. These constants are not valid with other methods of the control. The valid constants are:

➤ CdlCFBoth Displays both screen and printer fonts.

➤ CdlCFPrinterFonts Displays the installed printer fonts.

➤ CdlCFScreenFonts Displays the computer's screen fonts.

Other CommonDialog Methods

Besides the CommonDialog methods previously reviewed, the following methods are used to show available colors and printers:

➤ **ShowColor** Allows the user to select a color from the system color palette. To determine the color selected, query the **Color** property, like this:

```
myColor = CommonDialog1.Color
```

➤ **ShowPrinter** Displays a list of available printers.

The CommonDialog control also has a **ShowHelp** method, which is addressed in Chapter 11 in the section titled "Using The CommonDialog To Display Help."

The ImageList Control

As its main property, the ImageList control contains the **ListImages** collection, which contains **ListImage** objects. The ImageList control is basically a reference to images used by other controls. The images it references are Windows bitmaps, but you can use the **ExtractIcon** method of the **ListImage** object to convert the bitmap into an icon for those controls that expect an icon. For instance, assume you have a bitmap that you would like to use as your form's icon. You can do this with the following syntax:

```
Form1.Icon = ImageList1.ListImages(5).ExtractIcon
```

This example turns the bitmap referenced by the fifth **ListImage** object into an icon for use by **Form1**.

To assign an image to a **ListImage** object, use the object's **Picture** property and the following **LoadPicture** statement:

```
ImageList1.ListImages(3).Picture = LoadPicture _
    "C:\Graphics\Bitmaps\MyBitMap.BMP"
```

The most common use of the **ListImages** collection is as a source to the Toolbar control. For more information, search for "ImageList Control" in the Visual Basic Help files.

The ListView Control

The ListView control is used to display information in a graphical format. It is often used in conjunction with the TreeView control, which is discussed in the next section. Figure 4.6 shows the TreeView control in use in the left window and the ListView control in the right window.

The ListView control is contained in the COMCTL32.OCX file and can be added to your project by selecting Project|Components on VB's menu and then choosing Microsoft Windows Common Controls 6.0. Several controls, including the ProgressBar, Slider, ImageList, and TreeView controls, are also added when you select this component.

The ListView control provides you with four presentation options: large icons, small icons, list, and report. This is governed by the **View** property using the VB constants **ivwIcon, ivwSmallIcon, ivwList,** and **ivwReport,** respectively. In report view, you can specify that column headings are displayed by setting the **HideColumnHeadings** property to **True.** (Figure 4.6 shows the report view with column headings displayed.)

To supply icons, you first associate the **Icons** and **SmallIcons** properties with a valid ImageList control:

```
ListView1.Icons = imlIcons
ListView1.SmallIcons = imlSmallIcons
```

Each ListView control has a **ListItems** property, which is a collection of type **ListItem.** The **ListItems** property corresponds to the actual contents of the ListView control. Each line in the right window of Figure 4.6 is a **ListItem.** Two of the properties of **ListItem** are **Icon** and **SmallIcon.** The preceding code associated a ListView control with an Image control via its **Icons** and

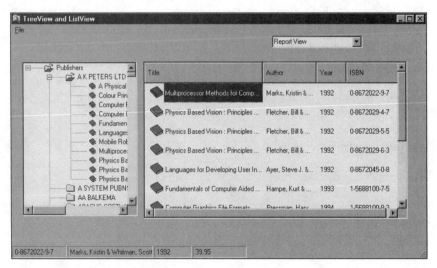

Figure 4.6   TreeView and ListView controls.

SmallIcons properties. You can now assign a specific icon to any individual **ListItem** that references the ordinal position within the collection or the icon's key:

```
ListView1.ListItems(1).Icon = 1
ListView1.ListItems(1).SmallIcon = "smlbook"
```

The ListView control has a **ColumnHeaders** collection property comprised of **ColumnHeader** objects. **ColumnHeader** objects are quite powerful. For instance, a user can click on one to sort the report by that column.

For more information on the ListView control, search for "ListView Control", "ListItems collection", and "ColumnHeaders collection" in VB's online Help files.

The TreeView Control

A TreeView control is a hierarchical representation of data. Both the TreeView and ListView controls can be seen in Windows Explorer. The left window of Explorer (the folders view) shows a TreeView control as it expands and collapses to show the computer's drives and directories. The right window is a ListView control that shows the contents of the currently selected folder. Each item in the TreeView is called a *node*.

The TreeView control's main property is the **Nodes** collection. Each **Node** object within the collection contains an image and some text. To associate graphics, you associate the **ImageList** property of the TreeView control with an ImageList control, similar to the way you associate the **Icons** and **SmallIcons** properties of the ListView control with an ImageList control. Then, you associate the **ImageView** property of each individual **Node** object with a specific image from the ImageList control using the ordinal position or key, like this:

```
TreeView1.Nodes(1).ImageView = 4
TreeView1.Nodes(2).ImageView = "open"
```

To add text, use the **Text** property.

Each **Node** can contain other **Nodes**. The **Child** and **Parent** properties of each **Node** object maintain the hierarchy of nodes. To add a new node as a child of another node, you would use syntax similar to the following:

```
Dim newNode As Node
Set newNode = TreeView1.Nodes (TreeView1.SelectedItem.Index).Child
```

This example uses the **Child** property of the currently selected **Node** object (determined by using the **SelectedItem** property of the TreeView control) to dynamically add the new **Node** object. An alternative is this:

```
Set newNode = TreeView1.Nodes.Add (ParentNode, tvwChild, "1234", _
   "Jane Doe", "woman")
```

In this example, **ParentNode** is a reference to an existing **Node** object. **tvwChild** is a constant that specifies that the relationship will be a child relationship. **"1234"** is the key of the node, whereas **"Jane Doe"** is the text. The key of the icon to be used is **"woman"**.

Set the TreeView control's **Sorted** property to **True** to sort the nodes.

For more information about the TreeView control, search for "TreeView control and Nodes collection" in the VB Help files.

The Slider Control

The Slider control is somewhat similar to an HScrollBar or VScrollBar control. It is a graphical representation of a "thumb" slider, which can be used to select either discrete values (such as 1, 2, 3, and so on) or a continuous range of values. Optional tick marks denote values. The **Max** and **Min** properties denote the maximum and minimum values. The **TickFrequency** property determines how many tick marks there will be. For instance, if the **Max** property is set to 10 and the **Min** property is set to 0, a **TickFrequency** of 2 will cause 6 ticks to be on the control (denoting the values 0, 2, 4, 6, 8, and 10). The **Value** property sets or returns the current value of the Slider control.

Use the **Orientation** property to set the control to a horizontal (**sldHorizontal**) or vertical (**sldVertical**) presentation.

The Slider control can be used to measure or alter a value. For instance, you can detect the alteration of the Slider control's **Value** property and use that value to alter something else, such as the size of a bitmap or the current position in a multimedia file. You use the **Change** event to detect a change in the **Value** property. **Scroll** is triggered whenever the control is scrolled.

For more information, search for "Slider control" in the VB Help files.

The UpDown Control

The UpDown control presents a pair of arrow buttons that the user can click to alter the contents of another control. The second control is known as a *buddy control*. A typical pairing of controls is a TextBox control with the UpDown control. You use the UpDown control's **BuddyControl** property to associate the TextBox control:

```
UpDown1.BuddyControl = Text1
```

Alternatively, you can use the **AutoBuddy** property to set the associated control. By setting this property to **True**, Visual Basic associates the control next lowest in the Tab order as the buddy control. If there is no control lower in the Tab order, VB uses the next control higher in the Tab order. The **BuddyProperty** property determines which property of the buddy control is altered when the UpDown control is used. If the **BuddyProperty** property is not supplied, the buddy control's default property is used. If the **SyncProperty** property is set to **True**, VB will ensure that the values of both controls are synchronized. Thus, you can use an UpDown control to change the number presented in a TextBox control.

The **Min** and **Max** properties control the minimum and maximum values. **Increment** maintains the amount that the value changes by every time an arrow is clicked. The **Value** control sets or returns the actual current value of the control.

The UpDown control is added with the Microsoft Windows Common Controls-2 6.0, available on the Project|Components menu.

The Toolbar Control

The Toolbar control is usually used in association with a menu to denote common menu choices. Select Microsoft Windows Common Controls 6.0 to add the Toolbar control to your project. When you draw the toolbar on the form, the Toolbar Wizard offers to build the control for you. If you choose to create the control manually, you need to add an ImageList control and add to the ImageList those icons that you plan to use in the Toolbar control. Set the **ImageList** property of the Toolbar control to the name of the ImageList control that will be supplying the icons.

The **Buttons** property of the Toolbar control is a collection of **Button** objects—one **Button** object for each Toolbar item. Set the **Image** property of each **Button** object to the **Image** number or key within the ImageList's **ListImages** collection:

```
Toolbar1.Buttons(3).Image = "save"
```

You set the **Key** property of the **Button** object so that it can be evaluated in code. To use the Toolbar control in code, you need to be able to determine which button the user pressed. The **ButtonClick** event of the Toolbar control is passed as an argument to the event procedure. Use a **Select Case** construct to evaluate the **Key** of the **Button** pressed:

```
Select Case Button.Key
  Case "New"
    ' do something
  Case "Open"
    ' do something else
```

The TabStrip Control

The TabStrip control is used to display property pages, often called *tab pages*. The **Tabs** property is a collection of **Tab** objects, each one being a property page, as shown in Figure 4.7.

Each **Tab** object acts as a container to other controls. The **Highlighted** property returns **True** when a given **Tab** object is highlighted. The **Caption** property is used to set the **Caption** of each **Tab**. If you have associated an ImageList control with the **ImageList** property of the TabStrip control, you can set the **Image** property of each **Tab** to an image in the ImageList control's **ListImages** collection.

The **MultiSelect** property of the TabStrip control can be set to **True** to allow multiple **Tabs** to be selected at once. The **HotTracking** property, when set to **True**, causes each tab to be highlighted as the mouse pointer passes over it (the text changes color). The **Style** property allows you to set the control's appearance. **tabTabs** gives the presentation shown in Figure 4.7. **tabButtons** causes the tabs to be replaced by buttons. When the buttons are pressed, the appropriate **Tab** object is displayed, and the button appears depressed. **vbButtonsFlat** uses Internet Explorer-type buttons. The **MultiRow** property allows the **Tabs** to be displayed on multiple rows. If you set this to **False**, Visual Basic will place all the **Tabs** in one row, truncating text as necessary. You can use the **Placement** property to set where the tabs will be displayed. Use **tabPlacementBottom**, **tabPlacementTop**, **tabPlacementLeft**, or **tabPlacementRight**.

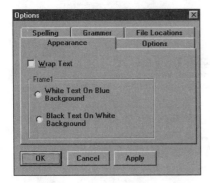

Figure 4.7   The TabStrip control.

Practice Questions

Question 1

> Which of the following is a step in assigning an icon to a Toolbar control?
>
> ○ a. `Toolbar1.Buttons(0).Icon = LoadPicture _`
>   `("myicon.ico")`
>
> ○ b. `Toolbar1.ImageList = ImageList1`
>
> ○ c. `Toolbar1(0) = LoadPicture ("myicon.ico")`
>
> ○ d. `LoadIcon Toolbar1.Selected, "myicon.ico"`

Answer b is correct. It is necessary to bind an ImageList control to the Toolbar control. Answer a is incorrect because you cannot assign an icon to a **Button** object using the **LoadPicture** method. Answer c is incorrect because it attempts to use the **LoadPicture** function and it does not reference the **Buttons** collection. Answer d is incorrect because there is no **LoadIcon** statement and there is no **Selected** method (or property) of the Toolbar control.

Question 2

> Your application has a menu item Save File and another Save File As. Which of the following methods of the CommonDialog control would be *most* appropriate to use for the Save File As menu item?
>
> ○ a. **Save**.
>
> ○ b. **SaveAs**.
>
> ○ c. **Open**.
>
> ○ d. The best would be to set **Action = vbCDSaveAs** because **SaveAs** has not been implemented as a method.

Answer a is correct. There is no separate **SaveAs** method of the CommonDialog control. You can set the **DialogTitle** to Save As, and you can set the **Flags** property to control the dialog's behavior. Answer b is incorrect because there is no **SaveAs** method. Answer c is incorrect because you would not use **Open** to save a file. Answer d is incorrect because there is no value for **Action** that opens a Save As dialog and because the question asks for a method not a property.

Question 3

> You have two PictureBox controls on a form. **Picture1** is display-
> ing the Clouds.bmp bitmap file. Which of the following techniques
> are viable for copying the picture displayed in the first control to
> the second PictureBox control? [Check all correct answers]
>
> ❑ a. `Picture2.Picture = Picture1.Picture`
>
> ❑ b. `Picture2 = Picture1`
>
> ❑ c. Drag and drop setting the **DragMode** and **DropMode**
> properties to automatic
>
> ❑ d. `Clipboard.SetData Picture1.Picture`
> `Picture2.Picture = _`
> `Clipboard.GetData(vbCFDIB)`

Answers a, b, and d are correct. Answer a is correct because you can assign the
Picture property of the first control to the **Picture** property of the second.
Answer b is also correct and is essentially synonymous with answer a because
Picture is the default property of the PictureBox control. Answer d is correct
because it uses the **SetData** method of the **Clipboard** object to copy the picture to the clipboard. Then, the **GetData** method is used to load the picture
into **Picture2**. Answer c is incorrect because there is no **DropMode** property
and because you would still have to do some coding to handle the dropping of
the picture on the second PictureBox control.

Question 4

> You have a ListBox control named **List1** that contains 100 values.
> The user has scrolled the ListBox control so that the fiftieth item
> is at the top of the display area of the control. How can you deter-
> mine in your code what that item is?
>
> ○ a. List1.Selected
>
> ○ b. List1.List (List1.ListIndex)
>
> ○ c. List1.Text
>
> ○ d. List1.List(List1.TopIndex)

Answer d is correct. **TopIndex** returns the index number of the item at the top
of the list box display. **List** is the array of all items in the list box. Therefore, the
expression returns the value of whatever is currently displayed at the top of the
list box. Answer a is incorrect because **Selected** is an array of type **Boolean** that
returns **True** for each item that is currently selected in the list box. Answer b is

incorrect because the expression returns the value of the item currently selected. Answer c is incorrect because it, too, returns the value of the item currently selected.

Question 5

> How can you capture an up or down arrow key while a ListBox has focus? [Check all correct answers]
>
> ❑ a. Use the form's **KeyPreview** event.
>
> ❑ b. Use the ListBox's **Scroll** event.
>
> ❑ c. Use the ListBox's **KeyPress** event.
>
> ❑ d. Use the ListBox's **KeyDown** or **KeyUp** events.

Answers b and d are correct. The ListBox control's **Scroll** event is triggered when an arrow key is pressed, thus allowing you to react to it. Likewise, the **KeyDown** and **KeyUp** events can be used to intercept an arrow key. Answer a is incorrect because **KeyPreview** is a property of the form—not an event. (Also, the form cannot intercept an arrow key in a ListBox control.) Answer c is incorrect because the **KeyPress** event is not invoked with the arrow keys.

Question 6

> What steps must you take to change the Tab order of controls at runtime?
>
> ○ a. It can't be done at runtime.
>
> ○ b. Invoke the **ReTab** method for each control that utilizes the form's **Controls** collection.
>
> ○ c. Alter the **TabIndex** property of the control or controls that need to be resequenced and all others will resequence themselves accordingly.
>
> ○ d. Invoke the **TabOrder** method of the form (using the **Controls** collection if desired) except that control arrays have to be sequenced at design time.

Answer c is correct. When you alter the **TabIndex** of any control, the other controls will move to reflect the change. Answer a is incorrect because the **TabIndex** is not a read-only property at runtime. Answer b is incorrect because there is no **ReTab** method. Answer d is incorrect because the form has no **TabOrder** method and the control array can be resequenced as any other controls.

Need To Know More?

The following sources provide some good overviews of VB controls. More important, I highly recommend that you develop an inventory of the intrinsic controls that you are not familiar with. Then, write a small application that manipulates those controls to ensure that you have a basic understanding. Of the ActiveX controls, it is particularly important that you be aware of the use of the CommonDialog control. Familiarize yourself with the controls available in the Microsoft Windows Common Controls 6.0 libraries (there are three of them).

 Craig, John Clark and Jeff Webb. *Microsoft Visual Basic 6.0 Developer's Workshop*, Microsoft Press, Redmond, WA, 1998. ISBN 1-57231-883-X. A good intermediate-level VB6 resource. I found the entire volume interesting and educational. The authors take a "How Do I?" approach to explaining various VB techniques. Chapters 12 and 13 discuss forms, dialog boxes, and the user interface.

 Davis, Harold. *Visual Basic 6 Secrets*, IDG Books Worldwide, Foster City, CA, 1998. ISBN 0-7645-3223-5. Harold has done a nice job with this book. Because Harold takes a different organizational approach to his book than I do in this book, you will find that the materials relating to this chapter are spread throughout *Visual Basic 6 Secrets*. Chapter 7 is devoted to the CommonDialog control, whereas Chapter 8 delves into most of the remainder of the user interface. Chapter 17 is a brief but good discussion of the human element in the user interface, whereas Chapter 18 discusses the multiple document interface and menus.

 Holzner, Steven. *Visual Basic 6 Black Book*, The Coriolis Group, Scottsdale, AZ, 1998. ISBN 1-57610-283-1. Steven has written an eminently readable book, and both intermediate- and advanced-level developers will find it to be a good source of information and techniques. Chapter 4 is an overview of using the Form and MDIForm objects. Steven takes a different approach from most texts here in that he uses the chapter to dive right into the creation and use of toolbars, status bars, and so on. It's a good chapter. Chapters 5 through 16 delve into the usage of different controls in more depth than you might ever want. Based on my review of those chapters alone, *Visual Basic 6 Black Book* should be part of any VB developer's library (and no, The Coriolis Group didn't "make me" say that).

Siler, Brian and Jeff Spotts. *Special Edition Using Visual Basic 6*, Que, Indianapolis, IN, 1998. ISBN 0-7897-1542-2. Brian and Jeff's book is a good intermediate-level text. Chapter 4 is devoted to using VB's intrinsic, controls calling them "default controls," whereas Chapter 12 is devoted to the exploration and use of Windows common controls.

 In the online books on the VB CD-ROM, go to Part 1 ("Visual Basic Basics"), and browse through the three "Controls" subtopics ("Controls For Displaying Text," "Controls That Present Choices," and "Controls That Display Pictures And Graphics"). Most of the concepts are basic, but you can scan them quickly for any points with which you might not be familiar. Look through Part 2 ("What Can You Do With Visual Basic?"), and pay attention to the first two subtopics ("Creating A User Interface" and "Using Visual Basic's Standard Controls"). Finally, review the Component Tools Guide and pay particular attention to the first two topics ("Using ActiveX Controls" and "Using The ActiveX Controls").

Visual Basic
Coding

. . . .

Terms you'll need to understand:

√ Collection

√ **Dictionary**

√ Class

√ Property procedures

√ Reference

√ **WithEvents**

√ Instantiate

√ **Implements**

√ Delegation and reuse

Techniques you'll need to master:

√ Knowing the new language features of Visual Basic 6

√ Being familiar with the Visual Basic 6 language

√ Using custom and built-in collection classes

√ Using the **Dictionary** object

√ Adding methods, events, and properties to a class

√ Obtaining a reference to a class

√ Exposing the event model of a class

√ Implementing the interface of one class in another

√ Using the Class Builder to create a class hierarchy

Chapters 3 and 4 deal with the mechanics of what makes up a Visual Basic application, from procedures and modules to the different controls and objects that you use to interact with the user. This chapter guides you through a quick summary of the VB language, beginning with a look at the language features new to VB6. Then, you'll delve into more advanced coding topics, including the use of collections, classes, and the new **Dictionary** object.

Visual Basic 6 Language Extensions

Although the main focus of change in Visual Basic 6 is in the areas of Internet development and database access, some welcome enhancements were added to the language, as well. The next couple sections review the enhancements of particular interest.

String Handling

A number of very useful and time-saving string-handling functions have been added to the Visual Basic programming language. These are summarized below.

MonthName

The **MonthName** function returns the name of the month supplied. An optional **Boolean** argument specifies whether to return the abbreviation for the month. **MonthName (12)** and **MonthName (12, False)** both return "December", whereas **MonthName (12, True)** returns "Dec". **MonthName** is fairly flexible in that it can extrapolate the numeric representation of a date in a particular month. For example, **MonthName (Val (Date))** returns "October" if the current date is during the month of October. **MonthName (Val(#12/31/1996#))** returns "December".

StrReverse

Another string-handling enhancement in VB6 is the **StrReverse** function. **StrReverse** reverses the specified string. **StrReverse ("California")** returns "ainrofilaC".

InStrRev

InStrRev is a welcome addition to performing a substring search within a string. **InStrRev** is similar to **InStr**, except that **InStrRev** searches from the end of the string. For example, it is common to need to parse a path and file name, as in the following example:

```
Dim sPath As String
Dim sFile As String
Dim sFullName As String
Dim iSlash As Integer
sFullName = "c:\program files\my project\project.exe"
iSlash = InStrRev(sFullName, "\")
sPath = Left$(sFullName, iSlash - 1)
sFile = Mid$(sFullName, iSlash + 1)
Debug.Print "Path: " & sPath & vbCr & _
  "File: " & sFile
```

The preceding code returns the following:

```
Path: c:\program files\my project
File: project.exe
```

The **InStrRev** function takes an optional argument—starting position. If the starting position is omitted, it defaults to -1, meaning that the search begins from the last character in the string. Otherwise, the search begins at the position specified and searches back from there. For example,

```
InStrRev ("abcabc", "c", 4)
```

returns 3.

Replace

The **Replace** function uses the following syntax:

```
Replace(expression, find, replacewith [, start[, count[, compare]]])
```

Visual Basic string comparison functions have an optional *compare* parameter that takes one of the following constants:

➤ **vbUseCompareOption** Uses the setting specified by the **Option Compare** statement.

➤ **vbBinaryCompare** Performs a binary compare.

➤ **vbTextCompare** Performs a text compare.

➤ **vbDatabaseCompare** Uses database settings (with Microsoft Access).

The **Option Compare** statement, if used, can be placed in any module but must precede any procedure declarations. You can specify **Binary**, **Text**, or **Database**. For example, **Option Compare Text** specifies a text-based comparison. All subsequent operations

> will use that setting unless explicitly overridden. In a text-based comparison, case does not count. For instance, **"A"** is considered equal to **"a"**. Thus, **If "cat" = "CAT"** evaluates to **True**. In a binary compare (the default), uppercase letters compare as less than lowercase letters (**"A"** is considered to be less than **"a"**). Thus, the statement **If "cat" < "CAT"** evaluates to **False**.

Replace searches through the string supplied as *expression*, finds occurrences of the substring *find*, and replaces each occurrence with the substring *replacewith*. If *start* is specified, searching begins from that position (*start*). If *count* is supplied, only the specified number of replacements is made. There is a gotcha with this function in that, counter-intuitively, if *start* is supplied, the string returned begins with the *start* position. Initially, I expected replacements to actually start at the *start* position but the whole string to be returned. The following shows some examples of how the **Replace** function works:

```
Debug.Print Replace("AACAA", "A", "B")      ' returns BBCBB
Debug.Print Replace("AACAA", "A", "B", 2, 2) ' returns BCBA
Debug.Print Replace("AACAA", "A", "B", 2)   ' returns BCBB
Debug.Print Replace("AACAA", "A", "B", , 2)  returns BBCAA
```

Split

Split parses a string by using a supplied delimiter that returns a zero-based array of substrings. For example, assume your application accepted command-line arguments using the **Command** function and your command delimiter is the slash character (/). The following will return all the command-line arguments:

```
Split(Command$, "/", -1)
```

The -1 argument is the number of items to return. -1 (the default) specifies to return all substrings.

In my testing, **Split** seemed to return one empty string. The following example creates an array of four items instead of the three items that you would expect:

```
Dim vArray As Variant
Dim vParse As Variant
Dim sTest As String
sTest = "/Open /Play /ShowAll"
vArray = Split(sTest, "/", -1)
For Each vParse In vArray
  MsgBox vParse
Next
```

Join

The **Join** function is the complement to **Split**. It takes an array and creates a single delimited string. If a delimiter character is not specified, then a single space is used as a delimiter. If we add the following two lines of code to the preceding example, you may expect that we will get four items. Instead, **Join** returns the original three-item list, as shown here:

```
sTest = Join(vArray, "/")
Debug.Print sTest  ' prints "/Open /Play /ShowAll"
```

Filter

Filter reads a one-dimensional array that returns another array that meets a certain search condition. The syntax is as follows:

```
Filter (inputStrings, value[, include[, compare]])
```

InputStrings is a one-dimensional array to be searched. *Value* is the substring to look for within each element of *inputStrings*. *Include* is set to **True** (the default), to include the strings that match, or **False**, to list only the strings that don't match. The following example finds only the cities in the state of Rhode Island using the optional *Compare* to perform a case-insensitive search:

```
Dim sCity(1 To 4) As String
Dim vArray As Variant
Dim vCity As Variant
sCity(1) = "Providence, RI"
sCity(2) = "New York, NY"
' note use of upper and lower case
sCity(3) = "pawtucket, ri"
sCity(4) = "hartford, ct"
vArray = Filter(sCity, ", RI", True, vbTextCompare)
For Each vCity In vArray
   Debug.Print vCity
Next
```

The code returns two cities—Providence and Pawtucket.

Round

The **Round** function takes a string containing a number that Visual Basic can recognize and returns a string containing the number rounded to the number of decimal positions specified (the default is zero). For example, **Round** ("1084.255", 2) returns 1084.26. If you round to a whole number, Visual Basic rounds as though you moved the number into an **Integer**. That is, if the decimal is exactly .5, even numbers round down and odd numbers round up. Thus, **Round** (**"$116.5"**) and **Round**(**"$115.5"**) both return **116**.

FormatCurrency And FormatNumber

The **FormatCurrency** function is similar to (but more functional than) the **Format** function. **FormatNumber** is identical except that the currency symbol is omitted. **FormatCurrency** takes a string and formats it as currency using the parameters specified and prepends the currency symbol specified in the computer's regional settings. The syntax is shown here:

```
FormatCurrency (expression [,numDigitsAfterDecimal _
   [,includeLeadingDigit [,useParensForNegativeNumbers _
   [,groupDigits]]]])
```

NumDigitsAfterDecimal specifies the number of digits to be displayed after the decimal point. The default is -1, which means that the computer's regional settings are used. The *includeLeadingDigit*, *useParensForNegativeNumbers*, and *groupDigits* arguments accept a value of **vbTrue**, **vbFalse**, or **vbUseDefault** (the latter means Visual Basic should use the computer's regional settings). *IncludeLeadingDigit* specifies whether a zero should be displayed before fractional values. For example, a value of **vbTrue** would display ".37" as $0.37. *GroupDigits* specifies whether a thousands separator will be used. If the string **sAmount** contains the value "18062.1", then

```
FormatCurrency ("18062.1", 2, , , vbTrue)
```

returns $18,062.10.

 The documentation incorrectly lists the groupDigits parameter values as **TriStateTrue**, **TriStateFalse**, and **TriStateUseDefault** instead of **vbTrue** and so on. **vbTrue**, **vbDefault**, and **vbUseDefault** are part of the **vbTriState** enum.

FormatPercent

FormatPercent is the same as **FormatNumber** except that the result is expressed as a percentage with a trailing percent symbol (%). Thus,

```
FormatPercent ("11.2222", 1, , , vbtrue)
```

returns 1,122.2%.

FormatDateTime

The **FormatDateTime** function formats a supplied string as date or time using a named date format (**vbGeneralDate, vbLongDate, vbShortDate, vbLongTime,** or **vbShortTime**). The meaning of each format is dependent on the computer's regional settings. The default is **vbGeneralDate**. On my computer,

```
FormatDateTime (Now, vbLongDate)
```

returns a string similar to "Monday, October 26, 1998".

Other VB Language Enhancements

Aside from the new string functions listed in the prior section, VB has added additional functionality. User-defined types (UDTs) can now be passed as arguments to public procedures. Public functions can return UDTs. Also, functions can now return arrays. The Microsoft Scripting Runtime library is included with Visual Basic, giving VB developers access to the **FileSystemObject** object.). Finally, the **Dictionary** object offers some enhancements over the collection class. Later, this chapter discusses the collection class followed by the new **Dictionary** object.

Review Of The Visual Basic Language

In this section, we'll quickly review elements of the Visual Basic language. As stated at the beginning of the chapter, the assumption is made that you are already familiar with the mechanics of VB coding. This section, then, serves to remind you of what is in the language. You may also wish to review the VBA library in the Object Browser. This section groups VB language elements in the same manner as VBA is organized in the Object Browser.

 Many of the VB functions that deal with strings come in two flavors—one that ends with a dollar sign ("$") and one that doesn't. An example is **Left$** and **Left**. The function that ends with the dollar sign returns a variable of type **String**, whereas the other function (without the dollar sign) returns a variable of type **Variant**. Because VB will generally perform data conversions automatically for you, using either form of the function will yield the same result. However, if you use the wrong version, VB has to perform an extra step (a data type conversion). This means that the program's performance takes a slight hit. In the following example, **Left** is used to assign the first five characters of **sAnimal** to **sAbbrev**. The variables are of type **String**, but the function returns data type **Variant**. So, VB has to convert the **Variant** back to **String**, as shown here:

```
Dim sAnimal As String
Dim sAbbrev As String
sAnimal = "Rhinoceros"
SAbbrev = Left (sAnimal, 5)
```

In my own testing, I calculated that a program optimized for fast code takes a 5.2 percent performance hit when using the **Left** function as opposed to the **Left$** function in the preceding example. The methodology I used was to create two versions of the program using only a standard module. I created a loop that performed the **Left** (or **Left$**) function 5 million times and ran each version of the program several times to try to eliminate environmental factors from the performance measurements.

Conversion

Conversion functions convert a value of a certain data type to another data type. (Chapter 2 reviews many of these functions.) **Cbool**, for example, converts a value to a **Boolean**. When converting a numeric value to a **Boolean**, VB considers any non-zero value to be **True**.

CVDate and **CVErr** convert values into variables of type **Variant** and subtype **Date** and **Err**.

VB provides functions to convert hex, octal, and decimal numbers to strings. **Hex** and **Hex$** functions return strings that represent the hexadecimal value of a number. **Oct** and **Oct$** return strings that represent the octal value of a number. **Str** and **Str$** return strings that represent decimal values of a number.

Val returns the numeric value of a number in a string. **Val** reads a string from left to right, attempting to convert the string's contents to a number, and stops when it hits the first nonnumeric character. As an example, **Val** ("123.456") returns 123.456, whereas **Val** ("123a456") returns 123. If the first character in the string is nonnumeric—such as **Val** ("$123")—then **Val** returns 0.

Fix and **Int** both return the integer portion of a number. Both will convert a string to a numeric value. **Int** (3.14) and **Int** ("$3.14") both return 3. However, **Fix** differs from **Int** in how it handles negative numbers. **Int** returns the next lower number, whereas **Fix** simply returns the integer portion of the number. **Int** (-3.14) returns -4, whereas **Fix** (-3.14) returns -3.

Date And Time

Date and Time functions allow you to manipulate date and time values, perform date arithmetic, and so on.

Date and **Date$** set or return the system date. **Time** and **Time$** set or return the system time. **Now** returns the current date and time, and **Timer** returns the number of seconds elapsed since midnight.

DateAdd returns a new date using this syntax:

```
DateAdd (interval, number, date)
```

Interval is a string representing valid intervals, such as "d" for day, "ww" for week, "w" for weekday, "m" for month, and so on. *Number* is the number of *intervals* to add or subtract. *Date* is the beginning date. So, **DateAdd ("m", 36, "Jan 1, 1999")** returns 1 Jan 2002 (36 months are added to Jan 1, 1999.)

DateDiff returns the number of intervals between two dates. For example, **DateDiff ("m", "Jan 1, 2002", "Jan 1, 1999")** returns -36 (which means that the second date is 36 months earlier than the first date).

DatePart returns the part of the date specified by the interval. For example, **DatePart ("y", "Feb 29, 2000")** returns 60 (y specifies the day of the year).

Day, Hour, Minute, Month, Second, and **Year** return a portion of a date or time. For example, **Year (Date$)** returns 1998, if the system date is in the year 1998.

File System

Visual Basic has a number of statements and functions that interact with the file system (such as **Open, Close,** and so on). While you are unlikely to be directly quizzed on the exam about how any of these statements and functions work, you may see some in the exam as part of a code that quizzes you about other topics. Most file system statements and functions work pretty much as you would expect. For example, **FileLen** returns the length of a file. Statements or functions that you might not be familiar with include:

➤ **FileAttr** Returns the open mode of a file previously opened.

➤ **Kill** Erases a file.

➤ **Loc** Returns the current read/write position in a file.

➤ **Reset** Closes all open disk files.

Financial

VB has a number of financial functions, such as **FV** (returns the future value of an investment), that are similar to Microsoft Excel functions. You are not likely to see these on the certification exam.

Information

The information functions mostly return information about variables. The information functions include the following:

➤ **IsArray** Returns **True** if the variable is an array.

➤ **IsDate** Returns **True** if the variable contains a date.

➤ **IsEmpty** Returns **True** if a variable has not been initialized. (There is no **IsNothing** function.)

➤ **IsNull** Returns **True** if a variable has a value of Null.

➤ **IsNumeric** Returns **True** if the value is numeric. For example, **IsNumeric** ("3") returns **True**, whereas **IsNumeric** ("3a") returns **False**.

➤ **IsObject** Returns **True** if a variable contains an object.

➤ **TypeName** Returns the data type name of a variable. If the variable is **Empty** or **Nothing**, then **TypeName** returns **Empty** or **Nothing**. Type-Name (**txtSalary**) returns "TextBox" if **txtSalary** is a TextBox control. **TypeName** (**sAnimal**) returns "String" if **sAnimal** is a **String**. If the variable is a **Variant**, then **TypeName** returns the sub-type.

Interaction

Interaction procedures interact with the system, users, or objects. Interaction procedures include **AppActivate**, **IIf**, **Environ**, **Environ$**, **Command**, and **Command$**.

AppActivate activates a specified window. You must supply the title in the application's title bar or the task ID (returned by the **Shell** statement) of the application. For example,

```
AppActivate ("Microsoft Word - Chapter 5.doc")
```

from a test VB application, activated the window in which I was editing this chapter.

IIf evaluates an expression that returns one result if the expression is **True** and another result if it's **False**. For example,

```
IIf (TypeName(vVar)="TextBox", "It's a TextBox!", "Something Else")
```

returns "It's a TextBox!", if **vVar** is a TextBox control.

Environ and **Environ$** return the string contained in the specified environmental variable. For example, **Environ$ ("Path")** returns the current **Path** environmental variable.

Command and **Command$** return the command-line arguments portion of the string that started the program.

Math

Math functions return mathematical results. Common math functions include the following:

➤ **Abs** Returns the absolute value of a number.

➤ **Int** Returns the integer portion of a number.

➤ **Mod** Returns the remainder of a mathematical operation. For example, **15 Mod 2** returns 1 (because 15 divided by two 2 equals 7 with a remainder of 1).

➤ **Randomize** Seeds the random number generator.

➤ **Rnd** Returns a random number between zero and one inclusive.

➤ **Sgn** Returns 1 if a number is positive and -1 if the number is negative. For example, **Sgn (myNumber)** evaluates to **True** if **myNumber** is positive.

Strings

Visual Basic is rich in string-handling functions. The following serves to summarize most of the key string-handling functions. (Also see the "Visual Basic 6 Language Extensions" section, earlier in this chapter.)

➤ **Asc** Returns the ASCII value of the first character in a string. **AscB** returns the value of the first byte in a string of byte data. **AscW** returns the first Unicode character in a string (if the system is not Unicode, **AscW** behaves like **Asc**).

➤ **Chr And Chr$** Give the character representation of the value supplied. **Chr (65)** returns A. **ChrB** and **ChrB$** return a string containing the single byte specified. **ChrW** and **ChrW$** return a string containing the specified character in the native (ASCII or Unicode) format.

➤ **LCase And LCase$** Return the lowercase equivalent of a string. **UCase** and **UCase$** return the uppercase equivalent of a string. For example, **UCase$** ("cat") returns "CAT".

➤ **Len** Returns the length of a string.

➤ **Left And Left$** Return the leftmost x characters of a string. For example, **Left$** ("California", 3) returns "Cal".

➤ **Right And Right$** Return the rightmost x characters of a string. For example, **Right$** ("Alaska", 2) returns "ka".

➤ **Mid And Mid$** Returns y characters beginning at position x of a string in the format **Mid$** (*string*, *x*, *y*). For example, **Mid$** ("Ontario", 2, 3) returns "nta". If the number of characters to return is omitted, the remainder of the string is returned. For example, **Mid$** ("Quebec", 3) returns "ebec".

➤ **LTrim And LTrim$** Return a string with leading spaces removed. **RTrim** and **RTrim$** return a string with trailing spaces removed. **Trim** and **Trim$** return a string with leading and trailing spaces removed. For example, **Trim$** ("   Boston   ") returns "Boston".

➤ **Space And Space$** Return a string padded with the number of spaces specified. For example, **Space$(4)** returns a string containing four spaces. **Space$(0)** returns an empty string but not a null string.

Arrays

VB provides several functions for creating and evaluating data arrays. These are summarized below.

➤ **Array** Returns a variant array containing the values specified. For example, **Array** ("Vermont", 4, txtSalary) returns an array containing three items.

➤ **LBound** Returns the lower bound of an array. For example, for an array declared as **sLNames (1 To 10)**, **LBound (sLNames)** returns 1. **LBound (Array ("Vermont", 4, txtSalary)** returns 0.

➤ **Option Base** Sets the default lower bound of an array. **Option Base 1** causes arrays not explicitly declared otherwise to begin with element 1, and **Option Base 0** (the default) causes arrays not explicitly declared otherwise to begin with element 0.

➤ **UBound** Returns the upper bound of an array.

The Collection Class

The VB definition of a *collection* is "an ordered set of items that can be referred to as a unit." Unlike arrays, collections can grow and shrink as necessary when you add and remove items.

Collections are implemented in two ways in Visual Basic. You can create your own collection objects to keep track of similar information, such as customers. Also, VB has many built-in collections, such as **Forms** and, in the ADO **Recordset** object, **Fields**.

Collection objects that you create are *not* the same as VB's built-in collections. For instance, look at this code:

```
' Declare two collection objects
Dim col1 As Collection
Dim col2 As Collection
Dim vPerson As Variant
' Create the first object
Set col1 = New Collection
' Add two people
col1.Add "Ann"
col1.Add "Bob"
' Set the second collection equal to the first
Set col2 = col1
```

The preceding code works just fine because both objects are of class **Collection**. However, the following code doesn't work—it generates a mismatch error:

```
Dim col1 As Collection
Set col1 = Forms
```

The code doesn't work because although **Forms** is implemented as a collection, it is actually a variable of type **Forms** and not **Collection**. **Forms** is not inherited from **Collection**.

Collection objects that you create yourself have one property (**Count**) and three methods (**Add, Remove,** and **Item**). Most but not all VB built-in collections also have the same property and methods.

The **Count** property returns the number of items in the collection. Some older VB built-in collections, such as **Forms** and **Controls**, are zero-based, meaning that the first item is number zero, the second item is number one, and so on. Some others, such as the ADO **Fields** and **Parameters** collections, are one-based. **Collection** objects that you create yourself are always one-based.

There are two methods of iterating through a collection, which are discussed next.

Iterating Through A Collection

I showed examples of iterating through a collection in Chapter 3 (see "Examining The Identity Of An Object" and Listing 3.1). The variable that you use to iterate the collection is called the enumerator.

The enumerator has to be an object or a variable of type **Variant**. If the collection is, in fact, made up of objects, you can get away with using a non-variant variable, as follows:

```
Dim coll As Collection
Dim oControl As Control
Set coll = New Collection
' Text1 and Command1 are valid control names
coll.Add Text1
coll.Add Command1
For Each oControl In coll
   Debug.Print oControl.Name
Next
```

It is more customary to use a **Variant**—it is also safer. When you use a **Variant**, there is less likelihood of introducing a bug, because you are using a consistent method to enumerate.

Every item in a **Collection** object is 16 bits long, because each is a **Variant** that references some other object (or an object variable, which is also a 16-bit address of an object). The object can be any Visual Basic object, such as a control or a form, or it can be any valid data type, such as **String** or **Date**, with one limitation—it must be supported by the **Variant** data type. Thus, user controls cannot be part of a **Collection** object. (But Visual Basic *does* have a built-in **Controls** collection on each form, as discussed in Chapter 3.)

Next, we'll discuss the methods of the **Collection** object.

Collection Methods

The three methods of the **Collection** object—Item, Add, and Remove—allow you to manipulate individual items. Each is introduced in the following sections.

The *Item* Method

The **Item** method returns a specific item either via its *index* or its key. The index is simply the equivalent of a subscript in an array. Thus, the fifth element in a one-based collection is item number 5.

When adding items to a **Collection** object, you can specify both the index and the key, as you'll see in just a moment. The key provides a very efficient way to look up an item in the collection. Let's assume that you have a collection of customers. You can find any item in the **Collection** object using the **Item** method, by supplying either a numeric argument—**colCustomers.Item (34)** retrieves the thirty-fourth item—or a string that you have previously assigned as a key:

```
colCustomers.Item ("Jones, Sally")
```

Because **Item** is the default property of the class, it can be omitted:

```
colCustomers ("Jones, Sally")
```

You can also use the *collection operator* as shorthand to reference the key of a collection. In this case, you omit the quotation marks, as shown here:

```
colCustomers!Jones, Sally.
```

If you use a numeric variable as a key, then you must first convert it to a string when retrieving something like the following:

```
colCustomer.Item (CStr (myNumber)).
```

Placing a numeric literal inside quotation marks is not the same as converting a numeric literal to a string using the **CStr** function.

To assign an item from a collection to another variable, you use the **Set** keyword (because you are referencing an object), as seen in the following code snippet:

```
Dim vMyVar As Variant
Set vMyVar = colCustomer (33)
```

The *Add* Method

You use the **Add** method to insert an item into a collection. Because a collection is not an array, it grows and shrinks dynamically.

You have a lot of control over where an item can be inserted in the collection. However, bear in mind that if you specify a numerical placement, it might be valid only until the next time an item is added. For instance, if you specify that an item is the eighth in the list and then you insert another item before it, the first item you added will then be ninth.

The syntax of **Add** is as follows:

```
collection_name.Add item [,key_value] [,before_value | after_value]
```

Item can be any data type, including an object. *Key_value*, *before_value*, and *after_value* are optional. *Key_value* must be a string because it serves as a way to find an item in the collection and must be unique (no other *key_value* in the collection can have the same value). The *before_value* and *after_value* clauses can be either numeric or string. If numeric, *before_value* and *after_value* must be in the range of 1 to **Count** − 1. If *before_value* or *after_value* is a string, it must be a valid key previously entered. This allows you to specify in which position in the collection an item is to be inserted. You can specify the *before_value* or *after_value* but not both.

Listing 5.1 shows how to set up a **Collection** object. Figure 5.1 shows the output of the code.

Listing 5.1 Populating a collection.

```
Option Base 1
' create an array of strings
Dim sCusts(5) As String
' populate the array
sCusts(1) = "Mrs. Maryjane Smith"
sCusts(2) = "Miss Donna E. Lemmings"
sCusts(3) = "Professor Alexander D. Vermacelli"
sCusts(4) = "Doctor Susan B. Anthony"
sCusts(5) = "Mr. Donald R. Desmond"
' create a collection
Dim colCustomers As New Collection
' add the items to the array with keys and positionally
colCustomers.Add sCusts(1), "Mary"
colCustomers.Add sCusts(2), "Donna", "Mary"
colCustomers.Add sCusts(3), "Alex", "Mary"
colCustomers.Add sCusts(4), "Sue", , "Donna"
colCustomers.Add sCusts(5), "Don", After:="Sue"
' create a variable to loop through the collection
Dim vVar As Variant
Dim iCtr As Integer
' loop through the collection
For Each vVar In colCustomers
```

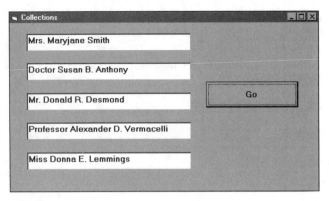

Figure 5.1   Demonstration of the use of a collection.

```
' assumes an array of txtResult text boxes!
    txtResults(iCtr) = vVar
    iCtr = iCtr + 1
Next
```

In Listing 5.1, the last **Add** uses a *named argument*. The fourth and fifth **Add** methods both use **After** instead of **Before**. The first case uses an extra comma to tell VB to skip over the **Before** parameter. The second example uses a named argument. Many VB methods allow named argu-ments. The advantage is that you can place your parameters in any order and can be more explicit (and more clear for the person trying to read the program) than using extra com-mas to skip over unused parameters. Named arguments are also helpful when arguments being passed to a function, sub, or method are ambiguous in their position (meaning that Visual Basic cannot determine the intended arguments from the values supplied).

The *Remove* Method

The **Remove** method, as its name implies, removes items from a collection. Specify the key of the item being removed such as this: **colCustomers.Remove "Donna"** or **colCustomers.Remove 3**.

The Dictionary Object

The **Dictionary** object is similar to the **Collection** object but adds more flexibility and is less likely to be the source of program errors. To use **Dictionary**, add a reference to the Microsoft Scripting Runtime library. Declare the object using the following syntax:

```
Dim dic As Dictionary
Set dic = New Dictionary
```

Alternatively, you can use the **CreateObject** function. **Dictionary** has four properties:

➤ **CompareMode** Specifies one of the following constants:

   ➤ **BinaryCompare**

   ➤ **TextCompare**

   ➤ **DatabaseCompare**

Each constant works the same as the string comparisons discussed earlier in this chapter. If you do not set the **CompareMode** property and use **Option Compare**, then the **Option Compare** setting is used. Otherwise, comparisons default to **BinaryCompare**. Note that the documentation incorrectly lists the constants and also incorrectly lists **vbOptionCompare** as a valid setting. You cannot alter this property after adding any items to the **Dictionary**.

➤ **Item** Sets or returns the **Dictionary** item for a given key. Unlike the **Collection** object, **Item** can be written to with the **Dictionary** object: **dic.Item("elle") = "Eleanor Rigby"**.

➤ **Key** Changes a key to a new value: **dic.Key("elle") = "Eleanor"**.

➤ **Count** Returns the number of items in the **Dictionary** object.

The **Dictionary** object has the following six methods:

➤ **Add** Adds a new item to the **Dictionary**. Supply the item and **Key**. The following examples set the **CompareMode** to text-based and add an item:

```
dic.CompareMode = TextCompare
dic.Add "ann", "Ann Smith"
```

➤ **Exists** Determines if a given **Key** is in the **Dictionary**. The following example searches for the item added in the previous example and takes advantage of the case-insensitive search in the **Option Compare** setting. The message box displays "Ann Smith" and uses the collection operator to reference the default property by **Key** value. Note that using this method omits the quotes:

```
If dic.Exists("Ann") Then
  MsgBox dic!ann
End If
```

➤ **Items** Returns a one-dimensional array of all items in the **Dictionary** object.

➤ **Keys** Returns a one-dimensional array of all keys in the **Dictionary** object; the following example illustrates the use of the **Items** and **Keys** methods to create arrays; the example then iterates through the arrays and prints each to the Immediate window:

```
Dim vArray As Variant
Dim vItem As Variant
' Create array of all items in dictionary
vArray = dic.Items
' Iterate through them
For Each vItem In vArray
   Debug.Print vItem.Key, vItem
Next
```

➤ **Remove** Removes an individual item by supplying its key as in dic.Remove ("ann").

➤ **RemoveAll** Removes all items from the **Dictionary** object.

Creating Classes

Chapter 2 discusses UDTs. Although UDTs are useful, they do not always give you all the programming power and flexibility that you might need. Imagine a UDT that equates to an employee record. Let's say that the UDT is instantiated as **strEmp**, and one of the fields is **strEmp.Age**. You do not want the **strEmp.Age** value to be less than zero. The UDT cannot enforce the rule that the age cannot be less than zero, and, although you could place code in every procedure that updates **strEmp** to validate the age, this is hardly convenient or productive. A business object in the form of a custom class provides you with the tools to encapsulate the data and provides a ready means to enforce the data's integrity (that is, you can use a custom class to not allow the **strEmp.Age** value to be less than zero). The following sections discuss the creation and usage of class modules.

Class Modules Revisited

Chapter 3 introduces you to class modules (see "Class Modules"). This section guides you through the creation of a class using a class module. Recall that a class is essentially the definition of an object. Visual Basic provides many pre-built classes, such as forms and command buttons. VB also allows you to create a class from scratch, providing you with the capabilities to define properties, methods, and events to fully encapsulate data and logic.

Think of the properties of the command button. **Default** is a property that defines whether the Enter key will invoke the command button's **Click** event. **Default** has two possible values—**True** or **False**. The logic to enforce this is *encapsulated* within the command button—there is no way to alter the value of **Default** without accessing the command button itself. If you build a class, you can similarly protect data values by encapsulating them within the class. It is in this way that you can protect the age field (mentioned at the end of the last section) from inappropriate changes.

Use the Project menu to add a new class module to your project. This new module is the basis for your new class. (Depending on the type of project, you will be presented with a dialog from which you can choose Class Module or a variety of templates.) The class module looks like a standard module because neither has a visual component.

As you can see in Figure 5.2, I have created a class module called **clsEmpDemo**. Notice that it has three properties—**Name, DataBindingBehavior,** and **DataSourceBehavior.** The properties of the class are dependent on the project type and, if present, the value of the **Instancing** property. (Chapter 10 discusses **DataBindingBehavior** and **DataSourceBehavior.** Other properties are discussed in this section.) Table 5.1 lists the class properties that are available in each project type.

Figure 5.2 Class properties.

Table 5.1	The class properties available by project type.				
Project Type	**Instancing**	**Data Binding**	**Data Source**	**Persistable**	**MTSTransaction Mode**
Std EXE	No	Yes	Yes	No	No
ActiveX DLL[1]	Private	Yes	Yes	No	No
	PublicNot-Creatable	Yes	Yes	Yes	Yes
	MultiUse	Yes	Yes	Yes	Yes
	Global-MultiUse	Yes	Yes	Yes	Yes
ActiveX EXE[2]	Private	Yes	Yes	No	No
	PublicNot-Creatable	Yes	No	Yes	No
	SingleUse	Yes	No	Yes	No
	Global-SingleUse	Yes	No	Yes	No
	MultiUse	Yes	No	Yes	No
	Global-MultiUse	Yes	No	Yes	No

[1] ActiveX DLL includes IIS, ActiveX Document DLL, ActiveX Control, and DHTML project types.
[2] ActiveX EXE includes the ActiveX Document EXE project type.

Data needs to be declared before you can encapsulate it into a custom class. The rules for doing so are the same as for any other type of module (see "Variable Declaration" in Chapter 2). If the data is declared as **Public**, then any other module has access to it. Thus, if the data is to be protected, you need to declare it as **Private**. You can then expose the data with **Public Property** procedures. These declarations become properties of the class. **Public Event** declarations become part of the class's event model, and publicly declared subs and functions become methods of the class.

The example shown in Listing 5.2 creates two UDTs—**EmpType** and **ErrType**—in the Declarations section of the class module. **EmpType** is instantiated as **strEmp**, whereas **ErrType** is instantiated as **strErr**. Further, the code creates a **Public Enum** called **RaiseRange** and declares a publicly viewable event, **ErrInfo**.

Listing 5.2 Declarations for the custom class.

```
Option Explicit
Public Enum RaiseRange
  Chump = 0.02
  Fair = 0.04
  Good = 0.06
  Wonderful = 0.08
End Enum
Private Type EmpType
  fname As String
  LName As String
  Age As String
  Dept As String
  salary As Currency
  Gender As String * 1
End Type
Private Type ErrType
  ErrNo As Integer
  ErrDesc As String
End Type
Private strEmp As EmpType
Private strErr As ErrType
Public Event ErrInfo(eno As Integer, edesc As String)
```

In Listing 5.2, **EmpType** and **ErrType** are defined as **Private** (you cannot have a **Public** UDT in a class module). **strEmp** is declared as **Private**, and the data contained therein cannot be acted upon without invoking properties and methods of the class module. This is encapsulation! (See the sections titled "Object-Oriented Development" and "Encapsulation" in Chapter 3 for a discussion of encapsulation.)

Adding Events To A Custom Class

When created, a Visual Basic class has only two events—**Initialize** and **Terminate**. However, adding an event to a class is relatively simple. You do so by adding the **Event** statement in the Declarations section, using the following syntax:

```
Event eventname [(arglist)]
```

Events are always **Public**. Events cannot have named arguments, **ParamArray** arguments, or other types of optional arguments, and they cannot return values.

Declared events are called by using the **RaiseEvent** keyword with the syntax

```
RaiseEvent eventname [(arglist)]
```

where *arglist* is a list of arguments that must be exactly the same as the list specified in the **Event** declaration.

> An *event source* is an object that raises events. You can create an object to handle the events using the **WithEvents** clause, like this:
>
> ```
> Private WithEvents objectname As classname
> ```
>
> *Classname* must be a valid (already existing) class. The *objectname* variable must be a module-level variable (such as a form or standard module). When *objectname* is declared, its events are available from the procedure drop-down list in the code window.
>
> You can declare user-defined events in a form. However, you need to declare references to the form itself, rendering this a tedious task.

In Listing 5.2, I added the **ErrInfo** event. Though I used the **Public** keyword, it wasn't mandatory—events are always public. (I always specify **Public** because it lends clarity to the program code.)

Adding Properties To A Custom Class

You use the **Property** keyword to define a *property procedure*. The **Property** keyword, then, becomes a method of the object to manipulate an object's properties in some way. There are three methods of declaring a **Property**, depending on what is being accomplished:

➤ **Property Get** Provides read access to the property.

➤ **Property Let** Provides write access to a non-object type property.

➤ **Property Set** Provides write access to an object type property.

The variations on declaring a property procedure look suspiciously like the variations on assigning a value to a variable. (The keyword **Let** is an optional method of assigning values—[**Let A = B**]—that is seldom used.)

The syntax for the **Property** statements are as follows:

```
[scope] Property Get propertyname ([arglist]) As datatype
[scope] Property Let propertyname ([arglist])
[scope] Property Set propertyname ([arglist])
```

followed by:

```
    [statements]
    [EXIT PROPERTY]
END PROPERTY
```

Scope is any valid visibility, such as **Public** or **Private**. Note that you can use **Friend** only in a class module. **Friend** has the effect of making the property viewable to all other modules except other classes implementing this class (implementing classes is discussed later in this chapter). There can be any number of statements in between **Property** and **End Property**, including any number of **Exit Property** statements.

 Module-level procedures cannot be declared with the **Static** keyword. Because there can be multiple instances of a class in memory at any one time, you may want certain properties or variables to maintain a common value across each class. You may also desire that a variable retain its value between calls to a class module. The latter is a little simpler than the former because a variable's data is not destroyed until the class is destroyed. However, Visual Basic provides no method to store a common set of data between all instances of a class. The only way to get around this is to declare a publicly accessible variable (or object) in a standard module, and then to provide corresponding **Property** statements in the class module to retrieve and update the value. This, however, violates proper object-oriented techniques in that the data is no longer encapsulated—it is accessible outside the classes because it is in a standard module.

Thus, to expose data members, you provide write access with **Property Let** or **Property Set** procedures (again, use **Set** for object data) and read access with **Property Get** procedures. Continuing with the example begun in Listing 5.2, Listing 5.3 provides read and write access to the employee's age.

Listing 5.3   Property Let and Property Get procedures.

```
Public Property Get Age() As Integer
Age = strEmp.Age
End Property
Public Property Let Age(newAge As Integer)
If newAge > 0 And newAge < 100 Then
  strEmp.Age = newAge
Else
  strErr.ErrNo = 3
  strErr.ErrDesc = "Age must be 1 - 99"
```

```
RaiseEvent ErrInfo(strErr.ErrNo, strErr.ErrDesc)
End If
End Property
```

In Listing 5.3, the **Get** procedure simply declares a publicly viewable property, and **Age** returns the value contained in **strEmp.Age**. The **Let** procedure accepts **newAge** as an argument and edits it for a valid range. If **newAge** is valid, **strEmp.Age** is updated. Otherwise, the **strEmp** information is filled in and the publicly viewable **ErrInfo** event is raised. The class exposes other properties in the same manner.

 You can add variables declared as **Public** to a class, and these can be part of its interface, as well. Declaring variables as **Public** does not provide any performance advantage over using **Property** procedures, because VB implements the public variables as **Property Get** and **Let** (or **Set**) pairs behind the scenes.

Adding Methods To The Class

You can add methods to a class by creating publicly viewable subs and functions. For the class being developed in Listings 5.2 and 5.3, I created a procedure to compute a raise using the **Enum RaiseRange**, as shown below:

```
Public Function ComputeRaise _
   (raisePct As RaiseRange, salAmt As Currency) As Currency
   ComputeRaise = raisePct * salAmt
End Function
```

Referencing The Class

To reference a class from within another module, you first declare a reference to it. Assuming the class name is **clsEmpDemo**, the following creates an object named **clsEmp** of type **clsEmpDemo**. Using the **WithEvents** clause allows the form module to access the class's event model:

```
Option Explicit
Private WithEvents clsEmp As clsEmpDemo
```

In the module's initialization code (such as a form's **Load** event), you will need to **Set** the object variable similar to the following:

```
Set clsEmp = New clsEmpDemo
```

As you can see in Figure 5.3, **clsEmp** can now be treated as any other Visual Basic object, with complete access to its event model in the code

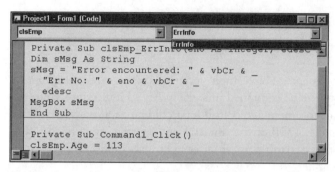

Figure 5.3 Using the **WithEvents** clause allows access to the object's event model.

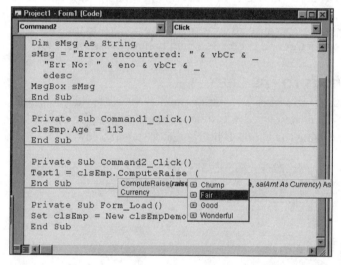

Figure 5.4 Auto List Members and Auto Quick Info pop up from the class.

editor. Likewise, you can address properties and methods of the object in code, as shown in Figure 5.4.

The following example shows you how to code an event procedure for an event exposed by a class—it is no different than any other event procedure:

```
Private Sub clsEmp_ErrInfo(eno As Integer, edesc As String)
Dim sMsg As String
sMsg = "Error encountered: " & vbCr & _
  "Err No: " & eno & vbCr & _
  edesc
MsgBox sMsg
End Sub
```

```
Public Function LetAge (newAge As Integer) As Variant
If newAge < 1 or newAge > 99 Then
  LetAge = CVErr (vbObjError)
Else
  LetAge = 0
  strEmp.Age = newAge
End If
```

Recall that **ErrInfo** event was declared in the class (Listing 5.2) with two parameters—**eno** and **edesc**—which are filled in by the class in the **RaiseEvent** statements. If I attempt, for instance, to set an employee's age using an invalid value, the class raises the **ErrInfo** event, which is then seen by and handled in any module using the class.

The following line of code calls the class's **ComputeRaise** method:

```
txtSalary = clsEmp.ComputeRaise(Chump, clsEmp.salary)
```

Other Class Properties

As noted earlier, and summarized in Table 5.1, the properties exposed by a class are dependent on the project type and the value of the **Instancing** property. **Instancing** dictates how an object in an ActiveX component is created and used. (Chapter 7 discusses **Instancing** at more length.) In a standard EXE, the only properties available are **DataSourceBehavior** and **DataBinding-Behavior**. There is no **Instancing** property. In ActiveX DLLs (including IIS, DHTML, ActiveX Document DLL, and ActiveX Control projects) as well as ActiveX EXEs (including ActiveX Document EXE projects), **Instancing** is always available.

Who Said You Can't Inherit?

Chapter 3 discusses a method of reuse known as *delegation*. You generally do this by implementing the logic of one class within another using the **Implements** statement. (I will come back to the term delegation in a moment.) For example, assume that you want to implement **clsEmpDemo** (built in the prior sections) within another class. The code to do so is shown below:

```
Implements clsEmpDemo
Private clsDemo As clsEmpDemo
```

The name of the implemented object is **clsDemo**, and its object type is **clsEmpDemo**. In the new class, all the procedures of **clsEmpDemo**, including those declared **Private** (but not those declared **Friend**), are available (as seen in Figure 5.5). In other words, **clsEmpDemo** *is* part of the new class. The classes

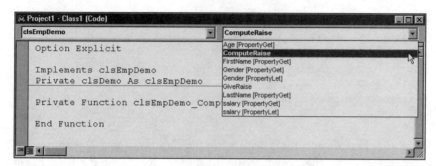

Figure 5.5 Using the implemented properties and methods of another class.

that are implemented are known as *inner objects*, and the container class is known as the *outer object*. Each object can, in turn, contain other objects nested as deeply as needed.

Implements allows a Visual Basic application to access the exposed *interfaces* of various types of classes, such as those created in VB or those in type libraries. An object's interface is its properties, methods, and events. When a property, method, or event is declared, the declaration becomes a *prototype* (it defines how the attribute is to be accessed). An interface, then, is a collection of prototypes that are encapsulated by the class referenced.

Visual Basic requires that you implement all **Public** procedures of an implemented class. You can, however, raise an error (**Const E_NOTIMPL = &H80004001**) when a procedure that you do not want to be exposed is called, so the calling procedure knows that the procedure it called is not implemented.

The container class need not contain any executable code at all. It can *delegate* some, none, or all processing to inner classes. Assume you have a class **clsAgeValidation** that has an exposed method called **EditAge**. You might have two more classes, **clsEmpInfo** and **clsCustInfo**, that both implement **clsAge-Validation**. The **clsCustInfo** can delegate all age validation chores to the contained **clsCustInfo**, whereas **clsEmpInfo** may perform its own age validation. Or, it might delegate some of the chore to **clsAgeValidation**, while also performing some additional validation. This is seen in Listing 5.4.

Listing 5.4   Implementing another class.

```
' clsEmpInfo
Implements clsAgeValidation
Private age As clsAgeValidation

Private Sub Class_Initialize
' create the new object
Set age = New clsAgeValidation
```

```
Private Sub EditAge (ByRef newAge As Integer)
' this is the implemented class
' Delegate to the contained class
Call age.EditAge (newAge)
' Also, add some edits
If newAge < 21 then
  ' age must also be over 21
  ' handle the error
End If
End Sub
```

Listing 5.4 shows the code for **clsEmpInfo**. A form that maintains employee information might reference **clsEmpInfo**. This class further implements **clsAgeValidation**. The outer class (**clsEmpInfo**) is required to implement all of the interfaces of the inner class (**clsAgeValidation**), as shown in the **EditAge** procedure. It is not, however, required to actually use it. In this example, **clsEmpInfo** does delegate some of the age validation (perhaps requiring that age be greater than 0 and less than 200) to **clsAgeValidation** but also performs some additional logic (requiring age to also be greater than 21).

There are some restrictions concerning classes implemented by other classes. The main restriction is that the exposed procedures cannot have an underscore in their **Name** properties. You can create classes stored in type libraries through the use of the Microsoft Interface Definition Language compiler or the VB MkTypLib utility. For more information, use the Find tab in the Help Search dialog and search for "Description Of Interfaces That Can Be Used With Implements (Read-Me)". The subject is outside the scope of both the certification exam and this book.

An alternative to using manually implementing classes is using the Class Builder utility, discussed next.

The Class Builder Utility

The Class Builder utility allows you to create and manipulate an *object model* using drag and drop. You can rearrange objects so that they are nested as deeply as needed (each inner class is implemented by its container class). The end result of rearranging the classes can be likened to a tree that can be traversed in either direction. The outer container always knows what the inner containers are, but the reverse is not necessarily true. The inner objects do not need to know to whom they belong (recall the principles of object-oriented development discussed in Chapter 3); instead, however, you should reference them through the **Parent** property. This returns a reference to the container object in the form *myObj*.**Parent**. To find the name of the container object then, you would use *myObj*.**Parent**.**Name**.

As you become more adept at object-oriented development, you will start to identify the procedures that can be *generalized* (applied to more than one situation) and move those particular procedures into class objects. Soon, you will have a nifty but unwieldy set of classes to use. The Class Builder utility is a good tool for visually deploying and maintaining your classes and their relationships to one another.

For instance, assume that your company verifies the ZIP code whenever an employee's address is maintained. Your company also verifies ZIP codes whenever a customer's or vendor's address is changed. So, you have an excellent situation where a **clsAddress** object would come in handy and can be used in all three cases. Let's further assume that you need to update an SQL database, check the return code, and perform the appropriate actions if an error has occurred. It is obvious that this can be generalized and used in multiple instances. You can quickly assemble these and other objects into a class hierarchy that looks something like Figure 5.6.

The structure shown in Figure 5.6 is easy to reproduce with the Class Builder utility. You invoke the Class Builder by selecting Add Class Module from the Project menu and then selecting the Class Builder from the dialog box that follows (or from the Add-Ins menu). If any classes are already in your project, they are included on the screen that follows but are not organized in any structure. You can move the classes around using drag and drop until you have achieved the structure that you want. Further, you can use the toolbar to add other classes or collections. You can see the events, properties, and methods in the right-hand pane and can edit any member by double-clicking it.

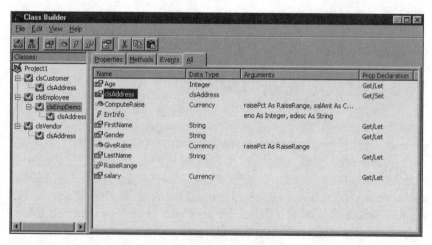

Figure 5.6 Class hierarchy. Notice that **clsAddress** is implemented by using three classes.

Reusing The Class

The ultimate goal of object-oriented development is, of course, reuse. You can use class modules that you create in other projects by choosing Add Class Module from the Project menu and then selecting the Existing tab. However, a better solution would be to create ActiveX components that can then be referenced in your project. Chapter 7 discusses the creation of ActiveX components.

Practice Questions

Question 1

> Which is not a property of the **Dictionary** object?
>
> ○ a. **OptionCompare**
>
> ○ b. **Item**
>
> ○ c. **Key**
>
> ○ d. **Count**
>
> ○ e. None of the above

Answer a is correct. While **Option Compare** is a Visual Basic compiler directive that specifies how string comparisons should be performed, there is no **OptionCompare** property of the **Dictionary** object (there is a **CompareMode** property). Answers b, c, and d are incorrect because **Item**, **Key**, and **Count** are valid properties of the **Dictionary** object. Answer e is incorrect because the correct answer is supplied.

Question 2

> Which of the following is not a valid property or method of a collection class that you create in code?
>
> ○ a. **Item**
>
> ○ b. **Count**
>
> ○ c. **Key**
>
> ○ d   **Remove**

Answer c is correct. **Key** is not a property or method of a collection class. Instead, it is a parameter of the **Add** method. Answer a is incorrect because **Item** is a property of a collection class. Answers b and d are incorrect because **Count** and **Remove** are valid methods of a collection class.

Question 3

> In a standard EXE project, which of the following is a valid value for a class module's **Instancing** property?
>
> ○ a. GlobalMultiUse
>
> ○ b. PrivateUse
>
> ○ c. NoUse
>
> ○ d. None of the above

Answer d is correct. In a standard EXE, a class module does not have an **Instancing** property. Answers a, b, and c are incorrect because the class module does not have an **Instancing** property so it cannot have a value. The question is tricky because not only does the class module not have an **Instancing** property in a standard EXE, but two of the choices listed aren't even valid values if there *were* an **Instancing** property. Most test-takers will automatically choose answer a because it is a valid value for **Instancing** in COM components (ActiveX EXEs, ActiveX DLLs, and so on), whereas choices b and c aren't.

Question 4

> Which of the following statements is valid inside a form module?
>
> ○ a. `Public Property Let Salary(newSalary As _`
> `        Currency)`
>
> ○ b. `Public Property Let Salary(newSalary As _`
> `        Currency) As Boolean`
>
> ○ c. `Public Property Let Salary()`
>
> ○ d. None of the above

Answer a is correct. You can place a **Property Let** statement inside any object module, including forms. Answer b is incorrect because it specifies a return value (**As Boolean**), which is invalid for a **Property Let** or **Property Set** statement. Answer c is incorrect because it specifies no argument(s). **Property Let** and **Property Set** statements must have at least one argument. Answer d is incorrect because a correct answer is provided.

Question 5

Which of the code segments will produce the following list? [Check all correct answers]

Ann Smith

Carol Jones

Bob Johnson

❑ a.
```
Dim colCustomers As New Collection
colCustomers.Add Item:="Ann Smith"
colCustomers.Add Item:="Bob Johnson", Key:="Bob"
colCustomers.Add Item:="Carol Jones", _
    Before:="Bob"
Dim vName As Variant
For Each vName In colCustomers
  Debug.Print vName
Next
```

❑ b.
```
Dim colCustomers As New Collection
colCustomers.Add Item:="Ann Smith", Key:="Ann"
colCustomers.Add Item:="Bob Johnson", _
    Key:="Bob", After:=1
colCustomers.Add Item:="Carol Jones", _
    Before:="Bob"
Dim vName As Variant
For Each vName In colCustomers
  Debug.Print vName
Next
```

❑ c.
```
Dim colCustomers As New Collection
colCustomers.Add Item:="Ann Smith", Key:="Ann"
colCustomers.Add Item:="Bob Johnson", Key:="Bob"
colCustomers.Add Item:="Carol Jones", _
    Before:="Bob", After:="Ann"
Dim vName As Variant
For Each vName In colCustomers
  Debug.Print vName
Next
```

❑ d.
```
Dim colCustomers As New Collection
colCustomers.Add "Ann Smith", "Ann"
colCustomers.Add "Bob Johnson", Key:="Bob"
colCustomers.Add "Carol Jones", "Carol", "Bob"
Dim vName As Variant
For Each vName In colCustomers
  Debug.Print vName
Next
```

Answers a, b, and d are correct. Answer a is correct even though no key is provided for Ann Smith. When Bob Johnson is added, he is placed following Ann Smith. Then, Carol Jones is added using the **Before** parameter to place her before Bob Johnson. Answer b is correct despite the funny syntax used for Bob Johnson. In the **After** parameter, a value of 1 is specified instead of "Ann". Recall that when you reference an item in a collection, you must supply either its key or its ordinal position. Answer d is correct despite the mixture of named and non-named arguments (which is perfectly valid). Answer c is incorrect because the code will not run. The line that adds "Carol Johnson" is invalid because it specifies both the **After** and **Before** arguments. You can supply one but not both.

Need To Know More?

 Aitken, Peter J. *Visual Basic 6 Programming Blue Book*, The Coriolis Group, Scottsdale, AZ, 1998. ISBN 1-57610-281-5. Peter is an excellent writer and manages to demystify that which Microsoft tries to make mysterious. Chapters 6 and 7 cover classes and collections.

 Craig, John Clark and Jeff Webb. *Microsoft Visual Basic 6.0 Developer's Workshop*, Microsoft Press, Redmond, WA, 1998. ISBN 1-57231-883-X. A good intermediate-level VB6 resource. I found this whole volume interesting and educational. The authors take a "How Do I?" approach to explaining various VB techniques. Chapter 5 is an in-depth discussion of object-oriented concepts using classes, collections, and even nested collections.

 Davis, Harold. *Visual Basic 6 Secrets*, IDG Books Worldwide, Foster City, CA, 1998. ISBN 0-7645-3223-5. Harold has done a nice job with this book. Chapter 3 discusses classes and object-oriented techniques in general. Chapter 4 is an overview of VB syntax. Chapter 14 continues the discussion of classes with more advanced topics, and Chapter 13 contains more advanced VB language topics.

 Holzner, Steven. *Visual Basic 6 Black Book*, The Coriolis Group, Scottsdale, AZ, 1998. ISBN 1-57610-283-1. Steven has written an eminently readable book, and both intermediate- and advanced-level developers will find it to be a good source of information and techniques. Check out Chapter 3, which covers the VB language. Chapter 27 discusses the creation of classes.

 MacDonald, Michael and Kurt Cagle. *Visual Basic 6 Client/Server Gold Book*, The Coriolis Group, Scottsdale, AZ, 1998. ISBN 1-57610-282-3. I always feel funny recommending my own materials (call me modest). Chapter 10 covers the creation of business objects, and, although the focus is on database applications, the concepts are applicable to database and non-database applications alike.

In the online books on the VB CD-ROM, locate the topic "Programming With Objects." Search for the terms "Collection", "Class", and "Dictionary". In the VB98.CHM Help file, expand the VB Language list and scan through the statements and functions for any VB language element with which you are not familiar.

 www.microsoft.com/support   Microsoft places the most current Knowledge Base online. Enter search terms such as "Dictionary", "Class Module", and "Collection" to view articles that detail tips (and sometimes fixes) that revolve around the issues discussed in this chapter.

Interapplication Communications

6

Terms you'll need to understand:

√ OLE

√ ActiveX

√ Automation

√ Linked and embedded

√ **Alias**

√ **hWnd, hDC**, and **hInstance**

√ **AddressOf**

√ **GetSetting, GetAllSettings, SaveSetting**, and **DeleteSetting**

Techniques you'll need to master:

√ Using DDE Visual Basic in a DDE conversation

√ Inserting OLE objects into an application

√ Using the OLE control

√ Initializing a string variable for use by the Windows API

√ Passing a null string to the Windows API

√ Obtaining a handle, device context, or instance

√ Creating a user-defined type to handle a C structure

√ Manipulating the Windows Registry

This chapter reviews the process of communicating with other applications, including use of the Windows API itself. The two primary means of communicating with other applications are DDE (Dynamic Data Exchange) and OLE (Object Linking and Embedding). Although DDE was the predecessor of OLE, it is still widely used. OLE, as a technology, is a springboard to ActiveX, which is also introduced in this chapter. In Chapter 7, we'll review creating ActiveX components with Visual Basic 6.

Interapplication Communications

In 1990, Bill Gates made a speech at Comdex in which he espoused his "document-centric" philosophy for the future of computing (and, not by coincidence, Microsoft Windows). Under this philosophy, users need to be concerned with only the document being worked on, not with the application(s) used to create the document. Thus, if a presentation at a board meeting requires the use of a word-processing document, spreadsheet, and a graph, the user should access all the files from one interface, not knowing or caring what applications are actually doing the work. The original implementation of this was DDE followed by OLE.

Dynamic Data Exchange

In Dynamic Data Exchange (DDE), two applications communicate with one another—one asks for data, and the other supplies the data. The application that asks for the data is called the *destination* or *DDE client*, whereas the application that supplies the data is called the *source* or *DDE server*. The process of communication is called a *DDE conversation*. The DDE client always initiates a DDE conversation by specifying a *DDE topic*. The DDE topic typically identifies the information being exchanged. Both the client and server need to be running when the conversation is initiated. Visual Basic can act as both a client and a server in a DDE conversation.

DDE communications occur asynchronously. There are three types of DDE communication—*cold link*, *warm link*, and *hot link*:

➤ **Cold link** Communications are opened, data is exchanged, and the channel is closed.

➤ **Warm link** The channel remains open, and the client is notified of any changes.

➤ **Hot link** The channel remains open, and the client is automatically updated when there are any changes.

The type of link to be used is implemented with the Visual Basic **LinkMode** keyword using the syntax

```
Object.LinkMode = Linktype
```

where *Object* is a Form, MDIForm , Label control, TextBox control, or Picture-Box control. When a control is used in a DDE conversation, **LinkMode** is one of the following constants:

➤ **vbLinkAutomatic** Hot link

➤ **vbLinkManual** Cold link

➤ **vbLinkNone** No DDE conversation

➤ **vbLinkNotify** Warm link

When **vbLinkManual** is used, data is exchanged only when the **LinkRequest** method is invoked. With a warm link, the **LinkNotify** event is triggered whenever linked data has changed, thereby allowing the object to use the **LinkRequest** method to update the data.

When a form is used as a source in a DDE conversation, **LinkMode** is either **vbLinkNone** (no DDE conversation) or **vbLinkSource**. In this case, the form is the DDE source (server) and acts as a warm link that allows any TextBox, Label, or PictureBox control to supply data to a DDE destination (client). The data sent when VB acts as the source, or received when VB acts as the destination, is the **Caption** property of the Label control, the **Text** property of the TextBox control, or the **Picture** property of the PictureBox control.

LinkTopic is used to describe the destination, and **LinkItem** describes the data being requested. Thus, the following code snippet will keep a text box updated automatically whenever the contents of an Excel spreadsheet cell change:

```
' describe the destination
Text1.LinkTopic = "Excel|Sheet1"
' establish the link
Text1.LinkItem = "R1C1"
' open the channel
Text1.LinkMode = vbLinkAutomatic
```

The **LinkTimeout** property is the amount of time (expressed in tenths of a second) to wait for the DDE server to respond. To specify to wait 10 seconds, you insert a value of 100. The maximum value is -1, which allows up to 1 hour and 49 minutes. If there is a timeout, a VB error occurs.

As we'll discuss next, several events are provided to monitor and control DDE communications.

The DDE Event Model

Visual Basic provides an event model for DDE communications:

➤ **LinkOpen** Occurs when a DDE conversation begins. If the VB application is the source, then you can set the **cancel** parameter on the form to a non-zero value to stop the link from happening. When the VB application is the destination, you can also set **cancel** to a non-zero value to stop the conversation from happening, though you are not likely to do so (because your application will have been the one requesting the conversation in the first place).

➤ **LinkExecute** Occurs when a command string is sent by a destination application and expects the source to fulfill the command. The command string is passed as an argument to the event procedure. If you have no **LinkExecute** procedure, VB informs the other application that you have rejected the request. A **cancel** argument is another parameter to the event procedure. Setting it to zero tells the other application that you have accepted the request, whereas setting it to a non-zero value tells the other application that you have rejected the request.

➤ **LinkError** Occurs when there is an error during a DDE conversation. An error is passed as an argument to the event procedure.

The **LinkExecute** method is used to send a command string to a DDE source. **LinkPoke** is used for a destination in a DDE conversation to send data to a client. For example, you could use the **LinkPoke** method of a TextBox control to insert some data into an Excel spreadsheet and then use the **LinkExecute** method to run an Excel macro that operates on the poked data. **LinkPoke** places the contents of the control (such as the text in a TextBox control) in the source application. Where the data is placed depends on the application and the current **LinkItem**. For instance, in an Excel spreadsheet, the data will be inserted into the cell specified in the **LinkItem** property. The **LinkSend** method is used to send the contents of a PictureBox control to a destination application. This method is needed in hot or warm links because VB does not notify destination applications when the contents of the PictureBox have changed. Therefore, it is your responsibility to send the data explicitly using the **LinkSend** method. The **LinkRequest** method is used by a TextBox, Label, or PictureBox control to request a source application to update the contents of the control. This isn't needed if a hot (automatic) link has been established.

Object Linking And Embedding

Before delving into the world of Object Linking and Embedding (OLE), you need to quickly nail down some definitions. Because the distinctions between some of these words are subtle, I have borrowed some of these definitions from the Visual Basic Help files:

➤ **OLE** The technology that allows an application to contain components from other applications.

➤ **Component** Any software that supports automation. This means the component can be accessed programmatically.

➤ **Automation** The technology that allows applications to provide objects to other applications in a consistent manner.

➤ **Automation controller** An application that uses objects provided by ActiveX components.

➤ **Automation server** An ActiveX component.

For all practical purposes, you can think of OLE and ActiveX as being synonymous. (Strictly speaking, an ActiveX component is an OLE Automation server.)

Interestingly, ActiveX and OLE version 2 communications occur synchronously, whereas OLE version 1 (like DDE) communicated in an asynchronous manner. This might seem like a step back, but asynchronous communications between two components can be tough to manage. In the asynchronous model, there is no automatic mechanism to be informed when the server receives or fulfills a request. This can make it tough to know when a request is fulfilled.

A VB project can act as either an OLE server or OLE client. When VB is the server, another application acts as the client and requests and receives data from the VB application. When VB is the client, it establishes communications with another application and receives data from that application. Further, the OLE server exposes its functionality (by exposing its objects) to the client. Thus, you can embed a Microsoft Word document into your VB application, and, when that document is active, Word's menus replace your own. For all practical purposes, when the document is active, the user is working inside Microsoft Word. Visual Basic implements OLE client technology through the use of the OLE Container control or by inserting an OLE object directly into the form.

Insertable Objects

You can insert an OLE object directly into your application from the Project|Components dialog. Select the Insertable Objects tab and then select

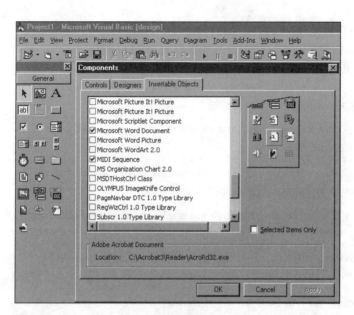

Figure 6.1   The Insertable Objects tab in the Components dialog box.

the required objects. Figure 6.1 shows the Insertable Objects tab in the Components dialog. Notice that the objects are added to the toolbox, where you can then draw them on your form as other controls. However, the object supports only a subset of the properties, methods, and events of the OLE control.

The inserted objects are supported only by the **GotFocus, LostFocus,** and **Validate** events as well as the **DragOver** and **DragDrop** events. As with intrinsic controls such as TextBox, the **Validate** event is similar to the **LostFocus** event except it occurs immediately before the focus on the object is lost. The event procedure supplies the **cancel** parameter, which you can set to **False** to prevent focus from shifting off the control. This gives you a chance to validate the contents of the object, save the file, and so on.

The **CausesValidation** property is set to **True** to cause the object to trigger the **Validate** event when it loses focus. The objects support the **Drag, Move, SetFocus, ShowWhatsThis,** and **ZOrder** methods.

How the object is used in the application depends on the object itself. For instance, in Figure 6.2, a number of OLE objects are inserted into a form. Double-clicking the Word document activates it. Word opens in the same space as the application. The Microsoft Note-It object displays its notes when you double-click it. The object exposes its Edit method via a right-mouse click. The Microsoft Photo Editor object activates in its own space—not within VB—via a double click.

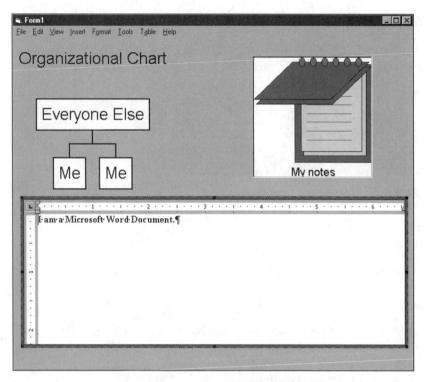

Figure 6.2 Form with several OLE objects inserted.

The OLE Container control is somewhat more flexible, though it uses a little more system resources. The next section discusses the OLE Container control.

OLE Container Control

You use the OLE Container icon directly from the toolbox to draw a container on the form. When you do so, Visual Basic prompts you for the object, as shown in Figure 6.3. You can create a new object or create an object from an existing file. When you create a new object, Visual Basic provides you with a list of OLE object types that you can create.

If you choose the Create From File option, you specify the file and can then choose whether to *link* or *embed* the file. A linked file is saved separate from Visual Basic and is managed by the other application, whereas an embedded object is saved within the VB application. Put another way, a linked file is available to other applications, whereas an embedded file can be edited only from the VB application.

The **OLEType** property corresponds to whether the object is linked or embedded. It has the possible values **vbOLELinked**, **vbOLEEmbedded**,

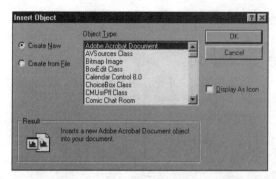

Figure 6.3 Inserting a new OLE object.

vbOLENone (the control does not contain an OLE object), or **vbOLEEither** (the control can contain either an embedded or a linked object).

You can also choose not to specify the object at design time. Instead, you can assign the object at runtime through the **Class** property. The class will be a value similar to "Word.Document.8" or "Equation.3".

By default, objects that support in-place activation open within the Visual Basic application. If the object does not support in-place activation, it opens in a separate window. You can override this by setting the **MiscFlags** property to **vbOLEMiscFlagsDisableInPlace**.

Other key properties and methods of the OLE Container control include the following:

➤ **Copy** Copies the OLE object to the clipboard.

➤ **CreateEmbed** Creates embedded OLE objects.

➤ **CreateLink** Creates linked OLE objects.

➤ **DoVerb** Performs an action on an object. For example, **OLE1.DoVerb (vbOLEShow)** opens an OLE object for editing. Although some objects will supply their own verbs, all should supply at least the following:

   ➤ **InsertObjDlg** Displays a dialog to users to allow them to select an OLE object.

   ➤ **ObjectVerbs** Specifies a zero-based array of all verbs that the object supports. The number of items is returned by the **ObjectVerbsCount** property. The first verb in the array is the default verb. **ObjectVerbsFlags** is an array where each item returns a value indicating the state of the menu associated with each verb. For example, a value of **vbOLEFlagDisabled** indicates that the menu item is disabled.

➤ **ReadFromFile** Loads an OLE object from a file created by using SaveToFile.

➤ **SaveToFile** Saves an OLE object to a file. (**SaveToOLE1File** saves an OLE object to a file in OLE version 1 format.)

Aside from the use of DDE and OLE to carry on "live" communications with other applications, you can use the functions exposed in the API of other applications, as I discuss for the remainder of the chapter.

Using API Functions

Many applications expose their services via an *API* (application program interface). These are sometimes referred to as external procedures or external functions. The process of exposing services is done via exported DLL (dynamic link library) functions and procedures. An exported function or procedure is one whose *prototype* is visible to other programs (such as your VB applications). A prototype is a function or procedure definition similar to what you provide when you create a function or sub in your VB application—it defines the name of the function or procedure, the expected arguments and data types, and the type of value to be returned (if any).

The Declare Statement

To create the prototype, you use the **Declare** statement with the following syntax:

```
Public | Private Declare Function func_name Lib "lib_name" _
    [Alias "alias_name"] ([arg_list]) As return_type
Public | Private Declare Sub sub_name Lib "lib_name" _
    [Alias "alias_name"] ([arg_list])
```

Use the **Sub** form when the API call will not return a value. Use the **Function** form when a value will be returned.

The keywords **Public** and **Private** are, of course, mutually exclusive and refer to the visibility of **Declare**. If the declaration is declared **Public**, all modules can access it. If the declaration is declared **Private**, only the module in which the declaration is defined can access the declaration. The declaration cannot have local scope. *Func_name* or *sub_name* is the name by which you will call the function or procedure. Unless you specify an alias (discussed shortly), it must be the same name as the function or procedure defined in the DLL being called. Use **Lib** followed by *lib_name* to tell Visual Basic in which DLL to look for the API function.

Alias supplies an alternate name for your program to use when invoking the DLL's function. If you create an alias, the "real" name of the function or procedure (as defined within the DLL) is supplied in quotation marks following the **Alias** keyword. The *func_name* or *sub_name* is the name you will use to call the function or procedure. Note that the name provided in **Alias** is case-sensitive. There are a few reasons why you might need to supply the alias. If the DLL's function name contains characters that are illegal in Visual Basic (such as the dollar sign), then you will need to create an alias. Also, the function name might be the same as a Visual Basic reserved word or an existing variable or procedure. Again, you would then need to create an alias. Finally, some functions that return a string have two versions: one for the ANSI character set and the other for the Unicode character set. In general, you should choose the form of a function that returns ANSI characters, whether you are working in Windows 9x or Windows NT.

Most API functions that return a string have two versions. Functions with names ending in "A" return ANSI strings, whereas those with names ending with "W" (for wide character) return Unicode characters. Although Visual Basic uses Unicode characters internally, it translates all Unicode strings to ANSI when making external procedure calls. Therefore, you should always use the ANSI version of an API function.

You must supply any necessary arguments enclosed within parentheses. If no arguments are expected, the parentheses should be left empty. If the function expects arguments, you place them in the parentheses using the same rules as Visual Basic procedures (discussed in Chapter 2).

You may encounter a situation where the function expects different data types depending on the context of how (or why) it is called. In this case, you specify a data type of **Any**. This causes Visual Basic to not do any type checking of the argument's data type.

Calling The API Function Or Procedure

After you have declared an external function, you invoke it much as you would any VB sub or function. The following code snippet demonstrates a VB **Declare** followed by a function call:

```
Dim iRslt As Integer
' declare a reference to the function
Declare Function myAPICall Lib "some.dll" Alias "_a_function" _
    (myVar As Long) As Integer
' call the function
iRslt = myAPICall (99000)
```

In this example, the name of the function within the DLL is "**_a_function**". Because it begins with an underscore character (which is illegal in VB), I have used the **Alias** keyword. The function accepts an argument of type **Long** and returns a value of type **Integer**. To call it, I assigned the result to the variable **iRslt**, which had been declared as an **Integer**. I passed the value 99000 as an argument.

String Handling With External Modules

String handling or, better put, string mishandling, is a common cause of problems when calling functions in external modules. A couple of definitions are in order:

➤ A *null string* is one with *no* value at all. It is not the same as an empty string.

➤ An *empty string* is a zero-length string ("") such as is returned by the function **Space$(0)**.

If you call a function that expects a string argument and you need to pass a null string, you can sometimes get away with declaring the variable as being of type **Any** in the **Declare** statement and then passing a value of zero when you call the function. This usually works because the function is generally expecting to receive the address of the string, and, if that address is zero, the function "knows" that the string is null. This can occasionally lead to subtle behavioral differences. It is a better practice to use the Visual Basic constant **vbNullString** instead.

 You may be asked a question about passing a string to an external module where the string has a null value or where it has a value of zero. *Null strings* and *zero-value strings* are synonymous terms. Either way, call the function using the VB constant **vbNullString**.

DLLs are usually developed in C, which uses *null-terminated* strings. This means that the end of the string is denoted by a null character. To accommodate this in VB, you need to allow for one extra character when passing a string to a DLL.

Data Type Considerations

The Windows API and most (or all) DLLs use C language data types. Additionally, they use some "derived" data types. These are roughly analogous to VB user-defined types. For instance, Windows API documents refer to **hWnd** (a handle to a window), which is a C **Long** data type renamed for the programmer's convenience. The names of the data types differ from C to

Visual Basic. Most of the C data types are recognizable and easily translatable. C data types that begin with "L" are generally "long pointers." Thus, **LPLong** is a long pointer to a **Long**. Because it is a pointer, it must be declared as **ByRef**. Where you see a function declared as **Void**, it means that the function does not return a value and should be declared in VB as a **Sub**. Though the naming conventions may look strange, most C data types map easily to VB data types.

The *LastDLLError* Property

Many external functions return a code to indicate success or failure. If the function failed, there is no Visual Basic error raised. However, the **LastDLLError** property of the **Err** object is filled in. Immediately after calling a function, the VB application should check this property and act accordingly. Use the DLL's documentation to determine the meaning of different return codes. I discuss the **Err** object in Chapter 8.

The external functions that you will call most often are in the Windows API itself. I discuss that next.

Communicating With Windows

Windows provides a wide variety of services to the developer. When we create a form in Visual Basic, the form is actually created by the operating system. VB merely "asks" Windows to create it. Windows exposes much of its functionality via its API, which is a series of functions, and procedures that provide such diverse services as printing a document and playing a MIDI music file.

 Any questions about the Windows API will query your ability to use the Windows API, but not your knowledge of the individual function names or calling syntax.

The Windows API is implemented in a series of DLLs. The Windows *core* is considered to be the KERNEL32.DLL, GDI32.DLL, and USER32.DLL. Services such as multimedia, ODBC, and so on are contained in other DLLs.

You can use the API viewer supplied with Visual Basic to copy declares (along with necessary structures [UDTs], constants, and so forth) into your program.

In the next sections, I review some of the issues you will encounter when communicating with Windows.

Windows Objects

Every item in Windows is an object—command buttons are objects as are menus and list boxes. (In the parlance of the Windows API, all objects are windows, but that starts to get confusing, so I will use the more generalized term *objects*.) Every object also has a *handle*, which is a *pointer* to the object. A pointer is an address, and a handle is a type of address. When you use the **ByVal** keyword to pass a variable to a function or procedure, you are actually passing a pointer to the variable. In the case of an object, we refer to the address of the object as its handle. Much as we create a variable in Visual Basic to reference a form or command button, the handle of an object is the API's reference to the object.

All Visual Basic controls and objects have an **hWnd** property, which returns a handle to the control or object.

Because handles to controls and objects can change, you should not store the value of a handle in a variable. Instead, use the property directly.

The following code snippet uses the **hWnd** property of a form to find the text stored in the **Caption** property:

```
Declare Function GetWindowText Lib "user32" _
    Alias "GetWindowTextA" (ByVal hWnd As Long, _
    ByVal lpString As String, ByVal cch As Long) _
    As Long

Dim lRslt As Long
Dim sVar As String * 101
lRslt = GetWindowText(hWnd, sVar, 100)
MsgBox (sVar)
```

In this code, **cch** is a variable used to define the length of **lpString**. Because the API expects a null-terminated string, the variable **sVar** has been defined as one byte longer than **cch**.

Note in the code snippet that **hWnd** has been passed, but no reference to the form was made. When a property or method is used without referencing an object, VB assumes you are referencing the form. It is the same as **Me.hWnd** or **form1.hWnd** (assuming the name of the form is **form1**).

Note that if a **UserControl** has its **Windowless** property set to **True, hWnd** returns 0.

If you use the Windows API to create an object, the API function will generally return a handle to the new object.

Windows uses handles to keep track of objects, tasks, and device contexts. I discuss the issue of Windows tasks in the next section.

Windows Tasks

Windows defines a *task* a little differently than you might expect. Any running application is a task, which seems natural enough. However, any loaded DLL, font, and so forth is also a task. Each task has an associated task ID. In API parlance, the task ID is known as an *instance*. Each instance is similar to a handle because it defines a memory address (and thus needs to be stored as a **Long**). To obtain the instance of the currently running VB application, access the **hInstance** property of the **App** object, as shown here:

```
' Display the current app's handle
MsgBox App.hInstance
```

Callback Considerations

Some Windows API functions are *callback* procedures—they call themselves recursively, interacting with the calling program. Visual Basic does not directly support this. However, you may pass the address of a Visual Basic procedure to the API in a standard module using the **AddressOf** function. The syntax is:

```
AddressOf procedure_name
```

When you pass the address of a VB procedure to an API function, the API function will call your procedure. The classic example most often used when discussing callback procedures is the enumeration of available fonts. The Visual Basic Help file contains an example under "AddressOf Operator Example", which is too lengthy to list here. For purposes of the exam, it is enough to know how to use the **AddressOf** function.

As noted earlier, Windows uses handles to track objects, instances, and device contexts. The next section discusses what a device context is and how the VB developer can use it.

Device Context

Windows performs its graphical chores using *device contexts*. Various drivers enable Windows to draw or print to different types of devices, such as screens and printers. The link between Windows and the specific device is called a device context. If you are going to use the Windows API to output graphics, you need to reference the appropriate context ID. Every form object in VB has a device context associated with it defined by the **hDC** property (literally, a handle to the device context). The following code snippet draws an ellipse on the current form by obtaining its device context. **X1, X2, Y1,** and **Y2** form a rectangle within which the ellipse will be drawn:

```
Public Declare Function Ellipse Lib "gdi32" _
    (ByVal hDC As Long, ByVal X1 As Long, _
    ByVal Y1 As Long, ByVal X2 As Long, _
    ByVal Y2 As Long) As Long

Dim lRslt As Long
' Set the form to use pixels
ScaleMode = vbPixels
' Set the form's foreground color
ForeColor = vbRed
lRslt = Ellipse(hDC, 1, 1, 200, 200)
```

In general, if an object can act as a container, then it can be drawn on and will have an **hDC** property. This includes UserControl, UserDocument, PictureBox, and PropertyPage. The **Printer** object has an **hDC** property as does the CommonDialog control (which returns the device context of the current printer). ActiveX objects typically have an **hDC** property.

The Windows Registry

Visual Basic applications should store program settings in the Windows Registry. When doing so, the settings will be within the key HKEY_CURRENT_USER\SOFTWARE\VB AND VBA Program Settings.

Assume you want to store some colors for your program. To do so, use the **SaveSetting** statement, as shown here:

```
SaveSetting "MyApp", "Colors", "Favorite", "Red"
SaveSetting "MyApp", "Colors", "Other", "Green"
```

The first argument is the application's name ("MyApp"). This is the key in the Windows Registry (underneath "VB AND VBA Program Settings"). If it does not already exist, it will be created. "Colors" is the section and appears underneath "MyApp" in the Registry. "Favorite" and "Other" are both values. "Red" and "Green" are settings. The results in the Registry are shown in Figure 6.4.

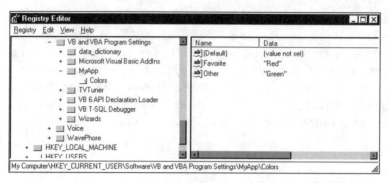

Figure 6.4 The Windows Registry after saving "color" settings.

To retrieve a value, use the **GetSetting** function, which returns a string, as shown here:

```
Print GetSetting(appname:="MyApp", _
  section:="Colors", Key:="Favorite", Default:="Unknown")
Print GetSetting(appname:="MyApp", _
  section:="Colors", Key:="Other", Default:="Unknown")
```

"MyApp", "Colors", and "Favorite" are the application's name, key, and setting, respectively. "Unknown" is a value to be returned if the setting is not found. In the example, the results are printed to the form.

To retrieve all settings, use the **GetAllSettings** function, which returns a two-dimensional array of type **Variant**. Do not define the variable as an array—VB converts it when the function is called. An example is shown in the following code snippet:

```
Dim myVar
myVar = GetAllSettings("MyApp", "Colors")
MsgBox myVar(1, 0) & " " & myVar(1, 1)
```

To delete a setting or section, use the **DeleteSetting** statement. To delete the Colors section, use the syntax:

```
DeleteSetting "MyApp", "Colors"
```

To delete just an individual setting, also supply the setting name:

```
DeleteSetting "MyApp", "Colors", "Other"
```

Practice Questions

Question 1

> How do you change the target of an OLE Container?
>
> ○ a. Alter the control's **Class** property.
>
> ○ b. At design time, remove the control and reinsert, or, at runtime, invoke a new **OLETopic.**
>
> ○ c. Invoke the control's **OLESetNew** method.
>
> ○ d. It can't be done.
>
> ○ e. None of the above.

Answer a is correct. You can dynamically alter the class of an OLE Container control's **Class** property to assign the OLE object. Answer b is incorrect because there is no **OLETopic.** Answer c is incorrect because there is no OLESetNew method. Answer d is incorrect because it can be done. Answer e is incorrect because the correct answer is provided.

Question 2

> You use the OLE Container control to create an Excel spreadsheet that is available to other applications without your Visual Basic application. Which is true of the OLE object?
>
> ○ a. It is embedded.
>
> ○ b. It is linked.
>
> ○ c. It could be embedded or linked depending on the value of the **OLEType** property.
>
> ○ d. None of the above.

Answer b is correct. Because the OLE object (the spreadsheet) can be edited by other objects, the object must be linked. Answer a is incorrect because if the object were embedded, other applications would not be able to edit it because the data is saved with the application. Answer c is incorrect because the object cannot be embedded. Answer d is incorrect because the correct answer is provided.

Question 3

> In a DDE conversation, the form can act as which of the following?
>
> ○ a. Source
>
> ○ b. Destination
>
> ○ c. Either source or destination
>
> ○ d. Neither source nor destination

Answer a is correct. The form can act as a source (server) in a DDE conversation. The destination application "talks" to the form and requests data from controls on the form. Answer b is incorrect because a form cannot act as a destination (client) in a DDE conversation. Answer c is incorrect because the form cannot be either a source or destination—it can only be a source. Answer d is incorrect because the form can be a source.

Question 4

> The Windows API provides two functions to return the directory where Windows files are located. Which two functions are they? [Check all correct answers]
>
> ❑ a. **GetWindowsDirectory**
>
> ❑ b. **GetWindowsDirectoryA**
>
> ❑ c. **GetWindowsDirectoryU**
>
> ❑ d. **GetWindowsDirectoryW**
>
> ❑ e. **GetINIDirectory**

Answers b and d are correct because Windows provides an ANSI and a wide character version of the function denoted by the *A* and the *W* characters at the end of the function names. Answer a is incorrect because you need to use the ANSI or wide character naming convention. Answer c is incorrect because the suffix for Unicode functions is *W* (wide character) and not *U*. Answer e is incorrect because there is no such function. The trick to this question is to reason out the correct answer, even if you do not know the names of all the API functions (though this is perhaps the most commonly used one). You are told that there are two correct answers. The fact that there are so many variations of **GetWindowsDirectory** clues you in to the fact that you need to choose from these. Further, any function that returns a string will always have an ANSI and a wide character version. If Windows provides an ANSI version, it always provides a wide character version. The last answer, e, was added to throw you off a little bit. An INI directory (if there were such a thing) would not necessarily have to be the Windows directory. Although the certification exam will not expect you to memorize the names of the API functions, you might encounter a question asking you to reason out which one(s) you might use from a supplied list of names.

Question 5

Which of the following is a valid **Declare** statement (assume the DLL is valid)?

○ a. `Static Declare Function myFunc Lib _`
      `"ABC.DLL" (myVar As String) _`
      `As Integer`

○ b. `Public Declare Function myFunc Lib _`
      `"ABC.DLL (ParamArray myVar () _`
      `As Variant, myVar2 As String) _`
      `As Integer`

○ c. `Private Declare Function myFunc Lib _`
      `"ABC.DLL" Alias ("_otherfunc") () _`
      `As Integer`

○ d. `Public Declare Function myFunc Lib _`
      `"ABC.DLL" Alias (As Any) _`
      `(myVar As String) As Integer`

Answer c is correct because there are no syntax errors. The funny-looking function name in the **Alias** clause is valid because the function has been renamed. Answer a is incorrect because it uses **Static**, which is illegal for this type of function. Answer b is incorrect because **ParamArray** must be last in the argument list. Answer d is incorrect because **As Any** is listed in the **Alias** clause—it should be listed as an argument, if used.

Question 6

> Assume you want to use the Windows API to draw on a form.
> Which property of the **Form** object might you use?
>
> ○ a. **hDC**
>
> ○ b. **DeviceContext**
>
> ○ c. **X1** or **Y1**
>
> ○ d. **Shape** (type **As Long**)

Answer a is correct because **hDC** returns the form's device context. Answer b is incorrect because **DeviceContext** is not a valid property. Answer c is incorrect because neither **X1** nor **Y1** is a valid property. Answer d is incorrect because **Shape** is not a property of a **Form** object (it is a control) and because properties are never expressed as functions (with parameters enclosed by parentheses).

Need To Know More?

 Appleman, Daniel. *Dan Appleman's Visual Basic 5.0 Programmer's Guide to the Win32 API*, Ziff-Davis Press, Emeryville, CA, 1997. ISBN 1-56276-446-2. This book will probably be revised and updated for VB6 but was not listed at this writing. Dan, president of Desaware Software, has been involved with Basic and Visual Basic for many years. This excellent volume is devoted exclusively to the subjects covered in this chapter. Of particular interest in prepping for the certification exam are Chapters 1, 2, and 3, where Dan lays the groundwork for communicating and exploiting the Windows API. If you happen to own the VB4-specific edition of this book, there is not a whole lot different in the VB5 edition. This book should be part of any VB developer's basic reference library.

 Simon, Richard. *Windows 95 Common Controls & Messages API Bible*, Waite Group Press, Corte Madera, CA, 1997. ISBN 1-57169-010-7. This book, the second of a three-volume set, discusses all the Windows messages and the common controls available to VB from the Project|Components menu. This book is an essential resource because it explains the meaning of those thousands of constants listed in the VB API Viewer utility. In addition, it illustrates the process of creating through API calls all the controls in the Microsoft Common Controls libraries. Volume 1 of this series is listed next. Volume 3 discusses multimedia and ODBC.

 Simon, Richard, Michael Gouker, and Brian Barnes. *Windows 95 Win32 Programming API Bible*, Waite Group Press, Corte Madera, CA, 1997. ISBN 1-57169-009-3. The definitive resource for Win32 development. This book, despite its title, is a valuable resource for NT developers that covers all WIN32 APIs common to Windows 95 and Windows NT as well as a discussion of how they differ. The book is geared to the C developer, but it still belongs on the reference shelf of most VB developers. The function prototypes given are easy enough to translate into VB **Declare** statements. This is the first of a three-volume library.

http://premium.microsoft.com/msdn/library/ The MSDN contains many good articles on the Windows API in general and its use with Visual Basic in specific.

 cerious.catalogue.com/manual/vbsample.htm If you want to see some real-world examples of using Visual Basic and DDE, see this Web site, which has some sample code that communicates with Thumbs Plus (a shareware graphics management program).

 teamserver.icat.com/Sybase/00000732.htm Here you'll find some code for communicating with Sybase Adaptive Server Anywhere (a relational database management system formerly called SQL Anywhere). Both products can be downloaded for a trial period, if you wish.

 www.inlink.com/~datadog/form3.htm Gary Friedman's home page (which has a lot of VB goodies) has an example of using a VB app as a DDE server (source).

Visual Basic ActiveX Components

7

. . . .

Terms you'll need to understand:

√ COM (ActiveX) DLL

√ COM (ActiveX) EXE

√ ActiveX control

√ Threading model

√ COM and DCOM

√ Instancing

√ Persistence

√ In-process and out-of-process

√ Version compatibility

Techniques you'll need to master:

√ Using the Object Browser to explore type libraries

√ Registering COM (ActiveX) components

√ Registering remote COM (ActiveX) components

√ Choosing the appropriate component type

√ Choosing the appropriate threading model

√ Generating remote server support files

√ Choosing the appropriate level of version compatibility

√ Choosing the appropriate instancing type

√ Persisting component states

Chapter 6 introduces the topic of using OLE to communicate with other applications. In that chapter, the other application was always an OLE Automation server (in other words, an ActiveX component). However, your Visual Basic application can also serve as an Automation server by creating an ActiveX component. This chapter focuses on the creation of ActiveX components.

 While taking the exam, my estimate was that somewhere around 20 percent of the questions related to the creation and usage of ActiveX components. This should not be a huge surprise, even for the Desktop exam, given the emphasis Microsoft places on COM and DCOM.

ActiveX Exposed

Chapter 5 shows you how to create a class module to which you can add properties, methods, and events. In Chapter 5, when the class was referenced in a form module, the editor "knew" what the class's event model was. The Auto Quick Info feature was smart enough to know the properties and methods of the class, and Auto List members were able to offer suggestions for allowable values for some parameters. What about ActiveX components that contain code that is not part of the program? How does Visual Basic understand the properties, methods, and events of ActiveX components that are referenced in code without having access to the source code? Enter the type and object libraries.

Type Libraries And Object Libraries

Components deliver services to clients by making classes available from which clients can create objects. Information about these classes is contained in type libraries. If you open the Object Browser (which is discussed in a moment), you can select any type library referenced in your project. The classes frame displays all the classes available in the library. In the VB library (strictly speaking, VB is an object library, which is addressed in a moment), **TextBox** is a class. When you add a TextBox control to your project, you are creating an object from the class. The members of the object (listed in the Members frame) are the properties, methods, and events of the object.

An *object library* (file extension .OLB) provides information to Automation controllers (your VB application) about available Automation objects (ActiveX controls, DLLs, and EXEs). A *type library* (file extension .TLB) contains "Automation standard descriptions" of exposed properties, methods, and events of other modules. When you create and compile an ActiveX control, a type library is also created, which allows other VB developers to browse the control's properties, methods, and events in the environment. A type library contains multiple object libraries.

If a type library isn't provided, you need to reference the component via a generic variable of type **Object**, which has binding implications. When a type library is supplied, VB can examine it and perform early binding, which means that the compiler can examine the control and include its properties and methods at compile time. Otherwise, VB does not "know" what properties and methods the control supports until you actually invoke a property or method at runtime. Because VB cannot include the properties and methods as part of the compiled program, it is forced to do late binding (essentially resolving references to the control at runtime), which is slower than access to early-bound controls.

It should also be noted that there are actually two types of early binding: *vtable* (virtual function table) and *DispID* (dispatch ID). If the type library provides a virtual function map (as all components created with Visual Basic do), then vtable binding is done. vtable binding is significantly more efficient than DispID binding for in-process components and somewhat more efficient than DispID for out of-process components.

As noted, type libraries and object libraries can be viewed through the Object Browser.

Manually Registering Type And Object Libraries

Though it is not a part of Visual Basic, you may see some references to RegSrv32 on your exam. Keep the following in mind:

➤ In order for an ActiveX EXE to be registered, it must support the **/RegServer** and **/UnRegServer** command-line arguments. ActiveX DLLs must have DLLRegisterServer and DLLUnRegisterServer entry points.

➤ To manually register an object, select Run from the Start button in Windows. Type in "RegSrv32 *file name*". Alternatively, you can add a shortcut to RegSrv32.EXE (the shortcut will be Regsrv32.exe "%1" including the quotation marks) in your SendTo folder. Then, right-click the file to be registered, choose Send To, and select RegSrv32.

The next section discusses the different types of ActiveX components that you can use or create.

Types Of ActiveX Components

There are three types of ActiveX components: ActiveX EXE, ActiveX DLL, and ActiveX control. If you are creating an ActiveX code component—a component with no visual interface—you will use the EXE or DLL. For a component with a visual interface to be used inside your application, you will choose an ActiveX control. (It is not necessary for an ActiveX control to have a visible manifestation.)

ActiveX controls run on a client computer. ActiveX EXEs and DLLs can run on a client computer or on a remote computer.

ActiveX DLLs and EXEs can be deployed across the Internet (Chapter 4 discusses this topic at more length). These can be ActiveX Documents, DHTML applications, or IIS applications.

All ActiveX components have certain features in common, including:

➤ Objects provided by the components can raise events visible to clients.

➤ Objects can be data aware. They can bind to any data source and can act as a data source to a client.

➤ They can provide constants via enumeration (**Enum**) visible in the Object Browser and the code editor.

➤ You can use the **Implements** keyword to provide standard interfaces to objects, thereby creating the potential for exposing objects provided by different components in a polymorphic manner. (See Chapter 5 for more details.)

➤ **Friend** functions allow objects to communicate internally within the component, without making those communications visible to client processes.

➤ Through the use of the **Instancing** property (discussed later in this chapter and in Chapter 5), you can allow a client to invoke methods of the object without explicitly creating the object.

➤ You can use the Procedures Attributes dialog from the Tools menu to choose a default property and method for each object. You can also create property categories such as "Appearance", "Behavior", "Data", and so on. This property affects how the property is displayed in the Properties window's Categorized tab.

The next section delves a little further into the subjects of ActiveX, COM, and DCOM.

More On ActiveX, COM, And DCOM

COM is the base model on which ActiveX components are built. COM defines how the object exposes itself and how this exposure works across processes and across networks. Conversely, DCOM allows an object to communicate across a network. Whereas COM relates to the object, DCOM relates to the communication. COM also defines an object's life cycle.

A COM component exposes itself via its interface. Some concepts fundamental to COM are:

➤ **IUnknown** The basic interface on which all interfaces are based, implementing reference counting and interface querying mechanisms running through COM.

➤ **Reference Counting** The technique by which an object's interface decides when it is no longer being used and is, therefore, free to remove itself. When the number of references falls to zero, the interface determines the object is no longer required.

➤ **QueryInterface** The method used to query an object for a given interface.

➤ **Aggregation** The way in which one object can make use of another. Chapter 5 discusses this in terms of classes implementing the interfaces of other classes.

➤ **Interface** The way in which an object exposes its functionality. Each interface is based on **IUnknown**. The methods of **IUnknown** allow navigation to other interfaces exposed by the object.

Chapter 5 reviews a number of definitions that relate specifically to ActiveX. You might recall that an ActiveX component is an Automation server (or OLE Automation server, if you prefer). An ActiveX component is an object that exposes its properties, methods, and events (via a type library) to Automation controllers (your programs).

Also in Chapter 5, we created a class module that encapsulated certain business functionality and used the module within an application. But, what if you wanted to reuse the class elsewhere? What if you wanted to locate the class on a middle tier of a three-tiered application with clients able to connect to it and use its properties, methods, and events? COM allows objects to expose themselves across process and network boundaries. DCOM provides the communication mechanism. Let's examine the issues involved in taking your ActiveX component and moving it elsewhere on the network (even if that network is the Internet).

Relocating The Business Object

Class modules are powerful weapons in the Visual Basic developer's arsenal. One of VB's key strengths is that it enables you to take a class module and compile it into an ActiveX server component. When that is done, the component can literally exist almost anywhere on the network and serve as a data provider for multiple clients. The advantages to this approach are numerous. The goal of the Microsoft Services Model is the partitioning of the application into three (and sometimes more) tiers:

➤ **client tier** The piece of an application that runs on the client's computer—typically the user interface.

➤ **business tier** Contains the business logic and typically handles communications with the database.

➤ **data tier** The data source itself.

Though you may be concentrating on desktop development, an argument can be made for separating out the business services into ActiveX components to be used by your client services. When you do so, the following terms become important:

➤ **Persistence** Refers to whether an object's state is saved between invocations. Persistent objects "remember" their settings, such as the values of properties, by saving them to disk. This "remembering" ability has advantages, particularly with remote objects, because it eliminates the need to set many properties and thus reduces the number of calls to the object. Objects that aren't persistent—nonpersistent objects—have the advantage of being simpler to design and implement, and are advantageous when there is no need to set properties. Depending on the project type, the class module has a **Persistable** property. The persisting of objects is discussed in more detail later in this chapter.

➤ **Process boundary** Refers to the way the operating system segregates separate processes where a process refers to an application, DLL, and so on. For the purposes of this discussion, a process is more akin to a separate program, such as Microsoft Word. The concept of process boundaries has implications in cross-process components.

➤ **Cross-process component** Refers to an executable program that makes its services available to other programs. The program runs in its own process space. Using DCOM, the two separate processes can communicate and share objects. Calls to an out-of-process component can be very expensive in terms of computer resources.

➤ **In-process component** Refers to a component that runs in the same address space as the application and is typically a DLL. Running a component as an in-process component saves a lot of overhead but means that the component cannot be shared with other processes.

➤ **Remote component** Refers to a component that runs on another machine on the network. This model exacts a toll in performance because it is not only cross-process, but it also involves network traffic. (On the other hand, the component is running on an entirely separate CPU from the application that is using it, which may offset—perhaps by a lot—the overhead incurred in communicating with it.)

➤ **Client** Refers to the application program or component that is calling or using the properties, methods, and events of another component.

➤ **Server (or, more accurately, ActiveX server)** Refers to the component whose services are being utilized.

➤ **Marshalling** Refers to the method used to invoke methods and properties of an out-of-process component. With in-process components, the client's stack space can be used to make the calls. With out-of-process components—that is, when process boundaries are crossed—the proxy on the client "gathers" parameters together to be passed to the out-of-process component and sends them to a stub on the server component. Counter-intuitively, you are better off passing **ByVal** parameters than **ByRef** parameters. With an in-process call, most VB developers use **ByRef**, because it involves passing only a pointer to a value or object (as opposed to sending a copy of, say, a 2,000-byte string). However, when making cross-process boundary calls, passing **ByVal** works against you. The other object needs to then make a call back to the client to get the value of the parameter. This means that parameters sent **ByVal** cause the process boundaries to be crossed twice instead of once.

➤ **Thread** Represents a separate line of communication within a process—almost like a process within a process. For instance, Windows runs 32-bit applications as separate threads within the Windows Virtual Machine (NT runs all applications as separate threads). Threads are normally protected from each other. You can create an ActiveX server that has separate threads for each client communicating with it.

➤ **Apartment model threading** Can be likened to a house with separate apartments. Each thread lives in its own apartment oblivious to what is going on in other apartments. This means that each thread has, for instance, its own copy of global data. Even if the component is single threaded, it still resides in its own apartment. You set threading options in the Project Properties dialog. Threading ActiveX components is discussed later in this chapter. Also, see "Apartment-Model Threading In Visual Basic" in the VB Help file for more details on options and trade-offs with different approaches.

Obviously, the remote ActiveX component can be only a DLL or EXE. By definition, the ActiveX control runs on the client computer. The next section discusses some of the issues involved in compiling the ActiveX component (whether running locally or remotely).

Compiling The ActiveX Component

Chapter 14 discusses the process of compiling the Visual Basic application. When compiling an ActiveX component, there are a number of options to set. You need to be familiar with the impact of each.

Compilation options are set in the Project Properties dialog, available from the Project menu. On the General tab, you set the Project Type. For ActiveX components, this will be ActiveX EXE, ActiveX DLL, or ActiveX Control.

Figure 7.1 shows the General tab for an ActiveX DLL project. The ActiveX DLL runs as an in-process component (meaning that it runs in the same memory space as the client). Note that the Unattended Execution option is available. With a DLL, this means that there will be no user interaction (that is, message boxes and the like are suppressed). Checking this option allows you

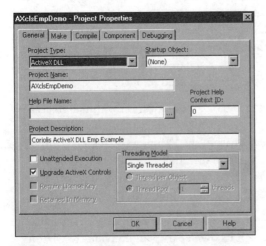

Figure 7.1   The ActiveX DLL project.

to mark the component as *thread safe*. This means that the component can provide objects on any of the client's threads of execution. In a sense, this provides the DLL the flexibility of the ActiveX EXE while maintaining the performance advantage inherent in an in-process component. Indeed, selecting Unattended Execution makes the Retained In Memory option available. Selecting this option comes at the expense of some overhead (in terms of memory usage) but provides the advantage of not needing to reload the component between uses. In an IIS application (which is an ActiveX DLL), this advantage is especially critical. Put into COM lingo, selecting Retained In Memory allows the component to maintain state between calls.

With the ActiveX DLL, you can choose between an apartment-threaded and single-threaded model. Because an in-process component cannot create its own threads, this option is not available for ActiveX DLLs. There is a trade-off between apartment-threaded and single-threaded DLLs. Single-threaded applications are thread safe—a multithreaded client (that is, a client that creates multiple objects from the same component) shares the same thread to the server (the component). This is almost as slow as an out-of-process call. One way to think of the advantage and disadvantage of each is this: With single-threaded components, there is just one copy of all global data that is shared by each client thread. The component's **Sub Main** is executed just once. With apartment-model threading, **Sub Main** is executed each time a new object is created from the component. There is a separate copy of all global data for each thread.

Figure 7.2 shows the General tab in the Project Properties window for an ActiveX EXE project. ActiveX EXEs run out-of-process, meaning that the available options are somewhat different than for an ActiveX DLL.

Figure 7.2 The ActiveX EXE project.

Apartment-model threading is not available for ActiveX EXE components because, by definition, ActiveX EXE components are meant to be shared by multiple clients. However, you can design the component to be multithreaded. Choose Thread Per Object to cause a new thread to be created each time a client creates an object. From a client's point of view, Thread Per Object is advantageous because it does not have to share a thread to the component. Each client has its own copy of global data. But, the component cannot control the number of threads created. Each thread uses resources on the server, and too many active threads will degrade performance.

If you select the Thread Pool option, you can specify how many threads to allow. The threads are *round-robined*. That is, the threads are shared among multiple clients in the order requested. Consider a component being shared by three clients across two threads. If Client 1 creates an object, it gets Thread 1. Then, if Client 2 requests an object next, the object is created and accessed on Thread 2. Now, assume Client 3 requests an object—it is created on Thread 1, meaning that Clients 1 and 3 are sharing the same thread. If Client 1 creates a second object, Thread 2 is used. Now, Client 1 is communicating on each thread. Each thread has its own copy of global data. Though Client 1 has created two objects from the same component, it has two different copies of the global data. Communications between client and component are always synchronous and *serialized*. This means that each request on each thread is processed in the order received while the client waits. If Client 3 sends a request across Thread 2 right after Client 1 sends a request across Thread 2, Client 3 has to wait until Client 1's request is fulfilled.

Choosing between the allocation of a single thread per object and a round-robin approach to threading is a matter of trade-offs of client performance and server performance as well as application requirements.

The Component tab of the Project Properties dialog allows you to specify component properties. For ActiveX EXEs, you can choose between the Standalone and ActiveX Component Start Mode options, as shown in Figure 7.3.

Specifying the Standalone option on the Component tab allows the application to start as a standalone application, like Microsoft Word. This option is not available for an ActiveX DLL because it can run only within the client's memory space.

Selecting the Remote Server Files option on the Component tab generates a VBR file containing information needed by the client to register the remote component. You can register the remote component on client computers by running CLIREG32.EXE.

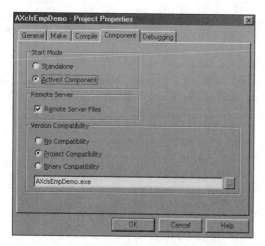

Figure 7.3   The Component options for an ActiveX EXE project.

The final option is Version Compatibility on the Component tab—a subject of confusion for many developers.

Version Compatibility

Version compatibility allows you to create components that have interfaces that are not the same as earlier versions while taking into account that previously written clients might "expect" the older interfaces. There are three levels of version compatibility that describe how the interfaces in your class modules should be handled:

➤ **Version identical** Specifies that the interfaces are all the same. Code inside procedures might be different, but that is transparent to the client.

➤ **Version compatible** Specifies that interfaces (objects, methods, and so forth) have been added, but the existing interfaces remain intact. Old clients can still use the component but will not take advantage of the new interfaces.

➤ **Version incompatible** Specifies that at least one element of the interface has changed or been removed. Clients written for the older version of the component cannot use the new version.

In all situations, you should be sure to use the Make tab in the Project Properties dialog box to increase the version number.

On the Component tab in the Project Properties dialog box, the options provided are:

➤ **No Compatibility** Specifies a version-incompatible component. Older versions of programs will not be able to use the component.

➤ **Project Compatibility** Specifies a version-compatible component. Project compatibility is normally used for new components, though you should also use this setting after creating a version-incompatible release. This causes new GUIDs to be generated at compilation.

➤ **Binary Compatibility** Causes VB to extract the interfaces from your original build, compare them to the current version, and create either a version-identical or version-compatible component. Using this option allows older programs to work with the new component even if its interface has changed.

Be careful with binary compatibility—if you create many versions of the component, the type library is filled with a version tree reflecting a different interface for each version. These are registered in the client's Registry, so the client can choose the correct interface. Having too many interfaces can slow down both the client and component.

On the other hand, you should carefully consider the wisdom of releasing a version-incompatible component. COM specifically allows for multiple interfaces, meaning that a better approach—should you need to modify the interface—might be to provide multiple interfaces. If you opt to proceed with a version-incompatible release, the new release will not contain any GUIDs that were contained with the older version. In this way, you are ensured that the client can still work with the older version. You should, however, consider changing both the project and file name to ensure that you don't overwrite older components that are required by other older components.

The next section discusses some aspects of component and object creation as they relate to the class module.

Properties And Events Of The Class Module

When you create an ActiveX DLL, the DLL runs in the same space as the client application. This is called an in-process component. (Note that ActiveX controls are also in-process components. The OCX file is a special kind of DLL.) When you create an ActiveX EXE, the EXE runs in its own memory space. This is called an out-of-process component.

An ActiveX EXE or DLL always includes one or more class modules. Objects are created from the class module (see Chapter 5 for a discussion about the mechanics of class module usage). The process of creating an object is called *instantiation*. Whether the component runs in-process or out-of-process dictates how objects can be instantiated. The class's **Instancing** property controls how objects are created from the class. The **Instancing** property can be one of the following values:

➤ **Private** Specifies that no object can access the properties and methods of the class—this is useful only for other objects within the same component.

➤ **PublicNotCreateable** Specifies that any other process can access the class but cannot actually create an instance of the class. In other words, other objects cannot use the **New** keyword or **CreateObject** to create objects from the class.

➤ **MultiUse** Specifies that the client can create multiple instances of the object.

➤ **GlobalMultiUse** Acts similarly to **MultiUse** except that the client can access properties and methods of the class without explicitly creating a new instance of it. The object is created merely by referencing it.

➤ **SingleUse** Allows any object to create objects from the class, but each object created causes a new instance of the class to be created.

➤ **GlobalSingleUse** Performs the same as **SingleUse** except that any reference to a property or method of the class causes the class to be instantiated without first explicitly creating it.

Because both **SingleUse** and **GlobalSingleUse** allow multiple instances of the same process on a computer, you cannot use the values for an ActiveX DLL.

If **Instancing** is any value other than **Private**, the **Persistable** property is available. The possible values are **Persistable** and **NotPersistable**. When the object is set to **Persistable**, it can save its state between executions and can load its state at instantiation. (*State* refers to the values of different properties.) Setting **Persistable** causes three new events to be added to the class: **ReadProperties**, **WritePropeties**, and **InitProperties**.

Individual properties can be persistable. To mark a property as persistable, use the **PropertyChanged** method, as shown:

```
Public Property Let postal(newpostal As String)
strAddr.postal - newpostal
PropertyChanged "postal"
End Property
```

When the **PropertyChanged** event is invoked, the **WriteProperty** event will fire when the class is terminated. The properties for which **PropertyChanged** has been invoked are each marked as "dirty," meaning that they have changed and can be saved using the **PropertyBag** object, as shown in the following code snippet:

```
Private Sub Class_WriteProperties(PropBag As PropertyBag)
PropBag.WriteProperty "postal", strAddr.postal, "00000"
End Sub
```

In the preceding example, the first parameter is the name of the property. The second parameter is the value, and the third is a default value. If the new value does not match the default value, then the value is written. If the two values match, the property does not have to be resaved.

The **ReadProperties** event is fired when the class is initialized. If the property bag is empty, the **InitProperties** event is fired.

If an object has never been instantiated, it cannot have saved its state (persisted), and the **InitProperties** event is triggered. You load default values in the **InitProperties** event, as shown here:

```
Private Sub Class_InitProperties()
postal = "00000"
End Sub

The "00000" is just a default value.
```

If the object has previously been persisted, then the **ReadProperties** event is used to restore the object's state:

```
Private Sub Class_ReadProperties(PropBag As PropertyBag)
postal = PropBag.ReadProperty("postal", "00000")
End Sub
```

In this example, "00000" is a default value to use in case "postal" is not found.

If the ActiveX component is a DLL, with an **Instancing** value other than **Private**, then there is a new **MTSTransactionMode** property available. This is used in conjunction with middle-tier components that use Microsoft Transaction Server. Possible values are:

➤ **NotAnMTSObject**

➤ **NoTransactions**

➤ **RequiresTransaction**

➤ **UsesTransaction**

➤ **RequiresNewTransaction**

Practice Questions

Question 1

> You are designing an application that will have many clients. The clients are in remote locations, so upgrading their applications is out of the question. The business rules are subject to change on a frequent basis. Which of the following are valid project types into which to encapsulate the business logic? [Check all correct answers]
>
> ❏ a. ActiveX control
>
> ❏ b. ActiveX DLL
>
> ❏ c. ActiveX EXE
>
> ❏ d. IIS
>
> ❏ e. None of the above

Answers b, c, and d are correct. All three provide code components that can be shared by multiple clients. An ActiveX DLL is an in-process component, whereas the ActiveX EXE is an out-of-process component. An IIS application is an ActiveX DLL. All three make available their classes from which the client can create objects. Answer a is incorrect because any changes to the ActiveX control would have to be distributed to each client computer. The ActiveX control runs on the client computer. Answer e is incorrect because correct answers are provided.

Question 2

> Which can you not do with an ActiveX EXE?
>
> ○ a. Apartment-model threading
>
> ○ b. Provide a thread for each object created
>
> ○ c. Share threads among multiple clients and objects
>
> ○ d. None of the above

Answer a is correct. You cannot have apartment-model threading with an ActiveX EXE. Instead, you choose between providing a thread for each object or creating a thread pool with the threads being shared. Answer b is incorrect because providing a thread for each object created is a valid ActiveX threading model. Answer c is incorrect because you can share threads among multiple clients and objects by using the thread pool option. Answer d is incorrect because the correct answer is provided.

Question 3

How can you register an ActiveX component?

○ a. Axreg32.EXE <filename> where <filename> is the component file.

○ b. Regedit.EXE /Import <filename> where <filename> is the component file.

○ c. Regedit.EXE /AX <type> where <type> is EXE, DLL, or OCX.

○ d. Regsrv32.EXE <filename> where <filename> is the component file.

Answer d is correct. You use Regsrv32.EXE to register an unregistered ActiveX component, supplying the name of the file. Answer a is incorrect because there is no such utility as Axreg32.EXE. Answers b and c are incorrect because Regedit.EXE does not have any switches (such as/Import or /AX) to register an ActiveX component.

Question 4

You have compiled an ActiveX component. One of the options you chose was Unattended Execution. Which of the following might have been the project type?

○ a. ActiveX control

○ b. ActiveX DLL

○ c. ActiveX EXE

○ d. Standard EXE

○ e. Both a and b

○ f. Both b and c

○ g. a, b, and c

○ h. a, b, c, and d

Answer f is correct. Both ActiveX DLLs and ActiveX EXEs make available the Unattended Execution options to suppress any messages (or cause them to be logged). Answers a, e, g, and h are incorrect because the Unattended Execution option is not available for ActiveX controls—the control runs as part of the application itself. Further, answers d and h are incorrect because Standard EXEs do not make the Unattended Execution option available.

Question 5

Clireg32.EXE successfully registers a remote component. When you compiled the component, what happened?

○ a. You selected the /client option on the Component tab of Project Properties.

○ b. You selected Remote Stub and Remote Proxy on the Make tab of Project Properties.

○ c. You added Microsoft DCOM Services as a library reference.

○ d. You selected Remote Server Files on the Component tab of Project Properties.

○ e. Either c or d.

Answer d is correct. To run Clireg32.EXE, you need to supply a VBR (remote automation) file. To generate this file, you select the Remote Server Files option on the Component tab of Project Properties. Answers a and b are both incorrect because the /client option as well as the Remote Stub and Remote Proxy options do not exist. Answer c is incorrect because there is no Microsoft DCOM Services library. Answer e is incorrect because it states that either c or d can be used, and answer c is invalid.

Question 6

> You have an in-process ActiveX component that saves its state
> between uses. Assuming **myText** is a valid property of the com-
> ponent, which of the following lines of code might appear in the
> component?
>
> ○ a. `SaveSetting "myText", "Hello World"`
>
> ○ b. `Set myText - PropRead ("myText", "Hello`
>   `World"`
>
> ○ c. `Let myText - PropRead (myText)`
>
> ○ d. `PropertyChanged "myText"`

Answer d is correct. The process of saving state is called persisting. Using the
PropertyChanged method sets the property value to "dirty," meaning that it
has changed and needs to be saved. In the component's **Class_WriteProperties**
event, you use the **WriteProperty** method of the **PropertyBag** object to save
the value of the property. When an object is instantiated from the class, the
ReadProperties event is triggered. There, you would use the **ReadProperty**
method of the **PropertyBag** object to read the properties' saved value. Answer
a is incorrect, because **SaveSetting** is used to store a setting to the Registry.
This is not the same as persisting an object. Answers b and c are both incorrect
because there is no **PropRead** function.

Need To Know More?

 Craig, John Clark and Jeff Webb. *Microsoft Visual Basic 6.0 Developer's Workshop*, Microsoft Press, Redmond, WA, 1998. ISBN 1-57231-883-X. A good intermediate-level VB6 resource. I found this whole volume interesting and educational. The authors take a "How Do I?" approach to explaining various VB techniques. Chapter 6 discusses the creation of ActiveX controls. Chapter 24 discusses the use of other ActiveX components, including Microsoft Word and Microsoft Excel. Chapter 27 discusses the creation of ActiveX components.

 Davis, Harold. *Visual Basic 6 Secrets*, IDG Books Worldwide, Foster City, CA, 1998. ISBN 0-7645-3223-5. Harold has done a nice job with this book. Chapters 20 through 23 cover the concepts of ActiveX through the creation of ActiveX code components. Chapters 24 through 26 cover ActiveX controls.

 Holzner, Steven. *Visual Basic 6 Black Book*, The Coriolis Group, Scottsdale, AZ, 1998. ISBN 1-57610-283-1. Steven has written an eminently readable book, and both intermediate- and advanced-level developers will find it to be a good source of information and techniques. Chapter 27 discusses the creation and use of code components. Chapter 20 discusses the creation of ActiveX controls and documents.

 The online books have extensive materials on ActiveX and the creation and use of components. Locate "Component Tools Guide," and expand that to "Creating ActiveX components."

 www.microsoft.com/activex For more information on ActiveX, go to the source.

 www.microsoft.com/support Microsoft places the most current Knowledge Base online here . Enter search terms such as "DDE", "OLE", and "ActiveX" to view articles detailing tips and sometimes fixes revolving around the issues discussed in this chapter.

Error Handling
In Visual Basic 6

8

Terms you'll need to understand:

√ **Err**

√ **Raise**

√ Error handler

√ Error handling hierarchy

Techniques you'll need to master:

√ Using the properties and methods of the **Err** object

√ Creating an error handler

√ Handling errors inline

√ Promoting errors up the error handling hierarchy

√ Raising custom errors

√ Using the **IsError** function

In this chapter, we'll look at handling errors in Visual Basic. The VB certification exam is likely to have a surprising number of questions measuring your knowledge in this area.

What Is An Error?

In a sense, nothing is an error if it is properly handled. Many things can go wrong in a program. Some of these things derive from logic flaws. You may not be able to do much about these except fix them when they are discovered. Others stem from the unexpected. Assume you are connecting to a database but the server isn't up. It's kind of silly to ignore that little fact and continue reading to and writing from the SQL tables. Errors that can be handled in your programs generally fall into four areas:

➤ Problems arising from external sources beyond your control, such as a printer jam.

➤ Problems arising from flaws in your code, such as a division by zero.

➤ Problems arising from circumstances that you did not envision (though these arguably often fall under the previous item). An example would be if a user runs an ill-constructed report that brings the network to its knees.

➤ Errors you deliberately create to avoid a worse situation. These are better classified under the category of error *handling* (rather than actual errors) because they usually arise out of a situation that you anticipated.

What Is Error Handling?

I like to think there are four areas of effective error handling, but they all have one aspect in common—the graceful degrading of an application so that the integrity of data is maintained and users are not faced with a vague message, such as the one seen in Figure 8.1. (The term *graceful degrading* is used to refer to a process whereby a program that encounters an error that cannot be resolved performs an orderly "shutdown" instead of an ugly "crash.")

The four areas of effective error handling are:

➤ Coding for the unexpected, such as the use of **Case Else**

➤ Anticipating specific errors and providing specific remedies in the code (such as checking return codes before issuing a **Commit**, following an SQL update)

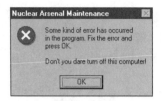

Figure 8.1   A vague and not very helpful error message.

➤ Specific **On Error** routines to handle events that cannot be handled in code (such as routines written to handle the possibility of a paper jam in the printer)

➤ Generalized error handling routines so that the application exits gracefully and informs the user of what has happened

The bulk of this chapter concentrates on these four areas (with most of the emphasis on the last two), with the caveat that component errors are touched on in Chapter 5 and database errors are looked at more closely in Chapters 9 and 10. First, I begin with a look at the **Err** object, which will be useful in most or all of your error-handling coding.

The Err Object

The **Err** object is a structure provided by Visual Basic. It is populated with data that your application needs to know to properly react to an error. (Alternatively, the application can populate the **Err** object, for instance, when it deliberately invokes an error in the debugging process.) The **Err** object has six properties: **Number, Description, Source, HelpFile, HelpContext**, and **LastDLLError**. I will review these in the next section.

The properties of **Err** are cleared after an error has been handled, such as when a **Resume** statement is encountered. They are also cleared when the procedure in which the error has occurred ends. Furthermore, you can also use the **Clear** method (**Err.Clear**) to clear the properties manually.

Whenever an error is encountered, you will want to examine **Err** to determine what has happened, in order to intelligently continue processing. Search for *Trappable Errors* in the VB Help file, where you will see a list of more than 115 error numbers defined. For example, **Err.Number = 9** is generated when a "Subscript out of range" error is encountered. Numbers 1 through 1,000 and all numbers over 31,000 are reserved by Visual Basic, although not all are used. Those numbers not used all equate to *application-defined* errors.

Properties Of The Err Object

The **Err** object's six properties provide the application developer with a fairly complete set of information about what went wrong. The **Number** property is helpful but only if the developer anticipates the particular error and provides the number in advance to the error-handling routine. Some errors simply can't reasonably be anticipated (such as **Err.Number = 47**, "Too many DLL clients"). Properties such as **Description** help overcome this limitation.

Number is a **Long** in the range from 0 through 65,635. For each **Number**, there is an associated **Description**. If the VB error number is not used, **Description** defaults to the string "Application-defined or object-defined error." The Visual Basic constant **vbObjectError** is used for creating user-defined errors, as you will see in the "Raising Errors" section later in this chapter.

Source is a string that contains the location where the error occurred. Unfortunately, this information is at a high level and does not tell you specifically at what line number and in what procedure the problem occurred. The actual contents of **Source** are dependent on where the error occurred. If it was in a standard module, the name of the project (as defined in project properties) is returned. If the error occurred in a class module, however, the class's name is also returned in the form *project.class*. If the error happened outside of Visual Basic in an OLE operation, the application where that error occurred fills in its own **Number** and **Source**, such as "Excel.Application".

HelpFile is a string containing the fully qualified path to a Help file. If a Visual Basic error occurs, the Help file will contain the path to the VBENLR98.CHM file.

The **HelpContext** is a string containing the Help Context ID associated with the error that occurred. If this field is blank, Visual Basic looks at the **Number** and uses the Help Context ID associated with that error. If the error is not a VB-trappable error, the VB Help Contents screen is displayed. The developer can populate the **HelpFile** and **HelpContext** properties in order to display appropriate application help.

 To display a Help button in the call to **MsgBox**, use **vbMsgBoxHelpButton**. If you want to display the VB Help file for an intrinsic error code, use the following code:

```
MsgBox Err.Number & ": " & Err.Description,
    vbMsgBoxHelpButton, "Error!", Err.HelpFile,
    Err.HelpContext
```

> The preceding code will display an OK button along with a Help button. Pressing the Help button will open the appropriate Help topic. For your own error handling, substitute your own Help file and Context ID.

The last property of **Err**—**LastDLLError**—is a **Long** and contains the result code of the last external call you made (to the Windows API or another DLL).

> An error in calling a DLL or in the execution of the procedure called does not raise a Visual Basic error event. Therefore, you should always examine the contents of **Err.LastDLLError** immediately after making an external call to ensure that you received the expected result or return code.

Methods Of The Err Object

Err has two methods associated with it—**Clear** and **Raise**. **Clear** is mentioned earlier in this chapter and behaves pretty much as you would expect: It clears (initializes) all the properties of the **Err** object. **Raise** is used to deliberately invoke a runtime error and is discussed in more length in "Raising Errors" later in this chapter.

Creating And Passing The Error Object

You may encounter situations in which you need to create an **Error** object and/ or pass the object as a result from a function. You can do both in Visual Basic. Assume you have a function whose purpose is to return an employee record as a **Recordset** object and that one of the parameters to the function is gender. You might declare the function (oversimplified here) as such:

```
Private Function GetEmpRec (gender As String) As Variant
```

In the body of the function, you will return either the requested **Recordset** object or an error:

```
If UCase$(gender) <> "F" And Ucase$(gender) <> "M" Then
   GetEmpRec = CVErr (2001)
   ' etc.
```

GetEmpRec is defined to return a variable of type **Variant**. The code tests that **gender** is valid, and if not, it uses the **CVErr** function to set the return value to a **Variant** of subtype **Err** (**VarType = vbError**). The **Err.Number** property is set to 2001—a user-defined error.

The result can be evaluated as shown here:

```
Dim vTest As Variant
vTest = GetEmpRec ("T")
If IsError (vTest) Then
  Select Case CInt (vTest)
    Case 2001
       ' invalid gender
  etc.
  End Select
Else
  Set rs = vTest
End If
```

The code assigns the result of **GetEmpRec** to **vTest** and then uses the **IsError** function to determine if the underlying data type is **Err**. If so, the **CInt** function is used to convert the result to an **Integer**, which can then be evaluated in a **Select Case** statement to handle the specific error.

In the following sections, I discuss some techniques for error prevention.

Preventing Errors

When errors occur, you don't want your users looking at an incomprehensible message box and then turning off their computers in frustration. It is only slightly more embarrassing to generate "An Unexpected Application Error (UAE) in Module Unknown" error message. There are three main strategies that you can use. The most effective strategy is to prevent those errors that you can. The next best strategy is *error anticipation* and the last strategy is to effectively plan for errors. There are a number of error-prevention strategies, which are briefly discussed in the following paragraphs.

The first defense against errors is common sense. Consider the next code snippet. If the text in **Text2** is non-numeric or otherwise equal to zero, the application will crash and burn:

```
' divide value in Text1 by value in Text2 and display result
Text3 = Str(Val(Text1) / Val(Text2))
```

The better approach is to use better coding:

```
' no division by zero errors!
If Val(Text2) <> 0 then
 Text3 = Str(Val(Text1) / Val(Text2))
End If
```

PCs' drop-through code results in hard-to-find bugs. The term *drop-through* code refers to poorly designed decision structures where the program does not anticipate the possibility of an unexpected condition. For example, a program might use an **If…Then** construct when handling customers to perform special processing on the postal code if the customer is Canadian, otherwise assuming the customer is American. What happens if an individual from Mexico places an order? The **If** statement tests to see if the customer is Canadian and, if he or she is not, "drops through" the code to perform the default logic as though the customer were American. The result, at best, is a fouled-up address. At worst, it's a program crash when a routine encounters an unexpected character in the postal code. It is a solid practice to always test for unexpected value with the **Else** statement in an **If** construct, **Case Else** in a **Select Case** construct, and so on.

 On the certification exam, read all code examples carefully looking for drop-through code possibilities.

Inline Error Handling

The single most commonly overlooked preventative measure (an ounce of prevention is worth…) is simply checking the return code of the operation being performed. This is called *inline error handling*. There are three types of inline error handling: Visual Basic functions, custom functions (those that you write yourself), and database updates.

Visual Basic functions seldom return a success or failure code. However, they return information that can be useful in preventing a subsequent error. For instance, the **InStr** function returns 0 if a substring being searched for is not found.

What about procedures that you write? You need to check for any possible unexpected results that tell the calling procedure that something went awry. You have two approaches to this. The first approach is to simply code a return value, as in the following code snippet:

```
Function OpenFile (fname As String) As Integer
On Error GoTo ErrHandler
Open fname For Input As 1
OpenFile = 0 ' Success
Exit Function
ErrHandler:
OpenFile = -1 ' Something went wrong
End Function
```

The preceding code snippet branches to the error handler (which I will discuss momentarily) in the event that the file open fails and returns a status code of -1 telling the calling routine that the operation failed. That's fine as far as it goes, but another approach would be to return a **Variant**, as seen in the next code snippet:

```
Function OpenFile (fname As String) As Variant
Dim iFNum As Integer
iFNum = FreeFile
On Error GoTo ErrHandler
Open fname For Input As iFNum
OpenFile = iFNum ' Success
Exit Function
ErrHandler:
' Return the error
OpenFile = CVErr(Err)
End Function
```

This code uses the ability of Visual Basic to type variants, using the **CVErr** statement. If the file open operation fails, the calling object can use the **IsError** function to determine if an error occurred:

```
If IsError (OpenFile ("fictitiousFile.txt")) Then
```

The advantage to this approach is that the function can pass two types of information. In addition to informing the calling procedure that an error occurred, it can pass the file number if the operation is successful. This is useful behavior more akin to how most other languages work. Unfortunately, the calling procedure does not know what the actual error is.

Still, there is one little bit of trickery you can do to have your Visual Basic error cake and eat it too:

```
Function OpenFile (fname As String) As Variant
Dim iFNum As Integer
iFNum = FreeFile
On Error GoTo ErrHandler
Open fname For Input As iFNum
OpenFile = Array(iFNum) ' Success
Exit Function
ErrHandler:
' Return the error info
OpenFile = Array(CVErr(Err), Err.Number, Err.Description)
End Function
```

In the preceding code, I made one modification. I use the **Array** function to either pass back to the calling procedure a complete set of error diagnostics (I could have added the error source and so on), or, in the event of success, I pass the file number as array element zero. To test the function, use the following example:

```
Dim vRslt As Variant
vRslt = OpenFile("c:\autoexec.bat")
If IsError(vRslt(0)) Then
  MsgBox "Error " & vRslt(1) & " occurred" & vbCr & _
    vRslt(2)
Else
  MsgBox "The File Number is " & vRslt(0)
  Close vRslt(0)
End If
```

The final area of error prevention is in the realm of database updates. I cover this topic in more detail in Chapters 9 and 10.

Handling Error Procedures

There is much we can do to prevent the more predictable errors from occurring. Some, though, might not be so predictable or Visual Basic might not provide a handy way of handling them inline. For those situations where we cannot handle errors in more of a preventative mode, we can use the VB error-handling procedures described in this section.

On Error

The **On Error** statement tells Visual Basic what to do when an error has occurred. It takes the syntax:

```
On Error GoTo 0 | linelabel | Resume Next
```

Either **GoTo** or **Resume Next** must follow **On Error**. If **GoTo** is used, either a valid line label within the current procedure, or 0, must be supplied. **On Error GoTo 0** has the effect of shutting off all error checking. **Resume Next** simply states that, if an error occurs, the program should execute the line immediately following the line in which the error occurred.

 If you do not have error checking turned on, *all* runtime errors, regardless of their severity, are fatal!

All error-handling routines must end in a **Resume** statement (or **End Sub** or **End Function**). If the **On Error** statement does not have **Resume Next**, then **Resume** must be coded elsewhere. Its syntax is

```
Resume [Next | linelabel]
```

where **linelabel** is a valid label within the current procedure. **Next** causes the execution to branch to the line immediately following the one where the error occurred. **Resume** with no qualification causes control to return to the statement in which the error occurred.

Error Handler States

Error handlers have three possible states—disabled, enabled, and active. When not turned on (such as following an **On Error GoTo 0**), the error handler is *disabled*. Following the execution of an **On Error GoTo** *linelabel* or **On Error Resume Next** statement, the error handler is *enabled*. After an error has occurred but before it has been handled (or before the current procedure had terminated), the error handler is *active*.

A properly constructed error handler will save the values of **Err**'s properties to program variables, in case another error occurs.

 Programmers generally put error-handling code at the end of the procedure. You should place an **Exit Sub** or **Exit Function** statement immediately above the error handler to prevent drop-through code.

The Error-Handling Hierarchy

An error handler can process only one error at a time. If a second error occurs while the error handler is active, control is passed to the calling procedure. As an example, assume procedure A calls procedure B and procedure B calls procedure C. If an error occurs in procedure C while procedure C's error handler is active, control will pass back to procedure B. If there is no error handler in procedure B, then control will pass to procedure A. Visual Basic will traverse the procedure hierarchy (which you can examine at any time in the Call Stack Window) until it finds an enabled but not active error handler. If one is not found, then a runtime error occurs.

After the error is handled, where execution resumes depends on how it is handled. Assume that an unhandled error occurs in procedure C, causing control to pass back to procedure B. If the error handler in procedure B ends with a **Resume Next** statement, then processing resumes with the statement immediately after the call to procedure C. The code in procedure C is *not* re-executed.

If the error handler in procedure B ends with a **Resume** statement, then control is transferred to the line in procedure B that called procedure C. In other words, C is rerun in its entirety.

The Generalized Error Handler

A procedure that is called to print a report should include an error handler that anticipates and handles printer errors, such as paper jams and out-of-paper. But, you cannot guarantee that life will always be that clear-cut. For example, while you are printing the report, a bug could lead to a subscript error.

Your program needs a generic way to handle these unforeseen errors without your having to write a monstrous block of code in every single procedure. The next choice is to take advantage of Visual Basic's "promotion" of errors to calling procedures, as discussed earlier.

Raising Errors

We can generalize error handling by employing the **Raise** method of the **Err** object. The syntax is:

```
Err.Raise Number [,Source, Description, HelpFile, HelpContext]
```

Raising an error in this manner is more flexible than using the **Error** statement, as shown earlier in this chapter. You are allowed to fill in the source, description, and so forth, as needed. This alone might give you reason to create your own error—you then have the option of providing even more rich information than that provided by VB. You might terminate an error condition by branching to a label where the only line is a **Raise** statement. Recall that if you do not **Clear** any properties of the **Err** object, they are intact. When you **Raise** an error, you are required to supply an error number, but all other information remains intact.

Assume that you have the previously mentioned print procedure and that you encounter an unexpected error. Your error handler will test for error conditions that it knows how to handle and will use **Raise** to promote other errors to the calling procedure, as in the following code snippet:

```
Select Case Err.Number
   Case 483 ' printer error
      ' do something
   Case Else
      Err.Raise Err.Numnber
End Select
```

This code creates a "new" error with the **Raise** method using the same error number that already occurred. Control will pass to the calling procedure. If that procedure doesn't know how to handle that kind of error, then it too will **Raise** the same error number until a generalized error handler is encountered.

You can also use **Raise** to create your own errors. If you want to test your error-handling procedures, you can write code to invoke an anticipated Visual Basic intrinsic error:

```
' cause division by zero
Err.Raise 11
```

Or, you can create your own custom errors:

```
Err.Raise, 1039, "MyApp.mySomething", _
  "Age must be greater than 21!"
```

Error numbers should be from 512 through 65,635 to avoid colliding with reserved errors. You can use the built-in constant **vbObjectError** to act as an offset:

```
Err.Raise vbObjectError + 527, "MyApp.mySomething", _
  "Age must be greater than 21!"
```

Practice Questions

Question 1

Form1 has a command button named **Command1**. The **Command1_Click** event contains the following code:

```
Sub Command1_Click ()
On Error GoTo ErrorHandler
Form2.Show
Exit Sub
ErrorHandler:
    MsgBox Err.Number, Err.Description
End Sub
```

The following code is in **Form2**:

```
Sub Form_Load ()
Dim a As Integer
On Error GoTo ErrorHandler
a = 3 / 0
Exit Sub
ErrorHandler:
Err.Raise Err.Number
End Sub
```

What happens?

○ a. Unhandled division by zero error

○ b. Unhandled duplicate line label error

○ c. Message box displays error number and division by zero error

○ d. Message box displays error number and duplicate line label error

Answer a is correct. A second division by zero error occurs in **Form2** with the **Err.Raise** statement. But, it is not promoted because the **Form_Load** procedure is not called by any other procedure. Put another way, the **Command1_Click** procedure in **Form1** is not running when the error is encountered. So, because there is no other error handler active, an unhandled division by zero error occurs. Answer b is incorrect because the line labels are not duplicate unless they occur in the same procedure. Answer c is incorrect because the second division by zero error is not handled. Control never reverts back to the **Command1_Click** event procedure. Answer d is incorrect because there is no duplicate line label error to handle.

Question 2

> Given the following code, what will be displayed in the message box? (Division by zero is error number 11.)
>
> ```
> Dim a As Integer
> On Error GoTo ErrHandler
> a = 3 / 0
> Exit Sub
> errhandler:
> MsgBox Error & ": " & Err
> ```
>
> ○ a. Property not found
>
> ○ b. Invalid Object Use
>
> ○ c. Division by zero: 11
>
> ○ d. 11: Division by zero

The correct answer is c. This is a bit tricky, but there is enough information provided to deduce the correct answer. **Error,** when used this way, is cast as the **Error$** function rather than the statement used to raise an error. Thus, it returns the description. Even if you did not know that, you should know that the default property of the **Err** object is **Number.** Because c is the only choice given that provides this as an option, you should be able to select the correct answer. Answer a is incorrect because there are no properties being addressed. Answer b is incorrect because there are no invalid objects. Answer d is incorrect because the default property of **Err** is **Number** and because **Error** returns the description.

Question 3

Assume the following code:

```
Option Explicit
Private a As Integer

Private Sub Command1_Click()
On Error GoTo errorhandler
Call procA
a = a + 3
Call procA
errorhandler:
Resume Next
MsgBox a
End Sub

Private Sub procA()
Call procB
a = a + 3
End Sub
Private Sub procB()
Call procC
a = a + 3
End Sub
Private Sub procC()
On Error GoTo errorhandler
a = (a + 3) / a
Exit Sub
errorhandler:
Err.Raise Err.Number
End Sub
```

Assume the command button **Command1** is pressed once. What is the value of **a**?

○ a. 5

○ b. 3

○ c. 8

○ d. None of the above

Answer c is correct—the final result is 8. In the **Command1_Click** procedure, control is transferred to **procA**, which immediately calls **procB**, which immediately calls **procC**. In **procC**, a division by zero error occurs because **a**, at that point, has a value of zero. **Raise** invokes a new error and control is transferred to **procB**, which does not have an active error handler, causing control to then transfer to **procA**. Because **procA** does not have an active error handler either, control passes back to **Command1_Click**. The error handler in **Command1_Click** becomes active. It has a **Resume Next** statement, causing the value of **a** to become 3. **procA** is called again as are **procB** and then **procC**. This time, there is no error. **procC** ends normally after computing **a** is equal to 2, because (2 + 3) / 2 = 2.5 (which rounds down to 2 because **a** is an integer). Control passes back to **procB**, which adds 3 (**a** is now equal to 5), and then to **procA**, which adds 3 again for a final answer of 8. The question is a little tricky because of the weird way integers round in Visual Basic (as explained in Chapter 2). You might have assumed **a** would round up to 3. To make things fair, I did not give a choice of 9 (which would have been the answer if 2.5 had rounded to 3 instead of 2). (Notice that the lack of an **Exit Sub** in **Command1_Click** causes execution to crash into the error handler. While this is sloppy, it is also harmless.) Answer a is incorrect because the procedures are called twice. Answer b is incorrect because the three procedures execute a second time. Answer d is incorrect because the right answer is provided.

Question 4

Which are valid methods of the **Err** object? [Check all correct answers]

❑ a. **Clear**

❑ b. **Source**

❑ c. **Raise**

❑ d. **Prior**

The correct answers are a and c. **Clear** and **Raise** are valid methods of the **Err** object. Answer b is incorrect because **Source** is a property. Answer d is incorrect because **Prior** is neither a property nor a method of the **Err** object.

Question 5

Look at the following code (which is very similar to the code in Question 3):

```vb
Option Explicit
Private a As Integer

Private Sub Command1_Click()
On Error GoTo errorhandler
Call procA
a = a + 3
Call procA
errorhandler:
Resume
MsgBox a
End Sub

Private Sub procA()
Call procB
a = a + 3
End Sub
Private Sub procB()
Call procC
a = a + 3
End Sub
Private Sub procC()
On Error GoTo errorhandler
a = (a + 3) / a
Exit Sub
errorhandler:
Err.Raise Err.Number
End Sub
```

Assume again that the command button **Command1** is pressed once. What is the value of **a**?

○ a. 5

○ b. 3

○ c. 8

○ d. None of the above

Answer d is correct. In this case, the program goes into an endless loop. The error handler in **Command1_Click** has a **Resume** statement, which causes control to be transferred back to the line that called **ProcA**. Unlike in Question 2, however, this time the value of **a** is still zero thus creating another error when control eventually gets to **ProcC**. The situation is never resolved and the program loops endlessly. Answers a, b, and c are all incorrect because the program never executes any code that would assign a value to **a** (except where the division by zero error occurs).

Need To Know More?

Finding solid guidance on robust error handling is very difficult. When I teach Visual Basic, error handling beyond the simple **On Error GoTo** statement is an area of much confusion for my students. Alas, students bring this or that text that they purchased in the bookstore, and invariably, the books devote two or three pages to what I consider a crucial subject. Some of the problem is that there really isn't much more than meets the eye. I am really hoping that VB eventually sports a universal error handler, perhaps an error event at the **App** object level. Such an event would be an error handler of "last resort." Till such a development happens, the VB developer needs to be especially judicious in the application of strict coding conventions, must give careful consideration to error prevention as I discussed in this chapter, and needs to perform rigorous testing and debugging. The following texts each stood out in my mind for one reason or another.

 Mandelbrot Set, The. *Advanced Microsoft Visual Basic 6*, Microsoft Press, Redmond, WA, 1998. ISBN 1-57231-893-7. *Advanced Visual Basic 6* was due to be printed just as this book was going to press. The VB5 version was superb, and I am sure the VB6 version will be as good. The VB5 version began with a chapter titled "On Error GoTo Hell," which was a really good treatment of the subject and is one of the best chapter titles I've seen. (Please note that the VB5 version of this book is on the MSDN CD-ROM that comes with the Enterprise Edition of Visual Basic 6.)

 Siler, Brian and Jeff Spotts. *Special Edition Using Visual Basic 6*, Que, Indianapolis, IN, 1998. ISBN 0-7897-1542-2. Brian and Jeff's book is a good intermediate-level text. Chapter 10 ends with what is really a cursory discussion of error handling. What I appreciated about the book was an eye to error handling and prevention throughout the text such as the "Control Error Handling" topic in Chapter 15 ("Extending ActiveX Controls").

 Search the online books on the VB CD-ROM for the terms "Err" and "error handling".

 Check out also the Microsoft Developer Network online at **http://premium.microsoft.com/msdn/library**, where there are many articles, book chapters, and updated documentation (as well as links to the Knowledge Base). Search for the term "error handling".

Data Access Models

Terms you'll need to understand:

√ ActiveX Data Objects (ADO)

√ Data Access Objects (DAO)

√ Remote Data Objects (RDO)

√ OLE DB

√ Open Database Connectivity (ODBC)

√ Schema

√ Batch update and batch collision

√ Lock

√ Concurrency

Techniques you'll need to master:

√ Understanding the basic use of SQL commands and concepts

√ Choosing between DAO, RDO, and ADO data models

√ Demonstrating a knowledge of the ADO event model

√ Creating and using a **Connection** object

√ Creating and using a **Command** object

√ Creating and using a **Recordset** object including creating the **Recordset** from a row-returning **Command**

√ Accessing the **Error** object and understanding what types of error information are accessed via the ADO **Error** object versus the Visual Basic **Err** object

√ Demonstrating an understanding of what processing occurs on the client versus what processing occurs on the database server

215

In this chapter and the next, we'll review database access techniques. Visual Basic 6 ships with an emphasis on data access via ADO (ActiveX Data Objects) and OLE DB. Although VB still supports data access via DAO (Data Access Objects) and RDO (Remote Data Objects), VB's future direction is clearly ADO and OLE DB.

In this chapter, we'll look at the mechanics of database access using ADO. We'll concentrate on the properties, methods, and events of the ActiveX Data Objects themselves. In Chapter 10, we'll review the controls and objects that are used to manipulate data.

Because database access is such a huge subject (my *Visual Basic 6 Client/Server Programming Gold Book* runs some 700 pages), I elected to concentrate on the core essentials in this chapter. In particular, I do not discuss the mechanics of DAO or RDO except to compare and contrast them with ADO. My reasoning is that most VB developers already have a basic understanding of DAO and RDO. So, where I do mention them, I try to capitalize on that knowledge to emphasize subtleties about ADO.

Visual Basic Data Models

Visual Basic provides many methodologies and controls to access data. Microsoft Jet has been the most commonly used method to access desktop databases, whereas RDO has gained popularity for remote database access via ODBC. Other options include using the ODBC API as well as the Visual Basic SQL Libraries (VBSQL). VBSQL provides a direct, or native, connection to Microsoft SQL Server.

ADO is Microsoft's newest method of connecting to a database. It interacts with OLE DB, which is a high-performance method of interacting with a wide variety of back-end data sources. When you are using ADO, the data source doesn't need to be relational. The OLE DB driver for the data source will generally expose the data in a relational manner. ADO is further enhanced to minimize traffic when communicating over a network, including the Internet. Its interface is based largely on OLE Automation. DAO and particularly RDO developers will adapt quickly to ADO. It is similar to DAO and RDO but offers a simpler yet more elegant data access model.

DAO, RDO, and ADO are called *data access interfaces* because they provide an object model of the database and expose it via properties, methods, and events of the objects (collectively, the interface).

As with DAO and RDO, Visual Basic provides the ability to place an ActiveData Control (ADC) directly on a form that lets your program quickly and easily manipulate the database. Although this provides a very rapid method to develop a database application, it is also somewhat less functional than what can be done in program code. In the following sections, we'll look at the key features of data access via ADO, using comparisons and contrasts to DAO and RDO where appropriate. RDO developers, in particular, will feel quite comfortable with most aspects of ADO. DAO developers will adjust rapidly also, although the event model is new.

The biggest difference between DAO and ADO is with the DAO Jet workspace. The Jet workspace provides many methods and properties not present in ADO, RDO, or even in DAO ODBCDirect. Much of the onus of maintaining users, groups, indexes, and so on rests on the DAO Jet workspace developer.

ABCs Of ADO

ActiveX Data Objects are a collection of objects used to connect to and manipulate a database. The object model summarized in Figure 9.1 shows two key differences between ADO and DAO/RDO. The most obvious difference is the nonhierarchical nature of ADO. The ADO **Recordset** object, as an example, exists independent of any other ADO object, whereas the DAO **Recordsets** collection is a property of the **Workspace** object. The next significant difference between ADO and DAO/RDO shown in Figure 9.1 is the streamlined model. ADO has only 7 objects compared to DAO's 16 objects (15 for DAO/Jet and 9 for DAO/ODBCDirect).

To use ADO, you need to declare a reference to Microsoft ActiveX Data Objects Library 2 (ADODB). Alternatively, you can use the Microsoft ActiveX

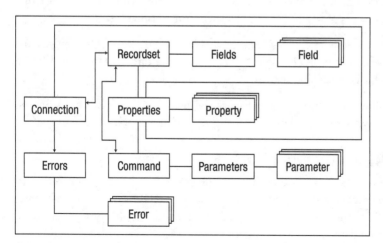

Figure 9.1   The ADO access model.

Data Objects Recordset Library 2 (ADODR), which is a scaled-down type library containing only the **Field**, **Property**, and **Recordset** objects and the **Fields** and **Properties** collections. (There is no **Recordsets** collection in ADO.)

 Note that whereas RDO has the **rdoResultSet** object, reflecting its ODBC and relational database orientation, ADO reverts to the DAO convention of record orientation. This reflects that OLE DB is not married to the concept of the relational database. The majority of Visual Basic developers deal with relational databases, so this chapter uses the term *row* instead of *record*.

Notwithstanding the scaled-down ADODR library, ADO sports four collections:

➤ **Errors** Consists of **Error** objects and contains information about the *most recent* database error.

➤ **Parameters** Consists of **Parameter** objects used in parameterized queries or in stored procedures.

➤ **Fields** Consists of **Field** objects with each **Field** object representing a column in a recordset.

➤ **Properties** Consists of **Property** objects, each of which represents a dynamic property of a **Connection**, **Recordset**, **Parameter**, or **Field** object.

As noted earlier, there is no **Recordsets** collection. Each **Recordset** object is independent of other **Recordset** objects. They can share a **Connection** object (via the **ActiveConnection** property) or can exist independently of a **Connection** object (by passing connection parameters in the **Open** method of the **Recordset** object). Likewise, there is no **Connections** collection. Each **Connection** object is independent of any other **Connection** object.

Table 9.1 cross-references DAO and RDO objects with their ADO equivalents. Note that there is no ADO object analogous to the **dbEngine** and **rdoEngine** objects. This is in keeping with ADO's nonhierarchical model.

In the following sections, we'll discuss the usage of ActiveX Data Objects, beginning with ADO's event model and then visiting each object in turn.

The ADO Event Model

The DAO access model exposed no events, meaning that communication to the database occurred in a synchronous manner. RDO exposes some events, and ADO expands on the RDO model to present a completely asynchronous, event-driven data access environment.

Table 9.1 DAO, RDO, and ADO object cross-reference.		
DAO	**RDO**	**ADO**
dbEngine	rdoEngine	N/A
Error	rdoError	Error
Property	N/A	Property
Workspace	rdoEnvironment	N/A
Database	rdoConnection	Connection
Connection	rdoConnection	Connection
Container	N/A	N/A
Document	N/A	N/A
QueryDef	rdoQuery	Command
Field	rdoColumn	Field
Parameter	rdoParameter	Parameter
Recordset	rdoResultSet	Recordset
TableDef	rdoTable	N/A
Index	N/A	N/A
User	N/A	N/A
Group	N/A	N/A
N/A	rdoPreparedStatement	N/A

To access the events of ADO objects that you declare in code, you need to use the **WithEvents** modifier, as follows:

```
Private WithEvents arsEmp As Recordset
Private WithEvents acon As Connection
```

Most ADO events either begin with "Will" or end in "Complete", denoting an event that is about to occur or an event that has just been completed.

Most of the events are triggered with arguments that provide you with details of what is going to happen or what did happen. For instance, the **WillChangeField** and **FieldChangeComplete** events are passed the arguments **cFields** and **Fields**. **cFields** is the count of the number of fields to be changed (or that were changed), whereas **Fields** is an array of variants containing the affected **Field** objects. Where there is the potential for an error, the arguments **pError** and **adStatus** are passed. **pError** is an **Error** object that contains information about the error if **adStatus** is equal to **adStatusErrorOccurred**.

The event procedures that occur prior to a database operation contain the **adStatus** parameter. Normally, you can set this parameter equal to **adStatusCancel** to prevent the operation from occurring. If for some reason it cannot be prevented, **adStatus** is set equal to **adStatusCantDeny**. If, when the event occurs, **adStatus** is any value other than **adStatusOK**, then the operation that caused the event to be invoked was not successful. For instance, if you attempt to change a field with an invalid data type, the **WillChangeField** event may fire, but **adStatus** will not have a value of **adStatusOK**.

ADO generates the following events:

➤ **CommitTransComplete** Occurs immediately after a commit operation on the **Connection** object.

➤ **ConnectComplete** Occurs immediately after connecting to the database.

➤ **EndOfRecordset** Occurs whenever there is an attempt to move beyond the end of a recordset. You can set the **fMoreData** parameter to **True** to cause a new record to be added when this event occurs.

➤ **ExecuteComplete** Occurs immediately after executing a command (the **Execute** method of the **Connection** or **Command** objects or the **Open** method of the **Recordset** object).

➤ **FetchComplete** Occurs after all records in a recordset have been retrieved during a lengthy asynchronous operation.

➤ **FetchProgress** Occurs periodically during a lengthy asynchronous retrieval of records, giving you the opportunity to cancel the retrieval. The **Progress** and **MaxProgress** parameters contain the number of records retrieved so far and an estimate of the number of records expected to be retrieved in total.

➤ **FieldChangeComplete** Occurs immediately after one or more **Field** objects that have changed due to the **Value** or **Update** methods of the **Recordset** object.

➤ **InfoMessage** Occurs whenever a connection event is generated and the operation was successful, but the data provider sends additional information.

➤ **MoveComplete** Occurs immediately after changing the current row in the **Recordset** object.

Under ADO, if changes are pending to a record and a new record becomes the current record (such as when a **MoveNext** method is invoked), the change is automatically applied. This is just the opposite of what happened in DAO and RDO; both discarded any pending changes. To force the changes not to be applied, use the **Cancel-Update** method of the **Recordset** object.

➤ **OnError** Occurs whenever a database error that is not the result of your VB code occurs. Generally, this means an error that occurs when no VB code is executing. The **sCode, Description,** and **Source** parameters provide you with details of the database status code, error description, and source (the query or command) that caused the error. You can set the **CancelDisplay** parameter to **True** to prevent the error from being displayed to the user.

➤ **RecordChangeComplete** Occurs immediately after one or more records in a **Recordset** object have been altered due to one of the following **Recordset** object methods: **AddNew, CancelBatch, CancelUpdate, Delete, Update,** or **UpdateBatch**.

➤ **RecordsetChangeComplete** Occurs immediately after changing the actual recordset due to the **Close, Filter, Open, Requery,** or **Resync** methods of the **Recordset** object.

➤ **RollbackTransComplete** Occurs immediately after a rollback operation on the **Connection** object.

➤ **WillChangeField** Occurs immediately prior to one or more **Field** objects that will be changed due to the **Value** or **Update** methods of the **Recordset** object.

➤ **WillChangeRecord** Occurs immediately prior to one or more records in a **Recordset** object that will be altered due to one of the following **Recordset** object methods: **AddNew, CancelBatch, CancelUpdate, Delete, Update,** or **UpdateBatch**. **WillChangeRecord** can be thought of as roughly analogous to the **Data** control's **Validate** event.

➤ **WillChangeRecordset** Occurs immediately prior to changing the actual recordset due to the **Close, Filter, Open, Requery,** or **Resync** methods of the **Recordset** object.

➤ **WillConnect** Occurs immediately prior to connecting to the database.

➤ **WillExecute** Occurs immediately prior to executing a command (the **Execute** method of the **Connection** or **Command** objects or the **Open** method of the **Recordset** object).

➤ **WillMove** Occurs immediately prior to changing the current row in the **Recordset** object.

The following sections outline the ADO objects. As you read, keep Table 9.1 in mind as you compare and contrast these objects to their DAO and RDO counterparts.

The Connection Object

The ADO **Connection** object is much like the RDO **rdoConnection** and DAO **Connection** objects. Its main function is to manage the physical connection to the database. Thus, all transaction management, for example, is done at the **Connection** level. Whereas multiple **Recordset** objects can share the same **Connection** object, transactions (and thus any database commits or rollbacks) affect all of them. I discuss the properties and methods of the **Connection** object next.

Connection Object Properties

The key properties of the **Connection** object are:

➤ **CommandTimeout** Specifies how many seconds to wait before an executing command times out and generates an error.

➤ **ConnectionTimeout** Specifies how many seconds to wait while attempting to connect to a database before generating an error.

➤ **ConnectionString** Supplies the information needed to connect to a database, similar to RDO's **Connect** property. This is a combination of four parameters:

➤ **Provider** Specifies the name of the OLE DB provider.

➤ **FileName** Specifies the name of a file containing connection information.

➤ **RemoteProvider** Specifies the name of the remote provider.

➤ **Remote Server** Specifies the path of the server in a Remote Data Services (RDS) connection.

The default **Provider** argument is "MSDASQL", which specifies an ODBC data source, as shown here:

```
Set acon1 = New Connection
acon1.Open ("PROVIDER=MSDASQL; dsn=My ODBC Test;" & _
"uid=Mike;pwd=MyPassword;")
```

As with RDO, the exact parameters may vary from database driver to database driver.

You can specify a **Database=** argument with either a DSN or DSN-less connection. For the former, the DSN already implies the database (as defined in the ODBC setup). Specifying a different database alters the DSN's definition.

Microsoft also delivers an OLE DB driver for Jet, which you would normally use when you need to join an ISAM data source for which no OLE DB provider exists to another OLE DB data source. The provider name is **Microsoft.Jet.OLEDB.3.51.** For Microsoft SQL Server, the provider name is "SQLOLEDB". For Oracle, use "MSDAORA". For the specifics of these and other OLE DB provider connection strings, see the Visual Basic Help file (for OLE DB providers provided by Microsoft) or the vendor's documentation.

➤ **CursorLocation** Determines where a cursor is to be located (similar to how you set the cursor library in RDO). You can set this value at any time on a **Connection**, but it is read-only on an open **Recordset** object. The value **adUseClient** specifies that a local cursor will be used. In other words, ADO will manage the cursor. This provides some flexibility in that the client-side cursor often has features not supported by a server-side cursor. (The value **adUseClientBatch** is synonymous with **adUseClient**.) If you are using RDS, you can specify only **adUseClient**. **adUseServer** specifies that the server will manage the cursor. For larger recordsets, this is more efficient, and the cursor is more sensitive to changes made by other users. However, you lose the flexibility of the client-side cursor. Note that **adUseNone** is obsolete and is retained for backward compatibility only.

➤ **DefaultDatabase** Specifies a default database for the **Connection**. This has implications when you join together two different data sources where you would normally have to qualify object names with the database name. Specifying a default database allows you to omit this information. (The **DefaultDatabase** property is not available with all OLE DB providers and is not available with RDS.)

➤ **IsolationLevel** Specifies the isolation level of the cursor. Isolation can be considered similar to variable scope in Visual Basic—it specifies how "visible" a cursor is. The defaults are **adXactCursorStability**, which specifies that your transaction cannot see the uncommitted changes of other transactions, and **adXactChaos**, which specifies that your transaction cannot overwrite pending changes of more highly isolated cursors. These settings are normally what you would want to use. For example, you would not want your transaction to update a row inserted but not committed because that insert could eventually be rolled back. The **IsolationLevel** property can be set at any time, but it doesn't take effect until the next transaction begins.

➤ **Mode** Specifies read and write permissions. You can set it only before making the connection to the data source. For RDS, it must be **adModeUnknown**. Other constants are:

  ➤ **adModeRead** Read-only

  ➤ **adModeWrite** Write-only

  ➤ **adModeReadWrite** Read and write

  ➤ **adModeShareDenyRead** Others are denied read permission

  ➤ **adModeShareDenyWrite** Others are denied write permission

  ➤ **adModeShareExclusive** No one else can access the data source

  ➤ **adModeShareDenyNone** No one can open the connection with any permissions

➤ **State** Returns the current state of the connection: **adStateClosed**, **adStateOpen**, **adStateExecuting**, or **adStateConnecting**. For example, to determine if an asynchronous command is still executing, you would code the following:

```
If acon.State = adStateExecuting Then
```

Connection Object Methods

The **Connection** object's methods are:

➤ **BeginTrans** Assists in transaction management. Calling one of these methods if the object does not support transactions causes an error (unlike with RDO), so you should verify the existence of the **Property** object **TransactionDDL**. Use **BeginTrans** to begin a transaction.

➤ **Cancel** Cancels the current asynchronous operation (**Execute** or **Connect**).

➤ **CommitTrans** Assists in transaction management. Calling one of these methods if the object does not support transactions causes an error (unlike with RDO), so you should verify the existence of the **Property** object **TransactionDDL**. **CommitTrans** makes all changes within the current **Connection** object permanent.

➤ **Execute** Executes a **Command** object. Its syntax is as follows:

```
connection.Execute CommandText, RecordsAffected, Options
```

CommandText is an SQL statement, table name, stored procedure, or some other provider-specific command text. **RecordsAffected** returns how many records were affected by the command (in the case of an error, this value will be -1). Use **adExecuteAsync** for **Options** to perform the command asynchronously. Alternatively, you can use **adFetchAsync**, which specifies that rows remaining after the initial cache has been filled should be returned asynchronously. Other constants that you can use with **Options** specify how to interpret **CommandText**:

➤ **adCmdText** Indicates that **CommandText** is a string that the data provider recognizes as a command—most typically an SQL statement.

➤ **adCmdTable** Provides the table name. ADO creates an SQL statement from the table name.

➤ **adCmdTableDirect** Returns all rows from the table.

➤ **adCmdStoredProc** Indicates that **CommandText** is a stored procedure.

➤ **Open** Establishes the connection to the data source. (Under RDS, the connection is not actually made until a **Recordset** is opened.) The syntax is as follows:

```
connection.Open ConnectionString, UserID, Password, Option
```

ConnectionString is described earlier in this chapter. **UserID** and **Password** specify the user ID and password for the connection. You can set **Option** to **adAsyncConnect** to cause the connection to occur asynchronously. All arguments are optional.

➤ **OpenSchema** Returns *schema* information, such as table structures, from the database. **OpenSchema** has no counterpart in DAO or RDO. When executed, **OpenSchema** returns a **Recordset** of type static-cursor, which is read-only. The following example creates a **Recordset** that lists all the views on the database:

```
Set arsSchema = acon.OpenSchema _
  (adSchemaTables, Array(Empty, Empty, Empty, "VIEW"))
```

Note the use of the **Array** function to pass arguments to the method. The query type is **adSchema**. Other possible values include **adSchemaColumns**, **adSchemaProcedures**, and so on. See the ADO Help file for a complete listing. The last argument specifies a selection criteria—in this case, "VIEW". Valid criteria vary by the type of query.

➤ **RollbackTrans** Assists in transaction management. Calling one of these methods if the object does not support transactions causes an error (unlike with RDO), so you should verify the existence of the **Property** object **TransactionDDL**. **RollbackTrans** undoes all changes within the current **Connection** object.

The Command Object

The ADO **Command** object is much like the DAO **QueryDef** and RDO **rdoQuery** objects. It represents a non-row-returning command to be executed by the data provider. Most typically (but not necessarily), this is an SQL statement or stored procedure. If the command is parameterized, the **Command** object has a **Parameters** collection. In the following sections, I discuss the properties and methods of the **Command** object.

Command Object Properties

The **Command** object has several properties:

➤ **ActiveConnection** Associates the **Command** object with a **Connection** object. Optionally, you can specify a connecting string (see the description of the **ConnectionString** property of the **Connect** object earlier in this chapter), in which case ADO will create a **Connect** object but will not assign it to a variable. Setting **ActiveConnection** to **Nothing** disassociates it from a **Connection**. Closing the connection causes ADO to set the **ActiveConnection** property to **Nothing** automatically. Assuming that you have created a **Connection** object named **acon** already, the following example sets the **ActiveConnection** property of **acmd** to **acon**:

```
acmd.ActiveConnection = acon
```

➤ **CommandText** Specifies a **String** that contains the command to be exec-uted, such as the following SQL **SELECT** statement:

```
acmd.CommandText = "SELECT * FROM employee"
```

As with the **Execute** method of the **Command** object, it could also be a stored procedure, a table name, or some other command recognized by the data provider.

➤ **CommandTimeout** Specifies how many seconds the command can execute before generating an error. A value of zero specifies that there is no timeout. The default is 30.

➤ **CommandType** Describes the type of command. (See Table 9.2.)

➤ **Prepared** Indicates a **Boolean** that, if set to **True**, causes the data provider to prepare (compile) the command before first running it.

➤ **State** Indicates the current state of the object. **adStateClosed** indicates that it is closed, whereas **adStateOpen** indicates that it is open. **adState-Executing** indicates that an asynchronously executing command is still executing.

Command Object Methods

The **Command** object has several methods. Use the object's **Execute** method to run the command. If the command returns rows, its result must be assigned to a **Recordset** object, as in the following example:

```
' ars is a recordset, and acmd is a command object
Set ars = acmd.Execute
```

You can use the **Cancel** method to halt an asynchronously executing command.

Use the **CreateParameter** method to create a new **Parameter** object using the following syntax:

```
Set parameter = command.CreateParameter (Name, Type, Direction,
Size, Value)
```

Table 9.2   Valid CommandType constants.

Constant	Description
adCmdText	Specifies that **CommandType** is a command, such as an SQL statement.
adCmdTable	Generates an SQL query that returns all rows from the table named in **CommandType**.
adCmdTableDirect	Returns all rows from the table named in **CommandType.**
adCmdStoredProc	Specifies that **CommandType** is a stored procedure.
adCmdUnknown	Specifies that the type of command in the **Command-Type** property is not known. (This is the default.)
adCommandFile	Specifies that **CommandType** is a saved (persisted) **Recordset**.
adExecuteNoRecords	Specifies that **CommandType** is a command or stored procedure that does not return rows.

When doing so, you must manually append the **Parameter** to the **Parameters** collection, at which time ADO will validate it. **Type** specifies the data type of the parameter, such as **adNumeric** (see the ADO Help file for a complete listing). **Direction** is similar to the DAO and RDO **Direction** properties—it sets whether a parameter is input, output, or both. **Size** specifies a maximum length or size where the data type is variable length. The **Value** argument sets the actual data value stored in the parameter as an optional **Variant**.

The next section discusses the use of parameters.

The Parameters Collection And Parameter Object

The **Parameters** collection and **Parameter** object work similarly to their DAO counterparts. **Parameters** represents all the parameters or arguments to a query or stored procedure. Each **Parameter** object has a **Properties** collection.

Suppose you have the following query:

```
SELECT * FROM Customer WHERE Cust_Gender = ?
```

The question mark is a placeholder for a parameter (M or F) to be supplied at execution time. The value you supply is represented by a **Parameter** object.

ADO will generate the **Parameter** objects for you automatically as a property of the **Command** object, as seen in this example:

```
' acmd and acon are previously declared command and
' connection objects
acmd.ActiveConnection = acon
acmd.CommandText = "SELECT * FROM employee where emp_gender = ?"
acmd.Parameters.Refresh
```

The code snippet uses the **Refresh** method of the **Parameters** collection, which tells ADO to examine both the query itself and the database to determine what data type to use and so on. If the query itself had been invalid, ADO would have generated an error message.

After ADO knows what parameters are required, you can assign the proper value and run the command. The following example assigns the result to a previously declared **Recordset** named **ars**:

```
acmd.Parameters(0).Value = "F"
Set ars = acmd.Execute
```

The first **Parameter** object has a **Name** property of "**Param1**". If there were a second **Parameter** object, it would be named "**Param2**". In the preceding example, the collection's ordinal position is used instead of the name.

You may wish instead to manually create the **Parameter** object and append it to the **Parameters** collection. This is because using the **Refresh** method can be an expensive operation against the database. The following code manually creates a **Parameter** object, appends it to the **Command** object's **Parameters** collection, and executes:

```
acmd.ActiveConnection = acon
acmd.CommandText = "SELECT * FROM employee where emp_gender = ?"
Set aparm = New Parameter
aparm.Type = adChar
aparm.Direction = adParamInput
aparm.Size = 1
aparm.Value = "M"
acmd.Parameters.Append aparm
Set ars = acmd.Execute
```

You can use the **CreateParameter** method to set its values all at once instead of setting them individually, as seen here:

```
Set acmd = New Command
acmd.ActiveConnection = acon
acmd.CommandText = "SELECT * FROM employee where emp_gender = ?"
Set aparm = acmd.CreateParameter _
  ("Sex", adChar, adParamInput, 1, "F")
acmd.Parameters.Append aparm
Set ars = acmd.Execute
```

In the following sections, I discuss the properties and methods of the **Parameter** object.

Parameter Object Properties

You should be familiar with the following **Parameter** object properties:

➤ **Attributes** Describes the **Parameter** with one of the following constants:

> ➤ **adParamSigned** **Parameter** accepts signed numbers.

> ➤ **adParamNullable** **Parameter** can accept **Null** values.

> ➤ **adParamLong** **Parameter** can accept very long binary or character data with the **AppendChunk** method.

➤ **Direction** Specifies the **Parameter** type, particularly for stored procedures. Normally, ADO can determine this automatically, but, to specify it yourself, use one of these constants:

➤ **adParamInput** For input parameters.

➤ **adParamOutput** For output parameters.

➤ **adParamInputOutput** For parameters that are both input and output.

➤ **adParamReturnValue** For parameters that are used as return values.

➤ **adParamUnknown** For indicating that the **Direction** is unknown.

➤ **NumericScale** Sets the scale of numeric values, whereas **Precision** sets the precision of numeric values. Certain SQL numeric data types, such as **adNumeric**, require that you set the precision and scale of the number. Scale refers to how many digits are in the number, and precision refers to how many of those digits are to the right of the decimal point. (A scale of 10 and precision of 2 means the number is 10 digits wide with 8 digits to the left of the decimal and 2 digits to the right of the decimal.)

➤ **Size** Sets the maximum width of character data types, such as **adVarChar**.

➤ **Type** Specifies the data type of the **Parameter** object, such as **adNumeric**. See the ADO Help file for a complete listing.

➤ **Value** Sets or returns the actual value of the **Parameter**. Its data type is **Variant**, so you can use any underlying data type.

Parameter Object Methods

Parameter has only one method: **AppendChunk**. The syntax for the method is

```
AppendChunk data
```

where *data* is the data you are appending to the **Value** property of the **Parameter**. The first time you call this method, any data in **Parameter** is overwritten. Subsequent calls add data to the end of the existing data. You use this method when you need to move large amounts of character or binary data into a **Parameter**. (The term "large amounts" is a bit vague. Using the **AppendChunk** method allows you to save memory by moving large chunks of data one piece at a time rather than as one large chunk.) When you use this method, be sure that the **Attributes** property has **adParamLong** set.

The **Recordset** Object

Recordset represents a set of records from the data provider and provides the ability to scroll through the records as well as add, edit, and delete them. ADO, like DAO, refers to records and fields (whereas RDO refers to rows and columns). Each field in a **Recordset** object is represented by a **Field** object. It also has a **Properties** collection.

The default property of **Recordset** is the **Fields** collection, and the default property of individual **Field** objects is **Value**. So, you can use shorthand to reference the value of any field using the familiar exclamation-point convention, as follows:

```
ars!emp_no ' The emp_no field in the recordset
```

ADO provides four types of **Recordset** objects:

➤ **Dynamic Cursor** Allows unrestricted movement through the **Recordset**. Depending on the data provider, you may or may not be able to use bookmarks to move.

 Note that a bookmark is *not* a record number. Databases use a *rowid* to keep track of where a particular row is located in the database. Most commonly, the database uses a "page" and record number to keep track of where each row is. The bookmark essentially records the rowid of the row.

➤ **Keyset Cursor** Is similar to the dynamic cursor, but prevents access to records that other users have added, and it prevents manipulation of records that other users have deleted.

➤ **Static Cursor** Creates a non-updatable **Recordset** that allows unrestricted movement but does not see changes made by other users.

➤ **Forward-Only Cursor** Is identical to the dynamic cursor, except that you can only move forward through the **Recordset**.

A given data provider may not support all cursor types.

As in RDO, **Recordset**s generate events (as discussed earlier in the chapter in the section titled, "The ADO Event Model") that help in asynchronous operations as well as in monitoring the state of the recordset. You should familiarize yourself with the use of those events. For instance, if you open a **Recordset** asynchronously, you will want to wait for the **FetchComplete** event before enabling any edit controls on your form.

As mentioned earlier, a key difference between ADO and DAO/RDO is that, under ADO, when your program navigates to a new record, any pending changes are automatically saved.

Recordset Object Properties

The **Recordset** object's key properties are:

➤ **AbsolutePosition** Specifies a 1-based reference to the current record number. Under DAO, **AbsolutePosition** is 0-based. **AbsolutePosition** can also contain the following values:

➤ **adPosBOF** Indicates that **BOF** is **True**

➤ **adPosEOF** Indicates that **EOF** is **True**

➤ **adPosUnknown** Indicates that the **Recordset** is empty or that the provider does not provide this property

➤ **BOF** If set to **True**, indicates the current record is before the beginning of the **Recordset**. If there are no records, **BOF** is **True**.

➤ **Bookmark** Specifies a variant with which you can record the current record and return to it, in the same way as in DAO and RDO. The following example saves the position of the current record, moves to the last one, and then moves back using the **Bookmark** property:

```
Dim vBookMark As Variant
vBookMark = ars.Bookmark
' Move to the last record
ars.MoveLast
' Move to saved position
ars.Bookmark = vBookMark
```

 Note that ADO does not have a **Bookmarkable** property as do DAO and RDO. Instead, you should use the **Supports** method (which I discuss later in this chapter) to determine if the **Recordset** object supports bookmarks.

➤ **CacheSize** Sets the number of records that are buffered locally. If you set **CacheSize** to 20 records, the first 20 records are read and cached locally when the **Recordset** is opened. Moving to the twenty-first record causes another set of 20 records to be retrieved. Use the **Resync** method to force records already cached to reflect changes made by other users.

➤ **CursorLocation** Specifies where the cursor is to be located. **adUseServer** specifies that the server's cursor services are to be used. This specification can be more efficient but may not have all the functionality of client-side cursors. Often, **AbsolutePosition** and **RecordCount** are unavailable when using a server-side cursor. **adUseClient** specifies that the cursor will be maintained locally. You must use a client-side cursor when doing batch updating.

➤ **CursorType** Sets the **Recordset** type as discussed earlier in this section. Valid values are **adOpenForwardOnly, adOpenKeySet, adOpenDynamic**, and **adOpenStatic**. For batch updates, use **adOpenStatic** or **adOpenKeySet**.

➤ **EditMode** Returns the edit mode of the current record:

> ➤ **adEditNone** Indicates that there is no edit in progress.

> ➤ **adEditDelete** Indicates that the current record has been deleted.

> ➤ **adEditAdd** Indicates that the current record is new.

> ➤ **adEditInProgress** Indicates that the current record is being edited, but the changes have not been saved.

➤ **EOF** If set to **True**, indicates the current record is after the end of the **Recordset**. If there are no records, **EOF** is **True**.

➤ **Filter** Specifies a variant that you can use to filter which records in the **Recordset** can become current. Setting the property to an empty string ("") or to **adEditNone** removes any filtering. You can use a filter such as "Emp_Gender = 'F' Or Emp_Salary > 80000" to cause only records meeting that criterion to be displayed. You can also set **Filter** to an array of **Bookmarks**. Finally, you can set **Filter** to:

> ➤ **adFilterPendingRecords** To view only records changed but not yet saved to the server (used in batch mode).

> ➤ **adFilterAffectedRecords** To view only records affected by the last **CancelBatch, Delete, Resync**, or **UpdateBatch** method.

> ➤ **adFilterFetchedRecords** To view only the most recently cached records.

> ➤ **adFilterConflictingRecords** To view only records that failed the last **UpdateBatch** attempt.

➤ **LockType** Sets the type of record locking using one of the following values:

➤ adLockReadOnly

➤ adLockPessimistic

➤ adLockOptimistic

➤ adLockBatchOptimistic

You cannot use **adLockPessimistic** for local cursors.

With pessimistic locking, the record is locked as soon as it is edited. With optimistic locking, a record is not locked until it's actually updated. Pessimistic locking is safer because you are guaranteed that no one else has changed the record. But pessimistic locking can cause performance problems because it denies that record (and often every other record on the database page) to other users until the transaction is complete. (Note that different databases lock at different levels. Whereas some databases use page-level locking schemes, others lock at the row level. If database resources start running short, locking may be escalated to page level or event table level, which would, in turn, deny the entire table to other users.) Optimistic locking is better for performance, but you have to take extra steps to ensure that the underlying record on the database was not changed by another user during the time that you retrieved and updated the record.

Batch updating means that you send a series (a batch) of updates to the database at the same time. This is normally more efficient. With batch updating, you must use optimistic locking with the **adBatchOptimistic** setting.

➤ **MaxRecords** Restricts the number of records retrieved.

➤ **PageSize** Allows you to break your **Recordset** set into logical *pages*. For instance, if you have a screen that displayed 20 records at a time, you might set this property to 20. This allows you to take advantage of the **AbsolutePage** property. By setting this property, you cause the **Recordset** to scroll to the first record of the specified page. **PageCount** returns the total number of pages in the **Recordset**. Note that the last page might not be full (there could be fewer records on it than specified in **PageSize**). The following example sets a page size of 20 and then moves to page 3; the current record will then be 41, which is the first record on page 3:

```
' Set page size
ars.PageSize = 20
' Move to page 3
ars.AbsolutePage = 3
```

➤ **RecordCount** Returns the number of records in the **Recordset**. If the **Recordset** does not support approximate positioning or bookmarks, then referencing this property will cause all records to be retrieved in order to determine an accurate record count. If this property is equal to -1, then ADO cannot determine the number of records.

➤ **Sort** Allows you to sort the **Recordset** object by any field after retrieval. **Sort** is available when **adUseClient** is set for **CursorLocation**. You can optionally specify the direction of the sort by appending **ASCENDING** or **DESCENDING** (the default is **ASCENDING**). The following example sorts employees by gender:

```
ars.Sort = "emp_gender"
```

 Using the **Sort** method is not the same as using the SQL **ORDER BY** clause. When you use an **ORDER BY**, the data is normally sorted on the database server prior to being returned to the client. The **Sort** method causes the recordset to be sorted on the client, which can have very adverse performance considerations. At worst, the **Sort** method could cause the entire recordset to be downloaded and then sorted locally.

➤ **Source** Contains the source of the data, such as the SQL **SELECT** statement or the name of the stored procedure.

➤ **State** Determines the current state of the **Recordset**. Possible values are:

➤ **adStateClosed**

➤ **adStateOpen**

➤ **adStateConnecting**

➤ **adStateExecuting**

➤ **adStateFetching**

➤ **Status** Returns information about the current record, returning one or more of the constants, as listed in Table 9.3.

Recordset Object Methods

The **Recordset** methods are similar to those available in DAO and RDO. The **Recordset** methods are:

➤ **AddNew** Adds a new record. You can optionally specify some or all of the **Fields** and **Values** arguments. The following example adds a new

Table 9.3	Status constants.
Constant	**Description**
adRecOK	The record was successfully updated.
adRecNew	The record is new.
adRecModified	The record was modified.
adRecDeleted	The record was deleted.
adRecUnmodified	The record was not modified.
adRecInvalid	The record was not saved because its bookmark is invalid.
adRecMultipleChanges	The record was not saved because it would have affected multiple records.
adRecPendingChanges	The record was not saved because it refers to a pending insert.
adRecCanceled	The record was not saved because the operation was canceled.
adRecCantRelease	The new record was not saved because of existing record locks.
adRecConcurrencyViolation	The record was not saved because optimistic concurrency was in use.
adRecIntegrityViolation	The record was not saved because the user violated integrity constraints.
adRecMaxChangesExceeded	The record was not saved because there were too many pending changes.
adRecObjectOpen	The record was not saved because of a conflict with an open storage object.
adRecOutOfMemory	The record was not saved because the computer has run out of memory.
adRecPermissionDenied	The record was not saved because the user has insufficient permissions.
adRecSchemaViolation	The record was not saved because it violates the structure of the underlying database.
adRecDBDeleted	The record has already been deleted from the data source.

record and uses the **Array** function to specify values of the **emp_salary** and **emp_gender** fields:

```
ars.AddNew Array("emp_salary", "emp_gender"), _
    Array (55000, "M")
```

➤ **CancelBatch** Cancels pending changes. You can add the following optional arguments to specify which changes are to be canceled:

➤ **adAffectCurrent**

➤ **adAffectGroup**

➤ **adAffectAll**

➤ **CancelUpdate** Cancels pending changes.

➤ **Clone** Creates a copy of the **Recordset**, including all saved bookmarks. You can optionally specify **adLockReadOnly** to make the cloned **Recordset** read-only. Otherwise, the cloned **Recordset** has the same locking as the original. When the cloned **Recordset** is opened, the current record is the first record.

➤ **Delete** Deletes the current record. If you specify the argument **adAffect-Group**, all the records that meet the current **Filter** criteria are deleted.

➤ **Find** Is similar to the **Find** method available in the DAO Jet workspace. The syntax is as follows:

```
Find (criteria, SkipRows, searchDirection, start)
```

The argument *criteria* is a valid SQL **WHERE** clause (omitting the word "WHERE") such as "**emp_gender** = 'F'". Use **Like** for pattern searches, such as: **ars.Find ("emp_lname Like 'F_*'")**. The optional argument **SkipRows** specifies how many rows to bypass from the starting position before searching. If you specify 5, for example, the search will begin on the sixth row after the starting position. Specifying a negative number will cause the search to begin *before* the starting position. **searchDirection** specifies in what direction to search. **adSearchBackward** causes the search to occur backward from the starting position. The default is **adSearchForward. start** specifies the position from which to start searching. The default is the current record. However, you can also specify a saved bookmark from which to start searching.

➤ **Move** Allows you to move an absolute number of records forward or backward. Specify a positive number as an argument to move forward or a negative number to move backward. You can optionally specify a starting point from which to move (the default is to move from the current record). The starting point can be a valid **Bookmark**. You can also use **adBookmarkFirst** or **adBookmarkLast** to move from the first or last record, respectively.

➤ **MoveFirst, MoveLast, MoveNext, And MovePrevious** Allow you to scroll to the first, last, next, and prior records, respectively.

➤ **Requery** Re-executes the **Recordset**.

➤ **Resync** Refreshes records in the **Recordset** to reflect the changes of any other users. You can optionally specify two arguments:

    ➤ **AffectRecords** Defaults to **adAffectAll** to refresh the entire **Recordset**. You can specify instead **adAffectCurrent**, which refreshes only the current record, or **adAffectGroup**, which refreshes the records that meet the current **Filter** condition.

    ➤ **ReSyncValues** Enables you to specify either **adResyncAllValues**, which causes any pending updates to be canceled, or **adResync-UnderlyingValues**, which specifies that changes are not overwritten and pending updates are not canceled.

Resync does not retrieve rows added by other users.

➤ **Save** Allows you to *persist* (save as a file) the **Recordset**. If the **Filter** property is set, only filtered records are saved to the file. The file is not closed until the **Recordset** is closed. Repeated calls to **Save** cause the records to be appended to the file. The syntax for the method is as follows:

```
recordset.Save FileName, PersistFormat
```

Currently, the only valid value for the **FileName** argument is **adPersist-ADTG**, which specifies a **Recordset** format. A saved **Recordset** can be opened later using the **Open** method of the **Recordset**.

➤ **Supports** Specifies which features the currently open **Recordset** supports. If you pass an argument of type **CursorOptionEnum**, the method returns **True** or **False** to determine if the feature is supported. The **Supports** method does not guarantee that the feature is available under all circumstances. For example, a **Recordset** may return **True** for

adUpdate, indicating that there is nothing in the type and location of the cursor that would preclude updates. However, the nature of the data in the **Recordset** set, such as a multiple table join, may mean that some fields will not be updatable. The following example determines if the **MovePrevious** method is supported:

```
If ars.Supports (adMovePrevious) Then
```

Constants that you can pass include **adAddNew, adApproxPosition, adBookmark,** and so on. See the Object Browser for a complete list.

➤ **Update** Saves changes made to the current record. You can also set values using the optional **Fields** and **Values** arguments, as in the **AddNew** method. When **Update** is called, the current record remains current. If the recordset is opened in batch mode, records aren't saved to the database until you call the **UpdateBatch** method. While in batch mode, calls to the **Update** method save the changes within the **Recordset** itself. If you scroll from one record to another, ADO automatically invokes the **Update** method.

➤ **UpdateBatch** Updates the database with pending changes. The argument **adAffectCurrent** causes only the current record to be updated to the database. **adAffectGroup** causes only changes to records that meet the **Filter** condition to be updated to the database. **adAffectAll** is the default and causes changes to all records to be updated to the database. If there are any batch collisions, a message is added to the **Errors** collection. Use the **Filter** and **Status** properties to find records with conflicts.

A *batch collision* occurs when a batch update fails for one or more records due to a concurrency violation. As an example, assume that you have a recordset consisting of 50 records. While you are processing those records on the client, another user changes one of those records as well. When you attempt to update the record to the database, the data provider detects that the underlying record has changed and rejects the update. This is called a batch collision—your change has collided with the change of another user.

The Fields Collection And Field Object

Each **Recordset** has a **Fields** collection that contains **Field** objects. Each **Field** object represents an individual field in the **Recordset**. The **Field** object contains basic information about the field, such as its value, data type, and size.

Each **Field** contains a **Properties** collection.

Field Object Properties

The **Field** object has the following properties:

➤ **ActualSize** Returns the number of bytes actually stored in the **Field**.

➤ **Attributes** Describes characteristics of the **Field**. Some of the more common **Attributes** constants include:

> ➤ **adFldUpdatable** Indicates that the **Field** can be updated.

> ➤ **adFldFixed** Indicates that the **Field** is fixed width.

> ➤ **adFldIsNullable** Indicates that the **Field** can contain **Null** values.

> ➤ **adFldRowVersion** Indicates that the **Field** object contains a time or date stamp, usually for concurrency purposes.

Use the Object Browser for a listing of other values.

➤ **DefinedSize** Contains the **Field**'s maximum width in bytes and is typically used for variable-length character fields.

➤ **Name** Provides the name of the field as stored on the database or as specified in the command that retrieved the data. Note that if you use the **AS** clause in the SQL **SELECT**, **Name** reflects the column alias. For example, if you specify **SELECT emp_id AS "ID"**, **Name** is equal to "ID" instead of **emp_id**.

➤ **OriginalValue** Contains the value of **Field** when first retrieved from the database.

➤ **Precision** Returns the number of digits in numeric **Field**s, such as **adNumeric**, whereas the **NumericScale** property returns the number of digits to the right of the decimal point.

➤ **Type** Contains a constant that indicates the **Field**'s basic data type, such as **adVarChar**.

➤ **UnderlyingValue** Retrieves the current value as stored on the database. This is a concern if another user has changed the record after you retrieved the **Recordset**.

➤ **Value** Lists the current value of **Field**.

Field Object Methods

Field has only two methods, **GetChunk** and **AppendChunk**, which are both used to manipulate long binary and character data fields. Use **GetChunk** to make iterative calls to retrieve data from a **Field** and store it in a variable. **AppendChunk** is used to iteratively add data to a long binary or character field.

The **Properties** Collection And **Property** Object

The **Connection, Command, Recordset, Parameter,** and **Field** objects all have a **Properties** collection that contains provider-specific **Property** objects. These properties are specific to a given data source provider.

The **Property** object has four properties:

➤ **Name** Identifies the property.

➤ **Value** Specifies the value of the property.

➤ **Attributes** Specifies one or more of the constants listed in Table 9.4.

➤ **Type** Specifies the data type of the property.

The **Errors** Collection And **Error** Object

The **Errors** collection consists of **Error** objects and is much like its DAO and RDO counterparts. Any time a provider error occurs, the collection is cleared, and one or more new **Error** objects is placed into the collection. Some provider messages are added to the **Errors** collection, but they do not halt program execution. Any time you perform an action that might result in an error or warning, you should first invoke the **Clear** method of the collection to clear any entries. Following the database operation, you should check the collection's **Count** property to ensure there were no messages.

ADO errors themselves (as opposed to errors generated within the database) are not entered into the **Errors** collection. Instead, they are handled by Visual Basic's normal runtime error-handling system.

The **Error** object has several properties and no methods.

Table 9.4 Valid Attributes constants for Property objects.	
Constant	**Description**
adPropNotSupported	Provider does not support the property.
adPropRequired	Value of this property must be set before data source is initialized.
adPropOptional	Value of this property does not need to be set before data source is initialized.
adPropRead	Property can be read.
adPropWrite	Property can be written to.

Error Object Properties

The **Error** object has these properties:

➤ **Description** Comes from either ADO or the data source provider itself and is a short description of the error condition.

➤ **NativeError** Specifies the data provider's own error code.

➤ **Number** Uniquely identifies the error (or warning) condition. **Number** is similar to the **Err** object's **Number** property.

➤ **Source** Specifies the name of the object in which the error was generated. Generally, this is the data provider itself.

➤ **SQLState** Corresponds to the ODBC SQL state, as documented in the ANSI SQL standards.

In the next section, we'll review the use of ADO in your Visual Basic application. The comments generally apply to DAO and RDO as well.

The Employee Maintenance Program

In order to allow a user to maintain data, you need to present the data to the user in some manner and perform the necessary, behind-the-scenes coding to validate the data and save changes to the database. In general, you will use various VB objects and controls to simplify this process (as with the ActiveData control) or to streamline it (as with the **DataEnvironment** object or class module) or both. The next chapter covers these issues. There are times, though, when you will need to exploit the power and control of a code-only solution. So, this section looks at portions of a real-world code-only program that displays data on a form and allows user input.

The application performs maintenance on employee records, as shown in Figure 9.2. At the bottom of the screen, there are four Image CommandButton controls for record navigation, similar to a Data control (their **Style** properties are set to **vbGraphical**, and each displays a bitmap). The box in the middle of the CommandButton controls is a Label control. The TextBox controls on the form are a control array named **txtFields**. The TextBox control for employee number is grayed and locked because **emp_no** is the primary key of the record. Space precludes long program listings (but see my book in the "Need To Know More?" section; it includes a CD-ROM that contains many complete programs).

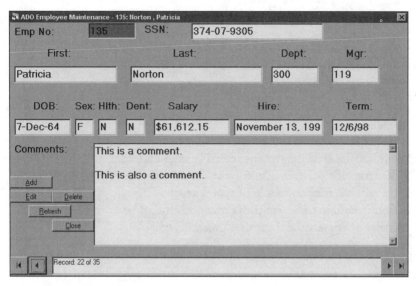

Figure 9.2   The Employee Maintenance form used to illustrate ADO procedures.

After declaring the ADO variables (**Recordset** and so on), you will generally want to connect to the database at program startup. Depending on how your application is organized, you will generally connect to the database in your form's **Load** event.

Next, you need to bind your data-display controls to the data source in code after you have created a **Recordset** object. In the following example, **txtFields** is a control array of text boxes, and **adoPrimaryRS** is a **Recordset**:

```
Dim oText As TextBox
' Bind the text boxes to the data source
For Each oText In Me.txtFields
   Set oText.DataSource = adoPrimaryRS
Next
```

Data validation is done in the **adoPrimaryRS_WillChangeRecord** event. As mentioned earlier in the chapter during the ADO event model discussion, the **WillChangeRecord** event occurs immediately prior to any action that would cause the current record to no longer be the current record. This includes not only some sort of move but also an attempt to close the form. The **adReason** is passed to the event as a parameter, which you can evaluate if necessary. If validation fails for any reason, you can force the record to remain current—for example, you can cancel the operation that is about to occur, such as closing the form—by setting the **adStatus** parameter equal to **adStatusCancel**.

If the user selects the add function, the following code executes:

```
With adoPrimaryRS
  If Not (.BOF And .EOF) Then
    mvBookmark = .Bookmark
  End If
  .AddNew
End With
```

The code verifies that the current record is valid by testing whether **BOF** or **EOF** is **True**. If not, then the current **Bookmark** is saved to a previously declared variable, **mvBookmark**, of type **Variant**. This allows you to move to the current record in the event the user cancels the add-record operation. The following code is executed if the user presses Cancel:

```
If mvBookmark > 0 Then
  adoPrimaryRS.Bookmark = mvBookmark
Else
  adoPrimaryRS.MoveFirst
End If
```

The code to handle a delete is shown next:

```
With adoPrimaryRS
  If Not (.BOF And .EOF) Then
    .Delete
  End If
  .MoveNext
  If .EOF Then .MoveLast
End With
```

This code verifies that the current record is valid and then deletes it. After you delete a record, the current record is no longer valid, so the code performs a **MoveNext**. Then, a test is done to ensure that we haven't moved beyond the end of the file.

The following line of code updates changed records in batch mode:

```
adoPrimaryRS.UpdateBatch adAffectAll
```

The **adAffectAll** argument specifies that all records should be updated to the database. (See the **Filter** property of the **Recordset** object earlier in this chapter.) In order to perform batch updates, the recordset must have been opened with a **LockType** of **adLockBatchOptimistic**. When you perform batch updates, the **Update** method does not save changes to the database—instead, it caches those changes until the next time you issue the **UpdateBatch** method. To cancel all pending changes, use the **CancelBatch** method.

To determine if there were any batch collisions (updates that failed due to concurrency problems), use code similar to the following:

```
adoPrimaryRS.Filter = adFilterConflictingRecords
If adoPrimaryRS.RecordCount > 0 Then
  '' do something
```

After you set the **Filter** property, the **Recordset** object's **RecordCount** property "sees" only those records that meet the criteria. Therefore, if the count is greater than zero, some of the updates failed. You can then run code similar to the following to see what changed:

```
Dim vField As Field
adoPrimaryRS.MoveFirst
Do Until adoPrimaryRS.EOF
  For each vField in adoPrimaryRS.Fields
    If vField.OriginalValue <> _
      vField.UnderlyingValue Then
      ' do something
    End If
  Next
  adoPrimaryRS.MoveNext
Loop
```

This code loops through each **Field** object in the **Recordset**. It compares the **OriginalValue** property (the value of the **Field** when first retrieved) to the **UnderlyingValue** property, which is the **Field**'s value as it is currently stored in the database. (The **Value** property stores the field's current value in your **Recordset**.)

Practice Questions

Question 1

> Under ADO, which of the following are valid collections? [Check all correct answers]
>
> ❑ a. **Connections**
>
> ❑ b. **Fields**
>
> ❑ c. **Parameters**
>
> ❑ d. **Recordsets**

The correct answers are b and c. **Fields** and **Parameters** are valid collections (as are **Errors** and **Properties**). Answers a and d are incorrect because **Connect** and **Recordset** objects are standalone—they are not part of collections (nor is the **Command** object).

Question 2

> Assume **rs** is a valid **Recordset** object. Which of the following lines of code will help you in determining if a **Recordset** supports the **Bookmark** property?
>
> ○ a. `If IsValid (rs.Bookmark) Then`
>
> ○ b. `If rs.Bookmark <> Nothing Then`
>
> ○ c. `If rs.Supports (adBookmark) Then`
>
> ○ d. `If Bookmark (rs) > -1 Then`

The correct answer is c—the **Supports** method returns **True** if the object supports the property or method supplied as an argument. In this case, **adBookmark**, which is the ADO constant to test whether the **Recordset** supports the **Bookmark** property, is passed. Answer a is incorrect because there is no **IsValid** function. Answer b is incorrect because the comparison will fail with an "Invalid Use of Argument" error and will tell you nothing about whether the property is supported. Answer d is incorrect because **Bookmark** is not a function.

Question 3

Examine the following table named "Employee":

Emp_No	Emp_Name	Emp_Salary
10	Ann	38000
20	Bob	40000
30	Carol	42000
40	David	44000

If the following code example is run, who will be the highest paid employee?

```
Dim rs As Recordset
Set rs = New Recordset
rs.CursorType = adOpenKeyset
rs.LockType = adLockBatchOptimistic
' con is an active connection
rs.Open "SELECT * FROM Employee " & _
    "Where Salary < " & _
  "(Select Max(Salary) From Employee)", con, ,
    , adCmdText
rs.MoveFirst
' Loop through recordset
Do Until rs.EOF
   rs!emp_salary = rs!emp_salary * 1.4
   If Left(rs!emp_name,1) = "C" Then
     rs.Cancel
   Else
     rs.Update
   End If
   rs.MoveNext
Loop
rs.Close
```

○ a. Ann

○ b. Bob

○ c. Carol

○ d. David

This is another nasty question that requires a careful reading of the code. The correct answer is d. David remains the highest paid employee because no records are updated. The key to answering this question correctly is to note that the

Recordset object is opened in batch mode with the **LockType** property. When operating in batch mode, updates to the database are made with the **UpdateBatch** method (which the code never executes). Thus, answers a, b, and c are incorrect. Follow the code as I discuss it. The third line sets a **CursorType** of **adOpenKeySet**, which is both updateable and navigable. So far, so good. The next line, as noted, sets the recordset to batch mode. The query is interesting but irrelevant. It exercises a sub-select that excludes David from the recordset. The sharp reader might conclude that, because some of the other employees are getting 40 percent raises later in the code, David will no longer be the highest paid employee. The certification exam is not likely to expect you to know advanced SQL, and if you see something like that, you should suspect that it is there to throw you off. The next several lines of code loop through the three rows in the recordset. Each employee is "temporarily" given a 40 percent raise. Some more irrelevant code specifies that if the employee's name begins with "C" (i.e., poor Carol), the raise should be cancelled. Otherwise, the **Update** method is invoked. In batch mode, the **Update** method merely buffers the changes made to the record—it saves the change to the **Recordset** object but not to the database. It is worth pointing out that invoking the method is superfluous because moving to a new record causes the change to be updated anyway. The **Recordset** object is finally closed. What is missing is the **UpdateBatch** method to apply the changes to the database. Since the database never gets updated, David remains the most highly paid employee (deserving or not!). The key to the question, then, is recognizing that changes to a recordset opened in batch mode are not updated to the database with the **Update** method.

Question 4

Assume that you want to store a large bitmap in the database. Which ADO method will be of interest to you?

○ a. **AddBlob**

○ b. **AppendChunk**

○ c. **LoadPicture**

○ d. **SavePicture**

The correct answer is b. The **AppendChunk** method is used to store very large character and binary data in a **Field** object. Answer a is incorrect because there is no **AddBlob** method. Answer c is incorrect because **LoadPicture** is a VB function not particularly helpful for this task. Answer d is incorrect because the VB **SavePicture** statement is not an ADO method and is not particularly helpful for the task at hand.

Question 5

> Assume you open a **Command** object using the OLE DB ODBC provider against a Paradox database. The table you select from is defined as having no primary key. The user is editing the current row in the **Command** object, which happens to be employee number 197. Because there is no primary key on the table, there is another employee 197 on the same table. After the user makes changes to the record, your program invokes the **Update** method. Which of the following statements is true?
>
> ○ a. The update will be rejected by Paradox.
>
> ○ b. The update will be rejected by the OLE DB provider.
>
> ○ c. The update will succeed.
>
> ○ d. The update will be applied to both records that are employee 197.
>
> ○ e. None of the above.

This is a nasty question—the correct answer is e. None of the answers is correct because you must assign the result of a row-returning **Command** to a **Recordset**. There is no **Update** method of the **Command** object. I saw a few questions on the certification exam that were worse—long, elaborate stories providing a lot of irrelevant details that are presumably designed to distract your attention from the main point. In this case, much is made about the fact that you are editing a Paradox database (which is meaningless) and that the table has no primary key (which is interesting and certainly complicates issues). You are even challenged with the meaningless information that there are two employee 197s. Alas, a careful reading of the question gives the answer away in the first few words: You do not use the **Command** object to edit records. Answers a through d are all incorrect because there is no **Update** method of the **Command** object. (Give yourself an honorable mention if you selected answer d. Too bad the test doesn't give credit for honorable mentions.)

Need To Know More?

 Craig, John Clark and Jeff Webb. *Microsoft Visual Basic 6.0 Developer's Workshop*, Microsoft Press, Redmond, WA, 1998. ISBN 1-57231-883-X. A good intermediate-level VB6 resource. I found the entire volume interesting and educational. The authors take a "How Do I?" approach to explaining various VB techniques. Chapters 23 and 32 are decent, if brief, introductions to database access and some of the newer VB6 wizards, but the book concentrates on DAO.

 Davis, Harold. *Visual Basic 6 Secrets*, IDG Books Worldwide, Foster City, CA, 1998. ISBN 0-7645-3223-5. Harold has done a nice job with this book. Chapters 31 through 33 provide a good overview of DAO and ADO, the newer VB database-oriented objects, and so on. Chapter 33, in particular, summarizes more advanced topics, including Visual Modeler and Microsoft Transaction Server (although you probably won't see either of these subjects on the Desktop exam).

 Holzner, Steven. *Visual Basic 6 Black Book*, The Coriolis Group, Scottsdale, AZ, 1998. ISBN 1-57610-283-1. Steven has written an eminently readable book, and both intermediate- and advanced-level developers will find it to be a good source of information and techniques. Check out Chapter 17, which covers file I/O. Also, turn to Chapters 24 and 25 for a discussion that starts with relatively simple database concepts and progresses to fairly in-depth code techniques using DAO, RDO, and ADO.

 MacDonald, Michael and Kurt Cagle. *Visual Basic 6 Client/Server Programming Gold Book*, The Coriolis Group, Scottsdale, AZ, 1998. ISBN 1-57610-282-3. I always feel funny recommending my own materials, but *Visual Basic 6 Client/Server Gold Book* is the only book that I have seen that provides in-depth coverage of some of the materials touched on in this chapter. Chapters 2 and 3 are good if you need a primer on SQL and database design. Chapter 11 covers advanced SQL topics, such as the creation and use of stored procedures and triggers. Chapters 5 and 6 are primers on the use of DAO and RDO. Chapter 7 covers the mechanics of ADO and OLE DB, and Chapter 8 details the migration of DAO and RDO applications to ADO. Chapters 9 and 10 cover advanced ADO and object-oriented techniques, including the creation of local and remote business objects.

Mandelbrot Set, The. *Advanced Microsoft Visual Basic 6*, Microsoft Press, Redmond, WA, 1998. ISBN 1-57231-893-7. *Advanced Microsoft Visual Basic 6* was due to be printed just as this book was going to press. The VB5 version was superb, and I am sure the VB6 version will be as good.

Vaughn, William R. *Hitchhiker's Guide To Visual Basic & SQL Server*, Microsoft Press, Redmond, WA, 1998. ISBN 1-57231-848-1. Be sure to get the sixth edition, which covers Visual Basic 6. Bill Vaughn's writings on the use of VB in database applications are always superb. Although the book concentrates on using VB with SQL Server, most of the material is equally applicable to other databases.

Search the online books on the VB CD-ROM for the term "database". In the VB Concepts Help file, check out the Data Access guide, which includes a number of tutorials. Also, check out the ADO200.CHM, RDO98.CHM, and DAO351.CHM Help files, which are ADO, RDO, and DAO specific. The quality of the VB Help files has slipped through the years, and you will encounter some broken links as well as a few inaccuracies. However, if you have patience, they are still good resources.

www.microsoft.com/support/ Microsoft places the most current Knowledge Base online here. Enter search terms such as "DAO", "RDO", and "ODBC" to view articles that detail tips (and sometimes fixes) that revolve around the use of external modules.

www.microsoft.com/data/ Check out this site for new ADO developments.

premium.microsoft.com/msdn/library/ Check out the Microsoft Developer Network online, where there are many articles, book chapters, and updated documentation (as well as links to the Know-ledge Base). There is a good article on data access with Visual Basic 6 at **premium.microsoft.com/msdn/library/devprods/vs6/vb/html/vbconDataAccessGuide.htm.**

Data Access Tools, Objects, And Controls

Terms you'll need to understand:

- ✓ **CursorType** property
- ✓ Data binding
- ✓ Data provider, data source, and data consumer
- ✓ **DataMember** property
- ✓ **RowSource**, **ListField**, and **BoundColumn** properties
- ✓ Hierarchical recordsets
- ✓ **BindingCollection** object

Techniques you'll need to master:

- ✓ Using the ADO Data control (Adodc)
- ✓ Binding controls to data sources
- ✓ Using the **DataMember** property to bind to one of multiple **Recordset** objects in a data source
- ✓ Using the DataCombo and DataList controls to display data from another table
- ✓ Creating and using the **DataEnvironment** object
- ✓ Using data-aware classes
- ✓ Using the **DataReport** object
- ✓ Using the **Format** object

Chapter 9 covers data access models in Visual Basic, concentrating on ADO properties, methods, and events. In this chapter, we'll discuss the usage of various Visual Basic controls with the database, as well as newly data-oriented and newly data-aware objects in Visual Basic. Again, although the emphasis on ADO reflects the trends within all of Microsoft's development products, many of the concepts generally apply to DAO and RDO as well. Where appropriate, this chapter compares and contrasts ADO techniques with those of DAO and RDO.

The Adodc

The ADO equivalent of the intrinsic Data control is the ADO Data control (Adodc). It provides a visible record-navigation control to the user while encapsulating the properties, methods, and events needed to connect to and maintain the database. To use the Adodc, you must add it to the toolbox using the Components dialog under the Project menu.

Adodc Properties, Methods, and Events

The properties of the Adodc are basically those of the **Connection** object, and the control can be considered a surrogate for the **Connection** object.

Recordset is a property of Adodc, and most of the normal recordset properties and methods are accessed via the control's **Recordset** property.

You should be familiar with the following key properties of the Adodc:

➤ **BOFAction** Specifies what to do if an attempt is made to move before the first record. **adDoMoveFirst** indicates to move to the first record (the default), whereas **adStayBOF** specifies that the record should move before the beginning of the file. This will create a runtime error, which you will then have to handle in code.

➤ **CursorType** Specifies which cursor library to use. With the Adodc, you don't have as many choices as when creating a **Recordset** object in code. Your choices are **adOpenKeySet**, **adOpenDynamic**, and **adOpenStatic**.

➤ **EOFAction** Specifies how to handle moving past the end of the file. The value **adDoMoveLast** indicates that the control should move to the last record. **adStayEOF** causes a move beyond the last record (which will then create an error), and **adDoAddNew** causes a new record to be added to the recordset.

Other Adodc properties are essentially the same as for the **Connection** and **Recordset** objects, discussed in Chapter 9.

Other than standard ActiveX methods, the only Adodc-specific method is **Refresh**, which causes the **Recordset** to be rebuilt.

The Adodc generates the same events as the **Recordset** object plus an **Error** event (when an entry is made to the **Errors** collection) and the usual events associated with ActiveX controls (**DragDrop** and so on). The Adodc equivalent of the Data control's **Validate** event is **WillChangeRecord**.

The following sections discuss data binding in Visual Basic 6.

Data Binding In Visual Basic 6

Before we jump into the particulars of data binding in VB6, you should be aware of three terms Microsoft uses in the database vernacular:

➤ **Data provider** Generally, a non-Visual Basic source of data, usually an ADO interface to the database, such as MSDASQL (for ODBC) or SQLOLEDB (for SQL Server).

➤ **Data source** An object or control that provides data. This can be a Data control (such as the Adodc), a class, or a **DataEnvironment** object.

➤ **Data consumer** An object or control that is bound to a data source.

In VB5, the only way that you could bind a control to a data source was in the context of a form. In other words, the data source (such as a Data control) had to be on a form. Now, any ADO data consumer can bind to any ADO data source, and the data source need not form based. All of Visual Basic's intrinsic controls that are data aware (as discussed in the next section) can act as ADO data consumers. New to Visual Basic 6 is the ability of non-form-bound items—such as class modules—to act as data providers. Additionally, class modules can act as data consumers. The following sections outline ways to bind controls to the database and how to use some of the controls' objects, including new objects, such as **DataEnvironment**.

Binding Controls To A Data Source

Many Visual Basic intrinsic controls can be bound to a data source. (Exceptions include the CommandButton, DirectoryListBox, FileListBox, Frame, Line, OptionButton, and Shape controls.) Each has four design-time data-related properties, as shown in Figure 10.1. **DataSource** specifies the control or object that is supplying the data. In Figure 10.1, the data source is an Adodc, but, unlike in earlier versions of Visual Basic, the data source can also be an object not associated with a form (such as a class or **DataEnvironment** object).

Figure 10.1 The data properties of Visual Basic controls.

DataField specifies which field from the data source is bound to the control. Normally, this is the field that will be displayed (with the DataCombo and DataList controls being notable exceptions, as discussed later in this chapter).

 You can now do all binding, except to the intrinsic Data control or the Remote Data control, at runtime. For instance, you can set the **DataSource**, **DataMember**, and **DataField** properties of a TextBox control during program execution.

New to Visual Basic 6 are the **DataFormat** and **DataMember** properties. **DataFormat** allows you to choose among a number of predefined data formats, such as **Date** or **Currency** (and within each of these, there are a number of choices). In past versions of Visual Basic, you had to format output in code. In Visual Basic 6, you can also choose a custom format that you define yourself. You could, for instance, define the format "@@@-@@-@@@@" to control the display of U.S. social security numbers, as seen in Figure 10.2. **DataMember** is used when a data source provides more than one **Recordset**. For instance, later in this chapter, we'll review the **DataEnvironment** object, which can have multiple **Command** objects. If you bind a control to **DataEnvironment**, the **DataMember** property allows you to choose which **Command** object to use.

The **DataChanged** property is a **Boolean** available at runtime that indicates whether data in the control has been altered. Additionally, you can set the **CausesValidation** property to specify whether the **Validation** event should trigger whenever data has changed and the control loses focus. This allows you to edit the changed data as soon as the user moves from the control, without incurring the overhead and awkwardness of depending on the **Change** event. Only controls that can be edited have the **CausesValidation** property and **Validation** event.

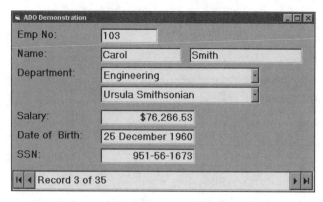

Figure 10.2   A VB form with controls bound to an Adodc. Note the
formatted social security number and the use of
DataCombo controls.

ADO Data-Aware Controls

Visual Basic supplies a number of useful ActiveX data-aware controls that you
can use on your forms. Note that many are supplied in two versions—one for
DAO and RDO and the other for ADO (the latter are labeled as OLE DB in
the Components Selection dialog). The next few sections outline the use of
key ADO data-aware controls that you should be familiar with.

The DataCombo Control

The DataCombo control is roughly the ADO and OLE DB equivalent of the
DBCombo control used with DAO and RDO. In general, comments made
about the DataCombo control also pertain to the DBCombo control.

Although the DataCombo control can be thought of as a "data-enhanced"
version of the intrinsic Combo control, its actual usage is a source of confusion
to some developers. Its purpose is to bind to a column in one table but display
data from another table in a manner more meaningful to the user. For example,
Figure 10.2 has DataCombo controls bound to the **emp_dept_no** and
emp_mgr_id columns on the Employee table. But, the data displayed on the
first DataCombo control is the **dept_name** from the Department table (whereas
the Employee table stores only a department number). The second DataCombo
control displays the **emp_name** from the Employee table that corresponds to
the employee's manager (whereas the employee's record stores only the manager's
employee number). The DataCombo control also allows the user to select any
department or manager for the employee being displayed.

To use the DataCombo control, you set the **DataSource** and **DataField** properties as with any other control. To accomplish this, five data-related properties

are needed. For example, other properties that must be set on the control displaying the department name are as follows:

➤ **RowSource** The data source from which the "expanded" data is being pulled. For example, a data source that selects the department name from the Department table.

➤ **ListField** The column from the second data source to be displayed, such as the department name (instead of the department number).

➤ **BoundColumn** The column that the control should use from the second Data control to relate to the **DataField** from the first Data control. For example, if you were displaying the department name instead, you would relate the two data sources using the department number.

Figure 10.3 shows the relationships between these properties.

Additionally, if the **DataSource** or **RowSource** properties are used to access a data source that supplies more than one **Command** or **Recordset** object, then the **DataMember** and **RowMember** properties are used to choose the specific member. This is illustrated in the next section's discussion about the DataList control.

The DataList Control

The DataList control is roughly the ADO and OLE DB equivalent of the DBList control used with DAO and RDO. In general, comments made about the DataList control also pertain to the DBList control.

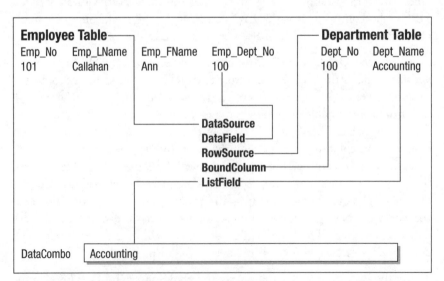

Figure 10.3 The DataCombo control and how it looks at two different data sources.

The DataList control is essentially a data-enhanced version of the intrinsic ListBox control. Whereas the DataCombo control occupies just one line on a form until expanded, the DataList control, like ListBox, always displays multiple lines at once.

Like the DataCombo control, the DataList control is most-often used to relate two data sources. Properties of the DataCombo control are set in the same manner as for the DataCombo control.

The DataGrid Control

The DataGrid control is roughly the ADO and OLE DB equivalent of the DBGrid control used with DAO and RDO. In general, comments made about the DataGrid control also pertain to the DBGrid control. The exception is that the DataGrid control has no unbound mode for displaying non-bound data.

The DataGrid control is highly programmable, and it is useful for displaying data in a grid or spreadsheet-like manner. The following lists key properties and methods of the DataGrid control:

➤ **Bookmark property** Returns the current row or can be used to move to a new row.

➤ **Caption property** The **Caption** property of a given **Column** is the column-heading name, and the **ColIndex** property is the ordinal position within the collection.

➤ **Col property** Returns the current column or can be used to move to a new column. To move to the third row in the seventh column, do this:

```
DataGrid1.Bookmark = 3
DataGrid1.Col = 7
```

➤ **Columns collection** Contains all the columns in the grid as **Column** objects. With the **Columns** collection, you can add or subtract a **Column** using the **Add** or **Remove** methods. You can address any particular column using its ordinal position (**Columns(4)**) or name (**Columns("curr")**). The name is the column-heading name.

➤ **CurrentCellModified property** A **Boolean** that returns or sets whether the current cell has been changed.

➤ **DataChanged property** Tells you whether the column on the current row has been modified.

➤ **NumberFormat property** Allows you to apply formatting in code. In the following example, the **Value** and **Text** properties might be equal to $1,273.99 and 1273.99, respectively:

```
DataGrid1.Columns("total").NumberFormat = "$  ###,##0.00"
```

➤ **SelBookmarks** A collection of all currently selected rows. This is especially useful when the user has selected a series of discontiguous rows that you wish to update, delete, or so on.

➤ **Text property** Reflects the actual contents of the current cell (for example, the **Text** property might be "$150.15", whereas the **Value** property is 150.15).

➤ **Value property** The actual contents of the **Column**.

You can organize the DataGrid into a collection of **Splits** which contains **Split** objects. Each **Split** is a logical view of the data. Using the **Columns** property of each **Split** object, you can specify whether columns should, for example, display or hide.

The DataRepeater Control

Strictly speaking, the DataRepeater control has uses beyond the display of data. The DataRepeater acts as a container for any user control you might create, repeating that control as many times as it will fit in the DataRepeater control. Figure 10.4 shows a user control (previously created and compiled

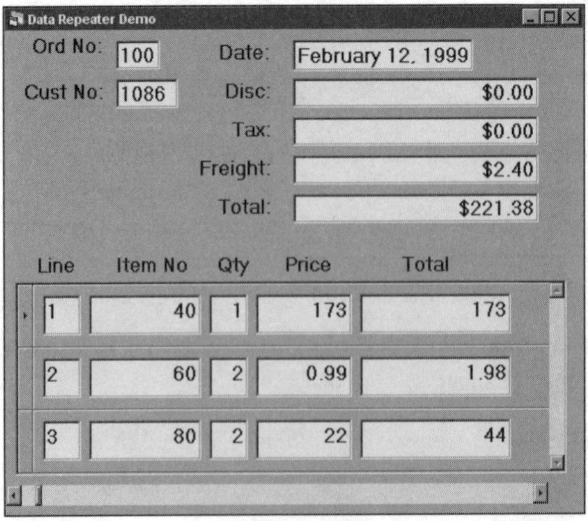

Figure 10.4 A form that uses the DataRepeater control to display multiple occurrences of a data-bound user control.

into an OCX ActiveX control) embedded into a DataRepeater control. The user control consists of five text boxes aligned in a single row. These text boxes are bound to the database. The user control has been resized to minimize the space required. And, the DataRepeater control is placed on the form and resized so that it's big enough to accommodate three "rows" of the user control. The **RepeatedControl** property of the DataRepeater control is used to specify the name of the control to be repeated.

The **DataSource** property and, if necessary, the **DataMember** property are used to bind the DataRepeater control to the data source. The code of the DataRepeater control must expose each data field as a public property. The **RepeaterBindings** property is comprised of **RepeaterBinding** objects. Each **RepeaterBinding** object is used to associate the publicly defined properties to fields from the underlying data connection.

The DataEnvironment Object

The **DataEnvironment** object is a real boon for Visual Basic 6 developers. It is a standalone object that encompasses one or more **Connection** objects, each of which can have one or more **Command** objects. If the **Command** object returns rows, **DataEnvironment** automatically creates **Recordset** objects (prefixing the name of the **Command** object with **rs** so that **cmdCustomer** generates **rscmdCustomer**). The object can be shared among forms, class modules, or other objects. Considering that prior releases of VB caused you to reinvent the wheel with every form that manipulated data, this is a huge improvement.

The **DataEnvironment** object exposes each **Command** object as a **DataMember**. **DataMembers** is a collection of **DataMember** objects, each of which represents a discrete data source. Objects that can provide multiple data sources, such as classes, User controls, and the **DataEnvironment** object, have **DataMembers** as a property.

Even better, all data-manipulation code can be encapsulated (indeed, *should* be encapsulated) to the **DataEnvironment** object to achieve a high degree of reusability along the way.

The **DataEnvironment** object can also be used from project to project, but the process of doing so is not intuitive (there is no Add DataEnvironment command on the Project menu). Use the Add File command from the Project menu, and navigate to your saved **DataEnvironment** module—it has an extension of .DSR.

The DataEnvironment Designer

The DataEnvironment Designer is used to create the **DataEnvironment** object. Wizards that can be invoked from the DataEnvironment Designer walk you through the process of creating **Connection** and **Command** objects. The process of creating a **Connection** object is self-explanatory, so I will not belabor the point here. For more information about the **Connection** object, refer to Chapter 9. To create a **Command** object, right-click on a **Connection**, and choose Add Command. You can also select Insert Stored Procedure and have the **Command** generated for you.

After you have added a **Connection** object, the Data View window, which shows each connection, opens. You can expand a connection to see tables, views, and so on. You can drag any of these objects to the DataEnvironment Designer, and the wizard will create a **Command** object. Figure 10.5 shows the development environment with the Data View, DataEnvironment, and so on, windows open.

If you elect to create (or modify) a **Command** object using the Properties dialog, you can create sophisticated and efficient **Command** objects. Using the General tab, you can select a type of object (stored procedure, table, view, synonym, or SQL statement). If you choose an SQL statement as the source of the **Command**, you can use the new SQL Builder dialog.

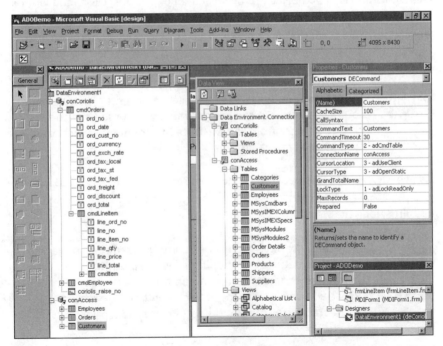

Figure 10.5 The DataEnvironment Designer and Data View windows.

You can create parent-child relationships between **Command** objects by selecting the Relations tab of the child **Command** and then selecting the Relate To A Parent Command checkbox. Next, select the name of the parent **Command,** and indicate the column(s) by which they are related.

The Parameters tab allows you to manipulate parameterized queries or stored procedures. Generally, ADO can determine direction, data type, and so on, but you can override the settings on this tab as well as supply a value, if desired.

The Grouping tab allows you to group your **Command** objects in a manner similar to the SQL **GROUP BY** clause. When you select the Group Command Object checkbox, the Fields In Command list box becomes available. You can select one or more fields to group by. When you aggregate (as discussed next), calculations are done on each break in your grouping. For instance, if you sum orders and choose to group by state, you can obtain a total of all orders for each state.

> Though grouping allows you to specify level breaks for aggregation as in an SQL **GROUP BY**, each grouping is more akin to a band in a report writer. You do not need to actually perform any totaling—the grouping can be merely an organized way to present data as meets your purposes.

The Aggregates tab allows you to perform various aggregation calculations, such as totals, averages, and so on. Each aggregate that you define becomes a **Field** object in the **Recordset** that is derived from the **Command**. You should give each aggregate an appropriate name and choose an aggregation function (Any, Average, Count, Maximum, Minimum, Standard Deviation, or Sum). Then, choose an aggregation level. The aggregation level options vary, based on the type of object, what grouping you have used (or not used), and so on. The Grouping option lets you further choose to aggregate on one of the fields that you have grouped by. The Grand Total option lets you take a grand total on the field that you indicate. If you are designing a child **Command**, then you can also choose to group by the parent **Command** and further choose a field within the parent **Command**.

Hierarchical Recordsets

When you create a parent-child relationship for row-returning **Command** objects, the result is a *hierarchical recordset*. (The **Command** object itself is more accurately thought of as a *hierarchical* cursor.) A hierarchical recordset is a recordset that returns data from two or more tables, and, although a hierarchical recordset is similar to a traditional SQL join, it is inherently more efficient. When you join two tables, data from the "parent" table is returned for each row of the "child" table. With a hierarchical recordset, data from the parent table is returned only once.

The hierarchy structure is created using Shape commands, which some Access users might be familiar with. You can right-click on a **Command** object in the DataEnvironment Designer and select Hierarchy Information to view either the Shape command generated or the actual ADO hierarchy. (I have found the Shape command generated to be buggy. You can copy from the Hierarchy Information into your application and modify the Shape command as needed.)

> To use Shape commands in your application, the ADO provider must be MSDataShape. This provider then interacts with the data provider to supply the shaping support. If you create hierarchical recordsets using the DataEnvironment Designer, Visual Basic determines the ADO providers for you. An example of a Shape command is shown later in this chapter in the section titled "Data-Aware Classes."

The Hierarchical FlexGrid Control

The easiest way to present hierarchical data is in a Hierarchical FlexGrid control (MSHFlexGrid). If you right-drag a **Command** object onto a form, one of the available options is to create a Hierarchical FlexGrid control. In most respects, a Hierarchical FlexGrid control is similar in operation to the DataGrid control. The key difference between the two controls is that the Hierarchical FlexGrid supports hierarchical recordsets. In Figure 10.6, which shows the MSHFlexGrid, you can see where I have created an aggregate, **SalesForState**, which sums sales by state. There are two levels of grouping occurring: state and customer number. In Figure 10.6, I have collapsed the detail for four customers in the middle of the grid as well as details for North Dakota and New York.

alesForState	cust_st		cust_no	cust_fname	cust_lname		ord_no	ord_date	ord_total
⊟		⊟					10077	1999-03-22	1569.31
							10140	1999-05-22	251.79
			1081	Zachary	Morton		10169	1999-06-20	24.82
							10234	1999-09-20	47.13
10572.74	ME						10276	1999-12-01	763.04
		⊟					10156	1999-06-07	1121.04
			1096	Priscilla	Spence		10159	1999-06-10	865.19
							10191	1999-07-16	397.27
⊞ 12217.96	ND								
⊞ 26298.18	NY								
⊟		⊞	1014	Barbara	Needham				
		⊞	1015	Carly	Oscar				
		⊞	1031	Zachary	Fitzsimmons				
		⊞	1033	Ben	Hale				
		⊟					10152	1999-06-03	235.56
			1045	Nancy	Bourke		10179	1999-07-04	618.56
20178.81	RI						10185	1999-07-10	1270.98
		⊟					10011	1999-01-12	344.06
			1065	Carly	Simons		10207	1999-08-05	326.53
							10261	1999-11-01	135.10
		⊟					10145	1999-05-27	604.42
			1088	George	Greggson		10153	1999-06-04	4.24

Figure 10.6 The Hierarchical FlexGrid.

Data-Aware Classes

Database-aware classes are capable of acting as data consumers and data sources. Whereas the **DataEnvironment** object is restricted to OLE DB data providers, a class module can interact with any type of data.

Class modules have two properties relating to their data awareness: **DataBindingBehavior** and **DataSourceBehavior**. To determine how the class binds to the data source, you can set **DataBindingBehavior** to **vbSimpleBound** or **vbComplexBound**. *Simple binding* means that the class is bound to a single field in an external database, whereas *complex binding* means that the class is bound to an entire row of data. You can set **DataSourceBehavior** to **vbDataSource** to cause the class to be a data source to other controls. In other words, you will then be able to instantiate the class and bind a TextBox or other controls to it, much as you would bind a control to a Data control.

The binding is actually done through a new object called the **BindingCollection**. As its name indicates, the **BindingCollection** is a collection of bindings to data source(s). The **DataSource** property of the **BindingCollection** is used to determine what object is actually providing the data—it must be a class or a User control. (The **DataSourceBehavior** of the class or User control must be set to **vbDataSource**.)

The next sections review the process of creating data-aware business objects using classes.

Creating A Data-Aware Business Object

A *business object* is a component that performs certain business logic. Strictly speaking, a business object that acts as a data source does not need to access a database. The class can have its own data properties by building **Recordset** objects in code and appending **Field** objects to the **Recordset** objects.

In the class from which you construct the business object, you will need to declare a number of objects, properties, and events—these comprise the object's interface. The following code declares a **Recordset**, **Connection**, and one publicly viewable event, **MoveComplete**:

```
Private WithEvents adoPrimaryRS As Recordset
Private WithEvents con As Connection
Public Event MoveComplete()
```

The class module normally has only two events: **Initialize** and **Terminate**. If you set the class's **DataBindingBehavior** to **vbComplexBound**, the following events are automatically added to the code:

```
Public Property Get DataSource() As DataSource
Public Property Set DataSource(ByVal objDataSource As DataSource)
Public Property Get DataMember() As DataMember
Public Property Let DataMember(ByVal DataMember As DataMember)
```

The **Initialize** event is shown next. It performs a connection to the database and then adds two items to the **DataMembers** collection:

```
Set con = New Connection
con.CursorLocation = adUseClient
con.Open "PROVIDER=MSDataShape;Data PROVIDER=MSDASQL;" & _
  "dsn=Coriolis VB Example;uid=coriolis;pwd=coriolis;"
  Set adoPrimaryRS = New Recordset
  adoPrimaryRS.Open "SHAPE {SELECT cust_no,cust_lname, " & _
  "cust_fname," FROM customer Order by cust_lname} AS " & _
  "ParentCMD APPEND ({SELECT ord_no,ord_date,ord_total " & _
  "FROM orders ORDER BY ord_date } AS ChildCMD RELATE "  & _
  "cust_no TO ord_cust_no) AS ChildCMD", _
  con, adOpenStatic, adLockOptimistic
  DataMembers.Add "Primary"
  DataMembers.Add "Secondary"
```

The **Recordset** uses a Shape command to create a hierarchical recordset using two tables. As such, there are two commands—**ParentCMD** and **ChildCMD**. Each command is appended to the **DataMembers** collection. Controls that bind to this class will select either the **Primary** or **Secondary** data member.

When a **DataMember** is added to the **DataMembers** collection, the **GetDataMember** event is triggered. It is in the **GetDataMember** event that you associate the actual data source (the **Recordset**) with the **DataMember**, as shown next:

```
Private Sub Class_GetDataMember(DataMember As String, _
  Data As Object)
Select Case DataMember
  Case "Primary"
    Set Data = adoPrimaryRS
  Case "Secondary"
    Set Data = adoPrimaryRS("ChildCMD").UnderlyingValue
  End Select
End Sub
```

In the preceding code, one of the arguments is **Data** as type **Object**. When called, **Data** will be set to either **adoPrimaryRS** or to the **UnderlyingValue** property of **adoPrimaryRS("ChildCMD")**. If you examined **adoPrimaryRS**, you would see that it has four **Field** objects: **cust_no**; **cust_lname**, **cust_fname**, and **ChildCmd**. **ChildCmd** is, of course, essentially another **Recordset**.

UnderlyingValue returns a reference to that **Recordset**. You will need to expose each of these fields as properties within the class. I discussed creating properties in Chapter 5.

Binding Controls To The Business Object

When using the class as a data provider, you'll need to bind controls on forms as you would with an Adodc. However, Visual Basic has no way of knowing that the class module will be a data provider as it does when an Adodc is placed directly on the form. Therefore, you need to set each bound control's **DataField** property to the names of a field provided by the class leaving the **DataSource** property blank. The association of the controls to the data provider has to occur when the form is instantiated, as shown next:

```
Private Sub Form_Load()
Set custClass = New clsCustOrder
Dim oText As TextBox
'Bind the text boxes to the data provider
For Each oText In Me.txtFields
    oText.DataMember = "Primary"
    Set oText.DataSource = custClass
Next
End Sub
```

In the preceding code, the **DataMember** property is set to the value of the object added to the **DataMembers** collection in the class's **Initialize** event. Then, each control's **DataSource** property is set equal to a class called **custClass**. In a sense, the class module becomes a reusable Data control—except that it has no visible components. There are no buttons provided to scroll through records and so on—you will have to provide your own navigation techniques.

In the next section, I discuss the **DataReport** object.

The DataReport Object

New to Visual Basic 6 is the **DataReport** object. Although I do not find it as easy to use or as flexible as Crystal Reports (still bundled with Visual Basic), **DataReport** has some advantages. One is that it generates some events for which you can code.

Creating a fairly sophisticated report is as simple as dragging a **Command** object onto it from the DataEnvironment Designer. But you might find it easier to set the object's **DataSource** and **DataMember** properties and then right-click on the report and select "Import Structure." This will cause the **DataReport** to add (or delete) bands to reflect the number of "children" in your **Command** object.

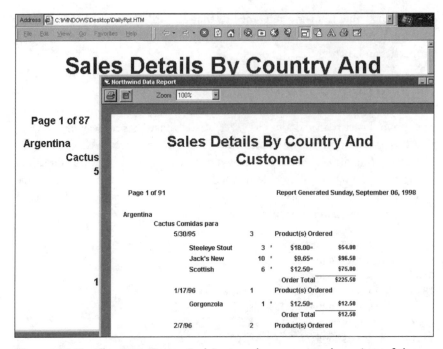

Figure 10.7 The **DataReport** object and an exported version of the report displayed in Internet Explorer.

The most valuable feature of **DataReport** is the **Export** method, which allows you to save the report as text, Unicode text, or HTML. Figure 10.7 shows a somewhat modified version of the sample Northwind report included with Visual Basic. The **DataReport** object is shown in front of Internet Explorer, which is displaying an exported version of the report.

The report generates these events: **Initialize, Terminate, Activate, Deactivate, AsyncProgress, Error, Resize, ProcessingTimeout,** and **QueryClose.** Unfortunately, there are no events generated for page change, band change, and so on. These seem so desirable that I have to believe they will be included in the next version of **DataReport.** Still, using the events available makes building reports on the fly (in code) feasible.

In the next section, I introduce the **Format** object.

The Format Object And Binding Collection

The final database topic in this chapter is the **Format** object, which allows you to format and unformat data between the database and bound controls. For instance, if your database stores the values "F" and "M" for a field called emp_gender, you can use a **Format** object to display "F" and "M" as "Female" and "Male".

To use **Format** objects, you need to add references to the Microsoft Data Formatting Object Library and the Microsoft Data Binding Collection. In code, you need to create a **BindingCollection,** as shown here:

```
Private bc As New BindingCollection
```

You also need to create **Format** objects. The following declares an object to format gender:

```
Private WithEvents fmtGender As StdDataFormat
```

Notice that the object supports events. These allow you to exercise fine control. The events supported are: **Changed, Format,** and **UnFormat.**

In the **Form_Load** event, you should code something like the following:

```
Set bc.DataSource = datPrimaryRS
Set fmtGender = New StdDataFormat
fmtGender.Type = fmtCustom
bc.Add txtGender, "text", "emp_gender", fmtGender
```

In the preceding code, the first line sets the **DataSource** property for **bc** to an Adodc on the form. The next line instantiates the **Format** object. The third line sets its **Type** property to **fmtCustom,** which allows for custom formats. Other options include **fmtBoolean, ftmGeneral, fmtObject,** and **fmtCheckbox.** If you choose **fmtCustom,** you can set the **Format** property to a format string that Visual Basic recognizes, such as "Short Date" or "$###,##0.00". Finally, the last line of code adds an item to the **BindingCollection.** It specifies that the **txtGender** control's **Text** property will be tied to the **emp_gender** field in the database using the **fmtGender** object.

The following example uses the **Format** event of the **fmtGender** object that is triggered anytime the value of **txtGender** changes:

```
Private Sub fmtGender_Format(ByVal DataValue As _
  StdFormat.StdDataValue)
If UCase(DataValue.Value) = "F" Then
  txtGender.Text = "Female"
ElseIf UCase(DataValue.Value) = "M" Then
  txtGender.Text = "Male"
Else
  txtGender.Text = "Unknown"
End If
End Sub
```

The **UnFormat** event occurs immediately before the control's value changes, in case you need to alter the underlying value to a data type that the database can handle. You can also use the **Changed** event if you need to perform any special processing.

Practice Questions

Question 1

> Which controls or objects can you bind to an ADO data source?
> [Check all correct answers]
>
> ❑ a. DataGrid
> ❑ b. Form
> ❑ c. TextBox
> ❑ d. RichTextBox

Answers a, c, and d are correct. The DataGrid, TextBox, and RichTextBox controls can all be bound to an ADO data source. Answer b is incorrect because you cannot bind a form to a data source.

Question 2

> Which of the following controls can act as a data source? [Check all correct answers]
>
> ❑ a. Adodc (ActiveX Data Control)
> ❑ b. Class module
> ❑ c. Standard module
> ❑ d. User control

Answers a, b, and d are correct. Answer a is correct because a Data control is always a data source whether it is DAO, RDO, or ADO. Answer b is correct because class modules can now act as data sources. Answer d is correct because User controls can also now act as data sources. Answer c is incorrect because a standard module cannot act as a data provider.

Question 3

Assume you use a **DataEnvironment** object as a data source. Which of the following are valid methods of displaying data from both the Employee and Department tables?

- ○ a. SQL join
- ○ b. Hierarchical **Command**
- ○ c. Both a and b
- ○ d. Neither a nor b

Answer c is correct. Although hierarchical **Command** objects are more efficient than standard SQL joins, you can still use an SQL join. Answer a is incorrect because an SQL join is not the only method of displaying data from two different tables. Answer b is incorrect for the same reason—a hierarchical **Command** is not the only method of displaying data from two tables. Answer d is incorrect because both a and b are valid.

Question 4

You create a **DataEnvironment** object named **deCustomer**, which displays customer name and address information. You then create a form on which you place an array of TextBox controls. Each TextBox is bound to a field from **deCustomer**. Where can you place code to validate data?

- ○ a. In **deCustomer**
- ○ b. In the form
- ○ c. Both a and b
- ○ d. Neither a nor b

Answer c is correct. You can write code inside of the **DataEnvironment** object or inside the form itself. Although it is a much better practice to encapsulate validation logic to **deCustomer**, there is nothing that precludes you from placing code wherever you want it. Answer a is incorrect because **deCustomer** is not the only place to do validation coding. Answer b is incorrect for the same reason—the form is not the only place where you can place validation coding. Answer d is incorrect because answers c and d are mutually exclusive.

Question 5

> You have a form on which you are displaying data from a class module that is acting as the data source. The user has made some changes to the current record, and you wish to discard those changes so as not to save them to the database. Which of the following techniques might you use to accomplish this?
>
>
>
> ○ a. Use the **CancelUpdate** method
>
> ○ b. Use the **Cancel** method
>
> ○ c. In the **UpdateComplete** event, use the **RollbackTrans** method
>
> ○ d. Set **adStatusCancel** to **True** in the **WillChangeRecord** event of the **Recordset**

Answer a is correct. The **CancelUpdate** method cancels any changes made and discards the record if it is newly added. Answer b is incorrect because the **Cancel** method is used to cancel an asynchronous operation. Answer c is incorrect because there is no **UpdateCancel** method. (Arguably, you can also say that the **RollbackTrans** method merely undoes changes made to the database and does not necessarily discard changes made to the **Recordset** by the user.) Similarly, answer d is incorrect. Setting **adStatusCancel** to **True** does not discard the user's changes—it merely cancels the action that caused the **WillChangeRecord** event to fire. The changes made to the record are still present.

Need To Know More?

 Craig, John Clark and Jeff Webb. *Microsoft Visual Basic 6.0 Developer's Workshop*, Microsoft Press, Redmond, WA, 1998. ISBN 1-57231-883-X. A good intermediate-level VB6 resource. I found this entire volume interesting and educational. The authors take a "How Do I?" approach to explaining various VB techniques. Chapter 15 is a good introduction to file I/O, particularly the new **FileSystemObject**. Chapters 23 and 32 are decent, if brief, introductions to database access and some of the newer VB6 wizards, but the book concentrates on DAO.

 Davis, Harold. *Visual Basic 6 Secrets*, IDG Books Worldwide, Foster City, CA, 1998. ISBN 0-7645-3223-5. Harold has done a nice job with this book. Chapters 31 through 33 provide a good overview of DAO and ADO, the newer VB database-oriented objects, and so on. Chapter 33, in particular, summarizes some more advanced topics, including Visual Modeler and Microsoft Transaction Server (although you should not see either of these subjects on the Desktop exam).

 Holzner, Steven. *Visual Basic 6 Black Book*, The Coriolis Group, Scottsdale, AZ, 1998. ISBN 1-57610-283-1. Steven has written an eminently readable book, and both intermediate- and advanced-level developers will find it to be a good source of information and techniques. Check out Chapter 17, which covers file I/O. Also, turn to Chapters 24 and 25 for a discussion that starts with relatively simple database concepts and progresses to fairly in-depth code techniques using DAO, RDO, and ADO.

 MacDonald, Michael and Kurt Cagle. *Visual Basic 6 Client/Server Programming Gold Book*, The Coriolis Group, Scottsdale, AZ, 1998. ISBN 1-57610-282-3. I always feel funny recommending my own materials, but *Visual Basic 6 Client/Server Programming Gold Book* is the only book I have seen that provides in-depth coverage of some of the materials covered in this chapter. Chapters 2 and 3 are good if you need a primer on SQL and database design. Chapter 11 covers advanced SQL topics, such as the creation and use of stored procedures and triggers. Chapters 5 and 6 are primers on the use of DAO and RDO. Chapter 7 covers the mechanics of ADO and OLE DB, and Chapter 8 details the migration of DAO and RDO applications to ADO.

Chapters 9 and 10 cover advanced ADO and object-oriented techniques, including the creation of local and remote business objects.

 Mandelbrot Set, The. *Advanced Microsoft Visual Basic 6*, Microsoft Press, Redmond, WA, 1998. ISBN 1-57231-893-7. *Advanced Microsoft Visual Basic 6* was due to be printed just as this book was going to press. The VB5 version was superb, and I am sure the VB6 version will be as good.

 Vaughn, William R. *Hitchhiker's Guide To Visual Basic & SQL Server*, Microsoft Press, Redmond, WA, 1998. ISBN 1-57231-848-1. Be sure to get the sixth edition, which covers Visual Basic 6. Bill Vaughn's writings on the use of VB in database applications are always superb. Although the book concentrates on using VB with SQL Server, most of the material is equally applicable to other databases.

 Search the online books on the VB CD-ROM for the term "database". In the VB Concepts Help file, check out the Data Access guide, which includes a number of tutorials. Also, check out the ADO200.CHM, RDO98.CHM, and DAO351.CHM Help files, which are ADO, RDO, and DAO specific. The quality of the VB Help files has slipped through the years, and you will encounter some broken links as well as a few inaccuracies. However, if you have patience, they are still good resources.

 www.microsoft.com/support/ Microsoft places the most current Knowledge Base here. Enter search terms such as "DAO", "RDO", and "ODBC" to view articles that detail tips (and sometimes fixes) that revolve around the use of external modules.

 www.microsoft.com/data/ Check out new ADO developments here.

 http://premium.microsoft.com/msdn/library/ Check out the Microsoft Developer Network online, where there are many articles, book chapters, and updated documentation (as well as links to the Knowledge Base). There is a good article on data access with Visual Basic 6 at **http://premium.microsoft.com/msdn/library/devprods/vs6/vb/html/vbconDataAccessGuide.htm**.

Implementing Online User Assistance

Terms you'll need to understand:

√   User assistance

√   ToolTip help

√   What's This help

√   Help strings

Techniques you'll need to master:

√   Using ToolTip help

√   Using What's This help

√   Using the StatusBar control to display help text

√   Using the CommonDialog control to display help

√   Displaying Windows Help and compiled HTML Help files

√   Adding help to your ActiveX components

Microsoft defines online user assistance to include the traditional Help files, the use of "What's This" and pop-up (ToolTip) help, and the passing of meaningful messages from server components to the user interface. In the requirements for exam 70-176, Microsoft also lists the ability to use HTML help for an application. In this chapter, we'll review each of these concepts. In addition, we'll look at providing a developer-assistance model for your ActiveX components.

Overview Of User Help

When designing your application, you want to think as though you are a first-time user of the program: How do I print that document? How do I save this file? What is the purpose of this button? Visual Basic provides five methods of providing this type of feedback to your users:

➤ ToolTips

➤ What's This help

➤ The StatusBar control

➤ Help files

➤ The CommonDialog control

ToolTips

ToolTips are sometimes known as *balloon help*. When ToolTips are implemented, a small box appears when the user pauses the mouse pointer over a control, toolbar button, and so forth.

ToolTips are easy to implement via the **ToolTipText** property of any control that can receive focus plus the **Form** object (but not the **MDIForm** object). The property is a string value, which should consist of no more than five or six words. It can be updated at design time or at runtime.

If the control has a menu shortcut, it should be included. For example, if the user held the mouse pointer over the Exit button, the ToolTip would state, "Exits the application (Ctrl+Q)".

What's This Help

What's This help displays a box of help text that is more detailed than ToolTips but not as detailed as a Help file. With What's This help, your user invokes the feature by clicking on a toolbar icon or a menu selection. The mouse pointer turns to a question mark and arrow. Then, the user clicks on the control of interest to bring up the pop-up box.

To implement What's This help, you need to enable it at the form level first. You do this by setting the **WhatsThisHelp** property to **True**. You can optionally set the **WhatsThisButton** property to **True**. Doing this causes a What's This icon to appear on the caption. However, if you do this, you must either set the **BorderStyle** property to **3 (Fixed Dialog)**, **2 (Sizable)**, or **1 (Fixed Single)**. You must also set the **MinButton** and **MaxButton** properties to **True** with the **ControlMenu** property also set to **True**. When the user clicks on the What's This button, the form invokes **WhatsThisMode**, which changes the cursor to the What's This pointer.

 You can invoke the **WhatsThisMode** programmatically as *form*.**WhatsThisMode.** You will typically do this from the toolbar or from the Help menu.

Next, each control for which you want to invoke What's This help must have its **WhatsThisHelpID** set to a valid Context ID for your Help file.

If you create a toolbar, you should assign one of the buttons for What's This help. You should also add a selection for What's This help under the Help menu.

Note that Windows 9x and Windows NT applications tend to invoke this feature inconsistently, if at all. For instance, Microsoft Word has only a menu choice. Visual Basic doesn't implement What's This help at all.

The StatusBar Control

You can add a StatusBar control to your application by adding Microsoft Windows Common Controls 6 (COMCTL32.OCX) from the Project|Component menu. The control will then appear on your toolbox. Select it, and place it on the form. You can then use the StatusBar control to display short help text to the user, as I explain next.

Right-click on the control to bring up its Properties dialog box. Select the Panels tab, and use the Insert button to create however many **Panel** objects you need. In Figure 11.1, I have an application that opens two instances of a form. The StatusBar control has three panels. The first two have a **Style** property of **sbrDate** and **sbrTime**, respectively. The third has a **Style** property of **sbrText**. In the **GotFocus** event of each control on the form, I added some code that indicates to the user what each control is used for, as shown in this code snippet:

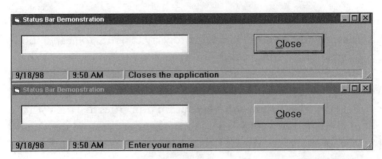

Figure 11.1 Using the StatusBar control to display user help. (On the first form, the command button has focus whereas the text box has focus on the second form.)

```
Private Sub Command1_GotFocus()
StatusBar1.Panels(3).Text = _
  "Closes the application"
End Sub
```

Alternatively, you can use the **MouseMove** event of a control (or form) to update the text on the StatusBar control. (The **MouseMove** event occurs whenever the mouse cursor passes over a control.) Each **Panel** object in the **Panels** collection of the StatusBar control itself has a **ToolTipText** property. The control's **ShowTips** enables or disables the **ToolTips** property of the individual panels.

 Note that in addition to knowing how to use the StatusBar to display information such as the date or simple help text, the exam may query you about the control's event model. The main thing to remember is that there is a **PanelClick** and a **PanelDblClick** event. Each receives a parameter, **ByVal Panel As MSComctlLib.Panel**, with which you can determine which **Panel** object was clicked.

Help Files

The most comprehensive help that you can display is contained in a Help file. When you open a Help file, you need to supply the Help Context ID so that the correct topic is displayed. The **HelpContextID** property of controls contains a string holding a valid Help Context ID. The Help file is specified as a property of the **App** object, as follows:

```
app.HelpFile = "c:\myhelp.hlp"
```

When the **HelpFile** and **HelpContextID** properties are set, Visual Basic launches the Help file whenever the user presses F1.

In the interests of being user friendly, you should think in terms of context-sensitive help. Every object to which a user can tab should have its **HelpContextID** property set.

If a control's **HelpContextID** is set to zero, Visual Basic looks at the control's container. If the container's **HelpContextID** is also set to zero, Visual Basic looks at the container's container (and so on). If a nonzero **HelpContextID** cannot be found, the F1 key is ignored, and help is not presented to the user.

You can present help in either the traditional WinHelp format (with an .HLP file extension) or as compiled HTML (with a .CHM file extension). You can use the HTML Help Workshop to create HTML Help files. Win Help files are compiled from rich text format (RTF) files.

The CommonDialog Control

The CommonDialog control provides a flexible means to present help data to your users. The control has four properties related to the display of help: **HelpContext, HelpCommand, HelpKey,** and **HelpFile.** There is a single method—**ShowHelp**—that interacts with all of these properties. Unfortunately, the CommonDialog control shipped with Visual Basic does not seem to recognize CHM files. Check the Microsoft (MS) Web site (**www.microsoft.com/vbasic/**) to see if MS has released a new version of this ActiveX control that supports the use of compiled HTML Help files.

The **HelpCommand** property of the CommonDialog control dictates in what manner the Help file will be displayed when the **ShowHelp** method is invoked. The property is set to one or more of the constants listed in the Object Browser, such as **cdlHelpContents**, which displays the Contents topic, or **cdlHelpContext**, which displays the help topic associated with the value assigned to the **HelpContext** property. (You cannot use **cdHelpContext** and **cdlHelpContents** together because they are mutually exclusive.) The following code snippet shows the CommonDialog control being used to display the Contents topic:

```
' set the properties
comdlg1.HelpFile = "c:\windows\help\myhelp.hlp"
cmddlg1.HelpCommnd = cldHelpContents
' display the Help file contents topic
cmndlg1.ShowHelp
```

The flip side of providing a user-assistance help model for your running applications is to provide assistance for the developer consumers of your ActiveX components.

Providing Help For Your ActiveX Components

You can provide help for your components through the use of Help files (which can be standard Windows Help files) and compiled HTML files. Additionally, you will want to create Help and Browser strings for the interfaces (events, methods, and properties) of your components to be viewed in the Property window and the Object Browser.

Providing Help Files For Your Components

Specifying a Help file for your component, be it an ActiveX control, EXE, or DLL, is as easy as entering the Help file name into the Help File Name box in the Properties dialog box of the component. You should also supply a Help Context ID that determines the topic to display when the user selects the ? (What's This) button in the Object Browser while your component's type library is being displayed.

Help And Browser Strings For The Component Interfaces

To create the Help string that appears when you select a property in the Property window, open the code window for your component, and on the Tools menu, select Procedure Attributes. In the Procedure Attributes dialog box (shown in Figure 11.2), you can enter a short description. Additionally, you can enter a Help Context ID to provide a topic to jump to when the developer presses F1. Repeat the procedure for all properties, events, and methods that are publicly exposed. (The Help strings for events and methods, as well as for properties, are viewable in the Object Browser.)

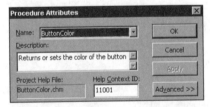

Figure 11.2 The Procedure Attributes dialog box can be used to enter a Help string and Help Context ID.

Help Strings For Objects

To create a Help string for the objects you create, open the Object Browser, select the type library of the component, and right-click on the object. Then, select References. Similar to the Procedure Attributes dialog box procedure in the last section, enter a short Help string as well as a Help Context ID to display when the user presses F1 after selecting the object. Note that you cannot create a Help string for any enumerated values that you create in your component.

Figure 11.3 shows a project in which I have added an ActiveX control that I created. In the Property window, I have selected a property, **ButtonColor**, which I defined to be a public property of the control. At the bottom of the Property window, the Help string that I entered is displayed. In the Object Browser, I have also selected the **ButtonColor** property, and the Help string is displayed at the bottom of the Object Browser window. The mouse pointer is hovering over the user control in the toolbox. The pop-up description is merely the name of the user control.

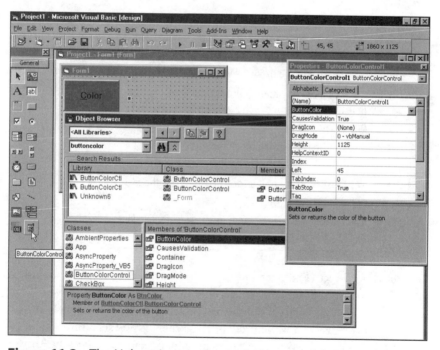

Figure 11.3   The Help strings in the ActiveX control that I created are displayed in the Object Browser and the Property window.

Practice Questions

Question 1

> Which of the following are valid Help file formats? [Check all correct answers]
>
> ❑ a. CHM (compiled HTML)
>
> ❑ b. DHM (compiled DHTML)
>
> ❑ c. HLP (Windows Help)
>
> ❑ d. OHP (OLE Help)

Answers a and c are correct. The valid Help file formats are compiled HTML and Windows Help. Answers b and d are incorrect because there are no such things as DHM and OHP formats.

Question 2

> What is the most significant issue with ToolTip help?
>
> ○ a. Because the **DelayInterval** property is fired synchronously, it can interfere with asynchronous database operations.
>
> ○ b. The ToolTip is the same for all buttons on the Toolbar control.
>
> ○ c. The **Mask** property of the ToolTip can render the text unreadable.
>
> ○ d. You are limited, as a matter of practicality, to how long the ToolTip can be.

Answer d is correct. The question needs to be read carefully. You are asked what the most significant *issue* with ToolTip help is. The only answer listed that is even vaguely accurate is d—the text provided in the ToolTip help should be fairly short. Answer a is incorrect because there is no **DelayInterval** property and the ToolTip does not affect asynchronous operations in any way. Answer b is incorrect because the ToolTip can be unique for all buttons on the toolbar. Answer c is incorrect because there is no **Mask** property for the ToolTip and the ToolTip is not a control.

Question 3

Assume you have a form on which there are a menu and a single Textbox control named **text1**. In the design environment, you set the Textbox control's **ToolTipText** property to "Enter your name". The menu has a menu item named **mnuFileExit**. You have set its **(mnuFileExit) ToolTipText** property to "Ends the application". In the **Form_Load** event, you have the following code:

```
text1.ToolTipHelp = "Enter your mother's name"
mnuFileExit.ToolTipHelp = "Don't you dare!"
```

When the application is run, what will happen when the user moves the mouse pointer over the text box and the menu item?

- O a. The ToolTip help will be changed.
- O b. The ToolTip help for **text1** will be changed but not the ToolTip help for **mnuFileExit**.
- O c. The ToolTip help for **mnuFileExit** will be changed but not the ToolTip help for **text1**.
- O d. None of the above.

Answer d is correct. The code will not run because menus do not have a ToolTipHelp property, and you couldn't have set the property at design time. Answers a, b, and c are incorrect—the code won't run.

Question 4

If you create an ActiveX control, where can you add Help strings that will display in the Property window and Object Browser? [Check all correct answers]

- ❏ a. In the control's **Initialize** event
- ❏ b. In the Procedure Attributes dialog box
- ❏ c. In the Object Browser
- ❏ d. In the control's **PropertyBag** object

Answers b and c are correct. Answer b is correct because you use the Procedure Attributes dialog box to enter Help strings for events, properties, and methods. Answer c is correct because you use the Object Browser to select an object and select Properties to enter its Help string. Answer a is incorrect because you cannot modify Help strings in the **Initialize** event. Answer d is incorrect because you do not use the **PropertyBag** object to maintain Help strings.

Need To Know More?

 Craig, John Clark and Jeff Webb. *Microsoft Visual Basic 6.0 Developer's Workshop*, Microsoft Press, Redmond, WA, 1998. ISBN 1-57231-883-X. A good intermediate-level VB6 resource. I found this whole volume interesting and educational. The authors take a "How Do I?" approach to explaining various VB techniques. Chapter 17 discusses many of the same subjects covered in this chapter. The authors name the chapter "User Assistance," which is a good beginning for a very good chapter. The authors cover the entire user-assistance model without belaboring it and then delve into the techniques of creating a Help file as either Win Help or compiled HTML. The authors point out that the compiled HTML Help Workshop has a wizard to convert your existing Win Help projects to HTML Help. I had somehow overlooked that when I used the tool. (Thanks, John and Jeff!)

 Davis, Harold. *Visual Basic 6 Secrets*, IDG Books Worldwide, Foster City, CA, 1998. ISBN 0-7645-3223-5. Harold has done a nice job with this book though some of the paragraphs listed with "Secrets" icons are fairly common knowledge. Chapter 34 covers Help files, including some information about compiled HTML Help files, and offers some helpful hints.

 In the online books included on the VB CD-ROM (specifically, the VBCON98.CHM file), search on "User Assistance Model". In the Programmer's Guide, look for "Adding Help To Your Application".

 Microsoft places the most current Knowledge Base online at **www.microsoft.com/support/**. Enter search terms such as "HTML Help" and "Win Help" to view articles detailing tips (and sometimes fixes) involving creation of Help files. In the VB section, enter terms such as "User Assistance".

 Check out the Microsoft Developer Network online at **http://premium.microsoft.com/msdn/library/**. There are many articles, book chapters, and updated documentation (as well as links to the Knowledge Base) at **http://premium.microsoft.com/msdn/library/devprods/vs6/vb/**.

Debugging
The Visual
Basic Application

Terms you'll need to understand:

√ Debug

√ Watch window

√ Locals window

√ Immediate window

√ Call Stack window

√ **Assert** method

√ **Debug** object

Techniques you'll need to master:

√ Suspending execution conditionally and absolutely

√ Changing variable values

√ Using the Watch, Locals, Immediate, and Call Stack windows

√ Using the **Print** and **Assert** methods of the **Debug** object

√ Debugging ActiveX components

Few activities are more important and less practiced than thorough debugging. Visual Basic provides a number of tools to make sure your programs run smoothly. Debugging a program in Visual Basic is largely a process of halting execution at appropriate places to see what is going on as your application is running and then taking corrective action. You will find several questions on the certification exam designed to judge your familiarity with exploiting these tools. You will also be expected to demonstrate knowledge of debugging in-process and out-of-process ActiveX components. Debugging and testing are the topics of this chapter on your road to VB certification.

Visual Basic Environment Modes

When in the design environment, you will always be in one of three modes:

➤ **Design** This is the mode where you draw forms, write code, and so on.

➤ **Run** This is the mode you will be in when your application is running within the environment. Most menu and toolbar items are unavailable.

➤ **Break** This is the mode you are in where you have suspended program execution. Many menu and toolbar items are not available, but the Debug menu and toolbar items as well as the Locals window, Immediate window, and so on become available.

The current mode is always displayed on the Visual Basic Caption bar. For example, in run mode, the caption might read *Project 1 - Microsoft Visual Basic: [run]*. Interactive debugging (debugging while the program is running) is done in break mode. Other types of debugging, such as using the **Debug** object, is done in run mode. In the next section, I discuss the interactive debugging tools available in Visual Basic 6.

The Debug Toolbar

Visual Basic provides a good selection of debugging aids under the Debug menu and makes them conveniently available on the Debug toolbar. If the toolbar does not show in your IDE, right-click in the toolbar area, and select Debug. The Debug toolbar is shown in Figure 12.1.

The debugging commands are shown below:

➤ **Breakpoint (F9)** This may well be the most useful debugging feature. By placing your cursor on a line of code and clicking on the toolbar, the breakpoint is toggled on or off. When the breakpoint is toggled on, the program automatically stops immediately *before* executing that line.

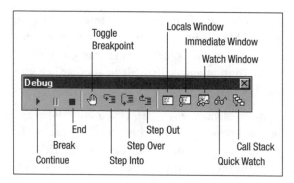

Figure 12.1   The Visual Basic Debug toolbar.

➤ **Step Into (F8)** This executes the next line of code and then pauses execution, even if that line of code is in another procedure.

➤ **Step Over (Shift+F8)** This executes the next line of code but does not enter other procedures. This means that other procedures are executed in their entirety as though each was one line of code.

➤ **Step Out (Ctl+Shift+F8)** This is an underused option that will cause all remaining lines in a procedure to be executed and pause execution on the next line of the calling procedure.

➤ **Run To Cursor (Ctl+F8)** This is not on the toolbar. It causes execution to continue up to the line where the cursor is placed.

➤ **Set Next Statement (Shift+F9)** This is also not on the toolbar. It allows you to place your cursor on a line of code and press Shift+F9 to specify the next line of code to execute.

➤ **Show Next Statement** This is available only under the Debug menu. As its name implies, it shows you which statement will execute next. (Normally, the next line of code is already highlighted in break mode. The color of the highlight is determined by the background color defined for Execution Point Text on the Editor Format tab of the Options dialog box.) The other buttons are covered in the next several sections.

The Debugging Process

You can set a breakpoint on any executable line of code. Executable lines of code include procedure declaration statements (including **End Sub** or **End Function**) but do not include variable declarations or comments. You can also press Ctrl+Pause at any time to suspend execution.

Visual Basic even allows you to alter many (but not all) statements while the program is running. The most notable exceptions to this are declarative statements. Adding or modifying a declaration often causes VB to restart the program from the beginning. Annoyingly, continuing a statement to another line also causes VB to restart the application.

Many program bugs come from problematic variables. If you knew what the values of your variables were at all times, you would not need to debug. In Chapter 8, I give you many pointers on preventing syntax errors and handling runtime errors. However, except for those of us who are perfect (such as myself), logic errors are a fact of life in programming.

Let's assume you are dividing values and get our "division by zero" friend as an error message. There are a number of tactics you can employ to determine where that nasty zero in the divisor is coming from. Namely, you can use the Watch, Locals, Immediate, and Call Stack windows, as I outline in the following sections.

The Watch Window

A topic you are sure to see on your exam is the Watch window, shown in Figure 12.2. You can add a watch on any variable or expression, which will cause a break (suspend program execution) when the expression is true or when the value changes. You can simply "watch" the variable. In all cases, VB continually displays the value of the variable (or expression). In Figure 12.2, an expression is set to break when the expression **dDivisor = 0** evaluates to true. While the program is executing, but suspended, you can click on the current value to change it, or click on the watch expression to edit it. Right-clicking on the Watch window allows you to add, edit, or delete a watch. Note that variable values are not available while "out of scope." Thus, if you are "watching" a variable defined in one procedure, it is not available while another procedure is being executed.

 The exam will query your knowledge of setting watches. You should be particularly familiar with the Add Watch (Edit Watch) window's Procedure and Module Context options. These control from where a variable's value will be visible *in the Watch window*.

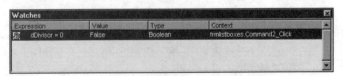

Figure 12.2 The Visual Basic Watch window.

Setting Watch Points

You can set specific watch points so that program execution breaks when a certain condition is true. The item being watched can be a variable or an expression.

The easiest way to add a watch is to highlight a variable and then select Add Watch. The Add Watch dialog box opens. You can then specify a watch type: Watch expression (in other words, monitor the value of the variable but take no action), break when the value is true, or break when the value is false. It is here that you can also alter the scope of the watch condition.

Breaking execution when a certain criterion is met is called *conditional breaking* as opposed to setting a breakpoint on a line of code, which is called *absolute breaking*.

The Locals Window

The Locals window is a built-in version of the Watch window. While stepping through code, you can select View|Locals Window at any time. A Watch window named Locals will be displayed containing all *in scope* variables (that is, all variables that are visible from the procedure currently being executed). Figure 12.3 shows the Locals window for a database application. All variables currently in scope are listed. In Figure 12.3, I have expanded **Me** (the form) to show all of its attributes, which include any form-level variables. In the figure, I drilled down to a **RecordSet** and to one of the **Field** objects.

 Be sure to understand the Locals window, especially the concept of variable scope.

The Immediate Window

In the Immediate window, you can type any valid Visual Basic line of code, but you cannot declare a new variable or object. The code is always executed in the context of the current procedure. This means that any statement behaves as though it is part of the code of the current procedure. Thus, if you alter a variable, the most locally defined version of that variable is the one that is operated on.

To print to the Immediate window, you can use the **Print** method of the **Debug** object or you can type **Print** methods directly into the window. Output from the **Debug** object is sent to the Immediate window without breaking execution and without disturbing the application's display space. Figure 12.4

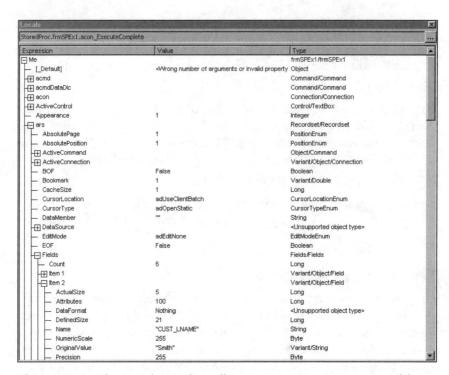

Figure 12.3 The Locals window allows you to examine any variable currently in scope, including objects.

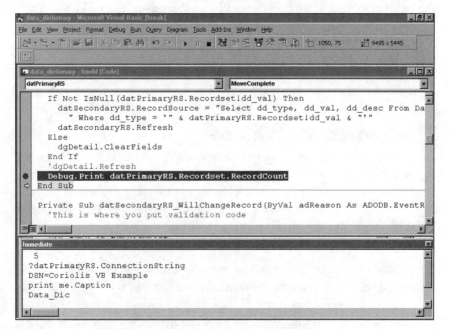

Figure 12.4 The Immediate window in Visual Basic.

shows the results immediately after a **Debug.Print** statement (I printed the record count for an ADO record set). I also used the **Print** method to display a **ConnectionString** property and the **Caption** property of the form. In the first example, I used the **?** shorthand for **Print**.

The Immediate window also allows you to call other procedures but only if doing so would be valid within the current procedure.

 The Immediate window, available since Visual Basic 1 (and back to its QuickBasic predecessors), has been intended to primarily be a debug-time tool. However, starting with VB5, it can also be used at design time to support ActiveX development.

The Call Stack Window

The Call Stack window is a useful, if imperfect, tool. It displays the name of all procedures executed, each preceded by the name of the object to which it belongs (such as, **frmTest.command1_Click**). This can be helpful when you are trying to follow complicated nested procedure calls. Unfortunately, if you have multiple occurrences of a given object, you cannot distinguish one from another.

The Debug Object

Debug is a Visual Basic object provided to support development. Statements referencing the **Debug** object are automatically stripped out of code when an EXE file is created. It has two methods: **Print** and **Assert**.

We have already seen the **Print** method in action earlier in this chapter. Its output always goes to the Immediate window.

Assert allows the developer to conditionally halt execution when the **Assert** line is encountered. The syntax takes the form **Debug.Assert** *expression*, where *expression* must evaluate to a **Boolean** (such as, **True** or **False**). Execution halts (and the **Debug.Assert** line is highlighted) when the expression is false. What you are doing is *asserting* that a statement is true and then having the program tell you if you are wrong. Assume you want to make the assertion that there are more than zero **Field** objects in a **RecordSet**. You might code the following:

```
Debug.Assert ars.Fields.Count > 0
```

In this example, if there are zero **Field** objects in **ars**, then program execution halts on this line of code (the line is not actually executed).

Debugging ActiveX Components

Debugging ActiveX components is only a little trickier than debugging standard EXE projects. For debugging purposes, there are two types of ActiveX components—out-of-process and in-process. (ActiveX components are discussed in Chapter 7.) If the ActiveX component runs as a separate process, it needs to be debugged separately from the project that uses it. In other words, if you create an ActiveX server and compile it so that it can be used by a standard EXE project, its code base is not part of the standard EXE and cannot be debugged from within the standard EXE.

The Visual Basic exam reflects the importance of component development and use by querying your ActiveX component knowledge, including its debugging.

Debugging The Out-Of-Process Component

To use an out-of-process ActiveX component in your project, you make a reference to it (see Chapter 7). Thus, it must first be compiled. It is the compiled code, of course, that is actually executed. To ensure that the code in the ActiveX component matches the compiled code being run by the calling application, you should set your breakpoints (and so on) in the ActiveX component and then run it using the Start With Full Compile option.

When you create an ActiveX component, a Type library is generated. When you add a reference to an ActiveX component, Visual Basic looks at the Type library to see what methods, properties, and events are available. If you do not recompile your component after making changes, the Type library cannot contain references to the added (or deleted) functionality.

Next, you will need to create a second instance of Visual Basic in which to run the test project that is using the out-of-process ActiveX component. As mentioned earlier, the out-of-process component should be started first. When you run the test project and reference the ActiveX component, the component's code will begin execution. You can then test as normal. Visual Basic will normally switch between the two projects as needed.

When you set a breakpoint in the out-of-process component and run the test project, if the component goes into break mode, the test project will receive a *Server Busy* message if it makes a reference to the component. You can then select the Switch To button to switch focus to the component.

Debugging With Multiple Clients

An ActiveX EXE project can support multiple clients. Sometimes, a problem might occur only when there is more than one client. In this case, you have two options to debug the component. The first is to run multiple instances of the development environment with the first being the out-of-process ActiveX EXE, and the second and subsequent instances being test projects. This is the easiest way to debug, but it could be taxing on your PC's resources when running the clients and server on the same machine. The second option is to modify the test project to simulate multiple clients by creating multiple connections to the server.

Debugging The In-Process Component

The in-process component runs in the same memory space as the calling application and so requires a different debugging strategy than does the out-of-process component. Like the out-of-process component, the in-process component needs to be compiled before debugging. This is because the test project needs to create a reference to it (in the case of the ActiveX DLL) or add it as a component (in the case of the ActiveX control).

After the component has been compiled, add the project to your test project. The test project will then be a project group. Run the project using the Start With Full Compile option to ensure that the test project uses the latest version of the component's code base. You can then debug as normal. Visual Basic will step from one project to the other as needed. You can set breakpoints, watch expressions, and so on in the test project and in any in-process component(s).

The component's code will not execute until it is first referenced by the test project.

Debugging In-Process And Out-Of-Process Components Together

Your project might use both in-process and out-of-process components at the same time. If so, you can debug the in-process components as described earlier, adding them to your project. Open an instance of Visual Basic for each out-of-process component being tested and execute each with a full compile. When all are running, start execution of your test project, remembering to first do a full compile there also.

ActiveX Documents

An ActiveX document can be created as either an in-process or out-of-process component. The process for debugging an ActiveX document is generally the same as for processing any non-ActiveX project with some additional caveats.

To test, run the project. A temporary VBD file is created. Switch to Internet Explorer (IE), navigate to the VBD file, and load it. (Normally, Visual Basic will launch IE and load the document for you.) You can then proceed with debugging as normal. Note that you do not need to create a sec-ond Visual Basic instance even if the project is an out-of-process component.

You should not halt execution of your test project within the Visual Basic en-vironment while the document is being displayed in IE. You should first make sure the document reference is released by IE. The VB Help file describes procedures for doing so without shutting down IE3 (by navigating to four other documents to clear IE's cache) but the simplest procedure is to simply shut down IE. You should be able to simply navigate to another document in IE4 and above. If you halt the project from within VB, an application error will result in IE.

After IE has been shut down (or references to the document have been cleared), you can then end the project in VB. Make changes as needed, recompile, run the project, and then use IE to display it.

Practice Questions

Question 1

Your project's Startup Object is **Sub Main**, which is in **Module1**. **Module1** looks like this:

```
Option Explicit


Private myVar As Integer


Sub main()


myVar = 18
Form1.Show


End Sub
```

Form1 has a single CommandButton, **Command1**. **Form1**'s code looks like this:

```
Option Explicit


Private Sub Command1_Click()
Dim myVar As Integer
myVar = 1


End Sub
```

You set breakpoints on the two **End Sub** statements (at the end of **Sub Main** and at the end of **Command1_Click**). When the program breaks the first time, you add a watch on **MyVar** and specify a context of All Procedures and All Modules. You then press the Continue button. While the program is running, you click **Command1**. What is the value of **myVar** displayed when the program breaks a second time?

○ a. 18

○ b. 1

○ c. The local **myVar** will have a value of 1 whereas the global **myVar** will have a value of 18.

○ d. **me.myVar** will have a value of 1 whereas **Module1.myVar** will have a value of 18.

○ e. <out of context>

The correct answer is a. Even though the variable was declared as **Private,** it is visible in the Watch window because you specified a context of All Modules. Answer b is incorrect because the local **myVar** is not listed—the global **myVar** is. Answers c and d are incorrect because only one value is listed in the Watch window. Answer d is incorrect because the watch context does not speak to scope; it speaks to when to monitor variable values. The question is tricky. Some developers will choose b or e reasoning that either VB will use the most local version of the variable or that, because **myVar** had been defined as **Private,** it would not be visible from within **Form1.** Strictly speaking, **Form1** is *not* aware of the value of the privately declared **myVar.** However, the debugging tools are. If you had set a watch on the local **myVar,** you could still monitor its values from other procedures and modules by changing the Watch window's context settings.

Question 2

You are working on a Standard EXE type of project. Assume that **clsTest** is a class module in your current project. Its code looks like this:

```
Option Explicit
Public sTest As String

Private Sub Class_Initialize()
sTest = "Hello World"
End Sub
```

Assume that **Form1** is the startup module in your project and that its code looks like the following:

```
Option Explicit
Private clsTestShow As Object
Dim iTestDim As Integer
Private Sub Form_Load()
Set clsTestShow = New clsTest
End Sub
Public Sub TestDebug()
Dim iCtr As Integer
End Sub
```

Finally, assume that you are debugging the project and set a breakpoint on the **Set clsTestShow = New clsTest** statement in the **Form_Load** event. You run the project until the breakpoint is encountered. In break mode, you open the Locals window. Which of the following variables is visible in the window? [Check all correct answers]

❑ a. **iCtr**

❑ b. **iTestDim**

❑ c. **clsTestShow.sTest**

❑ d. **clsTestShow**

The correct answers are b and d. The Locals window shows only those variables currently in scope. The question is a bit tricky because you need to remember that when Visual Basic encounters a break point, it halts execution immediately *before* that line of code executes. In this case, the **Set** statement has not yet run when VB goes into break mode. There is no instance of the class yet created, so the publicly viewable variable **sTest** has not been created.

iTestDim, answer b, is viewable because it has **Private** scope (even though it is declared with the **Dim** keyword). **clsTestShow** is also visible because it was declared as having **Private** scope though the value is actually **Nothing**. Note that even if I had declared the variable to be of type **clsTest**, it would still have a value of **Nothing**. Because this is not an ActiveX project, there is no available **Instancing** property, rendering the question of whether it is automatically created moot. It is not created until the **New** keyword is encountered. Answer a is incorrect because the variable **iCtr** is local to the **TestDebug** event procedure. It is not visible to the **Form_Load** event procedure. Answer c is incorrect because **clsTestShow** does not yet exist.

Question 3

The following event procedure is attached to a command button cleverly named **Command1**:

```
Private Sub Command1_Click()
Dim iCtr As Integer
For iCtr = 0 To 1
   iCtr = Not iCtr
Next
Debug.Assert iCtr = 1
End
End Sub
```

You execute the project by selecting Run from the toolbar. After you click on the command button, when does the program stop running or go into break mode?

- O a. When the **End** statement is encountered
- O b. When the **Debug.Assert** statement is encountered
- O c. When a Stack Fault error occurs
- O d. Never

The correct answer is d because the program goes into an endless loop. The first time that the **For** loop is executed, the variable **iCtr** has a value of 0. The **Not** statement changes the variable to -1. The variable ends up alternating between values of 0 and -1 with no chance to leave the loop, and so the program never stops running. Answers a and b are incorrect because the **End** and **Debug.Assert** statements are never executed. Answer c is incorrect because there are no stack space consequences of an endless loop. (The more likely place where you could run out of stack space would be in a procedure called recursively.)

Question 4

> You are working on an ActiveX document DLL project. All the code in the document is shown as follows:
>
> ```
> Option Explicit
> Private iEmpID As Integer
> Private Sub Form_Load()
> iEmpID = 33
> iEmpID = iEmpID - 1
> End Sub
> ```
>
> You set a breakpoint on the line of code that subtracts one from the employee ID. You then run the project and open the resulting VBD file in IE4. What happens?
>
> ○ a. The project runs just fine.
>
> ○ b. An error occurs.
>
> ○ c. The project runs but does not break when the subtraction is executed.
>
> ○ d. None of the above.

The correct answer is a. The project runs just fine, but it doesn't do a thing! The trick here is the reference to the **Form_Load** event procedure. You might jump to the conclusion that because an ActiveX document project cannot include a form, an error will occur. It doesn't. VB treats the procedure like any general procedure—it just happens to be named **Form_Load**. Because you don't call the procedure, it never executes. Sometimes you can get a hint to the correct answer by reading the question carefully. The question stated that *all* the code in the project was shown. When you see words like "all", your exam antennae should go up. Answer b is incorrect because there are no errors in the code. In particular, **Form_Load** is a valid procedure name even though there are no forms in the project (ActiveX document projects do not contain forms—they contain **UserDocuments; UserDocuments** do not have a **Load** event). Because the procedure is never executed and no code is ever executed (except the creation of the one private variable), there can't be an error. Answer c is incorrect also. The breakpoint is not encountered because that line of code is never executed. Answer d is incorrect because a valid answer is provided.

Need To Know More?

Craig, John Clark and Jeff Webb. *Microsoft Visual Basic 6.0 Developer's Workshop*, Microsoft Press, Redmond, WA, 1998. ISBN 1-57231-883-X. A good intermediate-level VB6 resource. I found this whole volume interesting and educational. The authors take a "How Do I?" approach to explaining various VB techniques. Chapter 26 ends with an interesting application of conditional compilation and compiler directives for debugging support. Chapter 27 provides some good guidance for debugging remote applications beginning on page 496. Chapters 6 and 7, which cover ActiveX components and Internet components, both take the time to discuss special debugging issues as well.

Davis, Harold. *Visual Basic 6 Secrets*, IDG Books Worldwide, Foster City, CA, 1998. ISBN 0-7645-3223-5. Harold has done a nice job with this book though some of the paragraphs listed with "Secrets" icons are fairly common knowledge. Chapter 15 covers both error handling and debugging. I was pleased to see that Harold is evidently an old-timer as he spends a few paragraphs discussing the brute-force debugging method of inserting message boxes at various places in code. While you won't see the technique on the exam, brute-force methods often end up being the most effective.

Holzner, Steven. *Visual Basic 6 Black Book*, Coriolis Group Books, Scottsdale, AZ, 1998. ISBN 1-57610-283-1. Steven has written an eminently readable book that both intermediate- and advanced-level developers will find to be a good source of information and techniques. Even more, the whole line of Black Books just plain looks slick. Steven does a nice job of covering error handling and debugging in Chapter 29.

Search the online books on the VB CD-ROM for the term "debug". There are a couple of good tutorials on the debugging process in general as well as the use of the **Debug** object and **Assert** procedures in general.

Check out also the Microsoft Developer Network online at **http://premium.microsoft.com/msdn/library/**, where there are many articles, book chapters, and updated documentation (as well as links to the Knowledge Base).

Compiling With Visual Basic 6

13

Terms you'll need to understand:

√ Pseudo-code

√ Machine-code

√ ActiveX EXE, ActiveX DLL, and ActiveX control

√ Project and group

√ Runtime engine

√ Conditional compilation

Techniques you'll need to master:

√ Compiling a project to different target types

√ Choosing appropriate optimizations

√ Using conditional compilation

Visual Basic 6 features an efficient, optimizing compiler. In this chapter, we will discuss various compilation issues.

The P-Word Vs. The M-Word

I don't agree with those who say that a language is not "professional" if it compiles programs into *pseudo-code*. Visual C, for instance, offers that as an option. Pseudo-code is not true *machine language* (those bits and bytes that the computer and the operating system understand), but it's a highly tokenized code that requires the presence of a runtime helper to assist in its interpretation.

Indeed, the loading of a runtime interpreter makes the program run somewhat slower. However, not all is as it seems on the surface. First, even our pseudo-code (usually referred to as *p-code*) programs contain a large amount of fully compiled code. Simple arithmetic operations tend to be fully compiled, while floating-point operations tend to depend on the runtime engine. Much more significant is the fact that modern client/server programs tend to spend most of their time either "idling" while waiting for user input or performing database operations. Compilation does not make the program idle any faster. The speed of database operations is almost fully dependent on the database itself and the connection engine (such as ADO and OLE DB).

Programs that perform many CPU-intensive number calculations will benefit the most from *native code*, which is code that the computer and operating system understand without the use of an intervening runtime engine. Programs that perform a lot of string manipulation or calls to the Windows API will not see much of a performance enhancement. The advantage of p-code is a smaller EXE file but at the trade-off of slower performance. A native-code EXE still requires the Visual Basic runtime engine, MSVBVM60.DLL, but makes many fewer (and often more efficient) calls to the DLL.

 Experienced programmers will debug their programs while compiling to p-code and do their final testing while compiling to native code, because it takes longer to compile to native code.

Compilation Basics (No Pun Intended)

The Visual Basic 6 compiler's technology is shared with that of Microsoft Visual C++ and is very efficient indeed. It is capable of producing *native code*.

Native code applications should still ship with MSVBVM60.DLL even though it is not longer used as a runtime interpreter. It is used, instead, as a true dynamic link library.

Visual Basic 6 supports only 32-bit executables (Windows 95/98 and Windows NT). Programs generated with Visual Basic 6 will *not* run under Windows 3.x.

The compiler assembles the various Visual Basic modules into an executable program. These modules collectively make up the project, a topic I discuss next.

Projects

A Visual Basic *project* is a collection of modules (form, class, and standard—see Chapter 3 for more information) grouped together in what is similar to a C++ *make file*. Every project requires a startup object, but there can be only one **Sub Main**.

Project names for ActiveX components have to be unique because they are stored in the Windows Registry as well as in the Object Browser. The project name is also used as a qualifier to describe classes within the project. The project name coupled with the class name (*project_name.class_name*) is the *programmatic ID* of the class. The name can contain no embedded spaces.

To set the properties of your project, select Project|*project* Properties (where *project* is the name of your project). I discuss the usage of the dialog box in the following sections.

The General Tab

You set various options in the General tab, as shown in Figure 13.1. Project Type can be a Standard EXE or an ActiveX EXE, ActiveX DLL, or ActiveX control.

The Help File Name and default Project Help Context ID are placed on this screen. The project description is entered as free-form text. When you create an ActiveX component, the description you enter is listed in the References or Components dialog box on the Project menu. There is a checkbox that allows or disallows ActiveX controls to be upgraded for this project. If you are creating an ActiveX control, you can also check Require License Key. If you select this, the user of the control must have the control registered in the Registry along with a copy of the VBL (Visual Basic License) file that is produced when the project is built. If you are creating a multithreaded application, additional choices allow you to select Unattended Operation, and to choose between one thread and a definable number of threads per object. (See Chapter 7 for more information.)

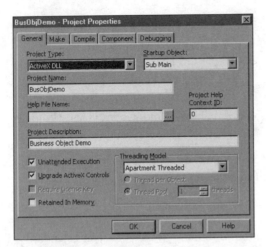

Figure 13.1 The General tab of the Project Properties dialog box for setting compile options.

The Make Tab

The Make tab of the Project Properties dialog box is shown in Figure 13.2. Here, you can set options that mostly reflect version information. You can set major, minor, and revision version numbers. Typically, a revision indicates bug fix releases (and possibly aesthetic changes). Minor releases are most typically functionality enhancements, whereas major releases denote releases with significant new functionality. When you are beta testing a project, the revision number is often used to denote the *build* (compile) number. There is a checkbox to auto-increment this number.

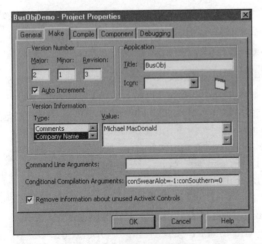

Figure 13.2 The Make tab of the Project Properties dialog box for compile options.

You can choose the icon that represents your EXE in its minimized state as well as within Windows Explorer. The Title field enables you to specify the name of the final executable file. It defaults to the project name, but you can specify a different name here. You can place text, such as comments, copyright, and other legal information, directly into your EXE.

The Command Line Arguments text box allows you to add some compilation switches, which are discussed in the "Compiling Your VB Application" section later in this chapter. The Conditional Compilation Arguments allows you to specify the value of conditional compilation arguments, which I discuss in the "Conditional Compilation" section at the end of this chapter.

The Compile Tab

The Compile tab (shown in Figure 13.3) is where you set your compilation options. Here, you choose between compilation to p-code or native code. If you choose native code, you can fine-tune optimizations. For the most part, you will want to optimize for speed. You can alternatively choose to optimize for space (minimize the size of the EXE or DLL file) or choose no optimization. The Optimize For Small Code option causes the compiler to *compact* a program by creating pointers to similar sequences of code, in a manner similar to how PKZip compacts files. This slows execution somewhat and is seldom beneficial. If your program will be running only on Pentium Pro processors, you may wish to select Favor Pentium Pros, which generates instruction sets optimized for the Pro. The Create Symbolic Debug Info checkbox allows the embedding of debugging information into the file, which can be used by many third-party debugging tools (such as Microsoft Visual C++ and Code View). If you are generating a DLL, you can specify the starting address, which the operating system will attempt to use.

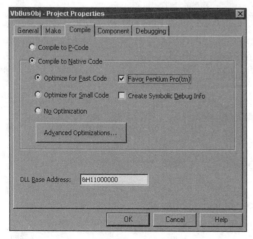

Figure 13.3 The Compile tab provides compilation options.

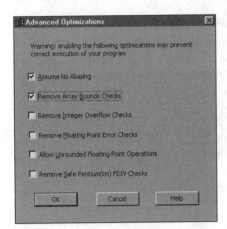

Figure 13.4   The Advanced Optimizations dialog box allows you to further refine compilation options.

The Advanced Optimizations Dialog Box

You can further fine-tune your compile with the Advanced Optimizations dialog box, shown in Figure 13.4, by selecting the Advanced Optimizations button. Be sure you know what you are doing before selecting any of these options, because program performance or reliability can be adversely affected. On the other hand, you might achieve better performance. For instance, the Remove Safe Pentium(tm) FDIV Checks option omits checks for the infamous division errors on very old Pentiums. This is overhead that is seldom needed, because there are relatively few of those CPUs and the actual number of errors was not large (and the sequence needed to create the errors is not likely to appear in most business applications). The Advanced Optimization options are as follows:

➤ **Assume No Aliasing** Specifies that the application does not use aliases. Allows optimization of string storage and certain loops. *Aliasing* means using a different name when passing a value from one procedure to another. Normally, you will leave this off.

➤ **Remove Array Bounds Checks** Tells VB not to perform array boundary checking. If there is no chance that you will exceed an array boundary, turn this on.

➤ **Remove Integer Overflow Checks** Disables Visual Basic integer overflow checking.

➤ **Remove Floating Point Error Checks** Improves speed somewhat by removing checks that **Single** and **Double** variables are within range.

➤ **Allow Unrounded Floating Point Operations** Allows the compiler to not round floating-point operations. Ironically, while this can increase accuracy, it can also adversely affect results due to potential comparison errors. The results will usually be subtle. Be sure to experiment.

➤ **Remove Save Pentium(tm) FDIV Checks** This option removes math-error checks due to the infamous floating-point division bug in old Pentium chips. Because few machines still have those old Pentium chips (they were all 60 and 66MHz) and because the error was unusual to begin with, you can normally set this option on to realize a slight performance boost.

The Component Tab

The Component tab (see Figure 13.5) is for ActiveX server applications and allows you to designate the Start Mode as standalone or as an ActiveX component. If the project is to be compiled into a standalone executable file (see "The General Tab" section earlier in this chapter), these options will be unavailable. I altered the project to be an ActiveX EXE so that the options could be seen in the figure. I discuss these options in Chapter 7.

After all of your project properties are set, you can proceed with compilation.

Compiling Your VB Application

To compile your application, select File|Make *project*.EXE (or *project*.DLL), where *project* is the name of your project. There are a number of optional arguments you can provide that are entered on the Project Build dialog

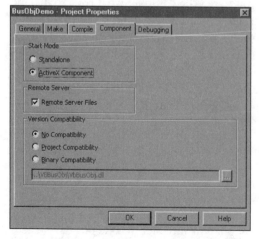

Figure 13.5 The Component tab allows you to set various options relating to ActiveX components.

Table 13.1 Other native code compilation switches.	
Switch	**Meaning**
/run or /r	Compiles and runs projectname.
/MAKE or /m	Compiles projectname to an executable (EXE) file.
/MAKEDLL or /l	Compiles projectname to an in-process ActiveX DLL.
/d or /D	Specifies to use conditional compilation constants.
compileconst	Provides the names and values of conditional compilation constants.
/cmd or /c	Places command-line arguments into the Make tab of Project Properties.
/?	Lists the available command-line arguments.

box, as summarized in Table 13.1. You can also compile from the command line, using

```
VB6 /MAKE | MAKEDLL projectname [/d compileconst]...
```

where *projectname* is the name of the project to compile to an EXE or DLL. You can specify other command line arguments, as on the Project Build page and summarized in Table 13.1.

In the next section, I discuss the Visual Basic runtime engine.

Conditional Compilation

Conditional compilation allows you to tell the compiler what code to include or not include depending on certain environmental conditions. Figure 13.2 (shown earlier in this chapter) shows you the Make tab, which is used for compilation. The Make tab defines the value of two conditional compilation variables: **conSwearAlot** and **conSouthern**. The first, **conSwearAlot**, was set to -1, while the second, **conSouthern**, was set to 0. When you are creating conditional compilation variables, their values should be set to -1 for true and 0 for false.

You can also set conditional compilation variables on the command line, as follows:

```
vb6.exe /make BusObjDemo.vbp /d conSwearAlot=-1:conSouthern=0
```

Finally, you can set conditional compilation variables in code preceding them with a pound sign (#), like this:

```
#conSwearAlot = -1
#conSouthern = 0
```

Conditional compilation variables set on the command line or in the Make dialog box are public in scope—they affect all modules in the project. Variables set in code are private in scope and affect only the module in which they appear.

To use the conditional compilation variables, use the **#IF...THEN #ELSE** directive. The pound signs tell the compiler that it should evaluate the statements. Consider the following code snippet:

```
#If conSouthern Then
   MsgBox "Hello y'all"
#Else
   MsgBox "Hello World"
#End If
```

The **#IF** statement determines whether to include the "Hello World" or "Hello y'all" messages in the final executable. For the second example, **#conSouthern** has a value of 0, so the "Hello World" message will be placed in the code and the other message will be stripped out of the executable.

Conditional compilation is usually used in portability issues. For instance, you might compile a different version for NT than for Windows 9x. You can compile different versions based on language. VB provides the built-in **Win32** constant, which evaluates to **True** on Windows 9x and NT but is of limited usefulness because VB apps deploy only to 32-bit platforms. **Win16** evaluates to **True** for Windows 3.x.

Practice Questions

Question 1

Which of the following are valid project types in the Project Properties dialog box? [Check all correct answers]

- ❏ a. ActiveX DLL
- ❏ b. ActiveX document
- ❏ c. ActiveX EXE
- ❏ d. ActiveX control

Answers a, c, and d are correct. Visual Basic supports the creation of standard EXEs, ActiveX EXEs, ActiveX DLLs, and ActiveX controls. Answer b is incorrect because an ActiveX document is not a project type—you would choose either ActiveX EXE or ActiveX DLL to create an in-process or out-of-process ActiveX document.

Question 2

Which of the following compilation optimization options are mutually exclusive?

- ○ a. Optimize for speed, and create symbolic debug information
- ○ b. No optimization, and create symbolic debug information
- ○ c. Remove floating-point error checks, and allow unrounded floating-point operations
- ○ d. None of the above

Answer d is correct because none of the choices is correct. The only optimization options that are mutually exclusive are optimize for size, optimize for speed, and no optimization. Answer a is incorrect because you can both optimize for speed and create symbolic debug information. Answer b is incorrect because you can choose not to optimize the code base for either speed or size and still create symbolic debug information. Answer c is incorrect because you can remove floating-point error checks while still allowing unrounded floating-point operations.

Question 3

> Which of the following methods are valid to deliver a localized version of an application? [Check all correct answers]
>
> ❑ a. Use conditional compilation with variables, such as **#conCanadian**.
>
> ❑ b. Format output using code like **Format$ (dateToday, "Long Date")**.
>
> ❑ c. Set the intrinsic **#Locale** constant to a value, such as **vbGeneral, vbArabic, vbHebrew**, and so on.
>
> ❑ d. Subclass **Format** objects, overriding the **DataDate** property, **DataCurrency** property, and so on, as required.

The correct answers are a and b. Answer a is correct because you can use conditional compilation with conditional compilation constants to have the compiler include or not include blocks of code. Answer b is also correct because you can use the **Format** function with named arguments (such as **Short Date**), which use settings from the Control Panel to determine how to display data. Answer c is incorrect because there is no intrinsic **#Locale** constant. Answer d is incorrect because, even if you could figure out a way to subclass the **Format** object, **DataDate, DataCurrency**, and so on are not valid properties.

Question 4

> How do you add copyright information to your program's executable code?
>
> ○ a. Add a Splash module to your code setting **TillRegistered = True**. Add the appropriate copyright warning message.
>
> ○ b. Use the Legal Copyright text on the Make tab in the Project Properties dialog box.
>
> ○ c. Submit the code to the appropriate local Microsoft office for verification. The office will also register the copyright.
>
> ○ d. Use a binary editor, and add the copyright information to the executable file, as appropriate.

The correct answer is b. The Make tab on the Project Properties dialog box allows you to enter a number of different comments into the executable file, including Legal Copyright. Answer a is incorrect because there is no such thing as a Splash module nor is **TillRegistered** a valid property. Answer c is incorrect because Microsoft has no copyright verification or registration services. Answer d is incorrect because you should never use an editor to change an executable file.

Need To Know More?

The nature of the subject of this chapter—compiling Visual Basic applications—is such that books don't tend to spend a lot of time discussing the subject. Still, the following resources may be helpful.

 Davis, Harold. *Visual Basic 6 Secrets*, IDG Books Worldwide, Foster City, CA, 1998. ISBN 0-7645-3223-5. Harold has done a nice job with this book, though some of the paragraphs listed with "Secrets" icons are fairly common knowledge. Chapter 2 discusses compilation of VB programs. Some aspects of compilation options are discussed in other chapters, primarily in the discussion of creating ActiveX components.

 Holzner, Steven. *Visual Basic 6 Black Book*, Coriolis Group Books, Scottsdale, AZ, 1998. ISBN 1-57610-283-1. Steven has written an eminently readable book that both intermediate- and advanced-level developers will find to be a good source of information and techniques. Steve discusses different compilation options in his overview of VB in Chapter 2.

 Siler, Brian and Jeff Spotts. *Special Edition Using Visual Basic 6*, Que, Indianapolis, IN, 1998. ISBN 0-7897-1542-2. Brian and Jeff's book is a good intermediate-level text. They devote Appendix B to a brief but sufficient coverage of compilation and distribution.

 Search the online books on the VB CD-ROM for the phrase "Native Code Compiler Switches". Also, search on the term "compiling" to bring up a variety of subjects related to the compiled application and compilation issues.

 Also, check out the Microsoft Developer Network online at **http://premium.microsoft.com/msdn/library/**, where there are many articles, book chapters, and updated documentation (as well as links to the Knowledge Base).

Distributing The Visual Basic Application

Terms you'll need to understand:

√ Dependency file

√ License file

√ Setup package

√ Package and Deployment Wizard

√ Install location macro

Techniques you'll need to master:

√ Using the Package and Deployment Wizard

√ Creating setup packages

√ Deploying packages to floppy disks and on networks

√ Deploying packages on the Internet

√ Indicating which files are to be included in the package

√ Indicating which files are to be marked as shared

Visual Basic 6 sports a nifty new Package and Deployment Wizard replacing the Setup Wizard that shipped with VB5. The certification exam will ask you some questions querying your knowledge of concepts in the use of the Package and Deployment Wizard and distributing your VB application in general. I cover these topics in this chapter.

The Setup Options

You run the Package and Deployment Wizard from the Add-Ins menu in VB or from the command line. When you launch the Package and Deployment Wizard, you have three choices:

➤ **Package** Create a setup package.

➤ **Deploy** Deploy a previously created setup package.

➤ **Manage Scripts** Rename, duplicate, or delete previously created package or deployment scripts.

The next sections show you how to use each option.

Creating The Package

The Package and Deployment Wizard creates CAB files that include your application and any necessary supporting files. It groups them into a package containing all needed information, such as the SETUP.LST file. You can create packages consisting of a single CAB file for distribution on a network, over the Web, or on a CD. You can also create smaller CAB files for distribution by diskette. Also included in the final package are files needed to install and uninstall the application.

When you first launch the Package and Deployment Wizard, the Active Project defaults to the current project. Pressing the Package button causes the wizard to compare all the components' dates to the last executable you created. If any component dates are newer than the executable, the wizard offers to recompile your application. I do not recommend doing this because you are essentially deploying untested changes. You should recompile the project from within VB, do your normal testing, and then return to the Package and Deployment Wizard.

The wizard next analyzes your project and locates all required components and dependencies. The components include all modules, ActiveX components, graphics, and so on. *Dependencies* are files that are required for your application to run, such as MSVBVM60.DLL.

For Internet deployments, the wizard will allow you to specify that dependency files, such as MSVBM60.DLL, are to be downloaded from an alternate site, if necessary.

After the project has been analyzed, VB offers to use a previously saved script file, if there is any. This allows you to save your settings between sessions. You can then choose between the creation of a standard setup package or dependency file. A *dependency file* is a text file with all dependencies listed. The file includes basic information in INF format, including the application version number and, optionally, a default Web address.

The standard setup package option prompts you for a folder to use to write out files. The Package and Deployment Wizard will create the CAB, SETUP.EXE, and SETUP.LST files in this folder. A subfolder, called SUPPORT, will be created. It will contain all the files in the CAB file, the SETUP programs, as well as a BAT file that can be run to re-create the CAB file if you modify the program.

Files To Be Included With The Package

After you have selected a folder to use, the Package and Deployment Wizard lists all the files that it determined you need. A button allows you to add other files as you see fit. You can also deselect files, if you wish. Figure 14.1 shows a package that I created. You can pause your mouse pointer over each of the files to determine why it is included in the package, as seen in Figure 14.1.

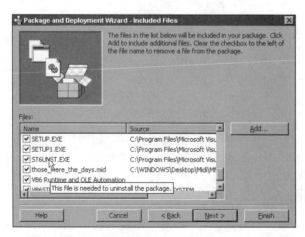

Figure 14.1   The Package and Deployment Wizard lists all the files it proposes to be included in the package as well as any that you manually add.

The VB6 Runtime And OLE Automation entry that you see in Figure 14.1 includes files required by all VB applications:

- ► ASYNCFILT.DLL
- ► COMCAT.DLL
- ► CTL3D32.DLL
- ► MSVBVM60.DLL
- ► OLEAUT32.DLL
- ► OLEPRO32.DLL
- ► STDOLE2.TLB

When creating an Internet deployment package, the wizard assumes that each of these files, except for MSVBVM60.DLL, is already installed in the target PC and, therefore, does not include them in the package.

When packaging ActiveX components for the Internet, you may consider not distributing files that your user already has. You can opt to link to the Microsoft Web site or to another site to download common components if they are not already present on the user's PC. This saves on download time and aggravation. Figure 14.2 shows this in action.

Other files added to all setup packages include:

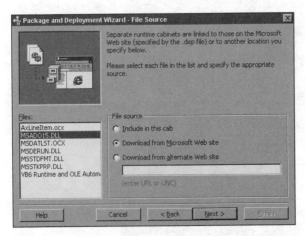

Figure 14.2 The File Source dialog box allows you to link to the Microsoft Web site or to an alternative Web site for common files to be downloaded to your user.

➤ **SETUP.EXE** This program is run by the user to pre-install files needed for your application to be installed on the user's machine, such as SETUP1.EXE.

➤ **SETUP1.EXE** This is the program that performs the actual application install and setup. You can modify its behavior as I show you later in this chapter. You can rename this file if you wish but be sure to change its name in the SETUP.LST file as well.

➤ **SETUP.LST** This text file contains installation settings and lists each of the files to be installed.

➤ **VB6STKIT.DLL** This is the dynamic link library (DLL) containing functions used by SETUP1.EXE.

➤ **ST6UST.EXE** This is the program to remove the application.

Distributing Microsoft Files

You need, of course, to have proper permission to distribute files that you did not create. You can distribute, without any runtime licensing fees, any EXE, OCX, or DLL file that you create with Visual Basic. Your Visual Basic license also allows you to distribute any files in the Graphics folder (icons, bitmaps, and the like) that are used with your application as well as any files from the ODBC subdirectory. You can also distribute any Microsoft file distributed with Visual Basic or Windows that the Package and Deployment Wizard deems to be a dependency. However, if you are using third-party controls, DLLs, and so forth, you will need to verify licensing restrictions with those vendors. Some components require a license key file to be distributed. I discuss this in the "Web-Based Deployments" section, later in this chapter.

If you use ADO, OLE DB, or ODBC components in your applications, the file MDAC_TYPE.EXE is automatically included in the setup package. This installs all necessary components onto your user's PC. If you are using DAO, the wizard prompts you for information regarding whether you are using ODBCDirect and so on, in order to determine the correct components to include.

Packages For Remote Components/DCOM

If you are creating an application that uses remote components (these used to be called OLE Servers), you will need to create two packages. One will be installed on the remote computer while the other will be installed on client computer(s). You need to ensure that the remote support (VBR) file is in the same directory as the project file.

To create a remote support (VBR) file, open the Project Properties dialog box in the remote project. Make sure the Remote Server Files box is checked on the Components tab of the dialog box, and then compile the project. The VBR file will be automatically generated.

To create the two packages, you will treat the two projects as a project group. Run the Package and Deployment Wizard twice—once for the client project and once for the remote project.

Scripting Safety Options

When you are packaging an ActiveX component, there is the possibility that the component will be scripted. For example, you can create an ActiveX control that, though you anticipate it being used in Standard EXE Visual Basic projects, might end up embedded in a Web page (by some other user). This raises safety concerns. As an example, assume you created an ActiveX control whose sole purpose is the creation of text files. Assume that one of the properties of the control is **fileName**. An unscrupulous user could embed your control in a Web page and, via scripting, pass a file name of COMMAND.COM. When another user downloads that Web page (and thus, your seemingly innocent control), he or she stands to have his or her COMMAND.COM file corrupted.

If you create a package for an ActiveX component, the Package and Deployment Wizard examines it to determine if it is safe or not—that is, if there is any possibility that it could cause harm to another PC. Generally, if the component exposes any properties or methods, the Wizard assumes it is unsafe unless you tell it otherwise. In the dialog box shown in Figure 14.3, you specify whether the component is safe for scripting and whether it is safe for initialization (which means that someone can run the component without harming the computer on which it is loaded). If you leave these questions with no values, then Internet Explorer (IE) will flash a warning message to potential users.

Specifying The CAB And Media Type

After you select the files to be included in the package, the Package and Deployment Wizard asks you whether you want to create a single CAB file or smaller CAB files for distribution on floppy disks. For the latter, you can choose the size (such as 1.44MB or 2.88MB). If you select multiple CAB files, the wizard will later create files as close to the specified size as possible. For instance, I created an install using the 1.44MB option. The first CAB file was 1,282K to allow for inclusion of SETUP.EXE and SETUP.LST files on the same diskette. The total size of the three files was 1.38MB. The second CAB file was 1.424MB, and the last CAB file was 135K.

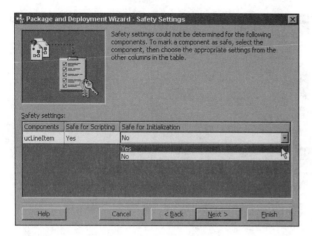

Figure 14.3   The ActiveX component's Safety Settings dialog box.

Next, you are prompted for the *installation title*. The installation title is displayed while the application is being installed on your user's machine.

Specifying Start Menu Items

The Package and Deployment Wizard will also generate the necessary instructions to add your application to the Start menu of your user's PC. You can add new program groups, items, and so on, as required.

Specifying The File Installation Locations

You are next prompted for the location in which to install each file. This is generally done with wild card macros, as seen in Figure 14.4. Table 14.1 lists each wild card macro and installation location.

For the $(AppPath) setting, the Package and Deployment Wizard will default to a folder in the Program Files folder, such as C:\Program Files\MyProject for a project called MyProject. You can override any of these macros by hard-coding the install path, but this is not recommended. You can also append a hard-coded path to a relative path. For instance, in Figure 14.4, I use $(WinPath)\Help to specify that the Help file for the application should be installed in the Help folder in the Windows folder.

Shared-File Handling

Shared files are those that other applications might use. An entry is made into the Registry to keep track of them. When your application is uninstalled by the user, the uninstall program checks the Registry for shared files and deletes them only if no other applications are using them.

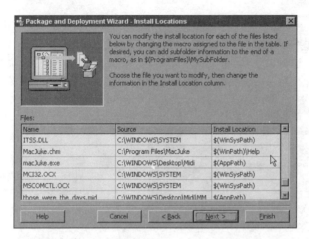

Figure 14.4 The Package and Deployment Wizard allows you to specify locations to install different files.

Table 14.1	Wild card macros for file install locations.
Wild Card Macro	**Location**
$(WinSysPath)	System or System32 folder under Windows or WinNT.
$(WinSysPathSysFile)	System or System32 folder under Windows or WinNT. This file will not be removed if the application is uninstalled.
$(WinPath)	Windows or Windoes NT folder.
$(AppPath)	Executable's folder.
$(CommonFiles)	Common Files folder, usually under Program Files folder.
$(CommonFilesSys)	System folder under Common Files folder.
$(ProgramFiles)	Program Files folder.
$(Fonts)	Fonts folder.
$(MSDAOPath)	For DAO only, stored in the user's Registry.

You specify which files in your application are shared, in the dialog box following installation locations, by selecting the components that are shared. The wizard will display only those files that it is unsure of. For instance, DLLs and OCXs are automatically marked as shared.

Creating The Actual Setup Package

The last steps in the use of the wizard involve specifying a script name, if you wish to save your settings, and then clicking on the Finish button. The Package and Deployment Wizard assembles the package and stores it in the folder that you specified earlier. The next task is to test the package.

Testing The Install Package

You will want to test your installation to ensure that it will work on your user's PC. You might want to refine the package somewhat, such as removing a file and modifying the SETUP.LST file.

Testing the install package is not as straightforward as it might seem. You should attempt to test it on as many machines and in as many environments as possible. Testing on your own machine is not a good indicator of whether your application will install correctly elsewhere. For instance, you might have certain DLLs installed on your PC that are not on other PCs. Your application might rely on the existence of a version of a DLL that is not on your user's PC. Only by testing in different environments and on different machine configurations can you detect these types of flaws and then act to correct them. In general, the wizard does a pretty good job of including those files that will be needed, but no program is perfect.

After you are satisfied that the package is adequately tested, you can deploy it.

Deploying The Package

After creating the package, you are returned to the main dialog box in the Package and Deployment Wizard where you can now click on the Deploy button. You are asked which previously created package to deploy. You have up to three options, depending on which type(s) of packages you have created: creating a Web install, a folder install, or a floppy disk install. If you have previously performed the deployment step, you can use a previously saved deployment script. I discuss the floppy disk and folder deployments next, followed by Web deployments.

Floppy Disk And Folder Deployments

If you have previously created a multiple CAB file package, your options for deployment will include floppy disks, folders, and Web publishing.

The floppy disk deployment will copy files to diskettes, offering to format each disk first. The first disk will contain SETUP.EXE, SETUP.LST, and the first CAB file. The CAB files are named using the first seven characters of your project name plus a single digit, such as MyProje1.CAB, MyProje2.CAB, and so on. File number two will go on disk number two, file number three will go on disk number three, and so on. Once you complete this step, you have only to mark the disks and then distribute them.

The folder deployment option asks you to specify a folder on your local machine or on the network to which you deploy the files. Generally, you won't deploy to your own machine, because that is where you would normally have created the files in the first place. However, it is common practice to create a network folder from which other users on the network can install.

The SETUP.EXE, SETUP.LST, and all CAB files are copied to the specified folder.

 In an organization where all users are connected to the network, folder deployments work best.

Web-Based Deployments

You can also select the Web publishing deployment method, if you will be distributing the file over the Internet. You are presented a dialog box in which to select those files to deploy. Generally, you will select all of them.

A second dialog box lists additional files that you might want to deploy. You are next asked to specify a destination URL to deploy to along with the Web publishing protocol (HTTP Post or FTP). You are also given the option of saving this information into your Registry and then of saving your script. Once you are finished doing this, the Package and Deployment Wizard posts your package to the specified Web site and generates an appropriate HTML page.

If any component requires a license, run LPK_TOOL.EXE found in the Tools directory on your Visual Basic 6 CD. This will create and output an LPK file for each component. See the output HTML file generated by the Package and Deployment Wizard for the Registry key that you will need to generate. Here's an example:

```
<HTML>
<HEAD>
<TITLE>AxLineItem.CAB</TITLE>
</HEAD>
<BODY>
<!--
If any of the controls on this page requires licensing, you must
create a license package file. Run LPK_TOOL.EXE to create the
required LPK file. LPK_TOOL.EXE can be found on the ActiveX SDK,
http://www.microsoft.com/intdev/sdk/sdk.htm. If you have the Visual
Basic 6.0 CD, it can also be found in the \Tools\LPK_TOOL directory.
```

The following is an example of the Object tag:

```
<OBJECT CLASSID="clsid:5220cb21-c88d-11cf-b347-00aa00a28331">
        <PARAM NAME="LPKPath" VALUE="LPKfilename.LPK">
</OBJECT>
-->

<OBJECT ID="ucLineItem"
CLASSID="CLSID:3D86AB0D-5AD3-11D2-9E8C-444553540000"
CODEBASE="AxLineItem.CAB#version=1,0,0,0">
</OBJECT>
</BODY>
</HTML>
```

Managing Scripts

The last option in the Package and Deployment Wizard is to Manage Scripts. Selecting this option brings up a dialog box with two tabs: Packaging Scripts and Deployment Scripts. Each lists previously saved scripts for the current project.

Using the command buttons provided, you can rename, delete, or duplicate scripts as needed. If you select the duplicate option, you are prompted for the name of the new script. This is useful if you wish to make minor changes based on a previously saved script without overwriting the original.

 Though managing scripts may seem trivial, be sure to understand the concept of reusing scripts.

The Setup Toolkit

There are times when you might want to alter the behavior of the Package and Deployment Wizard. You can add dialog boxes for registering users, installing optional components, and so forth. To do so, you should first make a backup of the setup1 directory, because you will be regenerating the Package and Deployment Wizard. All the files that you need are also in the setup1 directory. Open the VB project file SETUP1.VBP. You will need to manually specify all the project files and their dependencies to be installed on your users' computers.

 VB uses the **CopyFile** function to copy files to a user's computer. You should also use this function when creating your customized setup program, because it checks the date and version of files before overwriting them.

Practice Questions

Question 1

> When you are distributing ActiveX components that require a license, which type of file do you need to distribute?
>
> ○ a. LIC
>
> ○ b. VBR
>
> ○ c. LPK
>
> ○ d. OCX

Answer c is correct. You create an LPK file for distribution using LPK_TOOL.EXE. Answer a is incorrect because Visual Basic does not generate an LIC. Answer b is incorrect because VBR files are not used for licensing. Answer d is incorrect because an OCX file is an ActiveX control and not a license.

Question 2

> Assume you are distributing a multitiered project named CustMaint that uses ADO record sets to manipulate Oracle data. Which of the following files would you most likely not distribute?
>
> ○ a. MDAC_TYP.EXE
>
> ○ b. CUSTMAINT.VBP
>
> ○ c. CUSTMAINT.CHI
>
> ○ d. None of the above

Answer b is correct. The VBP file is the project file itself, which is generally of no use to the user and is not needed for the executable. Answer a is incorrect because the MDAC_TYP.EXE file is used to install necessary ADO and OLE DB components. Answer c is incorrect because the CHI file is the index to a compiled HTML Help file (CHM), which is perfectly reasonable to distribute. Answer d is incorrect because a correct answer is provided.

Question 3

> You create a floppy-based deployment package for 1.44MB disks. The total size of the generated CAB files is 2.71MB. How many floppies will the package require?
>
> ○ a. 1
>
> ○ b. 2
>
> ○ c. 3
>
> ○ d. The Package and Deployment Wizard does not support floppy-based install packages

Answer c is correct. While the CAB files will fit on two floppies, the SETUP.EXE and SETUP.LST files also need to be included, pushing the total space requirements over 2.88MB (the size of two disks) and thereby requiring a third floppy. Answers a and b are incorrect because the package will not fit on one or two 1.44MB floppy disks. Answer d is incorrect because the Package and Deployment Wizard supports floppy-based install packages.

Question 4

> What protocol(s) can you use in the Package and Deployment Wizard to distribute your application over the Internet? [Check all correct answers]
>
> ❑ a. FTP
>
> ❑ b. HTML
>
> ❑ c. HTTP Post
>
> ❑ d. UDP

Answers a and c are correct. You can use FTP and HTTP Post from within the Package and Deployment Wizard to deploy your applications over the Internet. Answer b is incorrect because HTML is not a protocol. Answer d is incorrect because the wizard does not use the UDP protocol.

Question 5

> You need to install a file onto your users' PCs into the System directory. Most of your users' Windows directories are named D:\Win95, but a few use the more conventional C:\Windows, instead. What is the best way to handle this, making sure that your file is installed into the proper location, within the setup package?
>
> ○ a. Use the $(WinPath) macro as the install-to directory. The proper location will be resolved at install time.
>
> ○ b. Customize the SETUP project using the **GetWindowsDirectory** API to ensure that the correct directory is selected.
>
> ○ c. Customize the SETUP1 project using the **GetWindowsDirectory** API to ensure that the correct directory is selected.
>
> ○ d. None of the above.

Answer d is correct because none of the supplied answers is the best. Instead, you should use the $(WinSysPath) macro, which will resolve to the System folder at runtime wherever it is installed. Answer a is incorrect because it specifies that you should use the $(WinPath) macro, which will not put the file into the System folder (although it will resolve to the correct location of the Windows directory). Answer b is incorrect because the SETUP.EXE program is a *boot-strap* program, which merely copies necessary files from the distribution media to the user's disk. It does not do the actual install. Also, there is no Visual Basic project file supplied for SETUP. Answer c is incorrect because there is a better way to perform the install. You can modify the SETUP1 project, recompile the program, use the **GetWindowsDirectory** API call (although **GetSystemDirectory** is a more direct function), and then make the coding changes required to locate the System folder. But, it is entirely unnecessary.

Need To Know More?

 Davis, Harold. *Visual Basic 6 Secrets*, IDG Books Worldwide, Foster City, CA, 1998. ISBN 0-7645-3223-5. Harold has done a nice job with this book though some of the paragraphs listed with "Secrets" icons are fairly common knowledge. Chapter 27 does a good job of creating Internet-based setup programs, scripting safety, and running controls in a Web page. Chapter 35 covers the setup creation process in a more general manner.

 Holzner, Steven. *Visual Basic 6 Black Book*, Coriolis Group Books, Scottsdale, AZ, 1998. ISBN 1-57610-283-1. Steven has written an eminently readable book that both intermediate- and advanced-level developers will find to be a good source of information and techniques. Chapter 30 covers the package creation process.

 Siler, Brian and Jeff Spotts. *Special Edition Using Visual Basic 6*, Que, Indianapolis, IN, 1998. ISBN 0-7897-1542-2. Brian and Jeff's book is a good intermediate-level text. They devote Appendix B to a brief but sufficient coverage of compilation and distribution.

 Search the online books on the VB CD-ROM for the term "setup" in the VB Concepts Help file. Also check out the SETPWZ98.CHM Help file, which, though named misleadingly, documents the Package and Deployment Wizard.

 Check out also the Microsoft Developer Network online at **http://premium.microsoft.com/msdn/library/**, where there are many articles, book chapters, and updated documentation (as well as links to the Knowledge Base).

Sample Test

This chapter provides pointers to help you develop a successful test-taking strategy, including how to choose proper answers, how to decode ambiguity, how to work within the Microsoft testing framework, how to decide what you need to memorize, and how to prepare for the test. At the end of the chapter, I include 70 questions on subject matter pertinent to Microsoft Exam 70-176, "Designing and Implementing Desktop Applications with Microsoft Visual Basic 6." Good luck!

Questions, Questions, Questions

You should have no doubt in your mind that you're facing a test full of questions. If the version of the VB6 Desktop exam that you take is fixed-length, it will include 70 questions, and you will be allotted 90 minutes to complete the exam. The passing score is 714 (71.4 percent). If it's an adaptive test (the software should tell you this as you begin the exam), it will consist of somewhere from 25 through 35 questions (on average) and take somewhere from 30 through 60 minutes. Remember, questions come in a few basic types:

➤ Multiple choice with a single answer

➤ Multiple choice with multiple answers

Though I have not yet seen them (nor has anyone I know), it is not inconceivable that you might run into these types of questions that have appeared on other Microsoft certification exams:

➤ Multipart with a single answer

➤ Multipart with multiple answers

➤ Simulations, whereby you click on a GUI screen capture to simulate using the VB6 interface

Always take the time to read a question twice before selecting any answer. Also, be sure to look for an Exhibit button, which brings up a window that contains longer code listings or screen shots that you'll need to consult in order to understand a question.

It's easy to assume that a question demands only a single answer. However, a lot of questions require more than one answer. Read each question carefully to determine how many answers are needed; also, look for additional instructions when marking your answers. When additional instructions are used, they usually appear in brackets, immediately after the question itself.

 Questions that require only one answer will have radio buttons for you to click on. Radio buttons are mutually exclusive—if you select one radio button, any previously selected button will be deselected. Questions where you are expected to provide more than one answer will have checkboxes for you to use to select your answers. You can select from one answer to all answers.

Picking Proper Answers

Obviously, the only way to pass an exam is to select correct answers. However, the Microsoft exams are not standardized, like SAT and GRE exams— Microsoft exams are more diabolical and convoluted. In some cases, questions are so poorly worded that deciphering them is nearly impossible. In such cases, you may need to rely on the process of elimination. There is almost always at least one answer out of a set of possible answers that can be eliminated due to any of the following scenarios:

➤ The answer doesn't apply to the situation.

➤ The answer describes a nonexistent issue.

➤ The answer is already eliminated by the question text.

After obviously wrong answers are eliminated, you must rely on your retained knowledge to eliminate further incorrect answers. Look for items that sound correct but refer to actions, commands, or features that do not apply to or appear within the described situation.

After this elimination process, if you still face a blind guess for two or more answers, reread the question. Try to picture the situation in your mind's eye, and visualize how each of the possible remaining answers might alter that situation.

You should guess at an answer only when you've exhausted your ability to eliminate answers but remain unclear about which of the remaining possibilities is correct. An unanswered question offers you no points, but guessing gives you at least some chance of getting a question right; just don't be too hasty when making a blind guess.

If you're taking a fixed-length test, you can wait until the last round of reviewing marked questions (just as you're about to run out of time or out of unanswered questions) before you start making guesses. If you're taking an adaptive test, you'll have to guess to move on to the next question if you can't figure out an answer some other way. Either way, guessing should be a last resort.

Decoding Ambiguity

Microsoft exams have a reputation for including questions that are difficult to interpret, confusing, or outright ambiguous. In my experience with numerous exams, I fully understand why this reputation is so prevalent. I'm not sure if the reason some questions are phrased so poorly is to limit the number of passing grades for those who take the tests. It may simply be that the tests are not well designed.

The only way to beat Microsoft at its own game is to be prepared. You'll discover that many exam questions test your knowledge of topics that might not be directly related to the issue raised in a question. This means that the answers offered—even incorrect ones—are as much a part of the skills assessment as the question itself. If you don't know most aspects of Visual Basic development well, you might not be able to eliminate obviously wrong answers because they relate to VB topics other than the subject or subjects addressed by the question.

Questions often give away their answers, but you have to be smarter than Sherlock Holmes to find the clues. Often, subtle hints appear in the text in such a way that they seem like irrelevant information. (Sometimes, irrelevant information is provided in an attempt to throw you off the trail.) You must inspect and successfully navigate each question to pass the exam. Look for small clues that seem incidental, such as control names, Registry settings, and so on. Small details can point out the right answers, but, if you miss them, you may find yourself facing a blind guess.

You will also run into some questions that are either very long—providing a lot of background—or that have answers that seem to be as much a matter of opinion as anything else. (Questions 70 and—to a lesser extent—68 on this practice exam are good examples.) My recommendation is that if the text is so long that you begin to get bleary-eyed, skip to the bottom where the question is asked and then go back and read the preceding text. You can then often hone in on the pertinent details. If the choices given seem to be a matter of opinion, go back and look for clues as to why Microsoft might consider one answer to be better than another.

Another common source of difficulty in the certification exams is vocabulary. Microsoft has an uncanny ability for naming some utilities and features cogently, yet it creates completely inane or arbitrary names for others—especially for those dealing with OLE/ActiveX technology and data access. Microsoft also has a tendency to adopt new naming conventions overnight. A great example of this is the use of the terms COM EXE and COM DLL, whereas the VB documentation uses the terms ActiveX EXE and ActiveX DLL. Be sure to brush up on the key terms presented in the appropriate chapters for these topics. You might also want to review this book's glossary before taking the test.

Working Within The Framework

Depending on the type of exam you get, questions may appear in random order. Many similar elements or issues are repeated in multiple questions. It's not uncommon to observe that the correct answer to one question is a wrong answer for another. As you take the test, take time to read each answer, even if you find the correct one immediately. Incorrect answers can spark your memory and help on other questions.

If you're taking a fixed-length test, you can revisit any question as many times as you like. If you're uncertain of the answer to a question, check the box that's provided to mark it for easy return later on. You should also mark questions you think may offer information that you can use to answer other questions. On fixed-length tests, test takers usually mark somewhere between 25 and 50 percent of the questions on average. The testing software is designed to let you mark every question if you choose, so use this framework to your advantage. Everything you'll want to see again should be marked; the testing software can then help you return to marked questions quickly and easily.

For fixed-length tests, I strongly recommend that you first read through the entire test quickly, before getting caught up in answering individual questions. This will help to jog your memory as you review the potential answers and can help identify questions that you want to mark for easy access to their contents. It will also let you identify and mark the tricky questions for easy return as well. The key is to make a quick pass over the territory to begin with—to know what you're up against—and then to survey that territory more thoroughly on a second pass, when you can begin to answer all questions systematically and consistently.

If you're taking an adaptive test, and you see something in a question or one of the answers that jogs your memory on a topic, or that you feel you should record if the topic appears in another question, write it down on your piece of paper. Just because you can't go back to a question in an adaptive test doesn't mean you can't take notes on what you see early in the test, in hopes that it might help you later.

 For adaptive tests, don't be afraid to take notes on what you see in various questions. Sometimes, what you record from one question, especially if it's not as familiar as it should be, can help you on other questions later on.

Deciding What To Memorize

How much material you must memorize for an exam depends on your ability to remember what you've read and experienced. For the most part, the test is reasonable in not requiring you to memorize obscure syntax variations. Yet, almost out of left field, you may be tripped up by a question asking you to memorize the value of a message box constant.

Important types of information to memorize include:

➤ Compiling and distributing applications, including handling licensing and registration issues.

➤ Using the VB wizards to accomplish key tasks, such as building classes.

➤ Creating and using ActiveX components.

➤ Creating a database application. Concentrate on ADO and understand the event model.

➤ Debugging and handling application errors are also hot topics.

Please note that although more than 70 percent of questions on the exam will come from the areas listed above, the Visual Basic 6 Desktop exam has other questions covering a very wide area. Don't be surprised to see the odd question on form activation, **GotFocus**, adding a menu item, and so on. Though they are not strictly part of the Visual Basic product (and thus not really discussed within this book), one person told me he had a couple of questions about Visual Source Safe, and I saw one about Visual Component Manager.

If you work your way through this book while sitting at a computer with Visual Basic loaded, you should have little or no problem interacting with most of these important items. Or, you can use The Cram Sheet that's included with this book to guide your rote memorization of key elements.

Preparing For The Test

The best way to prepare for the test—after you've studied—is to take at least one practice exam. I've included such an exam in this chapter. Give yourself 90 minutes to take the test. Also, keep yourself on the honor system, and don't cheat by looking at text that appears elsewhere in the book. After your time is up or you finish, check your answers against the answer key provided in Chapter 16.

For additional practice, visit Microsoft's Training And Certification Web pages at **www.microsoft.com/train_cert/**, and download the Self-Assessment Practice Exam utility.

 Microsoft's VB6 practice test was not available as this book was being prepared. You should visit the Microsoft Web site to see if it is available as you read this book.

Taking The Test

Relax. Once you're sitting in front of the testing computer, there's nothing more you can do to increase your knowledge or preparation. Take a deep breath, stretch, and start reading that first question.

You don't need to rush, either. You have plenty of time to complete each question and to return to those questions that you skip or mark for return (if you're taking a fixed-length test). If you read a question twice and remain clueless, you can mark it if you're taking a fixed-length test; if you're taking an adaptive test, you'll have to guess and move on. Both easy and difficult questions are intermixed throughout the test in random order. If you're taking a fixed-length test, don't cheat yourself by spending too much time on a hard question early on in the test, thereby depriving yourself of the time you need to answer the questions at the end of the test. If you're taking an adaptive test, don't spend more than five minutes on any single question—if it takes you that long to get nowhere, it's time to guess and move on.

On a fixed-length test, you can read through the entire test, and, before returning to marked questions for a second visit, you can figure out how much time you've got per question. As you answer each question, remove its mark. Continue to review the remaining marked questions until you run out of time or complete the test.

On an adaptive test, set a maximum time limit for questions and watch your time on long or complex questions. If you hit your limit, it's time to guess and move on. Don't deprive yourself of the opportunity to see more questions by taking too long to puzzle over questions, unless you think you can figure out the answer. Otherwise, you're limiting your opportunity to pass.

That's it for pointers. Here are 70 questions to practice on. As noted earlier, allow yourself 90 minutes. When you have finished, review the answers in the next chapter. For questions where you have to provide more than one response, give yourself credit only if you got all responses correct. Count the number of correct answers, and divide that number by 70. For instance, if you got 55 questions correct, divide 55 by 70 to compute your score of 78.6 percent. (Note that the test scores on a basis of 1,000 points, where 78.6 percent is a score of 786.) A passing grade is 74.5 percent (745). If you score above 80 percent, you are probably ready to take the real exam with a small cushion as a comfort factor. If you score above 90, you can probably be pretty confident of passing with no problems. A score of less than 80 percent is an indicator that you need more study or need to refine your exam-taking skills.

You may disagree with some of these answers. I have tested each line of code to ensure that the answers are accurate, and I have provided reasoning for why each answer is correct or incorrect. Additionally, a technical editor has reviewed each question, and a variety of other people have eyeballed each question. In the unlikely (I hope) event that you find a mistake, please drop me a line (**mike@mmacdonald.com**) or contact the publisher (**craminfo@coriolis.com**). Finally, be sure to visit **www.examcram.com**. As revisions are made, they are posted on that Web site.

If you fail, you should have a pretty good idea of what questions snowed you. Use these as a guide for additional study, and take the exam again. Whether you pass or fail, please drop me or the publisher a line and let us know.

Good luck.

Sample Test

Question 1

Consider the following code:

```
Dim sName()
ReDim sName(5)
sName(3) = "Smith"
Erase sName
```

Which of the following statements is true?

○ a. All memory is released. The array **sName** needs to be declared again using **ReDim** before it can be reused.

○ b. All memory is released. You can immediately reuse the array **sName** without further action.

○ c. The first four elements of the array **sName** are initialized (to empty strings), but not all memory is released. You can immediately reuse the first four elements of the array but have to use **ReDim** if you need to make the array larger.

○ d. You will receive an error message.

Question 2

Consider the following code:

```
#If fDebug Then
  Assert (dDivisor <> 0, "dDivisor = 0!")
#End If

Sub Assert(bExpr As Boolean, sMsg As String)
  If Not bExpr Then
    If MsgBox(sMsg & vbCr & _
      "Continue Processing?", _
      vbYesNo, "Assert") = vbNo Then
      End
    End If
  End If
End Sub
```

When is **Sub Assert** stripped out of the code?

○ a. When compiled to an executable.

○ b. When **#fDebug** is set to **False**.

○ c. When Break On All Errors is set in the Options dialog.

○ d. Never.

Question 3

Assume **rs** is an open ADO **Recordset** object consisting of 37 rows. Further, assume that it supports forward and backward navigation, bookmarks, and record counts. What will happen when the following code executes?

```
Dim iRecNo As Integer
With rs
  iRecNo = .RecordCount MOD 9
  .MoveFirst
  .Move iRecNo
  If .Bookmarkable Then
    Dim vBookmark As Variant
    vBookmark = .Bookmark
    .MoveLast
    .Bookmark = vBookmark
  End If
End With
```

○ a. The first record will be current.

○ b. The second record will be current.

○ c. **EOF** will be **True**.

○ d. **BOF** will be **True**.

○ e. Both **BOF** and **EOF** will be **True**.

○ f. An error will occur.

Question 4

Consider the following code:

```
form1.Show
Dim newFrm As form1
unload form1
```

What memory is used by the object(s) remaining in memory (do not consider the few bytes of overhead to reference the object variable)?

○ a. None. The form has been removed from memory.

○ b. None. Visual Basic will generate an error.

○ c. The memory used by **form1** is still being used.

○ d. A 16-bit "orphan" pointer (**newFrm**) is still being used.

Question 5

You wish to boldface the text on every command button on every open form in your application. Which code snippet will accomplish this?

○ a. Visual Basic does not support this functionality.

○ b.
```
Dim vButton As Variant
   For Each vButton In Controls
      If TypeOf vButton Is CommandButton _
         Then
            vButton.FontBold = True
         End If
      Next
   Next
```

○ c.
```
Dim iButton As Integer
Dim iForm As Integer
For iForm = 1 to UBound (Form)
  For iButton = 1 to UBound _
     (Form.CommandButton)
     Form.CommandButton _
        (iButton).FontBold = True
  Next
Next
```

○ d.
```
Dim vForm As Variant
Dim vButton As Variant
For Each vForm In Forms
   For Each vButton In vForm.Controls
      If TypeOf vButton = CommandButton
      Then
         vButton.FontBold = True
      End If
   Next
Next
```

Question 6

You have a form with a single TextBox control. As you can see in Exhibits 1 and 2 (Figures 15.1 and 15.2), the Cut and Copy menu items are enabled when text is highlighted and disabled when text is disabled. Where is the most likely place that the author attached code to accomplish this?

○ a. The TextBox control's **Change** event procedure.

○ b. The TextBox control's **Select** event procedure.

○ c. The Edit menu's **Click** event procedure.

○ d. The Edit Cut and Edit Copy menus' **Click** event procedures.

○ e. The menu's **Activate** event procedure.

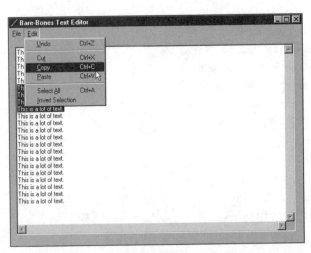

Figure 15.1 Exhibit 1 for Question 6.

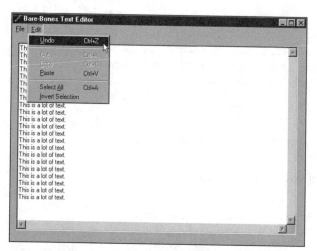

Figure 15.2   Exhibit 2 for Question 6.

Question 7

Which of the following are in-process COM components? [Check all correct answers]

❑ a. ActiveX DLL

❑ b. ActiveX EXE

❑ c. ActiveX control

❑ d. Standard EXE

❑ e. None of the above

Question 8

You are about to begin a new project for the ABC company. Here is the information that you have been given:

➤ The ABC company has 140 employees, but only 30 of them will use your new application.

➤ ABC company has an existing system that utilizes an SQL Server database. Some of the data may be corrupt.

➤ Your application needs to use the same SQL Server database.

➤ Some of the users need to access your new application as a standalone application, whereas others need to access some of the services it provides from an application that will be built at a later time.

➤ It is possible that the application to be built later might be done in Visual C++. Or, maybe it will be built with Visual Basic. The company doesn't seem to be too sure.

What type of project will you create?

○ a. ActiveX control

○ b. ActiveX DLL

○ c. ActiveX EXE

○ d. Standard EXE

○ e. Either a or b

Question 9

You have a form named **form1** on which is a CommandButton
named **command1**. Consider the following code snippet:

```
Private Sub Command1_Click()
    If TypeOf Me Is Form1 Then
        MsgBox "form1"
    End If
    If TypeOf Me Is Form Then
        MsgBox "form"
    End If
    If TypeOf Me Is CommandButton Then
        MsgBox "CommandButton"
    End If
```

What will be displayed in the message box(es)? [Check all correct
answers]

❑ a. **form1**

❑ b. form

❑ c. CommandButton

❑ d. "User-Defined Type Not Allowed"

Question 10

You have an application with the following code snippet:

```
#If Win95 Then
  MsgBox "Welcome Win95 user!"
#ElseIf Win32 Then
  MsgBox "Welcome Win32 user!"
#End If
```

The application is being run under Windows 95. Which message
box will be displayed?

○ a. "Welcome Win95 user!"

○ b. "Welcome Win32 user!"

○ c. Both

○ d. Neither

Question 11

You have created a Standard EXE project with Visual Basic that analyzes sales data from your company. You used the Package and Deployment Wizard to distribute the program throughout the Sales department, which includes Mary, Director of Marketing. Inside of a procedure that performs varios statistical analysis, you have this code snippet:

```
Dim myVar As Integer
myVar = 3
If  myVar = 3 Then Debug.Print myVar
```

Where will the output be displayed?

○ a. In the Watch window

○ b. In the Intermediate window

○ c. In the form

○ d. None of the above

Question 12

You have a form with one CommandButton named **Command1**. You enter the following code:

```
Private Sub Command1_Click()
    MsgBox 1
End Sub
Private Sub Command2_Click()
    MsgBox 2
End Sub
```

You then rename **Command1** to **Command2** and run the project. What will be displayed?

○ a. 1

○ b. 2

○ c. 1 then 2

○ d. 2 then 1

Question 13

Consider the following Visual Basic arithmetic operators:

➤ Addition (+)

➤ Division (/)

➤ Exponentiation (^)

➤ Modulus (**Mod**)

If a computation had all four types of operations, what would be the order in which the operations would be performed?

○ a. Modulus, then division, then exponentiation, then addition

○ b. Exponentiation, then division, then modulus, then addition

○ c. Addition, then exponentiation, then division, then modulus

○ d. The operators are evaluated in whatever left-to-right order they are encountered

Question 14

You are building a COM component that contains two classes, A and B. Suppose class A implements class B. Which of the following statements is true? [Check all correct answers]

❑ a. Class A cannot access the **Friend** procedures of class B.

❑ b. Class B cannot access the **Friend** procedures of class A.

❑ c. Class B must include all the **Public** procedures of class A.

❑ d. Class A cannot obtain a reference to class B unless there is a separate instance of class B.

Question 15

What Visual Basic statement supports using a VB procedure as a callback procedure?

○ a. **CallBack**

○ b. **hInstance**

○ c. **Back**

○ d. **AddressOf**

Question 16

Consider the following code:

```
Private Function ComputeAnswer (x As Integer, _
    y As Integer)
  x = x * 2
  y = y / 2
  ComputeAnswer = (x + y) ^ 2
End Sub
Sub Main
  Dim z1 As Integer
  Dim z2 As Integer
  z1 = 2
  z2 = 2
  MsgBox ComputeAnswer(z1, z2)
End Sub
```

You compile the program using the Assume No Aliasing option. Which of the following statements is true?

○ a. The value displayed in the message box is unpredictable.

○ b. The value displayed in the message box is 16.

○ c. The program will not compile.

○ d. The program might compute incorrect results on some older Pentiums.

Question 17

Where would you use the **IsMissing** function?

- ○ a. Database programs to test if a field has no value
- ○ b. COM components to see if implemented classes have been instantiated
- ○ c. Procedures to see if optional parameters are missing
- ○ d. Program code to see if objects referenced in collections or the **Dictionary** object have been destroyed

Question 18

What is the value of **a** after the following computation?

```
Dim a

a = (19 Mod 4) \ 2
```

- ○ a. 1
- ○ b. 1.5
- ○ c. 2
- ○ d. 2.375

Question 19

Consider the following code:

```
Dim myVar As String
myVar = vbNullString
If myVar = Null Then
  MsgBox "String is null"
Else
  MsgBox "String is not null"
End If
myVar = ""
If myVar = Null Then
  MsgBox "String is null"
Else
  MsgBox "String is not null"
End If
```

What two messages will be displayed?

○ a. "String is null" and "String is null".

○ b. "String is not null" and "String is null".

○ c. "String is null" and "String is not null".

○ d. "String is not null" and "String is not null".

Question 20

When compiling to native code, what are valid optimization options? [Check all correct answers]

❏ a. No Optimization

❏ b. Compile For Fast Code

❏ c. Allow Array Boundary Violations

❏ d. Create Symbolic Object File

Question 21

Which controls can be dragged at runtime? [Check all correct answers]

❑ a. Line

❑ b. CommandButton

❑ c. PictureBox

❑ d. TextBox

Question 22

You are creating an ActiveX control that is meant to be used in not only other Visual Basic projects but also other development environments. The control will be issued to run on Windows 95, Windows 98, and Windows NT. The code has this rather unlikely code inside of it:

```
Dim myVar1 As Variant
Dim myVar2 As Variant
Dim myVar3 As Integer
myVar1 = "1"
myVar2 = "one"
```

Which of the following statements are valid? [Check all correct answers]

❑ a. myVar3 = myVar1 + 4

❑ b. myVar3 = myVar1 + myVar2

❑ c. Dim myVar4 As Decimal
    myVar4 = myVar1

❑ d. myVar3 = Val(myVar1) + Val(myVar2)

Question 23

What does the ampersand (&) character do? [Check all correct answers]

☐ a. Acts as a type declaration character for data type **Long**

☐ b. Performs logical **Imp** operations on numeric data

☐ c. Concatenates

☐ d. Provides a visual cue of hotkeys

Question 24

How do you find all the fonts available to your application?

○ a. Enumerate the **Fonts** collection property of the **App** object.

○ b. Iterate the **Fonts** property of the **App** object using the **FontCount** property.

○ c. Enumerate the **Fonts** collection property of the **Screen** object.

○ d. Iterate the **Fonts** property of the **Screen** object using the **FontCount** property.

Question 25

You have an ADO record set named **rs** open; it contains some addresses. One of the fields is **City**. Which of the following will find the first occurrence of the city "Worcester"?

○ a.
```
With rs
    .MoveFirst
    .Find "=", .Fields("city"),"Worcester"
End With
```

○ b.
```
Dim search As String
search = "City = "'Worcester'"
With rs
    .MoveFirst
    .Seek (search, adExact)
End With
```

○ c.
```
Dim search As String
search = "City = 'Worcester'"
With rs
    .MoveFirst
    .Find (search)
End With
```

○ d.
```
Dim search As String
search = "City = 'Worcester'"
With rs
    .MoveFirst
    .Seek (search, adFirstMatch)
End With
```

Question 26

You have written a database application. You have a form where users can update records. However, you are concerned that a user might close the form before all changes have been saved. In what event of the form could you place code to handle this?

○ a. **Deactivate**

○ b. **Terminate**

○ c. **Unload**

○ d. **QueryUnload**

○ e. None of the above

Question 27

You have an application consisting of a form named **form1** and two CommandButton controls named **Command1** and **Command2**. The code is as follows:

```
Private Sub Command1_Click()
MsgBox "Hello World"
End Sub


Private Sub Command2_Click()
End
End Sub


Private Sub Form_QueryUnload(Cancel As Integer,
     UnloadMode As Integer)
Command1_Click
End Sub
```

What happens when the user presses **Command2**?

○ a. The application displays the message box and ends.

○ b. The application displays the message box but does not end.

○ c. The application repeatedly displays the message box because there is an endless loop.

○ d. The program just ends.

○ e. None of the above.

Question 28

You have an application that is remarkably similar to the one in Question 27, consisting of a form named **form1** and two CommandButton controls named **Command1** and **Command2**. The code is as follows:

```
Private Sub Command1_Click()
MsgBox "Hello World"
End Sub


Private Sub Command2_Click()
Unload Me
End Sub


Private Sub Form_QueryUnload(Cancel As Integer,
    UnloadMode As Integer)
Command1_Click
End Sub
```

What happens when the user presses **Command2**?

○ a. The application displays the message box and ends.

○ b. The application displays the message box but does not end.

○ c. The application repeatedly displays the message box because there is an endless loop.

○ d. The program just ends.

○ e. None of the above.

Question 29

You have created an ActiveX control project. You place a PictureBox, Image, and CommandButton control on the User control. The only code is this:

```
Private Sub Command1_Click()
Image1 = Picture1
End Sub
```

You set the **Picture** property of the PictureBox to a neat bitmap that you found on the Internet. You compile the project into an OCX file and add it to another Visual Basic project. In the new project, you have only a form on which you place your fabulous ActiveX control. You add no code to the form at all.

Next, you use the ActiveX Document Migration Wizard and convert your form to a UserDocument. You run the project inside of Internet Explorer and click on the CommandButton control. What happens?

○ a. Nothing.

○ b. The bitmap displayed in the PictureBox is displayed in the Image control.

○ c. The Image control is converted to a PictureBox control that displays the same bitmap.

○ d. You get a "Mismatch" error.

○ e. The Image control is converted to a PictureBox control, but it is empty (it doesn't display any graphic).

Question 30

Consider the following code snippet:

```
Dim myVar1 As Integer
Dim myVar2 As Integer
On Error GoTo Problem
myVar1 = "A"
On Error GoTo 0
myVar2 = "B"
Exit Sub
Problem:
Resume Next
```

What option would you have to set to force the program to break on the assignment to **myVar1**?

○ a. Go to the Tools|Options dialog, and set Break On All Errors.

○ b. Go to the Debug|Watch dialog, and set Break On All Errors.

○ c. Go to the Debug|Watch dialog, and set a break expression of **Not IsValid myVar1**.

○ d. You would have to remove the error handling in order to force the program to break.

Question 31

How can you debug an ActiveX EXE named MYTEST.EXE?

○ a. Run the ActiveX EXE project in the development environment. Open Microsoft Internet Explorer, and open the MYTEST.VBD file.

○ b. Run the ActiveX EXE project in the development environment. Open a second instance of Visual Basic. Create a standard EXE to test the methods of the ActiveX EXE.

○ c. Compile the ActiveX EXE. Create a new standard EXE, and use Project|Components to add MYTEST.EXE to your project. Use the project to test the methods of the ActiveX EXE.

○ d. Just run the ActiveX EXE in the development environment as you would any other non-DLL project.

Question 32

Which of the following is a logical scenario in which you set the **DataMember** property of a TextBox control?

○ a. When the data source uses the OLE DB Simple Data Provider (OSP)

○ b. When selecting the field or column of the result set to bind to

○ c. When binding to a complex data source

○ d. When binding to a **Format** object to present data in a graphical manner

Question 33

You have created an application with Visual Basic. After compiling it, you have run the Package And Deployment Wizard to create a CAB file for distribution. What step(s) do you take to compress the CAB file in a manner such that the Setup.EXE program you distribute can still install your application?

○ a. Compress the CAB files using a third-party utility, such as PKZip. Distribute the package as normal.

○ b. In the Deployment function of the Package And Deployment Wizard, choose the compress option. Modify the Setup program to run LZExpand on the user's PC to uncompress the CAB file. Distribute as normal.

○ c. Run LZCompress to compress the CAB file. Check the Expand On Install option in the Package And Deployment Wizard. Distribute as normal.

○ d. None of the above.

Question 34

You are designing an application with 100 users in 6 offices around the world. The main office is located in Detroit, Michigan, whereas other offices are in the cities of London, Paris, Sydney, Calcutta, and Rio de Janeiro. The main office is running on a Windows NT network, but the other offices run a mishmash of operating systems and equipment. The application you are designing is rather dynamic in that the business rules are subject to frequent change. Management has indicated that it is willing to make some changes in the computing environment—perhaps up to $400 or $500 per user. Of the choices listed, what is the best approach to building the application?

○ a. Create an IIS application project

○ b. Create an ActiveX DLL project

○ c. Create a standard EXE project

○ d. Create an ActiveX EXE project

○ e. Create a DHTML project

Question 35

You have created an ActiveX component to run on a remote computer. What project option causes the necessary files to be generated when the project is compiled?

○ a. None. Visual Basic 6 does not support the creation of remote ActiveX components.

○ b. None. Under DCOM, there is no difference between a local and a remote ActiveX component.

○ c. Remote Server Files.

○ d. DCOM Support.

Question 36

Each time you create a Visual Basic project, the Visual Basic objects and procedures library is automatically referenced. Part of that library is the TextBox control. In the Visual Basic objects and procedures library, the TextBox control is an example of a(n) _____?

○ a. Class

○ b. Member

○ c. Object

○ d. Type library

Question 37

You have created a COM component for which you are using the apartment-threaded model. Which of the following statements are not true? [Check all correct answers]

❑ a. Each thread can be shared with multiple clients in a round-robin manner.

❑ b. Each thread has its own copy of global data.

❑ c. Objects created on each thread are unaware of objects created on other threads.

❑ d. Threads can be limited in number in the Project Properties dialog.

Question 38

Examine the exhibit (see Figure 15.3). The application in the exhibit is an example of an Explorer-style interface. The right-hand pane uses what type of control?

○ a. Data

○ b. DataGrid

○ c. ListView

○ d. TreeView

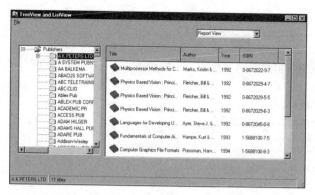

Figure 15.3   Exhibit for Question 38.

Question 39

You have created a COM component for which you have specified a thread pool of six threads. What type of component have you created?

○ a. ActiveX control

○ b. ActiveX DLL

○ c. ActiveX EXE

○ d. Standard EXE

Question 40

What does the **CancelUpdate** method of the ADO **Recordset** object do?

○ a. Cancels all updates to the database during the current transaction.

○ b. Cancels all updates to the database since the last commit.

○ c. Cancels all changes to the current record or discards a newly added record.

○ d. Cancels all previously committed changes to the database since the object was created (for ODBC data sources only).

Question 41

The Visual Basic **Dictionary** object is most like which of these choices?

○ a. The **Collection** class

○ b. The Object Browser Reference object

○ c. The system tables schema in Oracle or SQL Server

○ d. The ListBox control's **Item** property

Question 42

Using the ADO Data control (Adodc), what cursor types are available? [Check all correct answers]

❑ a. Dynamic

❑ b. Forward-only

❑ c. Keyset

❑ d. Static

Question 43

Which of the following statements is not valid (assume the **ErrHandler** is a valid line label)?

○ a. On Error GoTo 0

○ b. On Error GoTo ErrHandler

○ c. On Error Resume

○ d. On Error Resume Next

Question 44

What happens when the following line of code is executed?

```
Debug.Assert MsgBox("About to run sort!")
```

- ○ a. The message box is displayed in the compiled version of the program but not the debug version.
- ○ b. The message box is displayed in the debug version of the program but not the compiled version.
- ○ c. The message box is displayed in both the compiled and debug versions of the program.
- ○ d. The message box is not displayed in either the compiled or the debug versions of the program.
- ○ e. The program does not run correctly.

Question 45

When building COM components, what are some advantages provided by interfaces? [Check all that apply]

- ❑ a. Inheritance
- ❑ b. Early binding
- ❑ c. Guaranteed callback methods
- ❑ d. Data and object binding

Question 46

On **frmCustomer**, you wish to add a context menu. What seems like the best event to place it in?

- ○ a. The **Click** event of the particular menu you wish to display
- ○ b. The **GotFocus** event of the appropriate control
- ○ c. The **MouseDown** event of the form or appropriate control
- ○ d. The **KeyDown** event of the form or appropriate control

Question 47

Your application displays a pop-up menu. Which of the following is true?

- ○ a. The menu is displayed modally.
- ○ b. The menu is displayed synchronously.
- ○ c. The menu is displayed modeless.
- ○ d. The menu is displayed asynchronously.

Question 48

You have created a COM component that you wish to persist. What method should you use?

- ○ a. **Persist**
- ○ b. **Save**
- ○ c. **SaveSettings**
- ○ d. **WriteProperty**

Question 49

You have placed some controls on a form and wish to dock them on the bottom of the screen. Which is the best approach to doing so?

- ○ a. Set each control's **Docked** property to **vbDockBottom**.
- ○ b. Place the controls in a PictureBox control.
- ○ c. In the form's **Resize** event, adjust each control's location and, if necessary, size.
- ○ d. None of the above.

Question 50

You have created an in-process COM component with Visual Basic 6 and now wish to debug it. How do you do it?

○ a. Compile the component, install it on the appropriate computer, register the component with the client, and then run the client application within the Visual Basic environment as normal.

○ b. Open the Visual Basic client application, and then use the Add Project option to add the COM component project into the same instance of Visual Basic. Run the client application as normal.

○ c. Create a separate instance of Visual Basic. Run the COM component in the second instance of VB and the client application in the first instance.

○ d. Use the Application Performance Monitor to "watch" both programs stepping through and debugging code as necessary.

Question 51

Which of the following controls or objects are capable of displaying a bitmap? [Check all correct answers]

❑ a. CommandButton

❑ b. CheckBox

❑ c. Image

❑ d. **MDIForm**

Question 52

Examine the following code snippet:

```
Dim myVar As String

myVar = "All good things"
myVar = Trim(Mid$(myVar, _
    (InStr(1, myVar, "o") + 33 / 11.5)))
MsgBox myVar
```

What is displayed?

○ a. hings

○ b. ood things

○ c. things

○ d. d th

Question 53

Which code snippet will return all settings from the Windows Registry related to the "Test" application's "Colors" key?

○ a.
```
Dim myVar As Variant
Dim myStr As String
For Each myVar In AllSettings
   MyStr = GetSetting (appname := "Test",
      section := "Colors")
Next
```

○ b.
```
Dim myVar As Variant
Dim myStr As String
For Each myVar In AllSettings
   MyStr = Get (appname := "Test", section
      := "Colors")
Next
```

○ c.
```
Dim myVar () As Variant
MyVar = GetAllSettings(appname := "Test",
   section := "Colors")
```

○ d.
```
Dim myVar As Variant
MyVar = GetAllSettings(appname := "Test",
   section := "Colors")
```

Question 54

You have a form with an OLE container control named **OLE1**. Which of the following will create an embedded object?

○ a. CreateObject (OLE1, "c:\docs\mydoc.doc")

○ b. OLE1.CreateObject ("c:\docs\mydoc.doc")

○ c. CreateEmbed (OLE1, "c:\docs\mydoc.doc")

○ d. OLE1.CreateEmbed ("c:\docs\mydoc.doc")

Question 55

You have created a class module and are adding a property that is to be exposed for read/write access. What statement(s) will accomplish this?

◯ a. **Property Get** and **Property Let**

◯ b. **Property Let**

◯ c. **Property Get**

◯ d. **Property Let** and **Property Set**

Question 56

You are calling an API function that requires a string capable of storing 100 bytes of data. How should you declare the string to be passed?

◯ a. `Dim myVar As String`

◯ b. `Dim myVar As String ()`

◯ c. `Dim myVar As String * 100`

◯ d. `Dim myVar As String * 101`

Question 57

You have a created a class module and added an event **Processing_Complete (duration As Long)**. How would this event be invoked?

◯ a. `RaiseEvent Processing_Complete (1124)`

◯ b. `Event.Raise Processing_Complete 1124`

◯ c. `Raise Processing_Complete (1124)`

◯ d. It will happen automatically

Question 58

Which of the following will add a **Node** object to a TreeView control?

○ a. ```
Dim myNode As Node
Set myNode =
      TreeView1.Nodes.Add(,,"C:\","Root")
```

○ b. `Treeview1.Add ("C:\",tvwParent)`

○ c. ```
TreeView.Node.Add ("C:\",tvwParent,
tvwTextOnly)
```

○ d. `TreeView.AddNode ("C:\", tvwParent)`

Question 59

Assume you have a **DataEnvironment** object with a **Connection** object named **conOracle**. It contains two **Command** objects named **cmdEmployee** and **cmdCustomer**. **frmEmployee** has controls bound to **cmdEmployee**, and **frmCustomer** has controls bound to **cmdCustomer**. Both are open and both are editing **Recordset** objects derived from the two **Command** objects. In **frmCustomer**, the user presses a CommandButton control. In the event procedure, your code executes a **RollbackTrans** method. Next, the user clicks on a CommandButton control on **frmCustomer**, where your event procedure executes a **CommitTrans** method. Which of the following statements is true?

○ a. Changes to **cmdEmployee** are saved, but changes to **cmdCustomer** are lost.

○ b. Changes to **cmdEmployee** are lost, but changes to **cmdCustomer** are saved.

○ c. Changes to both **cmdEmployee** and **cmdCustomer** are lost.

○ d. Changes to both **cmdEmployee** and **cmdCustomer** are saved.

Question 60

Which is not an event of the TextBox control?

○ a. **GotFocus**

○ b. **MouseMove**

○ c. **Validate**

○ d. None of the above

Question 61

Assume that you create a new Visual Basic project, choosing an ActiveX control as the project type. To your control, you add the UpDown control followed by a ComboBox control and then a TextBox control. You set the properties of the UpDown control as follows:

```
AutoBuddy = True
BuddyProperty = Text
Min = 0
Max = 10
```

Next, you run the project and click on the up arrow on the UpDown control. Which of the controls on the form will change its display?

○ a. The ComboBox control

○ b. The TextBox control

○ c. The UpDown control

○ d. None of the above

Question 62

You have a form with four text boxes on it and need to intercept keystrokes for all four text boxes. Which of the following solutions is best?

○ a. Use the **KeyPreview** method of the form.

○ b. Use the **TestKey** event of the **OLE keyboard** object inserted into the form.

○ c. Use the **KeyDown** or **KeyPress** events of each of the text boxes.

○ d. Use the **KeyDown** or **KeyUp** properties of the form.

○ e. None of the above.

Question 63

Your form has two TextBox controls occupying the exact same space (one is on top of the other). Assuming the following code snippet, with which TextBox control(s) can the user interact (that is, into which TextBox control[s] can the user type)?

```
Private Sub Form_Load()
    Text2.ZOrder 1
    Text1.ZOrder 0
End Sub
```

○ a. Both

○ b. **Text2**

○ c. **Text1**

○ d. The one with the lowest **ZOrder** property, assuming the **TabIndex** for both is non-zero

Question 64

Your application has opened an ADO **Recordset**. In your code, you have coded an error handler that specifies **On Error Resume Next** followed by a line of code that invokes the **MoveLast** method of the **Recordset** object. Under which of the following circumstances might there be no records?

○ a. When **EOF** is **True** and **BOF** is **False**

○ b. When **BOF** is **True** and **EOF** is **False**

○ c. When both **BOF** and **EOF** are **True**

○ d. When both **BOF** and **EOF** are **False**

Question 65

How would you access an ODBC data source with the ADO Data control?

○ a. Use the RDO **UserConnection** interface.

○ b. Use the OLEDB Provider for ODBC.

○ c. Set the **DefaultCursor** property to **ODBCDirect.**

○ d. Use a translation table with SQL Server.

Question 66

Which of the following most accurately describes polymorphic behavior in Visual Basic?

○ a. It can't be done.

○ b. It represents the abstraction of an inherited object.

○ c. It is a way of implementing different functions using the same methods.

○ d. It requires either vTable or DispID binding.

Question 67

You create a COM DLL with Visual Basic and write a client program that references certain methods of the objects exposed by the DLL. The objects are explicity declared. What type of binding will result?

○ a. DispID

○ b. vTable

○ c. DispID if the COM DLL's Project Properties specified an apartment model

○ d. There is not enough information provided to determine what type of binding will occur

○ e. None of the above

Question 68

You have created an ActiveX control. The **InvisibleAtRuntime** property was set to **True** when you created it. It performs some currency exchange calculations for your order-entry application. The ActiveX control has a bug in it that causes it to crash every once in a great while with no discernible pattern. Because the crashes are so rare, you elect to proceed with the rest of your project and figure that some day (maybe after next year's Super Bowl), you'll get around to figuring out what the bug is.

You will include the ActiveX control as part of a COM component that is to be used by your order-entry application. The COM component is responsible for connecting to the database and retrieving, validating, and editing records. The COM component will also include code to validate user passwords and assign a "security level." (The security level is used to determine which screens the user is allowed to see and whether or not he or she can update the data.)

The order-entry application will leave almost all business logic to the COM component and will consist mainly of the user interface (forms, menus, and so forth). The COM component will be shared by multiple users on an application server.

What type of Visual Basic project will you choose to create the COM component?

○ a. ActiveX control

○ b. COM DLL

○ c. COM EXE

○ d. Standard EXE

Question 69

A Data Link creates which object(s)?

○ a. **Command**

○ b. **Connection**

○ c. **Recordset**

○ d. Either a or c

Question 70

You have a form named **frmCustomer**. On **frmCustomer**, there is a CommandButton control named **cmdOK** and a control array of TextBox controls named **txtFields**. This code is in the **Click** event of **cmdOK**. Other than the **Name, Index,** and **Caption,** you did not change any control properties at design time.

The project contains a **DataEnvironment** object named **deData**. **deData** is a single **Connection** object named **conSQLSrv**. There is also a single **Command** object named **cmdCustomer** that returns all customers in the database. One of the fields in the record is **cust_age**, which is numeric.

The Form has a module-level variable named **rsCustomer** that is assigned as follows:

```
Dim WithEvents rsCustomer As Recordset
```

The **Form_Load** event contains the following code:

```
Set rsCustomer = deData.cmdCustomer
cmdOK_Click
```

The following code is attached to the **cmdOK_Click** event procedure:

```
Dim vControl
For Each vControl in txtFields
    txtFields.CausesValidation = Not _
        txtFields.CausesValidation
Next
cmdOK.Enabled = False
```

The **Validate** event of **txtFields** contains the following code:

```
If Val(txtFields(Index).Text) < 0 Then
    MsgBox "Invalid Age"
    txtFields(Index).SelStart = 0
    txtFields(Index).SelLength = _
        Len(txtFields(Index).Text)
    Cancel = True
End If
```

(continued)

Question 70 *(continued)*

When you test the code, you notice that there are some problems. What are they? [Check all correct answers]

- ❏ a. The code does not run at all.
- ❏ b. **Recordset** does not support events.
- ❏ c. The code in **cmdOK_Click** has syntax errors.
- ❏ d. The **Validate** event cannot possibly execute.
- ❏ e. There are logic errors in the **Validate** event.
- ❏ f. Controls are not properly bound to the data source.

Answer Key

1. a	19. d	37. a, d	55. a
2. d	20. a, b	38. c	56. d
3. f	21. b, c, d	39. c	57. a
4. c	22. a, d	40. c	58. a
5. d	23. a, c, d	41. a	59. c
6. c	24. d	42. a, c, d	60. d
7. a, c	25. c	43. c	61. a
8. c	26. d	44. b	62. c
9. a, b	27. d	45. b, c	63. a
10. b	28. a	46. c	64. c
11. d	29. b	47. a	65. b
12. b	30. a	48. d	66. c
13. b	31. b	49. b	67. b
14. a, c	32. c	50. b	68. c
15. d	33. d	51. a, b, c, d	69. b
16. a	34. a	52. c	70. a, d, e, f
17. c	35. c	53. d	
18. a	36. a	54. d	

Question 1

Answer a is correct. The array **sName** is erased, and all memory is released. In order to reuse the array, you need to re-dimension it using **ReDim**. Answer b is incorrect because you cannot immediately begin to reuse the array without re-dimensioning it. Answer c is incorrect because the array is not merely reinitialized; all of the elements are deleted from memory. You cannot reuse the array at all until you re-dimension it. Answer d is incorrect because you will not receive an error message.

Question 2

Answer d is correct. **Sub Assert** is a valid subprocedure and is never stripped out of the code. The question is a bit tricky because the first three lines are stripped out of the code when the program is executed. However, **Sub Assert** is just a normal procedure with nothing to do with conditional compilation. Answer a is incorrect because the first three lines of code would be stripped out of the code when compiled to an executable but not the **Sub**. Answer b is incorrect because **#fDebug** is not a constant that you define—it is a built-in constant. Answer c is incorrect because the Break On All Errors option has nothing to do with conditional compilation.

Question 3

Answer f is correct because **Bookmarkable** is not a valid property of the ADO **Recordset** object. Instead, you should use the **Supports** method to determine if the **Recordset** object is bookmarkable. Answers a through e are all incorrect because the code will not run. Assuming that the **Bookmarkable** property had not been referenced, answer b would have been correct. The **MOD** operation would return 1. The **Move** method would move forward one record (to the second). That is the record that would have been bookmarked.

Question 4

The correct answer is c. The memory used by the form is not released until all objects referring to it have also been destroyed. Answer a is incorrect because memory is still being used. Answer b is incorrect because there is no error. Answer d is incorrect because though a pointer is still stored in memory, the form is also retained in memory. Also, object variables are 32 bits (not 16).

Question 5

Answer d is correct. The code iterates through the **Forms** collection and, for each **Form**, through the **Controls** collection. For each control that evaluates to a CommandButton, the **FontBold** property is set to **True**. Answer a is incorrect because Visual Basic does support this functionality. Answer b is incorrect because only those command buttons on the currently active form would be changed. Answer c is incorrect because forms and controls are not maintained in arrays—VB maintains references to them in collections.

Question 6

Answer c is correct. When the Edit menu is clicked on, you can use the TextBox control's **SelLength** property to determine if any text is selected and either enable or disable the Cut and Copy menu items as appropriate. You can use **Len(Clipboard.GetText)** to determine if there is any text on the clipboard to determine whether to enable or disable the Paste menu item. Answer a is incorrect because the **Change** event is not triggered as a result of the user selecting or deselecting text. Answer b is incorrect because the TextBox control does not have a **Select** event. Answer c is incorrect because you need to enable and disable the Cut and Copy menus before they are clicked on. Answer d is incorrect because there is no menu **Activate** event.

Question 7

Answers a and c are correct. An in-process component runs in the same process as the client. An ActiveX DLL runs in the same process as its client. An ActiveX control—an OCX file—is a special kind of a DLL and also runs in the same process as the client. Answer b is incorrect because an ActiveX EXE runs in its own process. Answer d is incorrect both because a standard EXE is not a COM component and because it runs in its own process. Answer e is incorrect because the correct answers are provided.

Question 8

Answer c is correct. The question provides mostly irrelevant information. The key is the fourth bullet, which requires that your new application be run standalone and, at some future point, provide services to an as-yet-unbuilt client. The ActiveX EXE is the only project type that satisfies this requirement. Answer a is incorrect because an ActiveX control cannot be run standalone. Likewise, answer b is incorrect because the ActiveX DLL cannot be run standalone. Answer d is incorrect because a standard EXE cannot provide services to other processes. Answer e is incorrect because neither answer a nor answer b is correct.

Question 9

Answers a and b are correct. The keyword **Me** returns a reference to the **Form** object, and so both the first and second tests (that **TypeOf** is **Form** and **Form1**) evaluate to **True**. Therefore, the message boxes display. Answer c is incorrect because **Me** does not return a reference to the CommandButton. Answer d is incorrect because there is no error.

Question 10

Answer b is correct. The code is performing conditional compilation and examines the operating system variable. Win95 is not a valid environment constant, so the test fails. Win32 is a valid environment constant, so the test evaluates to **True**, and the message box is displayed. Answer a is incorrect because Win95 is not a valid compiler constant. Answer c is incorrect because it is not possible to perform two branches in an **If...Then...Else** construct. Answer d is incorrect because a message box is displayed.

Question 11

Answer d is correct. Because the application is compiled (it must be compiled to use the Package and Deployment Wizard to distribute it), all Debug statements are stripped out of the code. Therefore, there is no output. Answers a, b, and c are all incorrect because there is no output. The question attempts to be tricky in two ways. First, you are buried with extraneous detail (Mary, Marketing, and so on). Second, the question attempts a little reverse psychology—the extraneous detail is so obviously irrelevant that you may miss the reference to use of the Package and Deployment Wizard.

Question 12

Answer b is correct. When you rename your control, the code in **Command2_ Click** will run. Answer a is incorrect because the code in **Command1_Click** is ignored. Answers c and d are incorrect because there is no way for both message boxes to display. The question is not particularly difficult, but it does underscore your need to know the VB development environment. On the live test, you will encounter several questions that are surprisingly trivial. I looked hard at some of those questions and wondered what it was that I was missing. I finally concluded that just as a cigar is sometimes just a cigar, some of the easier questions are just that: easy questions.

Question 13

The correct answer is b. Visual Basic has a predefined set of rules to determine the order of operations. Computations in parentheses are performed first. Then, any exponentiation operations are performed followed by: negation, division and multiplication, integer division, modulus, and addition and subtraction. If there is a "tie," operations are done from left to right. Answers a and c are both incorrect because they list operations in an incorrect order and would produce an inaccurate result. Answer d is incorrect because certain operations take precedence over others and are resolved in a left-to-right manner only if there is more than one operation of the same priority (such as two multiplication operations in the same computation).

Question 14

The correct answers are a and c. The controller of a class cannot see the **Friend** procedures of that class. When a class implements another class, it must include all **Public** procedures of the implemented class, and those procedures become methods of the implementing class. Answer b is incorrect because class A can access the **Friend** procedures of class B. Answer d is incorrect because the implemented class can obtain a reference to the implementing class.

Question 15

The correct answer is d. You can use the **AddressOf** statement to pass the address of a VB procedure to an API function, which then uses the address to make a callback to that procedure. Answer a is incorrect because there is no such VB statement. Answer b is incorrect because **hInstance** returns the address of the application and is a method of the **App** object. Answer c is incorrect because there is no such VB keyword.

Question 16

The correct answer is a—the value displayed in the message box is unpredictable. **Sub Main** declares the variables z1 and z2, each of which occupies 2 bytes of storage. When they are passed to the function **ComputeAnswer**, the memory address of those two variables is referred to as x and y. This is known as aliasing. Because the values are passed with an implicit **ByRef** (procedure arguments are passed **ByRef** by default), the procedure is passed the actual addresses of the two variables, which are then referred to by the names x and y. When you compile with the no aliasing option, you are telling Visual Basic that you will not perform any aliasing—using two or more variable names to refer to the same memory address. Therefore, you are not guaranteed that the correct values will be passed to procedures, and the computations are unpredictable. Answer b is incorrect because the no aliasing option will most likely cause Visual Basic not to "see" the correct values. Answer c is incorrect because the program *will* compile (even though it will not operate correctly). Answer d is incorrect because the allusion to programs not operating correctly on some older Pentiums is a reference to the infamous floating-point division bug on older 60- and 66MHz Pentiums. The Remove Pentium Safe FDIV Checks compilation option is concerned with that issue.

Question 17

The correct answer is c. You use the **IsMissing** function in procedures where one or more parameters have been declared using the **Optional** keyword. You use **IsMissing** to determine if the parameter was supplied. Answer a is incorrect because you would use the **IsNull** function to determine if a field has no value (assuming that the field was a nullable data type). Answer b is incorrect because, in a COM component, any implemented classes are automatically instantiated when the controlling class is instantiated. Answer d is incorrect because there is no function to determine if an object referenced in a collection or in the **Dictionary** object has been destroyed. (By definition, if such an object were destroyed, it would not be referenced in a collection or **Dictionary**.)

Question 18

The correct answer is a. This is a quick "Are you awake?" question. I saw a few of these types of questions on the exam where I found myself wondering, "Well, what's the catch?" Unfortunately, since you don't get to see what questions were scored right and which were scored wrong, you never know for sure. In this question, either the **Dim a** statement without specifying a data type or maybe the **Mod** operator could be considered tricky elements. In the case of the variable declaration, the data type defaults to **Variant**, which is no big deal. As to the **Mod** operator, that should not throw most developers either. The difficult part of this question to some VB developers is the use of integer division (the backwards slash \). The integer division operation throws out the decimal portion of the computation. Many VB developers seldom use integer division (I am in that camp), and some never use it, making it unfamiliar. The computation is solved this way: 19 **Mod 4** is equal to 3—modulus division returns the remainder. 19 divided by 4 is equal to 4 with a remainder of 3. Three is integer-divided by two with a result of 1. If regular division were used, the answer would be 1.5, of course. Answer b is incorrect because integer division was used. You might have chosen answer c if you inadvertently concluded that 19 **Mod 4** was 4 and then divided by 2. Likewise, you might have incorrectly selected answer d if you made bad assumptions about the meaning of the operators.

Question 19

The correct answer is d. Both **If** tests fail for a number of reasons. The first test fails because **Null** is a value that is really applicable only to data type **Variant**. To test a null string, use the constant **vbNullString**. Second, any comparison to null always returns **False** even when the item being compared is null. That is why you need to use the **IsNull** function. The second test fails because the string is no longer a null string—it is an empty string. Answer a is incorrect because the two tests fail. Answer b is incorrect because the first test fails. Answer c is incorrect because the third test fails.

Question 20

The correct answers are a and b. No Optimization specifies compilation will take place with no optimizations, such as Fast Code or Small Code. Compile For Fast Code specifies that compilation will optimize for speed at the expense of program size. Answer c is incorrect because there is no such option. However, there is the Remove Array Bounds Check option. Answer d is incorrect because it is not a valid option. There is a Create Symbolic Debug Info option.

Question 21

The correct answers are b, c, and d because the CommandButton, PictureBox, and TextBox controls can all be dragged. Answer a is incorrect because the **Line** object cannot be dragged.

Question 22

The correct answers are a and d. Answer a is correct because the addition operation checks to see if the first **Variant** has a recognizable number format and, if so, adds it to the second number. Answer d is correct because it adds the value of the two variables together. The result of the first **Val** function is 1, and the result of the second is 0. Answer b is incorrect because VB now looks at the first variable for a recognizable number format and, not finding one, attempts to concatenate the strings. However, the result is assigned to a numeric variable, which is illegal. Answer c is incorrect also because it attempts to declare a variable of type **Decimal**, which VB6 does not support. (To use the **Decimal** data type, you must create a variable of type **Variant** and then use the **CDec** function.)

Question 23

Answers a, c, and d are correct. Answer a is correct because the ampersand declares that a variable is of type **Long**. Answer c is correct because the ampersand acts as a concatenation operator. Answer d is correct because typing an ampersand followed by a character causes the character to be underlined, providing a visual cue that Alt plus the underlined character is a control's hotkey. Answer b is incorrect because the ampersand is not the **Imp** operator.

Question 24

The correct answer is d. The **Fonts** property of the **Screen** object is an array of available fonts. The **FontCount** property of the **Screen** object returns the number of fonts in the array. Answers a and b are incorrect because **Fonts** is not a property of the **App** object. Answer c is incorrect because **Fonts** is not a collection. This is an excellent example of some of the questions you will see on the exam in that the answers fall into two groups. One group has **Fonts** being a property of the **App** object, and the other has **Fonts** being a property of the **Screen** object. A number of the questions on the exam seem to do this—answer a (for example) is similar to answer c, and answer b is similar to answer d. In this particular question, not only do the answers fall into the **App** or **Screen** categories, but also, they fall into the "array" or "collection" categories (answers a and c propose that **Fonts** is a collection, whereas answers b and d propose that **Fonts** is an array). If I did not know the answer to this question, I might logically conclude that **Fonts** is a property of the **Screen** object (though VB is not always logical), but it would then be a coin toss between answers c and d.

Question 25

The correct answer is c. You would need to use the **Find** method of the **Recordset** object followed by the search criterion. Answer a is incorrect because the syntax for **Find** is garbled. Answers b and d are both incorrect because they use **Seek**, which is not a method of the ADO **Recordset** object.

Question 26

The correct answer is d. **QueryUnload** is the last event before the **Unload** event and gives you the opportunity to cancel the close, prompt the user to save the changes, and so on. Answer a is incorrect because **Deactivate** happens right before a form loses focus (is no longer active). Answer b is incorrect because **Terminate** is not an event of the form. Answer c is incorrect because **Unload** is not a proper place to attempt to cancel a form close. For instance, if the user closes Windows, the **QueryUnload** event, not the **Unload** event, can be used to cancel that. Answer e is incorrect because the correct answer is provided.

Question 27

The correct answer is d. When you use **End**, the form closes without events, such as **QueryUnload**, being triggered. It is a better practice to use **Unload Me** to ensure that the form's shutdown events are triggered. Answers a, b, and c are all incorrect because, since the **Form_QueryUnload** event procedure is never executed, the **Command1_Click** event procedure is also never executed. Answer e is incorrect because the correct answer is provided.

Question 28

The correct answer is a. Because the code in the **Command2_Click** event procedure specifies **Unload Me**, the **QueryUnload** event procedure executes. The call to the **Command1_Click** event procedure is executed as normal—you can have as much code as you want in the **QueryUnload** event procedure. The form will not unload until all of the code has completed. Triggering other form or control events occurs synchronously, meaning that the control is not transferred back to the calling procedure until the event procedure is completed. Answer b is incorrect because the application does end. Answer c is incorrect because there is no endless loop. Answer d is incorrect because the program does not end until the message box has displayed (until the code in **Command1_Click** has been executed). Answer e is incorrect because the correct answer is provided.

Question 29

The correct answer is b. This is another of those darned Microsoft questions with oodles of superfluous information. The only information that is important in this question is the assignment **Image1 = Picture1**. For both controls, the default property is **Picture**, so the bitmap displayed in the PictureBox is displayed as an Image control. Answer a is incorrect because the **Picture** property of **Image1** is set equal to the **Picture** property of **Picture1**. Answers c and e are both incorrect because controls cannot be converted to another type of control. Answer d is incorrect because there is no "Mismatch" error.

Question 30

Answer a is correct. You can go to the Tools|Options dialog box and set the Break On All Errors option to force VB to break, even if an error is properly handled. Answer b is incorrect because the Watch dialog allows you only to enter expressions to break on. Answer c is incorrect because the expression is invalid. Answer d is incorrect because you do not have to remove error handling.

Question 31

Answer b is correct. Because the ActiveX EXE is an out-of-process server, you need to create a second instance of Visual Basic to test it. Answer a is incorrect because you use Internet Explorer for ActiveX Document EXEs, not ActiveX EXEs. Answer c is incorrect because the ActiveX EXE is not a control that can be added via Project|Components. Answer d is incorrect because you need another application to test the ActiveX EXE, which is an Automation server component.

Question 32

Answer c is correct. You use the **DataMember** property to fully qualify the data source. For example, if you had a class that provided multiple data sources, you would use **DataMember** to set which object of the **DataMembers** collection to bind to. If you were binding to a **DataEnvironment** object, you would use **DataMember** to determine which **Command** object to bind to. Answer a is incorrect because the OLE DB provider is irrelevant to whether you would use the **DataMember** property of a control. Answer b is incorrect because you use the **DataField** property to specify to which field (or column) to bind. Answer d is incorrect because there is no **Format** object—there is a **StdFormatObject**. Strictly speaking, if you use the **StdFormatObject**, it is bound to the control's **DataFormat** property and not the **DataMember** property.

Question 33

Answer d is correct. You do not need to compress the CAB file because it is already compressed. The Setup.EXE program that the Package And Deployment Wizard adds to your setup package automatically extracts files from the CAB file. Answer a is incorrect because the Setup.EXE program will not be able to extract files from a zipped file. Answer b is incorrect because there is no compress option in the Package And Deployment Wizard—it occurs automatically. Also, you do not need to add LZExpand to your Setup program. Answer c is incorrect because you do not need to compress the CAB file, and there is no Expand On Install option in the Package And Deployment Wizard.

Question 34

Answer a is correct. With offices around the world and management (understandably enough) not willing to spend the money to connect each office via dedicated lines, you really have little choice but to run the application over the Internet. Moreover, you are told that the clients have a mishmash of operating systems and equipment. Creating an IIS application will allow you to present the user interface as a series of HTML pages inside of almost any browser on almost any operating system. As far as the client's equipment is concerned, connecting to your IIS application with a Web browser is no more taxing on the computer than using the Web browser to connect to any other Web site. Answers b and d are both incorrect because, although you can deploy the component (the ActiveX DLL or ActiveX EXE) on a server connected to clients via the Internet, clients may not be able to connect to it. This is because the clients may be running non-Windows operating systems. (You would also have to write client-side programs that use the ActiveX component.) Answer c is incorrect both because the clients might not be running Windows and because the frequently changing business rules would require that the standard EXEs be modified and distributed often. Answer e is incorrect because the DHTML application is dependent on Internet Explorer 4 or above being installed on the client computers, which, again, requires that they be running Windows.

Question 35

The correct answer is c. You can select Project|Properties, click on the Components tag, and select Remote Server Files to produce an ActiveX component that can be run on a remote server. A VBR file that clients can use to register the remote component (which is a necessary step, of course, in order to add a reference to it) will be created. Answer a is incorrect because VB6 does support the creation of remote servers. Answer b is incorrect because it does not really answer the question. Although DCOM may arguably make moot any difference between a local and remote component, it is still necessary to generate the VBR file in order for the client to reference the remote component. Answer d is incorrect because there is no DCOM Support option.

Question 36

The correct answer is a. If you open the Object Browser and select the VB library (VB6.OLB—the Visual Basic objects and procedures library), the TextBox is listed as a class. It is not until you actually create an instance of TextBox that it becomes an object. Literally, the library supplies the definition of the object. Answer b is incorrect because it is the properties, methods, and events of the TextBox class that are collectively the members of the TextBox class. Answer c is incorrect because the TextBox class in the library is not an object and does not become an object until it is instantiated as a control. Answer d is incorrect because the TextBox is part of a type library (more accurately, an object library)—it is not a type library unto itself.

Question 37

Answers a and d are correct. In the apartment-threaded model, threads are not shared among multiple clients. Also, you cannot restrict the number of threads in the apartment-threaded model. Answer b is incorrect because each thread does have its own copy of global data. Answer c is incorrect because objects created on each thread are unaware of objects created on other threads.

Question 38

The correct answer is c—the control in the right-hand pane is a ListView control. In an Explorer-style interface, the left-hand pane uses a TreeView control as a sort of macro-level look at the data. For example, Windows Explorer shows folders in the left-hand pane. The right-hand pane uses the ListView control as a sort of detail-level look at the data. Windows Explorer shows files in that pane. Answer a is incorrect because, though a Data control may be supplying the data, it is not the control in the right-hand pane. Answer b is incorrect because the right-hand pane is not a DataGrid control. Answer d is incorrect because the TreeView control is in the left-hand pane.

Question 39

The correct answer is c—the ActiveX EXE component type supports thread pooling. Answers a and b are both incorrect because ActiveX controls and ActiveX DLLs do not support thread pooling (which is the sharing of a limited number of threads for multiple client processes in a round-robin fashion). The issue here is how the component runs—in-process or out-of-process. In-process components run in the client's memory space and do not need to share threads with other clients. An ActiveX control is simply a special kind of DLL. The ActiveX EXE runs out-of-process and needs a mechanism to share threads with other multiple clients. The standard EXE project type has no need for a threading model. Thus, answer d is incorrect.

Question 40

Answer c is correct. **CancelUpdate** cancels any changes made to the current record and discards a record created using the **AddNew** method. If a record has been added, the record that was current prior to **AddNew** becomes current again. Answer a is incorrect because **CancelUpdate** is not related to a transaction. Answer b is incorrect because **CancelUpdate** is not related to when the last commit occurred. Answer d is incorrect because **CancelUpdate** does not undo saved changes to the database, and the cancel operation has nothing to do with whether the data source is ODBC or not.

Question 41

Answer a is correct. The **Dictionary** object is new to Visual Basic 6 and has much in common with the **Collection** class. It has extra properties and methods that make it in many cases preferable to using a collection. Answer b is incorrect because there is no Object Browser Reference object. Answer c is incorrect because the **Dictionary** object has nothing to do with system tables or database schemas. Answer d is incorrect because the **Dictionary** object and the ListBox control's **Item** property are not related.

Question 42

The correct answers are a, c, and d. The ADC dynamic, keyset, and static cursor types are supported as specified by the **CursorType** property. Answer b is incorrect because, though the **Recordset** object supports the forward-only cursor type, it is not implemented with the ADC.

Question 43

Answer c is correct. You cannot use **Resume** with **On Error**. Answer a is incorrect because the statement is valid—it turns off error handling (sets the error handler to **OFF**). Answers b and d are also incorrect because both statements are valid. Answer b turns on the error handler, transferring control to **ErrHandler** if an error occurs. Answer d also turns on the error handler, causing execution to resume with the statement following the statement that caused the error. Visual Basic does not support **On Error Resume** because that would cause the program to repeatedly execute the same instruction that caused the error, likely resulting in an endless loop.

Question 44

Answer b is correct for two reasons. First, references to the **Debug** object are stripped out of the program when compiled. Second, the **MsgBox** function when used in this manner implicitly returns the value 0 (which is as though the **vbOK** return were evaluated), which—to the **Assert** method—evaluates to **False**. Answers a and c are both incorrect because **Debug** is always stripped out of compiled programs. Answer d is incorrect because the **MsgBox** function returns 0 (effectively **False**). Answer e is incorrect because the code is valid. The question is tricky both because of the "oddness" of how **MsgBox** is used and because of the need to reason out how VB will treat the return value. Even more, some developers will look and see the use of parentheses (indicating that **MsgBox** is being used as a value-returning function) and, not seeing the return value assigned anywhere, will deduce that the program will generate a runtime error. (This is a neat little tool for debugging.)

Question 45

Answers b and c are correct. Interfaces provide for both early binding and guaranteed callback methods. Answer a is incorrect because, though interfaces do provide means for reuse, support for true inheritance is not provided. Answer d is incorrect because interfaces don't provide "data and object binding."

Question 46

Answer c is correct. You would use the **MouseDown** event, checking to see if the right button was pressed. If it was, you would use **PopUpMenu** to display the context menu. Answer a is incorrect because you would not evaluate the **Click** event on a menu to determine whether to display another menu (at least not a context menu). Answer b is conceivable but not realistic. You would not want to display a context menu each time the user tabs into a TextBox control, for example. Likewise, answer d is not practical—under Common User Architecture guidelines, use of the right-mouse button generally should result in a pop-up context menu.

Question 47

The correct answer is a. The pop-up menu is essentially a response window—no code is executed until the user either makes a selection or otherwise closes the menu. Answers b and d are incorrect because there is no request being made. In other words, displaying a menu is not an operation where a call is made in a synchronous or asynchronous manner. Answer c is incorrect because the menu is not displayed modeless—if it were, the user would be able to perform other actions in the program while the menu remained open.

Question 48

Answer d is correct. You should use the **WriteProperty** method of the **PropertyBag** object to persist a property of the component. Answers a and b are incorrect because there are no such methods. Answer c is incorrect because **SaveSettings** is appropriate only to save settings to the Registry.

Question 49

Answer b is correct. You should place the controls in a PictureBox control. Then, you can set the PictureBox control's **Alignment** property to dock the PictureBox to the bottom of the form. As the form is resized, the PictureBox remains docked with the controls inside of it. Answer a is incorrect because there is no **Docked** property. Answer c is incorrect because it is impractical, and a better answer is provided. Answer d is incorrect because a correct answer is provided.

Question 50

Answer b is correct. Because the component is an in-process component, you run it in the same instance of Visual Basic as the client application. When you add the project, you are creating a project group. Answer a is incorrect because it is almost nonsensical. If nothing else, you can't debug the compiled version of the component using Visual Basic. Answer c is incorrect because you do not need to open a second instance of Visual Basic. Answer d is incorrect because there is no such tool as the Application Performance Monitor (there is the Application Performance Explorer, which has nothing to do with debugging COM components).

Question 51

The correct answers are a, b, c, and d—each of the controls and the **MDIForm** object has a **Picture** property that allows you to display a bitmap. In the case of the CommandButton and CheckBox controls, you must first set the **Style** property to **vbGraphical**.

Question 52

Answer c is correct. The interactions of the nested functions need to be reasoned to solve this. The code uses the **Mid$** function to find a portion of the string. The second argument specifies that the first character of the substring is the one at the position defined by the **InStr** function. This initially returns 6 (o is the sixth character in the larger string). Then, you are asked to add to it the result of 33 / 11.5, which returns 2.869. Add 6 + 2.869, and the result is 8.869. This gets truncated to 8, so the substring begins at position 9 (the space between **good** and **things**). Because the optional length argument was omitted from the **Mid$** function, the calculation returns the rest of the string beginning at position 10. Then, the outer function (**Trim**) acts to remove any leading and trailing spaces, which gives the final result of **things**. Answer a is incorrect because it miscomputes the result of the mathematical operations. Answer b is incorrect because it does not take into account the modification to the beginning position. Answer d is incorrect because it assumes the math operation will be rounded down.

Question 53

Answer d is correct. To return all the Registry values for the given application and section, you would declare a variable of type **Variant** and then use the **GetAllSettings** function, as shown in answer d. Answer a is incorrect because settings aren't maintained in a collection, and the code uses an invalid function (**Get**). Answer b is incorrect because settings aren't maintained in a collection. Answer c is incorrect because you should not declare the variable as an array.

Question 54

Answer d is correct. **CreateEmbed** is a method of the OLE container control, which creates an object from the specified file. Answers a and b are incorrect because they use the **CreateObject** function incorrectly. Answer c is incorrect because **CreateEmbed** is not a VB function; it is a method of the OLE container control.

Question 55

Answer a is correct. You need to provide a **Property Get** statement to allow read access and then a **Property Let** statement to allow write access (if the property were an object, you would use **Property Set** instead). Answer b is incorrect because it provides write access only. Answer c is incorrect because **Property Get** allows only read access. Answer d is incorrect because **Let** is used for data type variables, and **Set** is used for object type variables. You cannot mix the two of them for the same variable.

Question 56

Answer d is correct. You need to create a string at least 1 byte longer than is needed to allow for the null termination character. Answer a is incorrect because the string needs to be preallocated to the correct size. Answer b is incorrect because you cannot pass a string array when it is not expected by the calling function. Answer c is incorrect because it does not allow for the null character at the end of the string. This question could be a little tricky to answer because of the wording of the question. One might reasonably assume that if the requirement were for a string long enough to hold 100 bytes, this would include the null termination character. However, the question specifies that the string should be long enough to hold 100 bytes of data. It is not reasonable to assume that the termination character would be part of the data.

Question 57

Answer a is correct. You would use the **RaiseEvent** function to invoke the event. Answer b is incorrect because **Event** is not an object and does not have a **Raise** method. Answer c is incorrect because **Raise** is used to invoke an error, not raise an event. Answer d is incorrect because an event that you define is not automatically invoked.

Question 58

Answer a is correct. A variable of type **Node** is created and then the **Add** method of the **Nodes** collection is used to add the node to the TreeView control. Answer b is incorrect because the TreeView control does not have an **Add** method. Answer c is incorrect because **Node** is not a property or method of the TreeView control. The control has a **Nodes** collection property. Answer d is incorrect because the control does not have an **AddNode** method.

Question 59

Answer c is correct. Any **CommitTrans** or **RollbackTrans** within the context of a single **Connection** object affects all objects that use the **Connection** object. In other words, a **CommitTrans** or **RollbackTrans** affects both **Command** objects. Answers a, b, and d are all incorrect because all changes made during the current transaction are discarded.

Question 60

Answer d is correct because all the events listed are valid. This question might be tricky for some VB developers. The **Validate** event is made available only when the **CausesValidation** property is set to **True**. The event occurs when the control loses focus.

Question 61

Answer a is correct. Because you specified **AutoBuddy** to be **True**, Visual Basic attempts to associate the control with the control that is next lowest in the Tab order. However, because you added the UpDown control first, there is no control lower in the Tab order (the **TabIndex** property of the UpDown control is 0). If there is no control lower in the Tab order, Visual Basic then attempts to use the control next highest in the Tab order. Because you added the ComboBox after the UpDown control, its **TabIndex** property is equal to 1, and the UpDown control uses the ComboBox. Answer b is incorrect because Visual Basic does not associate the UpDown control with the TextBox control. Answer c is incorrect because the appearance of the UpDown control does not change. Answer d is incorrect because the correct answer was provided.

Question 62

Answer c is correct because it is the only one that will work. The best way to do this is to use the **KeyPreview** property of the form, but this option is not provided. The key to this question is being familiar with properties, methods, and events, and then choosing among only the feasible solutions. Answer a is incorrect because, though it looks tempting, **KeyPreview** is a property not a method. Don't let yourself make a mistake by quickly jumping to the "obvious" answer without carefully reading the choices. Answer b is also incorrect because there is, in fact, no **OLE keyboard** object. Answer d is incorrect because **KeyDown** and **KeyUp** are events not properties. Answer e is incorrect because a valid choice is provided.

Question 63

Answer a is correct. As odd as it may sound, each control can still receive focus and even have data entered into it. The user just cannot see what is being typed. This question is tricky because answer a seems implausible, whereas answers c and d seem very plausible. This is another case where the choices have to be read very carefully. Answers b and c are both incorrect because both controls can, in fact, be edited. However, whereas answer b even looks wrong (because its **ZOrder** is set to 1), answer c is a logical but incorrect guess. It is logical because its **ZOrder** is 0, and it is incorrect because both text boxes can receive focus and be edited. Answer d is incorrect because **ZOrder** is a method not a property, and both controls can be edited.

Question 64

The correct answer is c. If both **BOF** and **EOF** are **True**, then the **Recordset** has no records. Answers a, b, and d are incorrect because if either **BOF** or **EOF** is **False,** then the **Recordset** has at least one record.

Question 65

Answer b is correct—the OLEDB Provider for ODBC data sources is used to connect to an ODBC data source. Answer a is incorrect because there is no RDO **UserConnection** interface. Answer c is incorrect because **DefaultCursor** is a property of the DAO Data control. Answer d is incorrect because you do not need to establish ODBC connections via SQL Server.

Question 66

Answer c is correct. Polymorphism is the use by several objects of the same method with different underlying functionalities. For example, you may have two objects, A and B. One maintains employee data on the database, whereas the second edits user input into a customer maintenance screen. If both have a **ValidateData** method (e.g., **A.ValidateData**), then the objects exhibit polymorphic behavior. Answer a is incorrect because VB does support the creation of objects with polymorphic behavior. Answer b is incorrect because inheritance is not required to implement polymorphism, and polymorphism has nothing to do with the "abstraction" of an inherited object. Answer d is incorrect because polymorphic behavior places no special restrictions on binding.

Question 67

Answer b is correct. vTable binding occurs when objects are explicitly declared, and the object library implements a virtual function table. All COM components created with VB implement a virtual function table. vTable is a type of early binding that is more efficient than DispID. Answer a is incorrect because DispID binding does not occur with components created by Visual Basic. Answer c is incorrect because compilation settings do not affect the creation of a virtial function table. Answer d is incorrect because there is enough information provided. Explicit object references result in early binding. The type of early binding (vTable or DispID) is determined by the component. Answer e is incorrect because the correct answer is provided.

Question 68

Answer c is correct. The main piece of information here is that the ActiveX control to be used as part of the COM component is buggy and tends to "crash." Since you do not wish the whole application to crash, you should be thinking in terms of an out-of-process component—an ActiveX EXE. If the control crashes the ActiveX EXE, it will not crash the application itself. Answer a is incorrect because you cannot share an ActiveX control among multiple users (or processes). Also, an ActiveX control is a DLL that runs in-process and could crash your application. (Further, you will see on the test that Microsoft does not term an ActiveX control as a COM component.) Answer b is incorrect because the COM DLL runs in-process and thus exposes your application to possible crashes when the ActiveX control misbehaves. Answer d is incorrect because a standard EXE is not a COM component. This question is a very good example of a type of question that you will see on the exam—it gives you information and asks you to conclude from the information provided what the best answer is.

Question 69

Answer b is correct. You use the Data Link to create a **Connection** object in the DataEnvironment Designer. Answers a, c, and d are incorrect because the Data Link is used to set up the **Connection**—not the **Command** or **Recordset** objects.

Question 70

Answers a, d, e, and f are correct. Answer a is correct because **rsCustomer** is set equal to **cmdCustomer,** which is a record that returns the **Command** object. The line of code should have been **Set rsCustomer = rscmdCustomer. deData** will automatically prepend **cmdCustomer** with the characters "rs" in creating the **Recordset** object. Answer d is correct because the **cmdOK_Click** event sets the **CausesValidation** property of each **txtFields** control to **False.** When form is loaded, the **CausesValidation** property retains its default value of **True** until the **cmdOK_Click** event. Answer e is correct because the code does not first verify that the data in the TextBox is customer age data. The same event fires for all **txtFields** controls because they are a control array. The code should have performed a **Select Case** statement to evaluate the value of the **DataField** property and apply the age edit only to that TextBox control containing the customer's age. Answer f is correct because nowhere are the **DataSource, DataMember,** and **DataField** properties of the TextBox controls set. (**DataSource** should have been set to **deData, DataMember** to **rscmdCustomer,** and **DataField** to a field from the Customers table.) Answer b is incorrect because the **Recordset** object does support events. Answer c is incorrect because there are no syntactical errors in the **cmdOK_Click** event, although the code does inadvertently suppress the **txtFields_Validate** event.

Glossary

· ·

Active client—A client capable of performing dynamic processing on the Internet within a Web browser via VBScript or ActiveX controls.

Active server—A server capable of performing server-side processing on the Internet via ActiveX components.

Active window—The window in the foreground that receives keystrokes. The title bar is highlighted.

ActiveX Automation—Automation implemented via ActiveX technology. *See also* Automation.

ActiveX component—An application that provides its objects to other applications. Also called an Automation server.

ActiveX control—Sometimes known as an OCX file or as an OLE control. ActiveX controls encapsulate functionality into objects that can be reused in development environments, Web pages, and so on. The CommonDialog control, for instance, is an ActiveX control.

ActiveX DLL—Also called a COM DLL. An ActiveX component implemented as a DLL. ActiveX DLLs are in-process servers and have a class object that exposes functionality of the ActiveX component. To use an ActiveX DLL, other applications create a reference to the class object and use its methods and properties to implement the services of the ActiveX DLL. *See also* ActiveX component and ActiveX server.

ActiveX Document DLL—An ActiveX DLL that includes user documents (but does not allow forms). *See also* ActiveX DLL and UserDocument.

ActiveX Document EXE—An ActiveX EXE that includes user documents (but does not allow forms). *See also* ActiveX EXE and UserDocument.

ActiveX EXE—Also called a COM EXE. An ActiveX component implemented as an EXE. ActiveX EXEs are out-of-process servers and have a class object that exposes functions of the component. To use an ActiveX EXE, other applications create a reference to the class object and use its methods and properties to implement the services of the ActiveX EXE. *See also* ActiveX component and ActiveX server.

ActiveX server—An Automation server implemented via ActiveX technology. *See* Automation.

AddressOf—A Visual Basic operator that computes the memory address of a procedure. This is usually used when passing the address of a procedure in an API call, particularly in callback operations.

ADO—ActiveX Data Objects. A collection of objects and their properties, methods, and events that allows you to access and manipulate databases.

Aggregation—A way in which one object can make use of another.

Alias—Used in Visual Basic **Declare** statements to provide the real name of an API function when the name is illegal in VB or otherwise inconvenient to use.

ANSI—The character set defined by the American National Standards Institute. Defines a 256-character set in which each character is comprised of 8 bits.

Any—A keyword used in various declarations (**Declare, Function,** and **Sub**) in place of the data type where an argument can be of any data type. This forces VB to not perform type checking on the data type.

API—Application Programming Interface. A library implemented via "exported" functions in a DLL that expose the library's services to other applications. Common examples include the Windows API, the ODBC API, and others.

Array—(1) A set of related elements that allow access to any of the elements via the array's sequentially indexed subscript. All elements of the array are of the same intrinsic data type. Arrays can be multidimensional and can be either fixed (containing a fixed number of elements) or dynamic (containing a variable number of elements). (2) A Visual Basic function that creates an array by providing a comma-separated list of values to a variable. X = **Array (8, 2, 1)** creates a one-dimensional array of variable X with three elements. *See also* Control array.

Assert—A debugging tool. VB provides **Assert** as a method of the **Debug** object, which tests whether an expression is **True** and, if not, halts program execution.

Asynchronous—A type of communication in which an object can send a request to another object and continue processing, without waiting for the first request to be completed. *See also* Synchronous.

ATL—Active Template Library. Template-based, C++ classes used for creating COM components.

Automation—A technology in which an application can expose its objects to other applications in a consistent manner.

Automation controller—An application that uses objects provided by an ActiveX component.

Automation server—*See* ActiveX component.

Binary—(1) Consisting of two possible values—zero or one. Computers perform binary operations in which a bit is either on (one) or off (zero). (2) A VB keyword used in file-open operations specifying that the file is opened in binary mode instead of text mode (sequential access).

ByRef—Dictates that a variable being passed to a procedure is passed by reference. In other words, the actual address of the variable is passed, allowing the procedure to alter the value of the variable. *See also* ByVal.

ByVal—Dictates that a variable being passed to a procedure is passed by a value. That is, a copy of the variable is passed and not the actual address. The procedure cannot alter the value of the variable. *See also* ByRef.

CAB file—A file with the .CAB extension that includes compressed files. Use the Extract program to extract any files within the CAB file. The Package And Deployment Wizard creates CAB files for distributing your application.

Call stack—In debugging, Visual Basic provides this method to view the call stack, which is a list of the procedures that have been called but not completed. Available from the View menu.

Child—(1) Depending on the context used, an object or process that is subservient to the parent or master. (2) A property of the **Node** object that returns the first child node on a TreeView control. (3) Visual Basic refers to MDIForm objects as parents, and forms with the **MDIChild** property set to **True** as children. (4) Controls on a UserControl object are referred to as child controls.

Class events—Events in a class module. Classes have only two built-in events—**Initialize** and **Terminate**. You can add events to your custom classes and invoke them with the **RaiseEvent** method.

Class modules—A code module that encapsulates functionality and data so it can be reused. Other modules that wish to use the functionality of the class module must declare a reference to the class and then access the class's publicly exposed methods and properties. The class module includes all the procedures and declarations within the class. A class module is saved with the .CLS extension.

Collection class—A special Visual Basic class that allows like objects to be grouped together. Collections allow grouped items to be indexed and enumerated via keys. Unlike arrays, collections shrink and grow as necessary. VB has a number of built-in collections, such as the **Forms** and **Controls** collections.

COM—(1) Component Object Model. Microsoft's application-development technology based on component reuse. The fundamental object model on which ActiveX controls and OLE are built. COM allows an object to expose its functionality to other components and to host applications. It defines both how the object exposes itself and how this exposure works across processes and across networks. COM also defines the object's life cycle. *See also* ATL. (2) Sometimes, communications (serial) ports are referred to as COM ports (such as, COM1, COM2, and so forth).

COM DLL—A COM-enabled DLL. *See also* ActiveX DLL.

COM EXE—A COM-enabled EXE. *See also* ActiveX EXE.

COMMIT—An SQL command that forces the database to permanently save all updates made to the database since the last **COMMIT** or **ROLLBACK**. Commit terminates a transaction. In Visual Basic ADO, the method used is **CommitTrans**. *See also* ROLLBACK.

Component—An object that can be reused in development.

Conditional compilation—A method of producing different executables based on the environment. In Visual Basic, tests are done in code and preceded by a pound sign (#) to determine whether statements are included in the final executable.

Container—(1) An object that contains other controls, such as the form, MDIForm, Frame, and PictureBox. (2) A property of Visual Basic controls that describes the container control.

Context-sensitive help—Help that is supplied by the application and is pertinent to an action currently being performed by the user.

Control array—A group of controls sharing the same name and events differentiated by their **Index** property. Unlike data arrays, indexes of control arrays do not need to be numbered sequentially (though the values must be unique within the control array).

Controls collection—A property of Form, MDIForm, PropertyPage, UserDocument, and UserControl. Defines the controls placed on the object. Visual Basic maintains these collections automatically.

CreateObject—A Visual Basic function that creates and returns a reference to an ActiveX object, such as a Microsoft Word document.

DAO—Data Access Objects. A collection of objects and their properties, methods, and events that allows you to access and manipulate databases.

Data array—*See* Array.

Data control—A Visual Basic control that connects to a database and supports methods to scroll through a recordset as well as to update, delete, insert, and so forth.

Data-bound controls—Controls bound to one or more columns in a database. Data-bound controls display the data from the column(s) they are bound to.

DBCS—Double Byte Character Set. A method of representing characters using 16 bits.

DCOM—Distributed Component Object Model. Microsoft's proposed standard for object interoperability. Under DCOM, any object can communicate with any other object regardless of the second object's location on the network.

DDE—Dynamic Data Exchange. A method of communication between two objects, DDE was the original fulfillment of Microsoft's document-centric philosophy. This allowed users to manipulate documents without needing to know which application created the data on the document. DDE is accomplished by opening links between a DDE client and a DDE server.

Delegation—A methodology used to achieve reuse in an application. In Visual Basic, classes can be combined so that the methods, properties, and events of one class can be used by another class. This process is known as delegation.

Dependency file—A required file that allows another file to operate correctly. Applications often require the functionality provided by dynamic link libraries. The DLLs are thus dependency files for applications.

DHTML—Dynamic Hypertext Markup Language. An extension to HTML that allows a developer to dynamically alter the presentation of a Web page without invoking the services of a Web server.

Digital signature—An electronic "signature" that certifies that an ActiveX control is safe to use. A digital signature is attached to an ActiveX control packaged for distribution.

DispID—Dispatch ID. A type of early binding used by Visual Basic when the object's type library does not provide virtual function tables. *See also* Early binding and vTable.

Dynamic HTML—*See* DHTML.

Early binding—The process of creating a reference to an object in such a way that the compiler can pre-allocate space and resolve references to the object. Early binding represents a more efficient way to access an object, at the expense of the object being "fixed" (that is, the allocation is specific). Early binding can be either vTable or DispID, with vTable being the faster of the two. Objects that are explicitly declared are always early bound, but it is the component that determines whether vTable or DispID is used. *See also* DispID, Late binding, and vTable.

Empty—A VB keyword indicating that a variable of type **Variant** contains uninitialized data.

Encapsulation—The process of placing data and functionality inside an object, "hidden" from other objects. Other objects can access the data and functionality only via the object's exposed methods. Visual Basic implements encapsulation via class modules.

Enum—A Visual Basic keyword used to create an enumerated variable. Enumerated variables can be declared only at the module level, and their values cannot change. Other variables can be declared as the enumerated variable's type.

Enumeration—(1) The process of iterating through a collection. (2) The process of creating enumerated variables. *See also* Enum.

Event-driven programming—A method of application development in which the program reacts to events, usually initiated by the user. Code is placed in event procedures, which are defined by user-driven events, such as clicking on a command button.

Execute—An ADO method that executes a **Command** object.

Expose—To make visible to other objects. An object makes its methods and properties visible to other objects by making them public.

Extender—A property of the UserControl that returns a reference to an **Extender** object. The **Extender** object holds the properties of the UserControl that are maintained by the container control (that is, Form, MDIForm, and PictureBox) on which the UserControl is placed. Examples of these properties are **Top** and **Left**.

Form modules—The procedures contained within a form object, including the event procedures of all the form's controls and any general procedures within the form. Form modules also include all declarations within the form. A form module is saved with the .FRM extension.

Forms collection—A collection of all forms within an application, maintained automatically by Visual Basic.

Friend—A type of declaration within a class module that makes the procedure declared visible (callable) by other modules within the project. **Friend** procedures cannot be called by controllers of the class (that is, other class objects that have implemented the class).

FTP—File Transfer Protocol. A protocol or "language" that two computers use to communicate between a client and an FTP server. FTP servers are typically organized by directories and allow files to be uploaded and downloaded.

Function—A type of procedure that can return a value to the caller.

GDI—Graphical Device Interface. A portion of the Windows API that controls graphical operations, such as printing and drawing to the screen.

Get—(1) A Visual Basic statement used to retrieve data from a file opened in binary or random access mode. (2) A qualifier to class procedures that exposes properties of class objects to other modules.

GetData—(1) A command that returns a graphic from the clipboard. (2) A method of the Winsock control that retrieves data from the input buffer during TCP or UDP communications.

GetObject—A function that assigns a reference to an ActiveX object from a file, such as a Microsoft Word document, to a variable.

GetSetting—A function used to retrieve the value of a key for an application in the Windows Registry.

GotFocus—An event that signifies that a Visual Basic control received focus.

Group—A Visual Basic file that contains multiple projects. Its file extension is .GRP, and it's sometimes called a project group.

GROUP BY—An SQL statement used to summarize data.

HAVING—An SQL statement used to restrict the result set of an SQL query, based on summarized computations.

hDC—(1) A handle to a graphical device context. (2) A property of a Form object, and several other Visual Basic objects and controls, that returns the handle to the object's or control's graphical device context.

Help Context ID—A string that acts as an index to a specific Help topic within a Help file.

HelpContext—The property of most VB controls that sets or returns the Help Context ID for the control.

HelpFile—A property of most VB controls that defines which Help file to display when a user presses the F1 key.

hInstance—(1) A handle (pointer) to the address of an application. (2) A property of the **App** object that returns a handle to the application.

HTML—Hypertext Markup Language. A standard cross-platform language used to set up Web pages. HTML listings consist of tags, text, objects, and applets. The Web browser interprets the tags to display a Web page.

HTML tag—A tag within a Web page used to control formatting or other aspects of the page's behavior. Most tags are paired, which means that one tag defines the beginning of a block, and the other tag defines the end of a block. Tags are enclosed in brackets. For example, the <B> and </B> tags define that all text between them is to be boldfaced.

HTTP—Hypertext Transfer Protocol. A protocol for communications on the World Wide Web.

hWnd—(1) A handle to an object in Windows. (2) A property of the **Form** object and most Visual Basic controls that returns a handle to the object.

Hyperlink—(1) A standard for navigating between documents on the World Wide Web. The object of a hyperlink is expressed as a URL (Uniform Resource Locator). (2) A Visual Basic object, with a **NavigateTo** method, used to jump to a given URL. (3) A property of ActiveX controls, the **UserControl** object, and the **UserDocument** object that returns a reference to the **Hyperlink** object.

ImageList—A Visual Basic control used in association with other controls to manage graphic files based on an index. The ImageList control is most typically associated with ListView, Toolbar, and TreeView controls.

Immediate window—A window available while you are debugging in the VB development environment that allows the display of data and the execution of procedures. The output of the **Debug.Print** statement is the Immediate window.

Implements—A Visual Basic statement that allows a class to implement the properties and methods of another class.

Inheritance—A method of reuse that allows an object to derive all the attributes of the class from which it is inherited. Visual Basic does not support inheritance.

In-place activation—The process of activating an object provided by an ActiveX component. By double-clicking on the object, a user can interact with the application that supplies the object without switching to a different application or window.

In-process server—A server that runs in the same memory space as its client. *See also* ActiveX EXE.

Instancing—A property of classes in ActiveX EXEs and ActiveX DLLs that defines the availability of class objects to other applications.

Instantiation—The process of creating an object from a class definition.

Interface—The mechanism through which an object exposes its functionality (properties, methods, and events).

Internet download—A file or document downloaded from a server via the Internet, or the process of downloading a file or document from a server on the Internet to a client computer.

InternetTransfer—A Visual Basic control that supports connections to FTP and HTTP servers. *See also* FTP, HTTP, and Winsock.

I/O—Input/output.

IUnknown—The basic interface on which all other interfaces are based. It implements the reference-counting and interface-querying mechanisms running through COM.

Kernel—A portion of the Windows API that provides Windows services, such as file I/O.

KeyDown—An event that detects when a key is pressed. The event occurs before the key has been released.

KeyPress—An event that detects when a key with an ANSI value is pressed.

KeyPreview—A property of the **Form, PropertyPage, UserControl,** and **UserDocument** objects that dictates whether keyboard events for the object are invoked before keyboard events for the controls.

KeyUp—An event that detects the releasing of a pressed key.

Late binding—The process in which an object reference cannot be resolved at compilation, forcing the compiler to add extra logic to resolve the reference at runtime. For instance, the following statement creates an object variable: **Dim myObject As Object**. Because the variable can later be assigned to any type of object (such as a control), the assignment will be done using late binding. However, the statement **Dim myObject As CommandButton** explicitly assigns the object variable, allowing the compiler to do early binding. Late binding is less efficient than early binding, but it allows for more flexibility in object assignment. *See also* Early binding.

Let—(1) A Visual Basic keyword used to assign a value to a variable, as in **Let A = 3**. Visual Basic does not require the use of **Let** in assignments. (2) A qualifier to property procedures within class objects that allows other modules to alter the value of a property.

License file—A VBL file distributed with ActiveX controls that allows the control to be used at runtime. If the license file is generated out of the setup process, the setup program will register the control in the Windows Registry.

Locals window—A window provided while you are stepping through code in Visual Basic to monitor all variables that currently have scope.

Marshaling—The mechanism that enables objects to be used across thread, process, and network boundaries, allowing for location independence.

MDI—Multiple Document Interface. *See also* MDIChild and MDIForm.

MDIChild—A property of the Form object that specifies that the form is a child of the MDIForm object.

MDIForm—A Visual Basic object that contains all Form objects whose **MDIChild** property is set to **True**. These forms are said to be children of the MDIForm. When an MDIForm closes, all the child forms also close. There can be only one MDIForm per project.

Microsoft Jet—An access method of the DAO **Recordset** object. Microsoft Jet is an engine that permits connections to relational databases as well as to non-relational databases via ISAM (Indexed Sequential Access Method).

Modal—A presentation format for forms. When a form is presented modally, nothing else can occur in the application until the form is closed.

Modeless—A presentation format for forms. When a form is opened modelessly, other forms in the application can also be accessed.

MSVBVM60.DLL—The Microsoft Visual Basic runtime engine. Visual Basic applications require this DLL, although applications compiled to native code access it much less often than those compiled to p-code.

Named arguments—A convention for supplying arguments to procedures by explicitly naming them. This allows for using arguments out of order. To use named arguments, supply the argument name followed by a colon, an equal sign, and then the value, as in: **myFunction (fontface: = "bold", fontsize: = 12)**.

Native code—A compilation option. Visual basic generates native code (machine-executable instructions) rather than p-code, which requires a runtime interpreter.

Nothing—A Visual Basic keyword used to disassociate an object variable from an object. For example: **Set myObj = Nothing**.

Null—(1) The absence of data. (2) A Visual Basic keyword indicating that a variable of type **Variant** has a value equal to null—it contains no valid data. This is different than **Empty**. *See also* Empty. (3) A null string is not an empty string. It is a string with a value of zero. To pass a null string to a DLL function, use the **vbNullString** constant.

Number type—The type of variable used for numeric data. The variable type determines the efficiency and accuracy of a number. Valid types are: **Integer, Long, Single, Double, Currency**, and **Decimal**. Although they are not used in numeric computations, the **Boolean, Byte**, and **Date** data types are numeric also.

Object—(1) A Visual Basic data type indicating the variable is of type **Object**, which can then be used to reference any other object, such as a control or class. (2) An instantiated item derived from a class definition. Objects include controls, forms, classes, and so on. *See also* CreateObject and GetObject.

Object Browser—A Visual Basic design-time tool that allows developers to browse type libraries for objects and definitions.

<OBJECT> tag—An HTML tag that denotes an embedded object, such as an ActiveX control. *See also* ActiveX control and HTML.

ODBC—Open Database Connectivity. A widely adopted Microsoft standard that allows access to different databases in a common manner using SQL.

ODBCDirect—A DAO type of workspace that allows connection to a database using ODBC rather than Microsoft Jet. *See also* Microsoft Jet, ODBC, and Recordset.

OLE—Object Linking and Embedding. An advancement on DDE that allows communication between objects. OLE is now called ActiveX. *See also* ActiveX, Automation, and DDE.

OLE Automation—A method of automating services of an OLE object to a requesting application. OLE Automation is now termed ActiveX Automation. *See also* ActiveX, ActiveX Automation, Automation, and DDE.

OLE DB—An evolution from ODBC. OLE DB is Microsoft's new standard for database access. ADO uses OLE DB. The OLE DB provider communicates with the database, whereas ADO communicates with OLE DB. The database doesn't need to be a relational database, though ADO exposes it as if it were relational.

OLE server—An object providing OLE Automation. An OLE server is now called an ActiveX server. *See also* ActiveX server.

On Error—A Visual Basic statement used to turn on and turn off error handling in applications.

OpenURL—A method that the InternetTransfer control uses to connect to a given URL (Uniform Resource Locator). *See also* InternetTransfer.

ORDER BY—An SQL clause that sorts a result set by one or more columns.

Order of operations—Defines the order in which mathematical operations will occur in a compound expression. In general, computations within parentheses are performed first. Multiplication and division operations take precedence over addition and subtraction. After that, operations are performed from left to right.

Out-of-process server—A server that runs in its own memory space. An ActiveX EXE is an out-of-process server.

Overloaded function—A function that behaves differently based on the number of arguments and/or data types of the arguments it receives.

ParamArray—Indicates that an argument is an optional array of type **Variant** and is comprised of an arbitrary number of values. Used with Visual Basic declarations.

<PARAM NAME=> tag—An HTML tag that can supply values used by an associated object.

Parent—(1) A property of most Visual Basic objects that returns a reference to the form, container, object, or collection that contains the object. (2) In an MDI application, refers to the MDIForm object.

P-code—Pseudo-code. A compile-time option that specifies the type of instructions that will be generated. P-code requires a runtime interpreter for the application to run; native code does not.

Persisting—The process of saving an object's state to disk.

Polymorphism—An object-oriented term indicating that an action can be used to communicate with different objects in a common manner to accomplish a common task. For instance, if an application wants to send the output of an object to a printer, polymorphic behavior dictates that the application can use the **Print** command without knowing or caring how the object accomplishes the task. Thus, an application can specify **Word.Document.Print** or **Excel.Worksheet.Print** and allow the object to handle the chore of sending the output to the printer.

Project—A collection of modules, controls, and so on comprising a Visual Basic application.

Project file—A file with the .VBP extension that contains the definition of a project. S*ee also* Project.

Property procedures—Procedures in a class module that allow the manipulation of class properties. There are three types: **Get, Let,** and **Set**.

PropertyBag—An object supplied by the container of an ActiveX control that allows behavior states to be saved between invocations of the object.

PropertyPage—The base object of an ActiveX control's property pages. You can use property pages to expose the properties of the control at design time.

QueryInterface—The method used to query an object for a given interface.

RDO—Remote Data Objects. A collection of objects used to manipulate remote ODBC data sources as well as Oracle and Microsoft SQL Server databases.

Recordset—An ADO and DAO object (called a **ResultSet** in RDO) used to manipulate data in a database at the record level.

Reference counting—The technique by which the interface of an object decides when it is no longer being used and is, therefore, free to remove itself.

RemoteHost—A property of the Winsock control that defines the name of the computer acting as the remote host (TCP and UDP communications) or the IP address of the computer acting as the remote host for TCP (TCP only).

RemotePort—A property of the Winsock control that defines the port on which the remote host listens for data.

Reuse—An object-oriented technique that reuses previously written and tested objects to make code more efficient. Inheritance is the most powerful reuse technique, but Visual Basic does not support inheritance. VB supports a more indirect method known as delegation. *See also* Delegation and Inheritance.

ROLLBACK—An SQL statement that discards all changes made to a database since the last **COMMIT** or **ROLLBACK**. ADO implements rollback with the **RollbackTrans** method. *See also* COMMIT.

Runtime engine—The MSVBVM60.DLL file that provides support functions for applications and runtime interpretation functionality for programs compiled to p-code.

SaveSetting—A function to save a key value in the Windows Registry.

Screen object—A VB object that represents the monitor screen. A screen object provides a number of methods to change the mouse pointer and so on.

Scripting and initialization safety—Ensures that properties of an ActiveX control embedded in a Web page can't inadvertently or maliciously be altered to cause damage to a client computer.

SDI—Single Document Interface. An application in which all forms are opened independent of one another. If one form closes, other forms remain open. *See also* MDI.

Select—Part of a **Select Case** conditional VB statement used to branch according to the value of a variable.

SELECT—An SQL statement used to retrieve data from the database.

Set—(1) An assignment operator for object variables. Assigns an object to a variable. (2) A qualification for a class procedure declaration that allows a variable of type **Object** to be assigned. *See also* Get and Let.

SetFocus—A method that allows a control to set focus to itself.

SQL—Structured Query Language. A query language used to access and manipulate relational databases.

Standard EXE—A Visual Basic project type that generates a standard executable file.

Standard module—A file with the .BAS extension that contains declarations and procedures.

Startup object—The object defined in the Project Properties dialog box to be the first item loaded in a Visual Basic project. In a standard EXE, this will be a form or **Sub Main**.

StateChanged—An event in the InternetTransfer control that occurs whenever there is a change in the state of communications, such as when a link has been established.

Static—A declaration for variables and procedures. When it is used to declare a procedure, all variables within the procedure retain their values between invocations of the procedure. When used to declare a variable (valid only with procedures), **Static** causes the variable to retain its value between invocations of the procedure.

StatusBar—An ActiveX control that provides panels to display information, such as date and time.

Sub—A declaration for a sub procedure. Sub procedures do not return values.

Synchronous—A method of communication that requires the caller or client to wait until the request has been completed before continuing execution. *See also* Asynchronous.

System modal—A window that is modal on a system-wide basis. The user cannot interact with any other application until he or she closes the window.

TabIndex—Sets or returns the Tab order for controls on a form or user control.

Table—A series of rows and columns that stores data in a relational database.

TCP—Transfer Control Protocol. The "language" by which computers communicate across the Internet.

ToolTip—A short phrase that indicates what an object does. It is displayed at runtime when the user pauses the mouse pointer over a control whose **ToolTipText** property has been set.

Transaction—A logical unit of work (LUW) in a database. A series of actions that can be rolled back or committed with the **Commit** or **Rollback** command. *See also* COMMIT and ROLLBACK.

TreeView—An ActiveX control used to display graphics and text hierarchically by using **Node** objects.

Twip—A screen-independent unit used to ensure that the placement and proportion of screen elements in your screen application are the same on all display systems. A twip is a unit of screen measurement equal to 1/20 of a printer's point. There are approximately 1,440 twips in a logical inch or 567 twips in a logical centimeter (the length of a screen item measuring one inch or one centimeter when printed).

Type library—A file containing Automation descriptions of objects, such as enumerated variables as well as objects' properties, events, and methods. Type library files have the .TLB extension. Object libraries, ending with the .OLB extension, contain multiple type libraries.

UDP—A protocol that does not require two computers to be continuously connected in order to communicate. Supported by the Winsock control. *See also* TCP and Winsock.

Unicode—A character set format comprised of 16 bits, native to Windows NT and used internally by Visual Basic 5. Unicode is sometimes called wide character.

URL—Uniform Resource Locator. An address of a computer on the Internet.

UserDocument—An object, similar to a form, used by ActiveX Document EXEs and ActiveX Document DLLs to present a user interface inside a Web browser.

Variable—A named memory location where Visual Basic stores values. Variables have different data types that dictate what types of information they can hold.

Variable accuracy—The ability of a variable to maintain numeric accuracy across computations. Generally, the larger the data type, the more accurate the result, but at the expense of performance.

Variable default—The default value of variables when they are initialized. For numeric data types, the value is zero. For strings, it is an empty string. For **Booleans**, the default is **False**.

Variable precision—The capability of a variable to maintain decimal accuracy (that is, the number of decimal places that can be accurately represented).

Variable promotion—Refers to the process by which Visual Basic increases the size of a temporary variable as needed during computations. Visual Basic will use the smallest data type possible.

Variable scope—Refers to the visibility of a variable through a project, as defined when the variable was declared.

Variant—A special type of variable that has a data type of **Variant** but can have any underlying data type. The data type **Variant** is Visual Basic's default for an undeclared variable type.

Variant array—An array of type **Variant**. Individual members of the array can have different underlying data types.

VBScript—A scripting language similar to Visual Basic for Applications (VBA) that is used in Web pages to create applets that run on a client computer.

Visual Basic data types—Visual Basic variables have data types that dictate what type of data they can store. Some examples are **String** for character data, **Variant** for varying data types, and a number of numeric data types. *See also* Number type, Variable, and Variant.

Visual Basic operators—Symbols or actions that perform operations on variables, such as addition, which is represented by the plus sign, and concatenation, which is represented by the ampersand character.

vTable—Virtual function table. A type of early-binding (faster than DispID) used when the component's type library provides virtual function tables. Components created with Visual Basic always provide vTable binding. *See also* DispID and Early binding.

Watch expressions—Expressions defined in the Visual Basic debugging environment. You can constantly monitor the values of variables or expressions when stepping through code or can instruct Visual Basic to break when an expression evaluates to **True**.

Watch window—The window used to monitor variables.

WhatsThisHelp—A method of providing short (usually a sentence or two) snippets of context-sensitive help. *See also* WhatsThisMode.

WhatsThisMode—A method of the Form and MDIForm objects that invokes WhatsThisHelp. The mouse pointer turns into a question mark, and the user can click on an object to view a short snippet of Help text.

WHERE—A clause of the SQL **SELECT** statement that restricts the result set by specifying filter conditions.

Wide character set—*See* Unicode.

Winsock—An ActiveX control that provides TCP and UDP services to a Visual Basic application. *See also* InternetTransfer, TCP, and UDP.

WWW—World Wide Web. A portion of the Internet that presents a graphical interface to display documents with a Web browser. WWW documents typically support point-and-click navigation via hyperlinks. Web servers are known as HTTP servers. *See also* HTTP, InternetTransfer, TCP, UDP, and Winsock.

Index

CORIOLIS HELP CENTER

Here at The Coriolis Group, we strive to provide the finest customer service in the technical education industry. We're committed to helping you reach your certification goals by assisting you in the following areas.

Talk to the Authors

We'd like to hear from you! Please refer to the "How to Use This Book" section in the "Introduction" of every Exam Cram guide for our authors' individual email addresses.

Web Page Information

The Certification Insider Press Web page provides a host of valuable information that's only a click away. For information in the following areas, please visit us at:

www.coriolis.com/cip/default.cfm

- Titles and other products
- Book content updates
- Roadmap to Certification Success guide
- New Adaptive Testing changes
- New Exam Cram Live! seminars
- New Certified Crammer Society details
- Sample chapters and tables of contents
- Manuscript solicitation
- Special programs and events

Contact Us by Email

Important addresses you may use to reach us at The Coriolis Group.

eci@coriolis.com

To subscribe to our FREE, bi-monthly on-line newsletter, *Exam Cram Insider*. Keep up to date with the certification scene. Included in each *Insider* are certification articles, program updates, new exam information, hints and tips, sample chapters, and more.

techsupport@coriolis.com

For technical questions and problems with CD-ROMs. Products broken, battered, or blown-up? Just need some installation advice? Contact us here.

ccs@coriolis.com

To obtain membership information for the *Certified Crammer Society,* **an exclusive club for the certified professional.** Get in on members-only discounts, special information, expert advice, contests, cool prizes, and free stuff for the certified professional. Membership is FREE. Contact us and get enrolled today!

cipq@coriolis.com

For book content questions and feedback about our titles, drop us a line. This is the good, the bad, and the questions address. Our customers are the best judges of our products. Let us know what you like, what we could do better, or what question you may have about any content. Testimonials are always welcome here, and if you send us a story about how an Exam Cram guide has helped you ace a test, we'll give you an official Certification Insider Press T-shirt.

custserv@coriolis.com

For solutions to problems concerning an order for any of our products. Our staff will promptly and courteously address the problem. Taking the exams is difficult enough. We want to make acquiring our study guides as easy as possible.

Book Orders & Shipping Information

orders@coriolis.com

To place an order by email or to check on the status of an order already placed.

coriolis.com/bookstore/default.cfm

To place an order through our online bookstore.

1.800.410.0192

To place an order by phone or to check on an order already placed.